Olivier de Clisson and
Political Society in France Under
Charles V and Charles VI

Olivier de Clisson and Political Society in France Under Charles V and Charles VI

John Bell Henneman

PENN

University of Pennsylvania Press

Philadelphia

University of Pennsylvania Press
MIDDLE AGES SERIES

General Editor
RUTH MAZO KARRAS,
Temple University

Founding Editor
EDWARD PETERS,
University of Pennsylvania

A complete list of books in the series
is available from the publisher.

Library of Congress Cataloging-in-Publication Data
Henneman, John Bell, 1935–
Olivier de Clisson and political society in France under Charles V
and Charles VI / John Bell Henneman.
    p.   cm. — (Middle Ages series)
Includes bibliographical references and index.
ISBN 0-8122-3353-0 (alk. paper)
    1. Clisson, Olivier de, 1336–1407.   2. France—Politics and
government—1328–1589.   3. Nobility—France—Brittany—Biography.
4. Soldiers—France—Biography.   5. Hundred Years War, 1339–1453—
Biography.   6. France—Relations—England.   7. England—Relations—
France.   I. Title.   II. Series.
DC97.C54H46   1996
944'.025'092—dc20
[B]   96-11190
                                                               CIP

FRONTISPIECE:
Olivier de Clisson. Detail from effigy on tomb.
Photograph by Michael C. E. Jones.

In memory of
RAYMOND CAZELLES
(1917–1985)
and
JOSEPH REESE STRAYER
(1904–1987)

Contents

Illustrations

Preface

MORE THAN TWENTY YEARS AGO, I began research for a study of military society in late fourteenth-century France, intending to compare the leading royal commanders with those who led the companies of free-lance soldiers (*routiers*) who caused great destruction during lulls in the Hundred Years' War. I soon discovered that the most influential royal commander was Olivier IV, lord of Clisson (1336–1407), who provided a link between the military leadership and an important party at court (the "Marmousets"). Then, in 1982, my respected friend Raymond Cazelles published a lengthy volume on the French nobility and political society during the reigns of John II and Charles V, yet never once mentioned Clisson. I determined to make a careful study of Clisson's career in order to determine his place in French royal politics and whether his omission by Cazelles was warranted.

The second, and least well-known of three great Breton warriors to hold the position of constable of France during the Hundred Years' War, Olivier de Clisson was a complex figure whose enormous wealth and difficult personality left a strong imprint on the politics of his time. To tell Clisson's story in the context of French royal politics is a daunting task because it requires bringing together three areas of study—politics at court, the aristocracy of Brittany, and the nobility of the royal household—in which other scholars (respectively Cazelles, Michael C. E. Jones, and R. C. Famiglietti) have a mastery of the documents that I cannot hope to equal. I have drawn heavily on their work, attempting to integrate their findings into my own research on Clisson and the Marmousets and to address questions that have not been of central importance in their work.

Abel Lefranc's "classic" study of Clisson nearly a century ago is now outdated because more documents are available and the narrative sources have been subjected to greater critical scrutiny. A pair of more recent works on Clisson, designed for a popular audience, by Georges Toudouze (1942) and Yvonig Gicquel (1981), draw heavily on nineteenth-century authors and share their excessive reliance on chroniclers that are not entirely reliable. The best known chronicler of the fourteenth century is, of course, Jean Froissart, an eminent literary figure, a marvelous storyteller, and a friend of several people who were close to Olivier de Clisson. Froissart presents Clisson as an extremely important figure at the French court, but his many inaccuracies compel us to treat his words with great caution, especially when they concern Clisson's sometime antagonist, the duke of Berry.

Olivier de Clisson's relationship with the duke of Brittany and with the tangled affairs of that duchy repeatedly complicated and prolonged the rivalry between England and France. Developments in Brittany occupy a large part of this book but are always treated in the broader context of French royal politics. For the authoritative treatment of Brittany itself in these years, one must turn to the important studies of Jean Kerhervé and Michael Jones.

Professor Jones is one of the three scholars (mentioned above) into whose specialties my research has intruded. To this eminent contemporary historian of medieval Brittany I owe a debt that is both professional and personal. My research has depended heavily on his monumental two-volume edition of the enactments of Duke John IV of Brittany, and his generous answers to my correspondence have led me to many important sources relating to Clisson and Breton history. Lacking his exhaustive knowledge of the Breton sources, I have made mistakes that he would have avoided, but I hope that my perspective can enrich our understanding of some areas that he has explored.

The late Raymond Cazelles was a friend, mentor, and supportive adviser from the time we first met in 1964 until the end of his life twenty years later. His suggestions and arguments greatly influenced my publications. We have disagreed about the competence and governing style of Charles V, but his death robbed me of a most valuable critic, and I feel very keenly the loss of his wisdom. He is one of two people to whose memory I have dedicated this book, the other being the great American medievalist Joseph R. Strayer, my former undergraduate teacher, who helped and encouraged me long after I was no longer his student.

The third scholar to whose friendship and research I owe a particular debt is R. C. Famiglietti, who initiated a correspondence with me nearly fifteen years ago. He has helped me ever since with a stream of useful archival and bibliographic references, information from his formidable data base on the French nobles during the reign of Charles VI, and his helpful comments on an early draft of this book.

Thanks to Professor Jones and Dr. Famiglietti, I learned of documents in a private collection at Château Grandville en Bringolo in the Côtes d'Armor region of Brittany. I wish to thank the Comte de Catuélan and his wife for their gracious hospitality in permitting me to examine documents in their family archives without making a prior appointment. I also appreciate the assistance of the staffs of the Archives Nationales and Bibliothèque Nationale in Paris and the Archives Départementales at Nantes, Rennes, Le Mans, Saint-Brieuc, and Vannes. At an early stage of this project, my research assistants at the University of Iowa, most notably Jill Harsin and Andrew Federer, provided many hours of labor collecting and classifying information about the leading French military commanders. For advice on mastering the new automated system at the Archives Nationales, I wish to thank Erwin Welsch at the University of Wisconsin Libraries and my longtime friend, Elizabeth A. R. Brown of the City University of New York, who provided me with help and advice in other areas as well. My brother, Edward O. Henneman, read part of the text and provided valuable critical comments. I also thank Edward Peters of the University of Pennsylvania for his strong support, and Daniel Rodgers of Princeton University for his crucial assistance with administrative arrangements that facilitated the funding required for publication. My colleagues on the excellent staff of the Princeton University Libraries have helped me in more ways than they realize. All these people have enabled me to make this a better book. The errors that remain are my own.

Over the years I have received financial support or released time that permitted me to visit the French archives and libraries: a "Research Assignment" from the University of Iowa in 1974, supplemented by an IREX travel grant; a fellowship from the John Simon Guggenheim Foundation in 1976; a Research Leave and travel funds from Princeton University in 1988; and a second Research Leave from Princeton in 1993. For help in funding publication of this volume, I am indebted to the History Department Subvention Account at Princeton University and to those who have contributed to it. In their editorial capacities at the University of Pennsylvania Press, Jerome Singerman and Mindy Brown were extremely helpful with their assistance at various stages. Eliza McClennen produced the maps, and certain photographs are reproduced here with the kind permission of Professors Michael C. E. Jones and Gwyn Meiron-Jones.

My wife Gerry has provided encouragement and support throughout my career, but on this project she played a particularly important role, operating both the car and the camera as we traveled through Brittany and the Vendée in 1993 exploring some of the important sites of Olivier de Clisson's career. I thank her for enduring so cheerfully my sometimes bizarre interpretations of road maps and the endless stream of Clisson anecdotes I inflicted upon her whenever we reached one of his former haunts.

Scholarly readers should be advised that my notes on the *Histoire* of Jean Juvenal des Ursins do not come from the most widely cited edition of that work, which was unavailable to me. I also have used an edition of Rymer's *Foedera* that differs from the one cited by many authors. Of the old Benedictine historians of Brittany, I have made heavy use of a reprint edition of Lobineau, which was almost continuously available to me when the important volumes of Hyacinthe Morice were housed in non-circulating collections with limited hours of access. References to currency in this volume are generally to the main royal money of account, pounds (*livres tournois*), each of which contained twenty *sols (sous)*, or to the gold franc, a coin that was supposed to equal one *l.t.*

It is always difficult to follow a coherent procedure in dealing with proper names. In general, I have anglicized the forenames of male royalty and great territorial magnates and have left other personal names in French, a practice conforming to the expectation of most American readers, but the dividing line between those lords whose names are anglicized and those with names left in French may appear arbitrary at times. In referring to French surnames and in alphabetizing them in Appendix 1 and in the Index, I have followed the style used by Philippe Contamine (see Chapter 1, note 4).

JOHN BELL HENNEMAN
Princeton, N.J.

I

Northwestern France in the Fourteenth Century: Crisis and Realignment

THE ANCESTRAL FORTRESS of the lords of Clisson is located in the extreme southeastern corner of Brittany on a lofty rock overlooking the Sèvre Nantaise some twenty miles upstream from the river's confluence with the Loire near Nantes. It was there that the greatest member of the family was born on 23 April 1336 and named for his father, Olivier III de Clisson, who held important lands in Brittany and elsewhere in northwestern France. The child's mother, Jeanne de Belleville, was an heiress who controlled a group of lordships in Poitou just south of the Breton border, stretching from Beauvoir-sur-Mer in the west to Châteaumur southeast of Clisson.[1]

Decades later, Olivier IV would be one of the kingdom's most powerful men, leading the military aristocracy of northwestern France and flaunting the assertive motto "because I like it."[2] Historians have been slow to recognize his importance, partly because of a reluctance to trust the chronicle of Froissart, but mainly because Clisson represented elements of French political society that did not leave "institutional footprints," such as membership in the royal council. For nearly forty years prior to 1360, this small council had been the forum for political debate in France. Kings altered its composition as they faced new political pressures, and the council came to mirror what the distinguished French historian Raymond Cazelles called *la société politique*—those people who influenced events, whose political power or opinions counted when the French royal government was deciding important matters of policy.[3] After 1360, however, the council became unusually stable, and certain men who acquired great influence in political society remained for a long time outside this body. One of these was Olivier de Clisson.

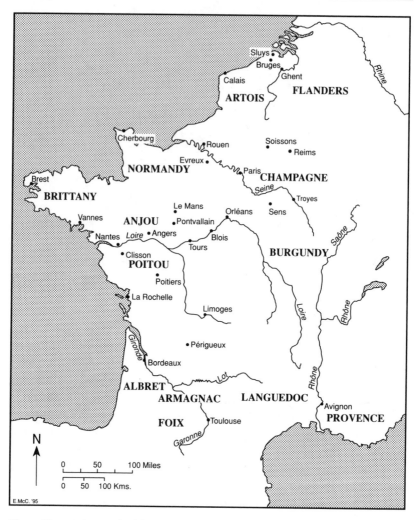

Map 1. France during the lifetime of Olivier de Clisson.

There was little reason to predict a great future for young Olivier IV in 1336, for he was the third son of his parents, each of whom also had a son by a previous marriage. His life and career were shaped by a series of traumatic developments that engulfed his region, his social class, and his family. A year after his birth, war broke out between France and England. This conflict, which continued intermittently for generations, came to be called the "Hundred Years' War." The early campaigns were expensive and inconclusive, but in 1341 the childless duke of Brittany died without naming a successor. A disputed succession plunged the duchy into a civil war that not only breathed new life into the Anglo-French conflict but also brought ruin to the Clisson family and made Olivier IV an exile in England by the age of eight. When he returned to the continent permanently in 1358, he was the sole remaining male heir of his parents and had to pursue his career in an environment quite different from the one he had left. The nobility of northwestern France, ravaged by an economic crisis, was undergoing a major political realignment that gave it a dominant role in the revival of French military fortunes. His exceptional military ability enabled Clisson to attain great power in this new political environment.

Political turmoil among the nobility was a striking feature of the Hundred Years' War because the conflict had a dynastic dimension. Philip IV of France (d. 1314) had left three sons, each of whom reigned briefly as king but left only daughters. Having decided against female succession to the throne in 1316, the French magnates went further in 1328 and declared that a woman could not transmit a claim to the throne. They chose as king Philip of Valois, the son of Philip IV's brother, and rejected the male offspring of Philip IV's female descendants—most notably his daughter's son, who was Edward III of England, but also any sons who might be born to Philip IV's granddaughters, such as the future Charles II of Navarre (1332–87). The decision to exclude the descendants of women did not provoke an immediate crisis over the royal succession, but it left open the possibility that excluded princes might later claim the throne. Philip VI (r. 1328–50) and his Valois successors had to contend with periodic challenges to their legitimacy. Efforts to enforce their authority encountered the threat of alternative allegiance: a dissident, while still professing loyalty to the French crown, might claim that the Valois were not true kings of France and transfer his allegiance to another prince. Edward III of England exploited this situation when he called himself king of France in 1340. Charles of Navarre subsequently became a magnet for the disaffected. Alternative allegiance would disturb the political society of Valois France until well into the next century.

This troubled political atmosphere required deft maneuvering on the part of the kings and led them to make frequent alterations in their council. The relative stability of the council between 1360 and 1375 was a striking departure from this practice, the implications of which will be discussed in Chapter 5. For the moment, it is sufficient to note that certain elements of political society acquired greater prominence in these years without gaining representation on the royal council. One such element was "military society," those members of the French nobility who were the leaders of a new salaried army that was coming into being during the 1360s. Besides the chief officers of the French armed forces—the constable, the two marshals, the admiral, and the master of crossbowmen—military society consisted of men who exercised authority by commanding the garrison of a fortress, governing a militarily significant district, or commanding troops in the field.[4]

Thanks to the survival of thousands of muster rolls, vouchers, and receipts that were used to control the payment of troops, it is possible to identify these important royal commanders and document their careers. Appendix 1 lists 188 men who served in positions of command over a number of years between 1360 and 1415. They formed the core of the "military society" that Olivier de Clisson would come to lead,[5] an influential group forged by a generation of politics, economic dislocation, and war. A large majority of them were drawn from an important regional aristocracy—the nobility of northwestern France. Some 70 percent came from a belt of territories that included most of the French coastline, extending from Artois and Picardy near the northern frontier, through Normandy, Maine, Anjou, and Brittany to Poitou and Saintonge in the west.[6]

This regional nobility, which became the bulwark of the royal army during the 1360s, had been a source of major discontent in the preceeding generation,[7] when Philip VI drew heavily upon Auvergne and Burgundy for his principal advisers, especially in the period 1335–43. When Philip moved away from this alignment between 1343 and 1347, hoping to placate discontent in the north and west, opposition to him began to coalesce around his son, John, who had strong ties to Burgundy and Auvergne.[8] Although nobles were more heavily concentrated in the north and west,[9] John II (r. 1350–64) continued to favor the center and east. A list drawn up at the time of his accession named 340 leading barons whose advice the king valued. The north and west, with their greater concentration of nobles, produced only 44 percent of the names on this list, while the center and east, with a much smaller population of nobles, provided 124 names, 59 of them from Burgundy (the most from any single region).[10]

Twenty years later, by contrast, nobles of the north and west dominated the list of royal commanders, supplying nearly five times as many as did the center and east.[11] One must not claim exaggerated significance for such numbers, but they do suggest that the core of royal support among the nobility shifted away from the center/east and towards the northwest during the 1350s. In fact, a significant number of the northwestern nobles holding military commands under Charles V, among them Clisson himself, came from families that had opposed the previous kings. It seems clear that a political realignment did take place and, as often happens, it did so in a context of serious economic dislocations. The devastating impact of war and plague gravely damaged the economic position of the nobles in northwestern France during Olivier de Clisson's years in exile and influenced the political environment in which he pursued his subsequent career.

The numerical importance of nobles varied from one region to another, but everywhere they made up a very small and declining fragment of French society—between 1.3 percent and 3.4 percent of the population in the early fourteenth century and between 1 percent and 1.6 percent 150 years later. In the regions of their greatest density they declined from slightly over 3 percent to slightly under 2 percent of a larger population that itself declined considerably in this period.[12] Even when facing economic problems, nobles remained the most fortunate 2 percent of society at large, but the medieval mentality understood "poverty" as a term related to the expectations of one's rank.[13] The concept of the "poor knight" or impoverished nobleman, something of an oxymoron to the modern mind, was fully intelligible in the fourteenth century. Within the fragment of society that was noble, the variations in wealth could be so enormous as to defy easy comprehension.[14]

Nearly all nobles in the first half of the fourteenth century still derived most of their income from the traditional rural lordship or *seigneurie*, an agricultural enterprise worked by small cultivators and generating revenue from tenancies (which produced rents) and demesne lands (which yielded agricultural products for the market). Revenues could be in cash or in kind, but cash now furnished the larger part.[15] The multitude of small lordships produced little additional income. Larger ones had potentially profitable jurisdiction but also the expense of administering justice. They enjoyed the profits of certain facilities that they controlled as monopolies, the most economically significant of these being mills.[16] The greatest lords had other valuable assets, like the right to exact tolls on merchandise or to hold fairs or exploit the resources of forests.[17] Any conditions that eroded seigneurial revenues and threatened noble purchasing power not only affected their political behavior but also jeopardized the very status of the lesser lords. This threat became a harsh reality during the fourteenth and fifteenth centuries, a time of crisis for seigneurial revenues or, as the Marxists would have it, a "crisis of feudalism."

Several recent studies have documented this crisis and its impact on
the regional aristocracy to which the Clisson family belonged. A critical region was Normandy, in the heart of that crescent of lands in northwestern
France that contributed most commanders to late fourteenth-century military society. Using documents unique to Normandy, Guy Bois was able to
calculate, for certain times in the fourteenth and fifteenth centuries, the approximate number of hearths (households) in eastern Normandy relative
to the total for 1314. He established a rough population index for each of
the following six periods:[18]

1314:	100	1357:	70	ca. 1412–13:	65
1347:	97	late 1370s:	43	ca. 1460:	30

These figures indicate two periods of catastrophic demographic decline,
the first lasting for a generation after 1347 and the second beginning shortly
after 1410. Between these two periods of disaster, northwestern France experienced a revival in which the population index rose about 50 percent in
less than forty years, a time coinciding with the second half of Olivier de
Clisson's life.

It is not difficult to find causes for the original demographic decline.
A terrible famine, accompanied by disease, afflicted northern Europe in
1315–17 and produced the first small dip in the index. The Black Death of
1348 was largely responsible for the sharp fall in the population index for
eastern Normandy between 1347 and 1357, and it is known to have afflicted
Anjou and Poitou as well. This first epidemic seems not to have penetrated
Brittany or Maine, but its next occurrence in 1361–63 ravaged most areas
that had escaped in 1348,[19] as well as Normandy, which also experienced a
third epidemic in the mid-1370s. Between these visitations of plague, Normandy also suffered from destructive warfare, and the Norman population
declined by an even greater percentage after 1357 than in the preceding decade.[20]

The first appearance of plague produced the most disruption and left
the most documentary evidence because it had a greater effect on the adult
population than later occurrences, which could have a devastating impact
on the children but were much less of a threat to those who had survived an
earlier epidemic. After 1348–49, the disease did not kill many members of
the political and military elite. The plague devastated population centers,
killing off many people and leaving survivors with more wealth to spend
and less incentive to save for the future. Strong inflationary pressures drove

up the prices of manufactured goods and the wages of (now scarce) skilled labor, while demand for agricultural products declined with the disappearance of so many consumers. Unable to sell their produce, peasants left their villages for the high wages in the towns, thus making rural depopulation a secondary effect of the plague.[21] After 1374 (apparently a very bad year), famine and plague proved to be less frequent and less damaging over the next thirty-five to forty years, and the population began to recover.

What makes this demographic curve particularly important is that when Bois examined the available evidence on wages, prices, and production, he found that these economic indicators roughly paralleled the demographic changes and also paralleled economic trends found in other regions for which no population index can be established.[22] Subsequent studies devoted to Anjou and Poitou produced data that seem to substantiate the conclusions reached by Bois for eastern Normandy.[23] Brittany appears to have suffered less from plague, but warfare and emigration affected its population and economy.[24] If the Norman demographic curve can be taken as a rough indicator of its condition, the seigneurial economy seems to have experienced about thirty years of stagnation prior to 1348, about thirty years of sharp decline after that year, and a slightly longer period of recovery thereafter, terminating in a new crisis that began a few years after the death of Olivier de Clisson in 1407.

Using a demographic model to gauge the changing seigneurial economy is controversial, of course, but the available evidence appears persuasive. Abandonment of marginal lands reduced the total rent that lords could collect, while depopulation forced them to lower the rates of assessment in order to retain much-needed tenants.[25] Revenues from tenancies in eastern Normandy plummeted, and by 1458 they were only 29 to 35 percent of what they had been in 1316.[26] This slump paralleled the long-term demographic trend, but did these rents recover when the population did in the late fourteenth century? Two very incomplete series of rents belonging to a hospital in Anjou suggest an affirmative answer. In each case, the level of the early 1330s is assigned a value of 100. In one case, the index was 51 in 1363–64 but rebounded to 84 in 1385–86. In the second case, there are no figures for several decades, but the index stood at 80 in 1385 and was on the way up, fluctuating between 86 and 90 during the years 1387–1402.[27]

Income from a lordship's demesne lands came from the sale of produce, particularly grain. If war or plague destroyed part of a local population, demand for grain would be reduced, yet grain prices over much of western Europe were a mirror image of the demographic curve, rising

between 1335 and 1375, falling between 1375 and 1410, then rising again.[28]
Such figures suggest that production decreased even more than demand
did when the population was falling and that the higher prices did not
mean increased seigneurial income. In the county of Tancarville, *total* revenues suffered more than those from rents,[29] leaving one with the impression that the economic value of the directly exploited demesne declined
more sharply than that of the tenancies.

Larger lordships with income from sources like justice, monopolies,
and forests could be affected not only by changes in population but also by
the physical damage of warfare and the impact of royal financial policies.
The economic effects of war on a locality could vary with circumstances.
A passing raid by a large force could destroy crops and the homes of peasants and receive considerable attention from the chroniclers, but it might
not have a lasting economic or demographic effect. On the other hand,
prolonged campaigning in a particular district could lead to permanent
damage, as could the mere presence of troops (even supposedly friendly
forces) living off the land. The critical moment came eight years after the
Black Death when, in September 1356, the Prince of Wales defeated John II
near Poitiers, killing or capturing large numbers of French nobles and dis-
crediting the military aristocracy in the eyes of the French populace. Many
captive lords owed large ransoms, and the king himself was among the
prisoners. The ransoms imposed a new burden on the seigneurial economy, but a more serious consequence of the defeat arose when the warring
monarchs made a truce and ceased paying their troops. Thousands of warriors were stranded on French soil and forced to live off the land, either as
outright brigands or as participants in local wars.

Unemployed companies of soldiers (*routiers*) compounded the violence in Normandy, where civil war raged between 1356 and 1364. A gradual restoration of order brought Normandy a respite until a new English
invasion led to periods of severe devastation after 1415.[30] In Brittany, the
war of succession (1341–64) was particularly damaging in the 1350s when
English troops were heavily involved, but order returned rather quickly
after 1364. Intermittent fighting between 1373 and 1395, which played a
central role in the career of Olivier de Clisson, did not approach the intensity of the earlier conflict except towards the very end (1394). The military
activity in Normandy and Brittany made the 1350s a time of frequent campaigning in the county of Maine, where the brigandage of unemployed
troops aggravated the situation in the 1360s.[31] Anjou experienced fewer
military problems than many other areas in the fourteenth century,[32] as

French garrisons at Craon and Château-Gontier generally held off the hostile forces in Maine until 1360. In that year, however, unemployed *routiers* began to ravage Anjou until lured southward by expeditions to Spain. Their return in 1368, however, proved very damaging for several years.[33] From the mid-1370s, the region experienced relative peace once again (especially after the Franco-Breton treaty of 1381),[34] until a grave new crisis began around 1424.[35]

Taken as a whole, the periods of military violence and those of relative calm closely paralleled the falls and rises of the demographic curve established by Bois. Besides its impact on the population, military activity had a direct but varying impact on seigneurial revenues, particularly those of the larger rural lordships. Mills were the most lucrative of the seigneurial monopolies, and while Michel Le Mené has warned against exaggerating their importance, his figures are from the fifteenth century, after they had experienced their greatest crisis.[36] Bois has shown that the crisis began in the fourteenth century and that warfare was a major factor. The "scorched earth" tactics of military campaigns created terrible hardships for peasants but also inflicted serious damage on the capital assets of the lords. Mills represented a major investment, since both water mills and windmills were expensive to construct and maintain. Because of high replacement costs, the most effective way for enemy forces to inflict lasting economic damage on a lordship was to destroy its mill.[37] Nonmilitary factors could also hurt the profitability of mills, whose revenues were especially sensitive to rural economic conditions. Their receipts depended on the price and production of grain while their expenses were largely a function of the wages paid to those who maintained them.[38] Revenue was based on the amount of grain milled and so declined when grain production did, as after a demographic slump; yet such a slump brought rising wages, which increased the cost of maintaining a mill. The demographic curve thus affected the profitability of mills even without the intervention of war. Periods of intense military action, which coincided with times of declining population, aggravated the situation. Damage from war that was costly to repair may have prevented a recovery of mill revenues during the demographic revival, especially if lords lacked the motivation and resources to undertake improvements.[39]

Depopulation, violence, and royal financial measures could affect other seigneurial revenues that were available only to the greatest lords. An important Angevin barony like Craon, which was somewhat comparable to Clisson, included a major castle and a town. Craon could realize substantial profits from justice, but not many nobles possessed such resources.[40] Like justice, tolls on commerce were a resource for relatively few lords, mainly those who controlled commercial centers or points of transit.[41] War and plague seriously disrupted these revenues, the former doing most damage in the countryside and the latter in the towns. Tolls and customs were on the quantity of goods sold, not their price, so that any serious price inflation hurt lords who derived income from this source.[42]

The nobility of northwestern France, in which the Clisson family was deeply rooted, thus appears to have experienced economic dislocations that paralleled the demographic curve in a number of respects. A first crisis followed the Black Death and ran its course during the first half of the 1370s. It was followed by a partial revival and then, in the fifteenth century, by a second severe crisis.[43] For this regional aristocracy, the late medieval "crisis" thus took the form of two separate ones. The intervening recovery, which coincided with the time of Olivier de Clisson's greatest power, has received less scholarly emphasis,[44] but its existence can be illustrated by fluctuations in the king's "ordinary" revenues, which were mostly seigneurial in character. Averaging over 473,000 pounds (*livres tournois*) annually in the years 1328–31, they had fallen to 47,235 in 1374, were back over 100,000 in 1384, and exceeded 180,000 pounds per year by the mid-1390s, only to fall in the fifteenth century, to around 50,000 in 1460.[45] When the seigneurial revenues of the crown experienced such adversity, the royal government looked for other ways of raising money, so that royal fiscal policies tended to have a heavier impact at the very time that the seigneurial economy was in its greatest distress.

There are not enough reliable statistics to prove the economic impact of royal fiscal policies, but contemporary critics of the policies certainly perceived such an impact. Before 1356, royal taxes bore mainly on the towns and aroused opposition even though they were very light. To obtain more money, the crown tried various fiscal expedients, including periodic enforcement of the laws prohibiting usury. In 1347, for instance, the government announced a "reform" that canceled the interest on all debts to usurious moneylenders but required immediate repayment of the principal to the crown. The process of collecting this money lasted fifteen years before concerted opposition brought an end to it. Most of the debtors who had reached settlements with the crown were nobles. The king's windfall from this expedient was thus a concealed tax on that part of the nobility that was already in debt.[46]

Nobles were even angrier about the crown's manipulation of the currency for profit. Royal mints had to cover their operating costs by issuing coins with a face value slightly higher than the price paid for the bullion. The crown could widen this gap by raising the assigned value of the coins or by "debasing" them (lowering their bullion content), thereby making a profit far greater than that needed to operate the mints. Introduced by Philip IV in the 1290s, this practice could yield enormous sums, but it caused an increase in the money supply and its impact was inflationary. Royal income from this source was another concealed tax, bearing mainly on wealthy people with fixed incomes. Nobles and clergy, with their dependence on seigneurial revenues, were quick to recognize its impact on their resources and led the demands for "strong money."[47] Philip VI's need for funds at the beginning of the Hundred Years' War, aggravated by a shortage of silver bullion, led him to weaken the currency seriously between 1337 and 1343, when the anger of the possessing classes compelled a drastically deflationary reform of the coinage. In the 1350s the crown began a bewildering series of manipulations that alternately weakened and strengthened the currency until highly vocal reformers not only demanded a stable coinage but also challenged the crown's right to alter it at will.[48]

The most erratic changes in the royal currency and the crown's campaign to squeeze money from noble debtors occurred in those years after the Black Death when the seigneurial economy was feeling the first effects of demographic losses. The intensified violence after 1356 and the costly ransoms owed by captured nobles coincided with the first really sharp increases in royal taxes. These were dictated by two compelling needs: the very large ransom required to secure the king's release and expensive military measures to control the *routiers*. They occurred in an atmosphere of class conflict; widespread hostility towards the nobility after 1356 achieved violent expression in the uprising of 1358 known as the *Jacquerie*.[49] The nobles thus had their first real encounter with royal taxes at a most inopportune time, for the late 1350s were not only a period of growing economic distress but also the time when they were held in the lowest public esteem. Thinking mainly of economic factors, Bois asserted that the problems of the lords created a general social crisis because the dominant class in society was losing the means of maintaining its rank.[50]

Although the greatest lords had the political influence to articulate the concerns of their class as a whole, it was not they who were threatened by the crisis, but rather the mass of petty nobles with one or two small lordships. Brittany, for instance, abounded in tiny fiefs with less than one hundred pounds in income.[51] No less than 149 small lordships were dependencies of the barony of Clisson,[52] while the Breton castle of Moncontour had around forty.[53] Olivier de Clisson's lordship of La Garnache in Poitou had sixty-eight noble dependencies, and his nearby possession of Palluau had over thirty.[54] If these cases appear exceptional, we may cite Le Mené's finding that the castellanies of Anjou had between fifteen and forty noble fiefs dependent on them.[55] Bois has mentioned the "miniscule" fiefs held by the *gros bataillons* of the nobility.[56] A confiscated lordship in Poitou granted to a royal follower in 1371 had an annual revenue of only 60 *l.t.*[57] Malcolm Vale points out that most nobles did not have castles, only *maisons fortes*—enough fortification to lord it over the rural inhabitants of their locality but no defense against a serious incursion by *routiers*.[58]

The nobility as a whole may have been a tiny elite among the lay population, but the castellans were a small elite within this group. Even among the castellans, moreover, there were significant variations in wealth. Le Mené used figures from the mid-fifteenth century when the value of Angevin lordships had declined considerably since 1400. For that later period he identified castellanies of a middling sort worth 200 to 300 pounds and three richer categories—those in the 500–800 pound range, those worth around 1,650 pounds, and a few great lordships worth 2,500–3,000 pounds.[59] Thus even within this elite subgroup the greatest lordships were worth ten times as much as the middling castellanies. Many nobles doubtless possessed more than one property, but this fact may have aggravated the gulf between the richest and poorest lords. The extreme variations of wealth within the nobility seem indisputable. The more difficult question is how large a portion of the nobles had an income so low as to face a threat to their status.

Contemporary documents used the terms "living nobly" and "pursuing the profession of arms" to define noble status.[60] For men of noble birth to maintain their status, they had to be well enough off to avoid manual labor and most types of commerce,[61] and they had to be able to afford the equipment of a mounted warrior. The pursuit of arms became increasingly costly in the fourteenth century, as improved missile weapons dictated protective gear more effective than the old chain mail, and the heavier plate armor made necessary larger and stronger horses. These changes made it more expensive to be a knight and may help explain Philippe Contamine's finding that only 15 percent of the French nobility ranked as knights in 1340 and just 10 percent did so by 1400.[62] Most nobles were only squires, and it is doubtful that many could afford the more expensive equipment. The question is how much income met the minimum required for a noble to support his family and maintain himself as a squire.

Contamine has found that defensive equipment for an ordinary man at arms cost about 25 *l.t.* in the 1360s, while the warhorse, then perhaps society's most potent symbol of status, cost a knight about 75 *l.t.* in this period, compared to around 36 *l.t.* for a squire's mount.[63] The squires in a detachment mustered at Saumur in 1370 had horses ranging in value from twenty-five to fifty pounds and averaging 37 *l.t.*[64] On one occasion, Contamine shows, living expenses for a "gentleman" on campaign came to 7 *sols tournois* per day, or about 127 pounds for a year.[65] Such figures, insofar as we can trust them, suggest that a squire with a single horse required over sixty pounds in initial capital and twice that much in annual income for his military role alone. To support a house and family and acquire a second mount naturally required more. It seems most unlikely that a squire could manage on less than two hundred pounds a year, even if he were lucky enough avoid capture or the loss of horse or equipment. It is in this context that the crisis of the seigneurial economy takes on real meaning. A noble with fiefs yielding three hundred pounds in income in the 1330s was in comfortable circumstances, but if his lordships yielded only half as much in 1364,[66] his status would be in serious jeopardy without income from an external source.

Vale has stated that "an annual income of 200 *l.t.* was not within the grasp of many nobles."[67] Even if we were to treat his appraisal as overly pessimistic and assume that only a third of the nobles fell below that line in the 1360s, we could still speak of a major crisis and understand the scourge of the *routiers*, who drew so many of their number from the nobility of war-ravaged regions with very small lordships. The daily salary for a squire in royal service was 10 *s.t.*, or around 180 pounds a year.[68] As the government gradually found ways to suppress the *routiers*, the growing number of nobles who needed more income than their lordships provided found it necessary to seek employment in the service of the king or a powerful prince.[69] In this economic context, the 1360s marked an important turning point in French political society, specifically in the royal relations with the nobility of the north and west.

French political society was not restricted to nobles, but they regularly formed its most important component. Political conflict generally involved competing groups of them or broader factions led by nobles. The old nobility had a very keen sense of honor and status,[70] and by the early fourteenth century many of its members were beginning to perceive threats to their traditional political and social role. Among these were increasing royal reliance on lawyers and financiers of nonnoble origin, inflationary manipulations of the currency, excessive donations of royal domain to favorites or cronies of the king, and fiscal measures that either blurred the distinction between nobles and other people or threatened seigneurial incomes.[71] For Cazelles, the nobles of the fourteenth century perceived themselves as having lost former powers and privileges, and he saw their anxiety reflected in increasing emphasis on endogamous marriage and efforts to become more of a caste.[72]

Demands for "reform" generally originated with dissident nobles who pressed the crown to correct these perceived abuses, but the demands were usually triggered by an event the government could not correct: a serious defeat on the battlefield. Nobles felt more threatened at such times because military defeat might call into question their ability to carry out their most obvious social function. A monarchy weakened by defeat was sure to face the wrath of noble reformers who took sharp notice of all recent developments they found threatening. Royal financial practices came under particular scrutiny at such times, as did the people from whom the king had been taking advice. Uncertain royal successions in 1316 and 1328 had created political tensions, and French military defeats in the years 1345 to 1347 led to demands for reform from a group of nobles and clergy whose familiar agenda Cazelles has identified: a strong and stable royal currency, control of finances by honest men, inalienability of royal domain, and enough control over the choice of royal councillors to prevent excessive influence on the part of the king's *familiers*.[73] Their reform program had support from nonnoble elements as well, since many Frenchmen distrusted the newer institutions of government, but for the nobles, "reform" coincided with the defense of their threatened liberties.[74]

While nonnobles looked to the monarchy as an institution that provided protection, public order, and justice, nobles had felt capable of providing themselves with these things, and for them political allegiance remained a largely personal matter. It is pointless to speculate on how much of their outlook was derived from a "feudal" tradition. Ties of blood, marriage, vassalage, and clientage, as well as loyalty to a particular king or to the royal house were all mixed in together, were personal in nature, and were strongly colored by perceived self-interest. The complex nature of these personal concerns will be especially evident as we try to understand the career of Olivier de Clisson, a western noble with strong loyalties and devoted friends, but also bitter enemies and powerful grudges. The northwestern nobles, who did not play an influential role under Philip VI, began to express discontent by the late 1330s, and in the next few years the royal

Parlement intervened, at times heavy-handedly, in their feuds and quarrels, including those involving the Harcourt, Tesson, and Clisson families.[75]

After the Valois succession created the possibility of alternative allegiance, this option attracted several powerful lords from the disaffected northwestern nobility, as Robert of Artois, Godefroi de Harcourt (Normandy), and Jean de Montfort (Brittany) swore allegiance to Edward III. Numerous ties linked the important families from different parts of this great crescent of lands. Members of families from the west often married into noble families of Picardy, Artois, or Hainault. The Clisson family, one of those dominating southeastern Brittany, had relatives in Anjou and Maine, lands in lower Normandy, and after 1330, important possessions in Poitou. The Norman lords of Harcourt held the viscounty of Châtellerault in the west as well lands as far north as the county of Hainault. The Brienne family, counts of Eu and Guines, had major possessions in Poitou. These last, along with the Craon family in the west, the Fiennes in the north, the ducal house of Brittany, and many ecclesiastical houses, held lands in England.[76] Most northwestern nobles, however, did not turn to England but expressed their discontent by demanding reforms in Paris and looking for leadership to the Évreux branch of the royal family.

The house of Évreux derived its prestige largely from Jeanne, queen of Navarre (d. 1349), the daughter of Louis X, but it was her husband, Philip (d. 1343), who possessed the *apanage* that gave the family its all-important Norman base—the county of Évreux. Their son Charles II of Navarre (1332–87), whom a sixteenth-century chronicler would nickname "the Bad," inherited a large clientele of discontented nobles. His father had been cultivating some of those in the north since the 1330s, giving pensions to the Coucy, Poix, Châtillon, Raineval, Fiennes, and Clermont-Nesle families, among others. In addition to these, Charles the Bad's own northern supporters included the families of Hangest, Trie, and Luxembourg-Ligny.[77] In Normandy itself, Charles had numerous followers by the 1350s. Among the families later represented in the royal military leadership under Charles V, we find the Clères, Paynel, Saquenville, Malet, Tournebu, Braquemont, and above all, the important house of Harcourt.[78] The Évreux family also supported a major intellectual institution, the College de Navarre at the University of Paris. First established by Louis X's mother and sustained by several generations of his descendants, it became an important stronghold for reformers.[79]

Those whose resentments led them to be tempted by alternative allegiance may have considered themselves still loyal to the crown of France, but to Philip VI they were guilty of *lèse majesté*, and the Hundred Years' War brought a sharp increase in the number of treason cases. Executions of prominent nobles for treason had been so rare that they created a sensation under the first two Valois kings.[80] Philip VI's more repressive policies towards disaffected northwestern nobles were attributed to the influence of his queen, Jeanne of Burgundy, who came to symbolize the crown's eastern orientation and was said to dislike Normans.[81]

When the French defeats of 1345–47 led to an outcry by reformist nobles, Philip VI added to his council several men associated with the Évreux family.[82] A plan to overhaul the government and build a well-financed royal army soon collapsed under the impact of the Black Death, and Philip's reign ended without further action. Soon after becoming king in 1350, John II angered the northwestern nobility by executing for treason one of its most prominent members, Raoul de Brienne, constable of France.[83] By this time the politics of alternative allegiance had undergone a change because Charles the Bad had now come of age. The young count of Évreux became king of Navarre in 1349 at the age of seventeen and subsequently married the daughter of John II. Only hardened rebels now supported Edward III, but many noble dissidents turned to the king of Navarre for leadership. Ties of clientage, patiently cultivated for fifteen years or more, enabled the house of Évreux to lead a formidable opposition party that gained in strength when John II replaced the executed constable with his favorite, Charles of Spain, an enemy of the Évreux family and inevitably resented by those with ties to the Brienne family.[84] Early in 1354, Charles of Navarre engineered the murder of Charles of Spain,[85] inaugurating a decade of Valois-Évreux hostilities that complicated the larger Anglo-French conflict and proved critical for the history of French political and military society.

The monarchy of Charles V eventually appropriated many of the reforms and reformers associated with the Évreux camp in the 1350s and achieved success after winning over important former dissidents from the northwestern nobility. After Charles died in 1380, however, his son's reign would be disturbed by a renewed rivalry between those who wished to continue the recent political tradition of Charles V and those who supported successive dukes of Burgundy whose roots were in the political society associated with the first two Valois kings. The conflicts between Valois and Évreux, between "corrupt" officials and advocates of reform, and between the north/west and the center/east often coincided with each other, but politics are rarely tidy and the three areas of conflict could also cut across each other. In the important Melun family, for instance, the influential archbishop of Sens was associated with noble advocates of "reform," but was not with Charles of Navarre. His brother Jean was count of Tancarville, which Cazelles has described as an island of anti-Navarrese sentiment in the duchy of Normandy,[86] and the Melun clan was connected to Charles of Spain.[87]

While continuing the policy of trying to defuse opposition by bringing new people into his council, John II still delegated great power to a few trusted men, mostly new nobles of bourgeois origin, who headed the major branches of the government.[88] They were highly unpopular and came under attack not only from noble and clerical reformers, but also from prominent Parisian bourgeois who resented and envied their successful careers.[89] Once drawn into what had originally been an antibourgeois reform movement, the Parisian leaders would come to play an important political role.

After the assassination of Charles of Spain, the king tried to accommodate his Évreux relations by adding pro-Navarrese lords to his council.[90] At the same time, he undertook peace negotiations with England in order to gain a free hand in dealing with Charles. In doing so, John II had to contemplate a dismemberment of his realm, for Edward III now regularly insisted on holding his French lands in full sovereignty so as to escape the jurisdictional claims of French officials. Charles of Navarre was bound to resist a settlement that would leave him isolated and make concessions to English claims that he considered inferior to his own. The Parisians and many reformers opposed a peace that would dismember the realm,[91] while many nobles, whether reform-minded or not, had a growing economic stake in a well-paid royal army. It is small wonder that draft treaties, both before and after 1356, ran into strong opposition. In the Estates General of December 1355, opponents of the monarchy were united, and they pushed through a number of reforms that served the interests of the dissident nobility more than anybody else.[92] These measures, however, were predicated on the collection of substantial taxes and, by the spring of 1356, those who were hostile to the taxes broke with the others and grouped themselves around Charles of Navarre, whose commitment to reform was far less strong than his hostility to the king.[93] In April, John II seized and imprisoned Charles, executing some of his supporters. Normandy plunged into open civil war.[94]

Defeat at Poitiers in September not only cost John his liberty but also decimated his council and the ranks of senior royal officers.[95] The young dauphin Charles, nominally in charge of the government during his father's captivity, bowed to the demands of the crown's opponents, and by March of 1357 the royal council was largely in the hands of reform-minded nobles, mostly from the north (Picardy and Artois) and from Normandy.[96] Many had associations with Charles of Navarre who, however, remained in prison until November 1357. When his partisans then secured his release, the nobles of Burgundy and Champagne angrily ceased cooperating with the reformers in the Estates. Charles the Bad, however, retained the support of the Parisians, who thought him best situated to protect the unimpeded navigation of the lower Seine that their economy required.[97] The citizens of the capital, who had their own agenda, were probably wrong in thinking he could pacify the surrounding countryside, but they were among the last to become disillusioned with this erratic prince. Blaming the military nobility for the brigandage, the Parisians murdered two marshals in the dauphin's presence during February 1358 and then, towards the end of May, played a supporting role in the anti-noble *Jacquerie*. These actions drove a sharp wedge between the noble and bourgeois reformers.[98]

The dauphin would be able to exploit this rupture, but without the money to pay troops he could neither suppress the *Jacquerie* nor subdue the Parisians. It fell to Charles the Bad to deal with the former, with a crushing victory at Mello and the aid of many northwestern nobles who were with him. Then, however, he entered Paris in triumph as an ally and collaborator of Étienne Marcel, leader of the Parisian bourgeois and now a sworn enemy of most nobles. Whether active reformers or merely class-conscious, nobles found it increasingly difficult to follow the king of Navarre, whose behavior continued to alienate supporters and turn them towards the dauphin.[99] The latter regained Paris later in the summer and by the end of 1359 the council again was dominated by reformist nobles, some of whom were formerly associated with the house of Évreux. The nucleus of this group, led by the Melun brothers, would remain intact for over fifteen years,[100] but the council gradually lost its role as the central forum for political debate.

For the hitherto dissident nobility, the year 1360 ended well. An Anglo-French treaty, drafted at Brétigny in May and ratified at Calais in October, required that hostages be sent to England to guarantee full payment of the royal ransom. Earlier drafts had proposed hostages drawn largely from the Navarrese camp—a scheme that, if implemented, would have rid John II of troublesome critics but which in fact guaranteed that the proposed treaties would meet strong opposition. The new treaty, by contrast, named as noble hostages many who were already prisoners in

England. The change in their status eliminated their need to pay ransoms. The bourgeois hostages came largely from towns that had supported Marcel and were considered anti-noble.[101] Finally, in December, the king promulgated an important fiscal package that must be seen as highly favorable to the nobility. It brought stability to the much-abused silver coinage, introduced a gold franc worth one *livre tournois*, and established taxes to pay for the royal ransom that bore primarily on the towns.[102]

There remained two final steps in the process that drew the formerly dissident nobility into the royalist camp: first, the decision, at the end of 1363, to finance a regularly salaried royal army; and second, two decisive battles in 1364 that ended the civil wars in Normandy and Brittany. The way at last was clear for nobles of the north and west like Olivier de Clisson to find employment and positions of leadership in the government of Charles V.[103]

2

The Breton Nobility
and the Succession Crisis

AT THE END OF THE 1350s, when the formerly disaffected nobility began to enter the royalist camp, Normandy and the north were well represented, but, as yet, the rest of the great crescent of northwestern lands—
Maine, Anjou, Brittany, and Poitou—was not. Some of this territory was
now in English hands, while in virtually all of it the closely interrelated
nobility was distracted by a disputed succession in the duchy of Brittany.
For twenty-three years (1341–64), the Breton war of succession consumed
the energies of these people and provided an important new theater of
operations for the war between England and France. This Breton conflict was one aspect of the monarchy's difficulty with the nobility of the
north and west. It also bore heavily on the socio-economic troubles of the
period, especially the emerging problem of uprooted soldiers (*routiers*). It
was also, of course, the critical factor in Olivier de Clisson's childhood and
youth and in the early military career of his older and more famous com-
patriot, Bertrand du Guesclin.

Brittany had long been a turbulent society, its nobility acquiring renown as fierce warriors. After the accession of John I as duke in 1237, however, the duchy enjoyed an uncharacteristic century of relative peace. In the
French-speaking eastern part of the duchy lay a tier of strong noble fiefs[1]
whose ruling families intermarried with neighboring dynasties in Maine,
Anjou, and Poitou. Thus the Laval family of Maine joined the Breton aristocracy after Guy VII de Laval married the heiress of Vitré in 1239.[2] The
Craon family of Anjou intermarried not only with the Laval but also with
the Breton families of Clisson and Lohéac.[3] In the mid-thirteenth century,
the Poitevin family of Chabot acquired by a marriage the lordship of Rais
(Rays, Retz) which lay in the frontier districts ("marches") of Brittany
south of the Loire and adjacent to neighboring Poitou and Anjou.[4] Be-

sides Rais, the most notable lordships in this sector were Machecoul and Clisson, the latter consisting of a castle and village near the southeastern frontier of the duchy.

The Clisson family had been obscure marcher lords until the late twelfth century, when they began a long rise to prominence fueled by a succession of brilliant marriages.[5] One such marriage united a lord of Clisson with Constance de Pontchâteau, from whom their son Olivier I inherited the castle of Blain, northwest of Nantes, which became the Clisson family's favored residence for a century.[6] After a serious falling-out with Duke John I, Olivier was forced to relinquish his lordships to his son Olivier II on 1 March 1262.[7]

Olivier II reigned as lord of Clisson for about thirty-five years, during which time he rebuilt the damaged château at Blain and married into a prominent Norman family, acquiring as his wife's dowry a part of the barony of Thury. This lordship, Le Thuit, would become significant in fourteenth-century politics.[8] The son of this marriage, Guillaume, remains an obscure figure because of his early death after being lord of Clisson for no more than a decade, but he too concluded a very favorable marriage, to the well-connected Isabelle de Craon (ca. 1282–1350), by whom he had two sons.[9] The older of these, Olivier III, was a widower in 1326, but his second marriage, around 1330, was to Jeanne de Belleville, the young widow of the lord of Châteaubriant and herself the heiress to a string of Poitevin lordships south of Clisson.[10] Their combined holdings made Olivier and Jeanne the leading seigneurial power in the marches. The couple had five children, two of whom, Maurice and Guillaume, had been born by 1334.[11] Although he was their youngest son, the future Olivier IV, born two years later, was the only one to survive his parents and inherit their fortune.

The marriages that led to the rise of the Clisson family were but one part of a series of marriage alliances that turned the aristocracy of Brittany and the marches into one vast interrelated network and made their conflicts very much a family affair. Duke Arthur II (r. 1305–12) made two important marriages. His first wife, heiress to the viscounty of Limoges, bore him three sons. His second wife, a widowed queen of Scotland and heiress to the county of Montfort l'Amaury, produced several daughters (including Béatrix, the future mother-in-law of Olivier IV de Clisson) and also a son, Jean de Montfort.[12] The latter, in 1329, married Jeanne, the sister of Count Louis I of Flanders, who promised as her dowry certain lands in his counties of Nevers and Rethel. She never actually received this dowry,[13] possibly because the count required the property for his own support after

Figure 1. Ruins of Blain castle. (Photograph by Margery C. Henneman)

being driven from Flanders in the 1330s. Her son's long effort to secure these lands or a comparable income would prove to be a continuing irritant in his relations with the French crown.

Arthur's oldest son, John III (r. 1312–41) inherited the ducal title but his marriages produced no children and one of his full brothers had died. In 1317, John endowed his other full brother, Guy, with a large *apanage* in northern Brittany, the county of Penthièvre, in exchange for Guy's claims to the viscounty of Limoges. The great Breton historian, Arthur de la Borderie, believed that John III harbored a strong personal dislike for his stepmother and her son, Jean de Montfort, who possessed only the small *apanage* of Guérande.[14] If so, the duke was left in a quandary when Guy died in 1331, leaving only a nine-year-old daughter, Jeanne. John is said to have considered giving Brittany to the king of France in exchange for other lands, but gave up the idea when the Breton magnates opposed it. In any case, when young Jeanne de Penthièvre reached marriageable age in 1337, a very suitable spouse was found in Charles of Blois, a nephew of the king of France. It is doubtful that such a marriage could have been arranged without the assumption that Jeanne would inherit the duchy of Brittany, but John III never produced the document or public pronouncement that might have spared his land a serious crisis.[15]

John III died on 30 April 1341 with the succession unresolved, and Montfort, who had apparently shown little prior interest in Brittany, was enough of an opportunist to advance a claim.[16] According to a much-repeated story derived from chroniclers, he seized the treasury at Limoges, then traveled rapidly through Brittany, gaining the submission of numerous towns and castles in the ducal domain.[17] Recent scholarship has largely discredited this entire version of the events of 1341,[18] but the English did initiate contact with Montfort in July.[19] Nearly four months after John III's death, in late August 1341, Philip VI opened hearings on the disputed succession, taking testimony from various Breton lords and hearing Montfort's case.[20] The exclusion of women from the royal succession, which had made Philip king, had no bearing on regional customs like those of Brittany, which did not bar female succession except that younger brothers were favored over older sisters,[21] but it was not clear whether a younger brother had a stronger claim than the heir of a deceased older brother. The duke of Brittany, however, had been made a peer of France in 1297,[22] and Montfort's lawyers claimed that a peerage should be subject to the rules of succession recently established for the French crown.[23] Michael Jones has pointed out the irony in this argument, for Montfort's descendants would steadfastly argue that Breton custom took precedence over whatever might be implied by the status of peer of France.[24]

On 7 September at Conflans, Philip and his court of peers handed down the verdict that Philip had favored: Charles of Blois and Jeanne de Penthièvre would inherit, and render homage for, the duchy of Brittany.[25] Edward III now moved quickly to encourage Montfort to resist this ruling, granting him the English earldom of Richmond, which had long belonged to dukes of Brittany. Once given this support, Montfort began seeking adherents in the duchy, but without much initial success. The Blois-Penthièvre party, however, had ties to the French monarchy that could arouse anxieties among those who clung to the Breton tradition of autonomy.[26]

Montfort did find one important early supporter in the person of the captain of Rennes, Amaury de Clisson, the younger brother of Olivier III.[27] Most of the Montfortists, however, were from the western part of the duchy and were townsmen or petty nobles rather than prelates or great lords. Such supporters were not enough to resist a French army that as-

TABLE I. The Houses of Valois and Brittany in the Fourteenth Century.

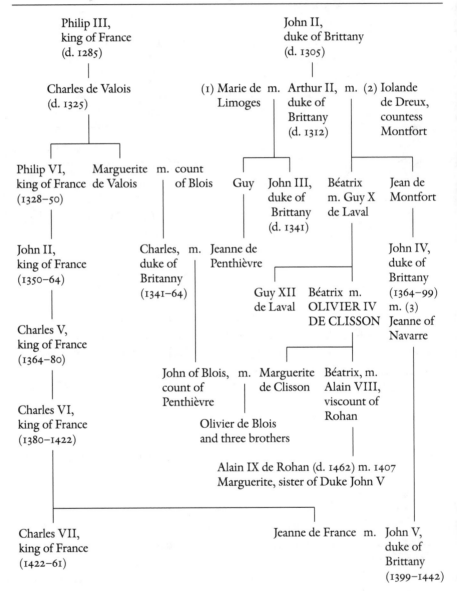

sembled at Angers in October, then took Champtoceaux and advanced down the Loire to blockade Montfort in Nantes. On 18 November 1341, the city capitulated and Montfort was captured. The crown then tried to obtain a negotiated compromise that would give him compensation in return for surrendering his claims to the ducal title.[28]

The disputed succession seemed on the brink of resolution after a short crisis. Why then did it turn into a civil war of twenty-three years' duration? La Borderie suggested a number of reasons, most notably Edward III's desire to make the conflict last as long as possible.[29] Edward's intervention surely was a critical factor, but certain characteristics of the Breton nobility also affected the situation. The great lords of Brittany had important interests in other parts of northwestern France, largely because of their many marital alliances, and these interests made them tend to support the "French connection" represented by Charles of Blois. But Brittany also contained a vast number of poor nobles whose interests were more parochial and whose economic needs were more urgent.[30] For this group, military employment had a particular allure, and they were receptive to opportunities afforded by the Anglo-Montfortists in what has been called "ideal terrain for small-scale guerilla warfare."[31]

It is doubtful that any of these factors could have led to a prolonged struggle if the victorious forces of Charles of Blois had maintained the momentum that could force Montfort to reach the agreement sought by Philip VI. Their failure to do so has generally been attributed to the courage and tenacity of Montfort's wife, Jeanne of Flanders. Perhaps the chroniclers exaggerated her military exploits, but she seems to have put up an unexpected resistance that slowed the French advance, and she also "sent at least two embassies to England." The result was an English alliance and a series of landings between March and October 1342 that eventually put thousands of English troops into the duchy.[32] In this way Jeanne effectively torpedoed Philip VI's hopes for negotiating a quick and favorable end to the dispute. It required all her skill and energy to keep going during the first half of 1342 because the bulk of the English army took a long time to arrive, but with a few supporters and a small English contingent, she held out in the Breton-speaking west until Edward III finally arrived in the fall. The Anglo-Montfortist coalition proceeded to establish control over a ring of coastal fortresses in southern and western Brittany, but the campaign had only mixed results and might have ended in disaster if the French army had been more aggressive.[33] In January 1343, England and

France concluded the truce of Malestroit that halted hostilities for two years[34] and left the Montfortists in a stronger position than a year earlier.

Once committed to the Breton conflict, Edward III had agents in France actively seeking support from those nobles in Normandy and Brittany who had grievances against Philip VI.[35] A key figure in this endeavor was Olivier III de Clisson, who not only possessed Pontchâteau, Blain, and Héric northwest of Nantes but also, with his wife, held the fortresses that straddled the duchy's southern frontier, dominated a rich countryside, and had good access to the sea.[36] His allegiance was a prize worth pursuing, and the English knew that his brother was already a leading Montfortist and his wife, a friend of Jeanne of Flanders.[37] Olivier had supported Philip VI and Charles of Blois, but he had run afoul of royal justice and was imprisoned briefly in 1341 for an unauthorized duel that was deemed an offense against the king's majesty.[38] He had suffered criticism and suspicion from the French side when he failed to hold Vannes against the English in 1342.[39] By December 1342, Clisson and several other marcher lords had decided to defect, and Edward III could write his son that he had Olivier's adherence and that of his son-in-law, the lord of Rieux, and his neighbors the lords of Rais, Machecoul, and Lohéac.[40]

During the long conflict, many important Breton lords would change sides occasionally to protect their interests or gain some advantage,[41] but to Philip VI, support for the Montfortists was tantamount to treason (*lèse majesté*) since it implied allegiance to Edward III rather than to himself.[42] Philip learned that the marcher lords had defected and did not think that the truce forbade him to punish traitors. Olivier de Clisson, thinking himself protected by the truce, attended a tournament in French territory during the summer of 1343. Philip had him arrested and brought to trial for treason, confiscated his lands in July, and had him beheaded in Paris on 2 August, ordering that the severed head be displayed at Nantes as a warning to others.[43]

To royal lawyers advocating drastic punishment for *lèse majesté*, Philip's action may have seemed entirely appropriate, but the execution of so prominent a lord produced consternation among the Breton nobility and may well have been a violation of the truce.[44] Clisson's wealthy widow, Jeanne de Belleville, was not a woman to be taken lightly. She had a keen sense of her rights and had brought action against her husband in 1334 when she felt he was not honoring their marriage contract.[45] She responded to Olivier's execution with a series of hostile actions during the summer that produced complaints in September about truce violations and led the

French crown to seize her property in November and declare her guilty of treason in December.[46]

The brief and garbled contemporary accounts do not permit us to trace Jeanne's activities with any assurance of accuracy, but as subsequent writers have embellished the story, it becomes worth retelling as a kind of metaphor, both for her personality and for that which Olivier IV would reveal in his mature years. One version has it that Jeanne, with her sons Guillaume and Olivier, left Clisson in a small vessel and traveled downstream to Nantes, where she took her boys to the Sauvetout gate, showed them the severed head of their father that was displayed there, and had them swear eternal hostility towards Philip VI and Charles of Blois. Subsequently, she and some adherents surprised and massacred a pro-Blois garrison holding Château Thébaut, just west of Clisson. Then they conducted raids by sea and destroyed French shipping, possibly in the estuary of the Penerf river. Her luck then ran out in a storm at sea, and for a time she and her boys were adrift in a small boat, where Guillaume died. At length, however, she made her way to Hennebont, the fortified port on the Blavet river where Jeanne of Flanders had been residing with the young Montfort heir.[47] In due course, she and Olivier followed the Montforts to exile in England.[48]

The two women and their young sons had sharply different experiences during their years in England, and it is regrettable that we do not possess more detailed information about this important period. Jeanne de Belleville seems to have fared very well. As early as September 1345, Jean de Montfort granted her lands taken from a partisan of Charles of Blois in Brittany,[49] and three years later Edward III gave her an important income from Bordeaux.[50] When the kings of England and France made a truce in the fall of 1347, Jeanne was deemed sufficiently important to be included on a short list of major English allies explicitly covered by its provisions.[51] To recover her confiscated lands in Poitou, Jeanne required a champion of proven military ability, and she found him in the person of Walter Bentley, one of Edward III's commanders, whom she married, probably in 1349. To give them further incentive, Edward III bestowed on the couple some of the former Belleville possessions now in French hands.[52]

The generous treatment accorded to Jeanne de Belleville stands in contrast to the experience of the countess of Montfort, Jeanne of Flanders. After some months in England as an honored guest, she was confined in Tickhill castle by December 1343. Except for a mysterious and abortive attempt to rescue her in 1347, she spent nearly thirty uneventful years in custody. Historians have long believed that she suffered a mental breakdown and was incarcerated because of insanity.[53] Recently, however, John Leland has challenged this view, presenting evidence that she was really a captive and speculating that Edward III wanted full control of Breton affairs, especially to raise taxes there, and that she was becoming an obstacle to his plans.[54] To make their foothold in Brittany as self-financing as possible, the English developed a system of "ransom districts," systematically exacting forced payments in money and kind from the unfortunate Breton populace in the areas they controlled.[55] This practice must have dampened enthusiasm for the Montforts and may well have encountered Jeanne's opposition.[56] If Edward's real aim was to prolong the English presence rather than settling the succession, this woman who so tenaciously upheld her husband's cause could have become an embarrassing liability instead of an ally. The possible explanations for her incarceration do not explain its long duration. Perhaps her health did deteriorate subsequently.

While their mothers were having such contrasting experiences in exile, the two young Breton lords were growing up at the English court. When Jean de Montfort died in 1345, his son of the same name, whom the English recognized as duke of Brittany, was five or six years old, while Olivier IV de Clisson was nine. Young Montfort, now without both his parents, was brought up as an important prince, but he remained a pawn in English policy and was utterly dependent on the goodwill and generosity of his self-interested host. Young Clisson, already hardened by the cruel experiences of 1343, was in a less dependent situation because his mother remained an important political figure with a good income.[57] All of Clisson's biographers have seized upon the remarks of an English chronicler to portray him as a tall, handsome, athletic young man, attractive to women and an extrovert who developed an early taste for military matters and began to act like a great lord. Montfort, by contrast, is portrayed as less robust, more calm and reflective, and ready to employ deception to attain his ends.[58] Whether or not their boyhood in England left him jealous of Clisson, as some have said,[59] the young claimant to the duchy of Brittany would have to contend with the fact that he and Olivier grew up as equals in an atmosphere that was not conducive to a lord-vassal relationship.[60]

The truce of Malestroit had left Blois in control of Nantes and Rennes as well as his wife's lands, and the French crown had managed to head off a full-scale rupture with the northwestern nobility. The Montfort cause appeared to languish, and after Philip VI proclaimed an amnesty in 1344, Charles of Blois recovered the loyalty of a number of important people, including Amaury de Clisson.[61] In January 1345, the Parlement finally ruled on the succession to the viscounty of Limoges, again favoring Jeanne de Penthièvre and Charles of Blois.[62] Soon thereafter, Jean de Montfort evaded his captors, rendered homage to Edward III for Brittany, and returned to the duchy to breathe new life into his cause.[63] Although he soon died (September 1345), the English, who now acted on his son's behalf, invaded Penthièvre and captured La Roche-Derrien in December. Not until a year and a half later did Charles of Blois and his supporters make a concerted effort to recover this place, but when they did, the English under Thomas Dagworth completely overwhelmed them. Charles was captured, while Amaury de Clisson met his death in what La Borderie has called a "massacre" of the Breton aristocracy.[64]

The battle of La Roche-Derrien, occurring so soon after important English victories over France at Auberoche and Crécy, and just six months before Edward III captured Calais, seemingly left Edward in a position to dictate his own solution to the Breton dispute. The heir to whom he had made a commitment was, however, still a young child who would need continued English assistance, and perhaps La Borderie was not entirely fair in stating that Edward only wished to keep the duchy in turmoil.[65]

The political and military situation was especially complicated in the strategic marches south of the Loire that the former Clisson-Belleville holdings had dominated. Edward tried to make use of Raoul de Caours, a somewhat shady character from the Guérande region. Caours was one of the Breton nobles who had accepted the French amnesty of 1344, but he soon changed sides again and by 1347 was Edward's lieutenant in northern Poitou with the promise of a substantial income from lands he recovered from the French.[66] Raoul campaigned with some success against the local French commanders, Foulques de Laval and Le Galois de la Heuse,[67] but his gains created a problem for the English because Walter Bentley was now Jeanne de Belleville's husband and expected to recover the lands of his wife and stepson. To forestall a private war between Caours and Bentley, Edward III ordered them to accept his arbitration, and on 20 October 1349 he ruled in favor of Bentley. Edward ordered his lieutenant in Aquitaine, the duke of Lancaster, who had favored Caours, to take Jeanne and her family under his protection and enforce the ruling of 20 October. Caours then defected again and arranged the ambush and the death of Dagworth in 1350.[68]

Bentley, already Edward III's commander in the marches, now received responsibility for all of Brittany as Dagworth's successor and inflicted a major defeat on a French-led army at Mauron on 14 August 1352.

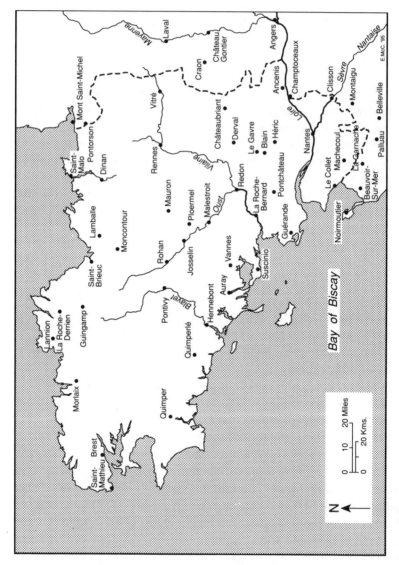

Map 2. Brittany and its southern marches.

The Breton magnates of the Blois-Penthièvre party again suffered heavy casualties, and their cause appeared prostrate. Edward III did not seek to terminate the conflict in favor of the young Montfort claimant,[69] but instead received an embassy from Jeanne de Penthièvre and actually agreed to a draft treaty recognizing his captive, Charles of Blois, as duke of Brittany in return for his homage. Charles even returned to the duchy for six months, leaving two young sons as hostages in England. This treaty, in fact, was not executed, and Charles obtained no more in the end than a truce.[70] In 1356 he finally gained his liberty in return for promising a large ransom, much of which was never paid.[71]

Walter Bentley proved considerably less successful in the strategic marches south of the lower Loire, despite his personal incentive for recovering his wife's lands. He failed to withstand the French in this region, and Edward had him replaced in April 1353 and imprisoned after he returned to England in June.[72] Perhaps the king feared that Bentley would be tempted to treat with the French in order to recover properties he could not conquer. About a year later, on 6 June 1354, Edward ordered him released and brought before the king in chancery. By late November, cleared of the charges against him,[73] Bentley was headed back to Brittany. This time, he brought along his eighteen-year-old stepson, Olivier IV de Clisson.[74] What sort of man had this young noble become? The most compelling account of his character remains that written long ago by Alexandre Mazas, who found Clisson to be quarrelsome and irascible, determined that people should bend before his will, and provoked to violence by the slightest resistance. More fond of power than of pleasures, Clisson was a man of great ambition who even enjoyed intimidating those he served. Mazas thought this last characteristic was strongly pronounced and distinguished him from most of his contemporaries.[75]

We know nothing of young Clisson's first two years back on French soil, a time of major military and political developments. In 1355, Edward, "the Black Prince" of Wales, led English forces from Gascony on a destructive raid into Languedoc. In April 1356 John II broke openly with the dissident Normans by arresting Charles the Bad and executing some of his followers. Then, in September, John suffered his disastrous defeat and capture at the hands of the Black Prince near Poitiers.[76] Two weeks later, on 2 October 1356, Henry of Lancaster, now commanding in Brittany, laid siege to Rennes. The terms of his release prohibited Charles of Blois from participating in the war until his ransom was paid, but Montfort and Clisson accompanied Lancaster, who continued his siege through what proved to be a harsh winter.[77] In January 1357 the ducal claimant presented Clisson, his mother, and his stepfather with the barony of La Roche-Moisan as a gift.[78] Some time thereafter, the celebrated Breton warrior Jean de Beaumanoir succeeded in capturing young Clisson, holding him for a ransom of twenty thousand *écus*. After about a year in captivity, Olivier secured his release and returned to England.[79]

Lancaster's chances of taking Rennes suffered a setback during the winter of 1356–57 when Bertrand du Guesclin succeeded in bringing supplies and reinforcements into the town.[80] A rising star in the camp of Charles of Blois, Du Guesclin had been a protégé of the murdered constable of France, Charles of Spain. He was fiercely anti-Navarrese, staunchly royalist, and he consistently supported the Blois-Penthièvre faction in Brittany.[81] The siege of Rennes was the first of several engagements in which he and Clisson were present on opposing sides. In 1357 the two future constables of France had little in common. An unlikely candidate for military hero, Du Guesclin was short in stature with a rather grotesque countenance, a self-made man from the lesser nobility whose exports often bordered on brigandage. Yet, he would become a beloved figure, remarkable for his ability to win the devotion of rough military men like himself. Clisson, although an exile still unproven in battle, was every inch the great noble, accustomed to wealth and comfortable in the court circles where Du Guesclin was forever an outsider.[82]

The captivity of John II lasted more than four years. It produced the political turmoil mentioned in the previous chapter and also marked the beginning of that period in which unemployed soldiers became the scourge of the French countryside.[83] Six months after his capture, John concluded a truce with England (March 1357), but Henry of Lancaster continued his siege of Rennes. It required a second royal order in July before he finally agreed to accept a payment to withdraw.[84] In England, John II began negotiations for his release. A draft treaty of 1358 provided that suzerainty over Brittany would pass to Edward III, and Jones has called this arrangement the apogee of Edward's power in the duchy.[85] This draft, and a successor in 1359, failed to gain acceptance by both monarchies, and the political and military situation underwent some changes before a definitive agreement was concluded in 1360.

It is regrettable that we know nothing of Olivier de Clisson's movements after he returned to England in 1358, for later developments suggest that French leaders were familiar with him by the time the treaty was ratified. Brought up to regard the Valois monarchy and its backers as his bitter enemies, he had had no opportunity for contact with them until the siege of Rennes. His captor, Jean de Beaumanoir, was a partisan of the Penthièvre party, and his sons would later be Clisson's close friends and associates. Unlike Du Guesclin, however, Beaumanoir had links to Charles of Navarre,[86] as did other French lords who would become aligned with the monarchy during the 1360s. It is possible that Clisson, after his return to England, made contact with those important prisoners, the *français de Londres* whom Françoise Autrand has called the "mafia" of John II, a group led by Guillaume and Jean de Melun, who wielded enormous power in the French government after their return in 1359.[87] At the age of twenty-two, Clisson was ready to assert himself in recovering his parents' former lands when he next returned to the continent,[88] but the conclusion of a treaty could deny him the opportunity for a military solution. Attainment of his objective might require contacts with well-placed people on the French side, and the Valois government was to show a strong and early interest in winning his support after 1360.

Unfortunately, the documents are silent until 8 October 1358, when Edward III ordered weapons for the archers who would be in Clisson's company when he made his imminent return to Brittany in the king's service.[89] Back on the continent, he received appointment as Edward's lieutenant in the marches south of the Loire.[90] Both his mother and stepfather had died by December 1359, when Edward acknowledged the homage of Olivier IV for their possessions and gave him custody of the castle of Pymmer (Kymmerch) in western Brittany, with its lands and revenues.[91]

England and France finally concluded their treaty of peace at Brétigny in the spring of 1360. Ratified with certain alterations at Calais in October, it deferred a Breton settlement pending further negotiations,[92] but it did provide for the restoration of properties confiscated from those who had been *bannis et adherens* of either side in the Anglo-French conflict. This provision made Olivier de Clisson eligible to regain the holdings his parents had possessed elsewhere in France.[93] Negotiations to settle the Breton conflict failed to produce any result, and on 22 June 1362 Edward III formally emancipated young Montfort and gave him responsibility for his duchy.[94] Montfort immediately offered proposals for a negotiated settlement, acquired from Edward a sizable advance of money, and returned to Brittany.[95] His arrival marked the first time the two rival claimants were there at the same time, but their negotiations produced only a prolongation of the truce on 23 September. La Borderie has blamed the intransigence of Jeanne de Penthièvre for the failure to reach a settlement.[96]

The adversaries took up arms again in 1363, with Olivier de Clisson among the Montfortist forces that hurried to prevent Blois from taking Becherel, but in July, at Evran, northwest of Rennes, they averted battle with a new truce and agreed to send envoys to negotiate before the Prince of Wales at Poitiers.[97] The plan was to partition the duchy and permit each claimant to use the title of duke. The embassies met at Poitiers in November, with Clisson being among Montfort's representatives. They in turn arranged for a meeting between Blois and Montfort at Poitiers in February 1364, where Montfort pressed his rival to ratify the plan proposed at the truce of Evran. Charles, however, refused to speak to him directly and rejected the proposed settlement.[98]

Again the Montfortists took the field, aiming to secure the remaining enemy fortresses near their stronghold of Vannes. Montfort captured Suscinio and La Roche-Periou, then laid siege to Auray. Besides Clisson, his army included such famous English captains as John Chandos, Robert Knolles, Hugh Calverley, and Walter Huet.[99] In September 1364, Charles of Blois marched to relieve the siege of Auray, accompanied by many of the great lords of Brittany as well as Bertrand du Guesclin, who had recently beaten the Navarrese at Cocherel. Auray occupies a high bluff overlooking a river, so the besiegers held a favorable position. While Blois and his men would have to advance up a slope, they did have superior numbers, and Montfort wanted to even the odds by a surprise attack on the enemy camp. The twenty-eight-year-old Olivier de Clisson opposed this plan, thinking it preferable that the Montfortists hold their strong position and force the enemy to advance against it. Such advice was to become a hallmark of Clisson's military tactics, and it gained support from the veteran English commanders.[100]

The battle of Auray, fought on 29 September 1364, was a bloody affair that gave Clisson a reputation for being a brave and savage warrior who inflicted many casualties with his fearful ax and continued to fight even after being pierced in the eye. Thanks largely to Chandos, who commanded Montfort's rear guard, the battle produced total victory for the Montfortists, as Charles of Blois met his death and Du Guesclin was taken prisoner.[101] Olivier de Clisson had avenged his father's death, and Montfort, as John IV, was now the unchallenged duke of Brittany. Although a serious defeat for French policy towards the duchy, this dramatic termination of the long conflict made possible the entry of important Breton lords into French military society and a greater role for Olivier de Clisson in royal politics.

3

Clisson's Reconciliation
with the Crown

IN THE DECADE OF THE 1360s, Olivier de Clisson gradually made his peace with the French monarchy and then became estranged from Duke John IV of Brittany. As Charles V's government became reconciled with the nobles of the north and west and built a successful military establishment on their support, Clisson participated in the process and became a respected figure in French political and military society. His break with the duke, which would have serious consequences for French politics as the two men became bitter enemies, was a somewhat later development, related to the first by one common thread—Clisson's strong and celebrated dislike for the English. Some historians have said that he had harbored a "profound hatred" of them since his years of exile in England,[1] but this view seems questionable, since he and his mother had been well treated by the English and had good reason to resent the French crown. A more likely explanation is that Clisson's Anglophobia arose during the handling of his family's confiscated property after 1360 and was fanned by jealousy over continued English influence in the Brittany of John IV.

Many dissident nobles had suffered loss of property by becoming involved with the English, but the largest confiscation had been the lands of the Clisson-Belleville family. The treaty of Brétigny in 1360 required the French to restore confiscated lands, within a year in most cases, but it was sometimes difficult to execute this provision, especially when the property had been granted to other people. Because of such complexities, the process could be slow, and an especially prompt restitution of confiscated lands to a particular individual must be seen as a mark of favor with political implications, not merely the fulfillment of a legal obligation.

The French crown showed a particular interest in becoming reconciled with Clisson and winning his loyalty and support. According to Siméon

Luce, the dauphin Charles began wooing Clisson at an early date, returning his part of the Norman barony of Thury in September 1360.[2] Luce may
have been wrong about the date,[3] but it is significant that the dauphin, as
duke of Normandy, took this initiative before the end of 1360, possibly
even before John II ratified the treaty at Calais in October. As ratified, the
treaty required restitution of confiscated lands in virtually the same form
as in the original agreement at Brétigny.[4] Clisson's Norman lordship was
only a fragment of what the crown had taken from Olivier III, but most
of the paternal inheritance lay in Brittany, excluded from the treaty pending a negotiated settlement of the disputed succession. The crown was not
yet in a position to restore those lands, but there remained the large maternal inheritance in northern Poitou. West of Belleville were the lordships
of Beauvoir, Noirmoutier, La Garnache, and Palluau. To the east lay Montaigu, Châteaumur, Les Essarts, Les Deffens, and others. These holdings
occupied most of the rich open country between the castles of La Roche-
sur-Yon in Poitou and Clisson in the Breton marches.[5]

    At the beginning of 1360, the twenty-four-year-old Olivier de Clisson
was Edward III's commander in the marches, where Edward doubtless
hoped that he would be more effective than his stepfather, Walter Bentley,
in reconquering Jeanne de Belleville's former possessions. Then England
and France concluded their treaty, which eliminated the need for conquest
because it specified that the French cession of Poitou to England would
include the *terre de Belleville*.[6] Edward III had already granted to Clisson
and received his homage for a fragment of these lands (Beauvoir-sur-mer),[7]
but in view of the debate that followed, it appears that the king gave him
no assurances that he would recover any more of the maternal heritage
after England acquired the lands under the terms of the treaty. Some of
them were destined for Olivier's sisters,[8] but he felt entitled to more than
Edward had bestowed. Perhaps the English ommission was mere careless-
ness; or did Edward consider Clisson well enough rewarded and certain to
remain an enemy of the Valois or, to the contrary, did he harbor suspicions
about Olivier's loyalty?

    These questions remain unanswered, but the French had made Clis-
son well aware that the treaty entitled him to restitution of lands confiscated from his parents, and he was not a man to take lightly any frustration
of his expectations. With the Breton civil war still unresolved, Clisson had
great value to the English as an ally. Their failure to give him assurances
about the Poitevin lands must be seen as a first step in alienating him.
The French soon maneuvered them into aggravating the situation. Having

chosen to treat the prompt restitution of Clisson's lands as a serious obligation, John II's government contrived to generate a major dispute over what constituted the "land of Belleville."

Towards the end of July 1361, the French king officially notified the clergy, nobles, towns, and inhabitants of Poitou that their region was being ceded to England.[9] John Chandos, who was to represent Edward III in receiving the allegiance of these lands, spent a few weeks in Paris before proceeding, rather unhurriedly, to Poitou. He began traveling through the region, taking possession and receiving homages in the name of the king of England, beginning at Poitiers and reaching Saint-Maixent on 28 September.[10] At this precise moment, the king of France ordered a number of properties returned to Olivier de Clisson, citing the treaty's restitution clause. They included not only the Angevin castle of Champtoceaux but also part of his mother's Poitevin inheritance—Beauvoir and La Garnache, which were to be returned only if they were not part of the "land of Belleville and its appurtenances."[11] In adding this disclaimer, John II was being disingenuous, since he had every reason to know that the lands in question *did* form part of the *terre de Belleville*.[12]

The matter became an issue in November when Chandos, having completed his work around Thouars, interrupted his itinerary to spend some time at Saumur with the French marshal, Jean le Meingre ("Boucicaut"). Olivier de Clisson arrived at Saumur and presented John's letter of restitution. Chandos wrote to Edward III for instructions, and the cession of Belleville was added to a list of issues that Edward presented to the French for resolution early in 1362. John II's government duly responded to the English queries, explaining the restitution to Clisson by enclosing a copy of the aforementioned royal letter that pretended uncertainty as to whether Beauvoir and La Garnache were part of the *terre de Belleville* mentioned in the treaty. The English already found themselves saying that the French were wrong in restoring the lands to Clisson[13]—an awkward position they should have been able to avoid. Numerous Poitevin nobles were accepting English suzerainty as required by the treaty. The English desire to give the territorial cessions priority over the general restitution clause[14] should have caused no problem with Clisson, but his case became a special one the moment he showed the royal letter to Chandos at Saumur.

That incident suggests some collusion between Clisson and the French, but the latter had been laying the groundwork with their solicitous concern to execute the treaty's restitution clause promptly in his case beginning with his Norman barony in 1360. The Valois government doubtless recognized the ambiguity in a treaty that required French restitution of confiscated lands but simultaneously ceded some of those lands to England. The treaty lacked the usual French formula "and its appurtenances" after the word "Belleville," and a royal lawyer may have thought this small loophole was sufficient to introduce the uncertainty about Belleville suggested in John II's letter of restitution. Any suspicions on Clisson's part that the English might block the recovery of his inheritance were welcome to the French. By returning some lands to Clisson, they effectively challenged the English to make him a better offer, but the English appear to have been thrown off balance by the French action. Their response was to demand the cession of Belleville to England rather than Clisson, thereby falling into the trap.

French scholars have emphasized the debate over whether the *terre de Belleville* consisted of the entire collection of lordships formerly held by Jeanne (which was surely correct), or only the small castellany of that name, as the French began to suggest.[15] The distinction was important economically, for the English reckoned the annual income of Jeanne's entire inheritance at thirty thousand pounds while the lordship of Belleville proper was worth only two hundred.[16] The correspondence exchanged in January–February 1362, however, gave no indication that the French had adopted the narrow definition and it is not clear when they did so because the document that sets it forth is not precisely dated.[17] As 1362 wore on, however, so did the dispute over Belleville, and it became involved in the activities of four French princes who were hostages in England and highly desirous of release. The king was anxious to get them home before they negotiated a damaging treaty with Edward III, but in November they did precisely that, promising, among other things, to turn over to England "the land of Belleville with all castles and fortresses and their appurtenances" that were in French hands at the time of the treaty of Brétigny.[18] The question was far from settled, however, and dragged on for five more years without resolution.

The length and the growing intensity of the dispute over Belleville can only have driven a wedge between Olivier de Clisson and his erstwhile English allies. We may suspect some collusion between him and the French government by the fall of 1361, but the English could have ended it by giving him some assurances about the recovery of his maternal inheritance. When they failed to do so and allowed the matter to drag on, Clisson began to regard the English, and especially their local representative, John Chandos, as his adversaries. Their failure to pursue a speedy resolution of the Belleville question would cost them a valuable ally.[19]

The debate over Belleville was still in its early stages and Duke John IV was still in English exile when Olivier de Clisson continued his family's tradition of advantageous marriages. On 12 February 1362, at Vitré, he contracted to marry Béatrix de Laval, John IV's first cousin and the sister of Guy XII, lord of Laval, an important magnate whose wife was Clisson's half-sister, Louise de Châteaubriant.[20] Not only did this union connect Olivier to both of the competing Breton ducal houses and many prominent families of western France, but his wife's dowry, when it was paid, further augmented his possessions and his political leverage.[21]

Thus by the time that John IV returned to Brittany in the summer of 1362, Olivier de Clisson was well established as a prominent member of the Breton aristocracy.[22] As we have seen, he remained John's loyal partisan, participating in the campaigns of 1363 and 1364, as well as serving on the embassy to Poitiers in the fall of 1363.[23] At the decisive battle of Auray in 1364, he was the one important Breton lord who fought on the winning side, and he won renown as a ferocious warrior but also lost an eye fighting for the Montfortists.[24] According to traditional stories, however, trouble began at the victory celebration when Clisson arrived late and was offended to find the duke sharing his cup with Chandos.[25] The victorious John IV, who owed his duchy to English support, was probably justified in giving Chandos major credit for the victory at Auray, but after nearly three years of tension over Belleville, Clisson was in no mood to see him exalted as a hero.[26]

For his part in the victory, Clisson expected a reward: he hoped the duke would give him the important forest lordship of Le Gavre, which adjoined his ancestral fortress of Blain. More than a century later, at an inquest into the tangled claims to Le Gavre, the investigators recorded a commonly repeated tale that John IV had promised the property to Chandos. Once again Clisson found this English commander obstructing what he considered his legitimate territorial ambitions. He is said to have exploded angrily that "je donne au diable si ja Anglois sera mon voisin," and then led a "great company of *gens de guerre*" to destroy Le Gavre and bring back some of the rubble to be used in repairing Blain.[27]

While Clisson's irritation at Chandos antedated the duke's return to the continent, many other conflicting claims to Breton lands created problems for John IV after his victory. Expected to reward his supporters in the succession dispute, he also needed to secure the loyalty of Breton lords who had formerly opposed him. These were prepared to recognize the victor of Auray, but in return for their allegiance they expected to recover lands they had lost to confiscation or conquest. Michael Jones has written of

Figure 2. Ruins of Clisson castle. (Photograph by Margery
C. Henneman)

"spectacular cases of Englishmen carving out seigneuries for themselves"
in Brittany during the civil war.[28] Robert Knolles, an important English
commander during periods of Anglo-French hostilities and a dreaded captain of free-lance companies (*routiers*) during periods of nominal peace,
had substantial possessions in Brittany until 1373, including the lordship of
Derval, whose former owner wanted it back. Another of John IV's English
allies, Walter Huet, acquired various properties, making his base the little

port of Le Collet, near the mouth of the Étier river on the Breton-Poitevin frontier.[29]

Such English commanders were an important buttress to John IV's authority, but their ambitions complicated the duke's efforts to establish good relations with his former opponents in the Breton nobility. Olivier de Clisson was only one of those who resented the continuing English presence, and he at least recovered Blain and other family possessions without returning the barony of La Roche-Moisan, which had been confiscated from an anti-Montfortist lord.[30] While John IV struggled to overcome the resentments caused by conflicting claims to property, Charles V could continue cultivating northwestern nobles with Breton interests. The lords of Rais and La Suze, who had lost Breton possessions to English adventurers, found employment with the king of France.[31]

La Borderie felt that the situation in Brittany after the battle of Auray was not much different from that of 1347 after La Roche-Derrien, in that the Penthièvre apanage was still intact, the cities of Rennes and Nantes firmly in the hands of the anti-Montfortist faction, and the ducal claimant of the house of Blois a prisoner in England. The difference, as he saw it, was a general reluctance to continue fighting that led Jeanne de Penthièvre to initiate peace talks.[32] It was not quite that simple, however, since the relations between England and France, a decisive factor throughout the conflict, were very much different in 1364, and continued strife in Brittany could jeopardize their treaty. The French government was anxious to terminate the conflict and within a month of the battle ordered the archbishop of Reims and a marshal of France to bring the Breton factions to the negotiating table.[33]

To win full legal recognition as duke, John IV had to come to terms with the French crown, and while he may have chosen to regard such a settlement as a treaty between equals, he had to confront the distasteful prospect of rendering to Charles V the homage required of a peer of France.[34] The ensuing negotiations therefore were rather difficult, but in April 1365 John IV and Jeanne de Penthièvre concluded the treaty of Guérande. Jeanne relinquished her claims to the duchy, recognized John IV as duke of Brittany, and agreed to render homage to him for her *apanage* of Penthièvre, which would remain in her possession intact. Confiscated lands on both sides would be restored and pardons granted. John promised to pursue the liberation of Jeanne's two sons who remained hostages in England. The oldest of Jeanne's sons would inherit the duchy if John IV should fail to produce male heirs. Jeanne would retain the viscounty of Limoges and its appurtenances with the promise of John IV's support if the

Prince of Wales tried to impede her possession. John would provide Jeanne with an annual income of 10,000 *l.t.* from lands he held in France outside the duchy. Finally, John IV was to render homage to Charles V for the duchy of Brittany in the manner that his predecessors as dukes had done.[35]

As a definitive settlement for Brittany, the treaty of Guérande would be a failure. John IV made no effort to secure the release of his cousins who were hostages in England, nor did he honor his promise to support Jeanne's possession of the viscounty of Limoges. He quickly fell behind in providing her with the promised income because most of the revenues in question were to come from lands the crown could not return to him—those making up what was to have been his mother's dowry. Wrangling over this property would continue for the rest of the century.[36] The treaty also ignored certain jurisdictional issues that would be crucial to the duchy's relations with the French crown. In the fall of 1365, John IV convened the Breton Estates at Vannes as part of his effort to consolidate his position and begin rebuilding his duchy. The assembly authorized him to collect a hearth tax (*fouage*), probably based on assessments already rendered obsolete by war and plague. Collection of ducal taxes inevitably caused friction with the great magnates, who had fiscal pretensions of their own and had lived for nearly a generation without being troubled by ducal officers.[37] In Brittany, as elsewhere in France, such friction would cause some nobles to appeal to the royal courts, whose jurisdiction the dukes were unwilling to recognize.

The problem of jurisdiction would arise only gradually, but it was related to the issue that was crucial to the ratification of the treaty, namely John IV's homage to the the king of France. This homage, of course, was the essential ritual that would ensure French recognition of his title and presumably eliminate Brittany as a base for brigandage or English action against France, but it occasioned endless debate as to the proper form. What the French required from a peer did not appear compatible with the duke's sense of Breton autonomy.[38] Because of problems over the homage, the king delayed his approval of the treaty until May of 1366.[39] The duke did not give his ratification by rendering homage until December 1366, and even then the ceremony carried ambiguous wording. Considerable negotiating preceded both occasions, and Olivier de Clisson was a member of each ducal embassy.[40] Charles V, while accepting the duke's evasive posture on the technicalities of the homage, appended to the agreement copies of earlier Breton homages and a statement that nothing in the present agreement would preclude liege homage.[41] While ratification of the treaty was under negotiation, John IV had protected himself by making an alliance with the Black Prince who, as Prince of Aquitaine, was now the ruler of neighboring Poitou.[42]

Jean Froissart thought that the battle of Auray and the treaty of Guérande were what permitted Olivier de Clisson to recover his family's confiscated lands in France and become so trusted an adviser of Charles V that "whatever he wished was done in France and nothing was done without him."[43] Writing many years later, Froissart remained ignorant of what had transpired with respect to Clisson's property between 1360 and 1364 and may have exaggerated his influence on Charles V, who never appointed Clisson to the royal council. Nevertheless, the chronicler's informants obviously considered Clisson influential, and Froissart was basically correct in associating the restoration of his fortune and his influence at court with the period after the treaty of Guérande. Only the end of the succession crisis permitted him to regain securely his father's former lands in Brittany. It was, moreover, only in 1365 that the Laval family began to transfer the property designated three years earlier for Béatrix's dowry.[44] Not until early 1366 did they confirm, and Charles V approve, their principal donation of two thousand pounds in income from the receipts of Champagne.[45] Clisson had rendered homage to Charles V for these revenues by 2 May 1366.[46] With his new renown as a formidable warrior, his fortunate marriage, and the great wealth now in his possession, Olivier seemed to his biographer to be blessed by Providence.[47]

However he may have felt about the duke's generosity to Englishmen after Auray, Clisson was still very much John IV's man, hosting him at Blain during the winter of 1364–65,[48] and representing him the following spring in negotiations with the Prince of Wales.[49] He was with the duke at Vannes in mid-March 1366,[50] and on 22 March John IV named Clisson and William, Lord Latimer, to an embassy that would discuss with Charles V's government the delayed ratification of the treaty of Guérande.[51] It was this mission that secured the king's ratification and gave Clisson the opportunity to render homage for his wife's dowry.[52] It also marked his first personal encounter with Charles V, and while this meeting cannot have turned him instantly into a member of the king's inner circle as Froissart implied, the royal interest in him must have been evident to observers. The thirty-year-old Clisson now possessed a substantial fortune if one considers his wife's dowry, the inheritance from his mother and Bentley in 1359, his recovered paternal holdings, the ransoms he probably collected after Auray, and the revenue from Beauvoir and La Garnache. His wealth, connections, and strategically located lands made him worth cultivating for the same reasons that Edward III had pursued his father in 1342. He had not secured this wealth at the time of his earliest contacts with the French in 1360–62, but his undeniable importance in 1366 was augmented by his recent record of proven military and diplomatic competence.[53]

The agreements of December 1366 finally appeared to settle the vexatious Breton question, but three eventful years would pass before Olivier de Clisson moved definitively into the Valois camp. Two major problems confronting the French government dominated the complex drama of these years: (1) the struggle to contain the dangerous brigandage of *routiers* left unemployed by the treaties of peace, and (2) the French desire to secure an ally in Spain. The Valois government had made a strenuous effort to ransom Bertrand du Guesclin, who had surrendered to Chandos on the field of Auray.[54] Having been liberated, Du Guesclin in 1365 received the task of assembling an army of *routiers* and leading them out of the country. Their goal was to overthrow King Pedro I of Castile, an enemy of France, and replace him with his half-brother, Henry of Trastamara. The project met with complete success,[55] but the ouster of their ally gave serious concern to the English, particularly the Black Prince in nearby Aquitaine.

Edward began assembling an army that included many of the lords in Aquitaine who had recently passed from French to English suzerainty, as well as other distinguished captains who had fought for the Montfortists at Auray but had since lacked military employment. Among them was Olivier de Clisson. The Anglo-Gascon forces entered Spain early in 1367 and in the spring won a resounding victory at Najera over the forces of Trastamara and Du Guesclin, with the latter again being taken prisoner.[56] During Du Guesclin's subsequent captivity in Aquitaine, he and Clisson had a chance to become acquainted, possibly for the first time, after fighting on opposite sides in several engagements over the past decade.[57] The Najera campaign proved to be a Pyrrhic victory for the Black Prince. It ruined his health and his finances, and its military results would be reversed in just two years.

The French again had to confront what Autrand calls "organized crime," as thousands of *routiers* poured back into the kingdom.[58] With Du Guesclin facing a costly ransom,[59] the royal governmment desperately sought a leader who could deal with the brigands and turned to Olivier de Clisson. The French attempt to cultivate Clisson had obviously been part of the ongoing dispute with England over the *terre de Belleville*. After November 1362, the "treaty of the hostages,"[60] while never executed, remained the basis for all further discussions, and early in 1367 the two kings agreed to have their representatives meet and devise a settlement that would give Edward III lands of comparable value by Easter 1368.[61] Some meetings occurred, but the English then wanted a delay and did not meet the French representatives as scheduled on 6 June 1367. The commission never completed its work,[62] and Charles V now evidently felt free, in September 1367, to reaffirm his father's restitution of La Garnache and Beauvoir, reissuing John II's letter of six years earlier.[63]

Siméon Luce considered this action to mark Clisson's "definitive" reconciliation with the monarchy,[64] but we can best view it as another landmark in a complex process. In January 1368, Charles V authorized Clisson to retain the royal taxes collected in the communities making up his Norman lordship of Le Thuit.[65] This grant was doubtless intended to help finance the expedition against the *routiers* for which Charles enlisted him. Aided by Robert de Beaumanoir, the younger son of his former captor, Clisson raised a force of troops and spent the spring of 1368 fighting the companies in Touraine, Vendomois, and Maine. His own troops were a rough, undisciplined lot, probably recruited from the ranks of the *routiers* themselves, for our knowledge of the campaign is based largely on pardons issued later to men who had committed crimes while in Clisson's service.[66] This military activity came to the attention of the Prince of Wales, who had serious problems of his own in 1368 and had a scheme that might attract Clisson away from French service.

Hoping to restore his finances in Aquitaine after the costly expedition to Castile, the Black Prince had convened the Estates of his principality in January 1368. This assembly granted him a *fouage* (hearth tax) of ten *sols* per hearth to be levied for five years, and on 26 January Edward formally announced this grant and ordered its collection.[67] The tax aroused strong opposition, particularly among those southwestern lords who had been subject to French suzerainty prior to 1361. Their ringleader was John I, count of Armagnac, whose son-in-law, the duke of Berry, was a brother of Charles V. Armagnac had served the Valois against England but then accepted the Black Prince as his overlord and accompanied him on the Castilian expedition. Armagnac was hard-pressed financially, however, first because he and his local allies owed large ransoms to the count of Foix, who had captured them in a private war some years earlier, and second because the Black Prince had not reimbursed their expenses for the Spanish campaign.[68] John decided not to permit the *fouage* ordered by the prince to be collected in his lands. This decision, followed by appeals to the court of Charles V, would have major consequences for Anglo-French relations.[69]

Angered by Armagnac's opposition, the Prince of Wales wished to confiscate the county and bestow it on someone else. A new count of Armagnac would have to win the land by conquest, and Edward offered this reward to Olivier de Clisson, promising him whatever aid was needed to help him conquer Armagnac.[70] Since the *routiers* included many Bretons and Du Guesclin had shown that money and leadership could turn them into an effective army, the prince probably thought that Clisson, a wealthy Breton with an excellent military reputation, could mobilize these troops to intimidate dissident lords in Aquitaine. In any event, Clisson did not accept the offer. Roland Delachenal was probably correct in thinking that one of Edward's motives was to retain him in the English camp,[71] but Clisson's disenchantment with them was now far advanced.

His next opportunity to express hostility to the English came towards the end of 1368 when he frustrated the designs of the Prince of Wales by intervening in a transaction that involved the viscounty of Limoges. The treaty of Guérande guaranteed Jeanne de Penthièvre's possession of this fief, but by this time the Limousin had passed under the authority of the Black Prince, who had other ideas about the viscounty. Jeanne and her husband had incurred an enormous debt during the war of succession, secured in part by the viscounty of Limoges, and in 1366 she arranged to make annual payments of 7,000 *l.t.* to Jean Goldbêtre, a moneylender from Bruges.[72] Her ability to make the payments, however, depended on her timely receipt of the 10,000 *l.t.* that John IV was to pay her each year, and this annuity was to be drawn from the revenues of lands not yet in the duke's possession. Consequently, John IV's payments to Jeanne fell into arrears despite royal efforts to take over some of them.[73] Her scheduled payments to Goldbêtre also fell behind, and in July 1368, the Prince of Wales, now deeply involved with the dissident Gascon lords, ordered that the viscounty of Limoges be seized and sold to pay off the debt to Goldbêtre.[74] This order triggered a series of hearings and depositions before Edward's seneschal of Limousin, Thomas de Roos, but in December 1368 the prince ordered that the viscounty be sold to none other than Robert Knolles, the English soldier of fortune who had fought for John IV at Auray.[75] At this point, Olivier de Clisson stepped in and paid off the debt, borrowing some of the money for this purpose from Barthélemy Spifame (as he was known in French), a Lucchese moneylender who had become a bourgeois of Paris and purveyor to the royal family.[76]

Clisson's intervention in this case enabled him to express hostility to Englishmen like Knolles, who had gained a foothold in Brittany, and to do a favor for the French government, which hardly welcomed the installation of an English *routier* chieftain at Limoges in lieu of the pro-Valois countess of Penthièvre. His action posed no threat to the duke of Brittany, with whom he remained on good terms for another year, but it served to remind John IV that he had not honored his promise, in the treaty of Guérande, to support Jeanne's right to the viscounty of Limoges. Having worked on the duke's behalf to secure ratification of this pact, Clisson became increasingly irritated as its provisions were not implemented, possibly believing that his honor was involved.

His wealth permitted Clisson to rescue Jeanne de Penthièvre from the loss of her lands and to become her creditor and banker. In overseeing her finances, he acted as her lieutenant in Brittany.[77] A much-cited document mentioning this title concerns a minor financial transaction, says nothing about his actual appointment, and gives no hint that his duties had a political dimension.[78] His lieutenancy seems to have entailed purely financial services to Jeanne and it is difficult to perceive it as challenge to John IV.[79] Certainly his relations with the duke had not been entirely cordial since his outburst following the victory at Auray, but the main source of friction was over conflicting fiscal pretensions. Clisson now held Champtoceaux as a vassal of the duke of Brittany,[80] and in the fall of 1368 the duke issued orders to prevent him from collecting taxes on the dependents of the castle.[81] Difficulties between the duke and the Breton magnates over finances were fairly common, and it is difficult to agree with those who have seen the ducal order as punitive in character.[82] The duke could grant or withhold permission for vassals to take money from their men, and in exercising that right he was merely taking a small step in reasserting ducal authority over a nobility accustomed to excessive independence during the long civil war.[83] His action with respect to finances at Champtoceaux did not bring about a break with Clisson and cannot plausibly be linked to Clisson's financial rescue of Jeanne de Penthièvre several months later.

The period from the spring of 1368 to that of 1369 was an important one for Anglo-French relations. John of Armagnac and his fellow Gascon lords had appealed to Charles V against the exactions of the Prince of Wales, and the French crown was orchestrating the process very carefully in order to gain the largest possible number of adherents who would support the reopening of hostilities with England. In June 1368, following a meeting of princes, prelates, and senior royal officers, the crown agreed to hear appeals from the counts of Armagnac and Périgord and the lord of Albret. By the time Albret formally submitted his appeal in September, many other southern nobles, clergy, and towns were joining the appellants. In mid-November 1368 Charles V issued his formal summons to the Prince of Wales to appear at the Parlement in Paris on 2 May 1369.[84] When the appointed day arrived, many lords and towns from Aquitaine had representatives in Paris, while the Black Prince ignored the summons. The king waited another week and then added to these representatives a great council of his own advisers and accepted the appeal, effectively abrogating the treaty of Brétigny.[85]

While the two monarchies were heading towards this rupture, the French scored important successes abroad. In March 1369, Du Guesclin led another army of *routiers* into Castile and defeated Pedro I. This time Trastamara murdered his half-brother and seized the Castilian throne as Henry II. By June, he had concluded an important naval treaty with the king of France.[86] Meanwhile, after difficult negotiations, the French reached an agreement with Count Louis II of Flanders, whose heiress, Marguerite, married Charles V's younger brother, Philip the Bold, duke of Burgundy.[87]

These successes and the anticipation of Castilian naval assistance must have influenced the French government's decision to launch a major effort at sea. France had long maintained an important naval arsenal, the *Clos des Galées*, at Rouen, and during the 1330s her navy had created serious problems for the English.[88] Since then, however, this fleet had deteriorated, and French seapower had become restricted to local initiatives, becoming what Delachenal called a "marine des villes."[89] Now, however, as renewal of the Anglo-French war became imminent, Charles V hoped to expose the English to the sort of misery foreign troops had been inflicting on the French countryside. As early as April 1369, Charles launched an effort to revive the fleet, and he personally spent an extended period in and around Rouen, overseeing the process. The ostensible reason for assembling ships and provisions was to prepare an invasion of England.[90] This naval buildup required a number of months. On 1 July, the twenty-seven-year-old Philip of Burgundy agreed to lead a force of one thousand lances in an attack on England.[91] The king then summoned the Estates from a limited geographical area to meet with him at Rouen towards the beginning of August. The interests of the military nobility clearly dominated this assembly, which supported a proposal for offensive warfare and chose to replace the royal hearth tax with high, unpopular indirect taxes.[92]

In the meantime, however, Edward III had decided to launch a new invasion of France. His twenty-nine-year-old second son, John of Gaunt, duke of Lancaster, contracted on 11 June to serve for six months in France, and he reached Calais by 26 July with a modest number of troops, expecting the king to follow him in about a month.[93] After some discussion, the French government decided to send Burgundy and his troops to oppose Lancaster. Philip was under strict orders not to give battle without a direct command from the king. After several weeks of confrontation in late August and early September, Edward III's retinue (but not the king himself) reinforced John of Gaunt's forces, and Burgundy withdrew his troops from a strong position. His departure left Lancaster free to take the offensive, and John's troops pillaged the land southwestward as far as the Seine, apparently aiming for Harfleur. Unable to penetrate its defenses, Lancaster returned to Calais and thence to England.[94]

What are we to make of these months of military activity? Olivier de Clisson strongly opposed invading England, at least according to Froissart, who called him "li uns des especiauls dou conseil du roy." His knowledge of the English and the French lack of seafaring experience led him to give this advice, which was consistent with his preference for defensive over offensive warfare.[95] Did he also advocate the policy of not permitting Burgundy to give battle? He would be associated with just such a strategy the following year, but if he had such influence in 1369 he must have exercised it before the end of August, since thereafter he was not with the king. The royal government may have doubted Philip's military ability;[96] Delachenal called his withdrawal in September "inexplicable."[97] In Jean Favier's view, the English considered Lancaster's expedition speedy and successful compared with Edward III's expensive campaign of 1359, leading them to favor similar raids in the future, whereas the French concluded that their refusal to give battle in 1369 was a useful strategy to pursue in the future.[98] Historians tended to view the English raids after 1369 as costly mistakes that consumed resources without attaining any strategic objective, but John Palmer pointed out that they were so destructive that Charles V's strategy left much of his realm devastated.[99]

The proposed French naval expedition itself raises certain questions. The king seems to have cared more about it than anybody else,[100] but did he seriously contemplate an invasion aimed at conquest, or did he picture a more realistic goal such as raids that could terrorize the English coastal towns and disrupt the organizing of expeditions to the continent? Announcing any sort of expedition to England had propaganda value in France, particularly when it came to getting support for taxes in Normandy and other coastal areas. I have argued elsewhere that the government had this fact in mind when it summoned the Estates to meet at Rouen, where they could observe the preparations underway at the *Clos des Galées*.[101] Was John of Gaunt's expedition to Calais intended to disrupt French invasion plans? One chronicler thought so,[102] and Delachenal felt that Lancaster's subsequent march towards Harfleur proved it. A major project in the Norman ports over a period of months was unlikely to escape English intelligence.[103] James Sherbourne, on the other hand, doubts that Lancaster's expedition had this objective and suspects that the English may have been unaware of the French naval preparations since they did not organize coastal defenses.[104] Perhaps they saw that a serious French attack was not yet feasible.

Throughout 1369, Olivier de Clisson had to juggle his multiple responsibilities as counsellor to the duke of Brittany, financier of the countess of Penthièvre, and occasional royal adviser and commander. The reopening of Anglo-French hostilities increased his difficulty in honoring all these commitments and forced him to make hard choices. His Poitevin inheritance became vulnerable when the English attacked La Roche-sur-Yon, which they had been claiming for eight years. The fortress capitulated towards the beginning of August, just before Amaury de Craon's relief expedition could arrive.[105] Meanwhile, a force of *routiers* accepted three thousand francs to evacuate the fortress of Château-Gontier in the county of Maine,[106] and the crown ordered Amaury de Craon to pursue them when they decided to join others at Saint-Sauveur-le-Vicomte, a strategic Norman fortress in the Cotentin that belonged to John Chandos.[107] Charles V, who had pronounced the confiscation of French lands belonging to Chandos, was very anxious to capture this stronghold, and he ordered Craon, Clisson, and others to besiege it. According to the official royal chronicler, the siege had to be halted when Clisson and his men abruptly departed. The king angrily ordered resumption of the siege, but the place could not be taken.[108]

Clisson's departure from the siege of Saint-Sauveur illustrates his growing difficulty in serving both the duke of Brittany and the king of France. Charles II of Navarre, who hoped the renewal of Anglo-French hostilities might work to his advantage, had left his Spanish realm and returned to Normandy, arriving by mid-August at his port of Cherbourg just north of Saint-Sauveur.[109] One chronicler reports that Clisson left the siege in order to meet with Charles, and, while Abel Lefranc credited him with dissuading Charles from an English alliance, he apparently was acting as an emissary of John IV.[110] The king of Navarre long maintained cordial relations with the Breton duke, who would one day become his son-in-law, and in 1371, before he returned to Spain, Charles named John IV his lieutenant in northern France.[111] Clisson completed his mission to Cherbourg in time to be with the duke at Nantes on 10 September.[112]

The renewal of Anglo-French hostilities was especially awkward for the duke of Brittany. His homage to Charles V, which gave him legal title to his duchy, carried with it an obligation to support the king of France against his enemies. Yet John owed Edward III significant debts in money and gratitude and retained English advisers in Brittany. Either king might seriously damage his position. The research of Michael Jones has shown how John IV endeavored to play off the rival kings against each other in order to safeguard the integrity of his duchy, but there remains some basis for the older tradition in French scholarship, represented above all by La Borderie, that believed the duke to be largely pro-English and anxious to conceal these sentiments from the French.[113] As Olivier de Clisson grew increasingly suspicious of John's English sympathies, his relations with the duke deteriorated. John had not come to the military aid of Charles V in 1369, and some thought he was ready to allow English troops to pass through Brittany en route to Poitou.[114]

Thinking it imperative to redefine his obligations in a way that would serve Breton interests without antagonizing Charles V, John appointed a new embassy to the king on 25 October 1369, consisting of his chancellor, the bishop of Saint-Brieuc and his "dear and faithful cousin," Olivier de Clisson.[115] This mission achieved results by January 1370, some three months later. On the twenty-third of that month, Charles V agreed that John could discharge his military obligation by remaining in Brittany ready to defend the duchy against English attack.[116] He also promised John an income of one thousand pounds in lieu of certain French lands that had not been returned to him, and he agreed to take over the obligation to pay seven thousand pounds of the income the duke was supposed to furnish Jeanne de Penthièvre.[117] Three days later, the ducal emissaries swore in John's name that he would adhere faithfully to his obligations as the king's man and subject and would not make war on Charles.[118] In the document describing this oath, Olivier de Clisson is identified as John IV's councillor. It would be the last service he would render to the duke for more than twenty-six years.

The oath of loyalty Clisson swore to the king on John's behalf was a solemn act of the sort that medieval noblemen took seriously because their honor was involved. Those who wished to break such an oath generally

felt obliged to demonstrate just cause for doing so and often sought ecclesiastical dispensation. Having taken an oath of loyalty on John IV's behalf,
Clisson could reasonably believe that his own honor had been called into
question if the duke were to violate that oath. As a member of John IV's
council, he was well aware of the continuing English presence in Brittany
and had found it irritating. After the oath of January 1370, however, continued contacts between John IV and the English court would cease to be
merely irritating and would become a question of perjury. Whereas Clisson's reconciliation with the French crown had occurred gradually over the
course of a decade, his break with John IV was a good deal more sudden
than historians have thought. It occurred within a few months of the oath
of January 1370, as he and Charles V became convinced that John was supporting England against France.

It was probably in the spring of 1370 that Charles V dispatched his
secretary, Hutin d'Aunoy, to Brittany to express royal concern that an
English fleet might arrive in Brittany. John responded on 2 June with further assurances of his loyalty,[119] but by this date Clisson and the king had
initiated a remarkable stratagem that was calculated to make the duke sub-
stantially more vulnerable to French military pressure in the event that he
proved disloyal in the war against England. This scheme, which Charles V
unveiled on 14 May 1370, involved an exchange of strategic properties.
Only the king was in a position to initiate this transaction, but whoever
conceived of the plan had to have (1) strong suspicions about John IV's
loyalty, (2) a solid grasp of strategic military considerations in Brittany
and lower Normandy, and (3) a certainty that Olivier de Clisson could be
trusted completely to serve Charles V. That person was most likely Clisson himself, who not only had a solid military reputation with the French
government but also knew John IV's policies better than anyone else in
close touch with the royal court. The king's cousins, the counts of Alençon
and Perche, held modest *apanages* near the border of Normandy and Brittany. They also possessed the county of Porhoët in the heart of Brittany,
centered on Josselin castle, a fortress towering over the waters of the Oust
river less than forty kilometers northeast of the duke's favored residence
at Vannes.[120] If the king could acquire Josselin and place it in the custody
of a trusted commander, he could exert an intimidating military influence
in central Brittany, while his cousins could present a formidable bulwark
against the English and Navarrese in lower Normandy if they held additional strongholds in that region.

What Charles V made public on 14 May was an arrangement whereby the counts of Alençon and Perche would relinquish Josselin in return for four thousand pounds in annual revenues and various Norman lands—the castles of Exmes and Caniel, and Clisson's ancestral barony of Le Thuit.[121] The two counts ratified this exchange of lands,[122] and Charles V confirmed the transaction on 24 May. Although the king stated that the two counts were transferring Josselin to him and his successors "for the evident profit of our kingdom,"[123] the real recipient of Josselin was to be Olivier de Clisson, who would hold it for the king in return for relinquishing Le Thuit and the 2,000 *l.t.* in revenues from his wife's dowry.[124] In a series of documents of July and August 1370, Charles V issued the orders necessary to put into execution the transfers of Norman lands to the counts of Alençon and Perche.[125]

The actual transfer of Josselin into Clisson's custody, however, posed serious problems. He was to hold the stronghold in hereditary homage and fealty from the duke of Brittany, under the sovereignty and jurisdiction (*ressort*) of the king. John IV, however, had strong objections to recognizing royal sovereignty and jurisdiction, and he doubtless realized that in engineering this transaction the crown was posing a threat, jurisdictional as well as military, to the Breton independence he was trying so hard to maintain. He appears to have done what he could to obstruct the transfer before finally agreeing to turn over Josselin to Clisson by the end of August.[126] In Paris, meanwhile, Clisson promised on 21 July that once he acquired Josselin he would relinquish it to the king on demand should John IV become aligned with the Charles's enemies. This "treaty" (as Lefranc has called it)[127] marked the definitive rupture between John IV and Olivier de Clisson, firmly establishing the latter as the king's man in the event of conflicting allegiance.

John IV can only have regarded the Josselin transaction as a major betrayal. Referring to Clisson's "great disobediences," the duke took possession of some of his lands and ordered his own men to collect revenues that Clisson normally would have received.[128] The two men would henceforth be bitter enemies, and their feud would have a major influence on French political society for the next generation. Medieval nobles could be arrogant, easily offended, and quick to anger, but the length and intensity of this feud seems striking even by the standards of the time. Despite the differences in their personalities and experiences, Clisson and the duke had formerly shared years of exile and a strong sense of being wronged by the house of Valois. Their interests had diverged, however, since 1364. The triumphant John IV was concerned with protecting the integrity of

his duchy in the face of pressure from the rival monarchies and the pretensions of the Breton aristocracy. Clisson had become rich and powerful at
the very moment when the duke required his subordination. Respected,
trusted, and rewarded by the king, Clisson was not receiving similar treatment from his duke. Having developed intense dislike for the English,
he had become progressively more royalist, but we can only speculate on
his precise role in initiating the Josselin transaction.[129] If Clisson thought
John's continued dealings with the English violated his oath to Charles V,
the duke surely thought that the arrangements regarding Josselin were a
violation of Clisson's homage and fealty to his lord.[130]

John's sense of being betrayed may have received strong reinforce-
ment a year or so later, if we are to believe a confession extracted in 1378
from Jacques de Rue, a henchman of Charles of Navarre. This individual reported that on a visit to Brittany in 1371, Charles told the duke that Clisson
had been pursuing an amorous relationship with his duchess.[131] If John IV
heard and credited such a tale, it can only have intensified his hatred for
Clisson. So it was that two important political figures, both with strong
and unforgiving personalities, became bitter enemies, with major consequences for French political society and Anglo-French relations.

4

Clisson in the Service of Charles V

THE JOSSELIN TRANSACTION, which triggered Clisson's complete break with John IV in the summer of 1370, eventually strengthened the French military posture in both Brittany and lower Normandy, but it did not signal an immediate improvement in Valois fortunes. Until the end of 1370, the French were on the defensive and barely holding their own except in Gascony, where the war had started. In that sector, the appellant lords coordinated with the king's brother Louis, duke of Anjou, who was royal lieutenant in Languedoc. Their offensive produced important gains by the end of 1369[1] and received additional leadership when Du Guesclin, recalled from Spain by Charles V, reached southern France in the summer of 1370.[2]

At the northern end of Aquitaine, the French fared less well. In Poitou, each side gained an important stronghold, but most of the local nobility largely remained loyal to the Black Prince.[3] The situation in the Limousin was more complicated. Jeanne de Penthièvre's viscounty of Limoges was but a small part of the district, concentrated on the castle and town of Limoges itself but not including the old *cité* under the bishop. Clisson had prevented the viscounty from being sold to Knolles, but the Black Prince had occupied most of it anyway.[4] In the summer of 1369, Jeanne formally ceded it to Charles V,[5] and on the same day (9 July), Charles secretly ceded it back to her.[6] The Prince of Wales remained the legal lord of Aquitaine until the French crown actually confiscated the duchy later in the year,[7] and the transaction with the viscountess of Limoges must have been intended to help recruit the lords of the region back into French obedience. Some important ones, like Raymond de Mareuil and the viscount of Rochechouart, did "turn French" about that time.[8] The castle of Limoges remained in English hands, however, and when the duke of Berry could not take it in 1370, he negotiated with the bishop and obtained the surrender of the *cité* in August, only to depart almost immediately without leaving it adequately protected.[9] This surrender enraged the Black Prince, who brought an army to Limoges in the third week of September and sacked the *cité* with considerable slaughter.[10]

News of the sack of Limoges arrived in Paris at a time when the government and people were already beleaguered by a destructive English raid from the north. Rather than entrusting this expedition to a commander of royal rank, Edward III turned to a veteran of lesser social standing, as he had done during the Breton war of succession. His choice fell on Robert Knolles, the formidable captain who still held the Breton lordship of Derval. Knolles and his *routier* bands had terrorized central France and upper Languedoc during the years of John II's captivity.[11] We have seen that he fought for the Montfortists at Auray and very nearly acquired the viscounty of Limoges in 1368 before Clisson intervened. Now, in the summer of 1370, Knolles brought a strong English force to France. Leaving Calais late in July, he headed southeast, burning and pillaging. After making a demonstration before Arras, he passed through Vermandois, and then turned west, evidently planning to pass south of Paris and proceed to his lands in Brittany.[12]

Charles V's government was still committed to what Delachenal has disparaged as "timid counsel,"[13] and it appears that Olivier de Clisson had a good deal to do with it. Although Clisson had been in Paris on 21 July when he promised to hold Josselin for the king, he spent the next few weeks campaigning in the Limousin, where the duke of Berry wrote to him on 30 July and 12 August. He was among the French commanders at Paris when Knolles approached the capital in September and it is possible that he could not appear in Brittany to take possession of Josselin at the end of August.[14] Clisson was still the strong supporter of a defensive strategy, and his influence in French military circles was now evident. Froissart considered him the leading spokesman for the policy of not engaging Knolles's forces,[15] an approach that doubtless displeased some of the other commanders as well as being ruinous to the French countryside.

The French and their historians have long associated the military successes of the 1370s with the leadership of the nonmilitary Charles V and his "good constable," Bertrand du Guesclin. The essential feature of Charles V's strategy, however, was a preference for defensive tactics over pitched battles. Not only was Du Guesclin far from Paris in 1369 and 1370 when the crown twice decided not to engage an English invasion force, but the strategy itself was hardly compatible with his previous career as an impetuous warrior. It resembled more closely the behavior of a Chandos or a Knolles, and was probably suggested by a military man well versed in the methods that had succeeded for the English. There is no reason to dispute the accuracy of Froissart's informants who attributed the defensive policy to Clisson. Fond of recounting great military engagements, the chronicler would have been very curious about the French refusal to give battle and is unlikely to have attributed the policy to the wrong person.

Those who thought it shameful to do nothing in the face of enemy raids cannot have liked this strategy, and news of the sack of Limoges compounded the government's difficulties. The old constable, Robert de Fiennes, asked to be relieved of his duties. To determine his successor and to discuss how best to provide for the defense of the kingdom in its present extremity, Charles V summoned Bertrand du Guesclin to Paris and hastily convened a "great council," augmenting his usual body of appointed councillors with other influential people, including some bourgeois of Paris. With their advice and that of his brother Louis of Anjou, who had arrived from Languedoc, Charles named Du Guesclin constable of France on 2 October 1370, in what Autrand has called a *coup médiatrice*.[16]

Both Charles V and Du Guesclin himself had some misgivings about whether a man from the petty nobility would have sufficient prestige to command the French armies and hold the obedience and respect of princes and well-born nobles. There was, in fact, little opposition from this quarter. He was admired by the aristocracy although, ironically, it may have been his main military weakness—reckless and undisciplined bravery in pitched battles—that they most respected. His opponents, as it turned out, were people of another sort—the lawyers and financial officers close to Charles V, men of modest backgrounds who would become known as the "Marmousets." They never really trusted him and cannot have been pleased when, after they had been overruled and he had accepted the office, Du Guesclin urged the king to raise money quickly by means of a forced loan from wealthy bourgeois and royal officials.[17]

Du Guesclin's political ties were to the old anti-Navarrese party associated with one of his predecessors, Charles of Spain,[18] and he had been a steadfast supporter of the defeated Penthièvre faction in Brittany. He is remembered by posterity as a great French hero, but his actual military record was at best uneven. His Norman victory over the Navarrese in 1364 soon was balanced by his Breton defeat at Auray, while his successful Spanish expedition in 1365 had to be repeated four years later because of his defeat at Najera. In campaigns led by princes or great nobles, Du Guesclin tended to rush into battle and become involved in the melee, perhaps hoping to win their recognition for great feats of arms, but usually with bad results. This kind of unrestrained individualism undermined the cohesion and discipline essential to successful cavalry operations and was a factor in several French disasters. When campaigning with *routiers*, however, Du Guesclin was another man. He understood the motives and methods of those who were lesser nobles like himself and made careers as warriors, and his greatness lay in his ability to lead, as well as to fight, such people. Since the immediate enemy to be confronted in 1370 was Robert Knolles, Du Guesclin was probably the best qualified man to take over the French army. During the later 1360s, his work in mobilizing companies of *routiers* to fight campaigns in Spain and Languedoc had made him extremely valuable to Louis of Anjou and to Charles V.[19]

Having been named constable of France, Du Guesclin wished to recruit the Breton lords who had been his comrades in support of Charles of Blois during the war of succession.[20] Some of these, like his cousins, the Mauny brothers, had continued in his service in Spain and Languedoc. Others, however, were men of higher social and economic standing, and while they remained anti-English and suspected their duke's policies, the Breton war was over and Du Guesclin had no particular claim on their services. The key to recruiting the great lords of Brittany for the French cause was Olivier de Clisson who, far more than Du Guesclin, belonged to their circle and also had many relatives among them. He had rendered important services to the widow of Charles of Blois, had become a royal adviser on military matters, and had broken with John IV over the latter's English leanings. He also enjoyed the support of precisely those royal advisers who had their doubts about Du Guesclin.

These considerations may help explain an alliance that Du Guesclin made with Clisson at Pontorson three weeks after becoming constable. On 24 October, each declared, in a formal document, that he would defend the other as a brother, against anybody who attacked him or "voudroit desheriter par puissance," except the king of France, the viscount of Rohan, and those other lords from whom they held lands. If either man heard anything that might be damaging to the other, he would inform him. They also agreed to an equal division of such profits as booty and ransoms.[21] Although Luce, in passing, called it a "curious pact,"[22] and others have noticed some of the differences between the two men, most historians seem to have thought it unexceptional that two Breton nobles in royal service should make such a pact.[23] The context of this arrangement warrants closer scrutiny.

Du Guesclin and Clisson came from rather different backgrounds,

were not well aquainted personally, and had fought on opposing sides in
several campaigns. They were not obvious candidates for a close friendship
and tight alliance, but Clisson's recent break with the duke of Brittany gave
them a common enemy. The pact offered Clisson an ally against John IV's
efforts to seize any of his lands; it offered Du Guesclin a well-placed defender against rumors spread by his detractors at court. It is even conceivable that the pact was suggested to the two commanders by someone in
the royal government astute enough to see its potential advantages.[24] It
was a beneficial arrangement because their different strengths and weak-
nesses enabled each man to make a positive contribution to the alliance.
Clisson was conservative about giving battle and preferred the tactics he
had learned from the English. Du Guesclin, when working with the *routiers*, was adept at such tactics, but his undisciplined approach to pitched
battles had worked against him.[25] After forming close ties with Clisson, he
would avoid large engagements and enjoy considerable military success.
Du Guesclin wanted the assistance of the Breton aristocracy, while Clisson had the connections to deliver the support of what Luce called his
"powerful clientele."[26] Du Guesclin had the hard-won prestige of a valiant
knight in combat, but he was distrusted by some of Charles V's advisers.
These very people were friendly with Clisson, but the latter's prickly personality was no match for Du Guesclin's evident personal magnetism. Du
Guesclin's personal style may have helped legitimize Clisson's defensive
approach in the eyes of those who tended to value booty and glory ahead
of tactics.

The alliance of Du Guesclin and Clisson created a "two-headed Breton
high command"[27] and delivered to the service of Charles V a formidable
contingent of Breton lords who would play a central role in the French
military establishment of the 1370s. Their immediate impact would have
serious consequences for the hitherto successful raid of Robert Knolles.
The latter's movements, well-chronicled up to the beginning of October, are less easy to follow thereafter. The count of Alençon, his position
strengthened by what he had acquired in the Josselin transaction, was holding lower Normandy with a large force,[28] and Knolles, whose forces were
scattered through the county of Maine, apparently decided to move on to
Brittany.[29]

Despite the efforts of several modern historians to make sense of the
various chroniclers and to correct their errors,[30] it is very difficult to piece
together the contemporary accounts of what took place in December 1370.
It seems clear that Du Guesclin and Clisson fell upon and crushed one of

Knolles's contingents, commanded by Thomas de Granson, at Pontvallain, near Le Mans, probably on 4 December 1370.[31] This quick victory under the new constable, even in a minor engagement, had great psychological value for the government in Paris after the reverses of recent months.[32] The two Breton commanders seem to have inflicted further damage on the forces of John Cresswell, another of Knolles's lieutenants, later in December before Du Guesclin took up quarters at Saumur, while Clisson remained in the field and decimated an English detachment sent to reinforce Knolles and to carry home some of his booty. Precisely where and when these actions occurred remains unclear,[33] but chroniclers assert that the English now were calling Clisson "butcher."[34]

Having thus brought a bad end to the latest expedition sent from England, the Breton-dominated French forces in the Languedoil could turn their attention to the lower Loire and the northern part of Aquitaine, continuing to fight the minor engagements in which they were most effective. From early 1371 until early 1372, Clisson was governor of La Marche,[35] and in August 1371 he was royal lieutenant in Poitou and its marches.[36] A document of mid-September called him royal lieutenant in Touraine, Anjou, and Maine.[37] Clisson's defensive strategy was geared to dealing with an English raid, but now he was in a campaign that entailed reducing fortresses and recovering enemy-held lands. Towards the end of August 1371, Charles V ordered him to move to the relief of Moncontour, one of the few French-held fortresses in Poitou and now under siege by Thomas Percy. Moncontour fell before Clisson could come to its rescue. Now faced with the need to conduct a siege, he lacked the necessary equipment and was hampered by the absence of crossbowmen.[38] To remedy this deficiency before the campaign of 1372, the crown retained a contingent of fifty Genoese crossbowmen to serve with Clisson's large personal retinue of fifty-seven knights and 399 squires.[39]

This force remained inactive for months but Clisson, with his great wealth, was able to keep the troops paid. He became the crown's perpetual creditor, and on 24 March 1372 Charles V undertook to reimburse him by awarding him the ransoms owed by several English garrisons.[40] Du Guesclin, who did not have such a personal fortune, was in no position to advance such sums to his men, despite his constable's salary of two thousand francs per month. He was continually railing at the government over inadequate financial support and even threatened to resign his office, according to one chronicler.[41] The need to keep the troops paid was obvious to both Breton commanders, but their respective financial circumstances

determined their different responses and probably also their respective relations with the king's financial officers.

Apparently by design, the French army did not take the offensive
in Poitou until well into the summer of 1372. On 14 June, Clisson, Du
Guesclin, and the other leaders were still at Loches, well upstream on the
Loire.[42] What they were waiting for was a decision at sea, for the English
were sending the earl of Pembroke and a large fleet to La Rochelle. The
French galley fleet under Rainier Grimaldi and another squadron sent by
the king of Castile were hoping to intercept this force. The decisive battle
off La Rochelle on 22 and 23 June was a major English defeat,[43] and it
effectively sealed the fate of Edward III's continental possessions north of
the Gironde.

In less than a month, the French secured the submission of most of
Poitou, Saintonge, and Angoumois.[44] It took only a few days to recover
Moncontour at the beginning of July. An attack on Saint-Sevère led to
its capitulation on the twenty-ninth, and Bertrand du Guesclin entered
Poitiers in triumph on 7 August.[45] The campaign had its ugly incidents.
One of Olivier de Clisson's close friends, a Breton squire named Geoffroy
Payen, fell into English hands at Saint-Sevère. He was taken as a prisoner
to Benon, which Clisson invested in the second week of September. The
English commander of Benon, David Hollegrave, decided to execute some
of the prisoners, Payen included. This action so enraged Clisson that he
swore never to give quarter to any Englishman and is said to have killed
fifteen English prisoners following the fall of Benon.[46] It may have been
this episode rather than the earlier one in 1370 that earned him the name
of butcher among the English.[47]

Philip, duke of Burgundy, arrived at Poitiers on 28 August 1372, and
three weeks later he joined with Du Guesclin, Clisson, and the dukes of
Berry and Bourbon in concluding the treaty of Surgères with the prelates
and nobles of Poitou and Saintonge, who promised their full allegiance
to the king of France if the English did not come to their aid by the
end of November.[48] For the rest of the year, the five French commanders were busily campaigning to recover large amounts of territory for the
French crown.[49]

While Du Guesclin and Clisson were occupying themselves in the
French reconquests south of the lower Loire, relations between Charles V
and the duke of Brittany were building towards a crisis that would sharply
affect the lives and careers of the two Breton lords and their compatriots.
The French suspicions that had given rise to the Josselin transaction of 1370

Map 3. Poitou and adjacent regions.

were reinforced by the fact that Knolles retained his stronghold of Derval and could use Brittany as a haven when his expedition to France disintegrated at the end of the year. The French stance towards Brittany became more menacing when they occupied Walter Huet's former stronghold, Le Collet.[50] On 23 April 1371, John IV ordered his garrison at Champtoceaux on the Loire to hold firm against French pressure.[51]

John tried without success to expel the English garrison from the fortress of Becherel, but in the fall of 1371 he was actively negotiating with Edward III. The English king offered to return Becherel, but only as part of a treaty that would require John to perform liege homage and deliver up a number of Breton strongholds to English forces. Agreement to such conditions would undermine all of his efforts to restore the autonomous position of his duchy, and he was unwilling to accept them.[52]

Yet while he refused to become a mere pawn in the English war effort, John IV had real grievances against the king of France. He was particularly offended by those proposing sainthood for his defeated rival, Charles of Blois, whose canonization would make John the persecutor of a holy man. As Jones has pointed out, the duke's second childless marriage might be perceived in some quarters as a judgment of God.[53] Charles had a reputation for saintliness that equaled his military incapacity, and as early as 1368 the Franciscans at Guingamp, where he was buried, began circulating reports of miracles, perhaps as part of their rivalry with the generally Montfortist Dominicans.[54] Having received a complaint from John IV, Pope Urban V's reaction was to forbid the friars to circulate their tales of miracles and martyrdom; but Jeanne de Penthièvre encouraged them, and in 1369 Charles V asked the pope to hold an inquiry.[55] Urban then reversed himself and authorized the inquiry, but agreed in 1370 that it should be held outside Brittany at Angers, where Louis of Anjou opened hearings in August 1371.[56]

The increasingly tense relations between John IV and Charles V are documented by a series of diplomatic exchanges, but several important texts are undated and certain others are now lost, being known today only through references to them in other documents. Michael Jones has painstakingly reconstructed these Franco-Breton negotiations, which seem to have consumed the better part of 1371 and 1372.[57] The earliest surviving document in the sequence indicates that the duke had complained to the king about the proposal to canonize Charles of Blois and the failure to execute provisions of the treaty of Guérande involving lands claimed by John in other parts of France. He had also insisted that he was a loyal and obedient subject of the king and that Charles V should not believe Olivier de Clisson or anyone else who said otherwise. The king's rejoinder called attention to the English possession of strongholds like Becherel and Derval and to the presence of Englishmen on the duke's council. He disclaimed involvement in the canonization proceedings, expressed his displeasure at the duke's hostility to Clisson, said Clisson had never impugned his loyalty, and pointed out that when he had entered royal service Clisson had been in favor with John IV and had been retained to fight the companies, not the duke. He wanted the duke to reach an accord with him and said that Clisson was prepared to appear before the duke once the English were removed from the ducal council.[58]

Charles was being less than forthright about some of these points, and the same was true of John IV when he responded. The duke protested (probably sometime in the fall of 1371)[59] that he was not aiding the enemy and had no intention of helping men like Knolles and Lancaster wage war against France. The garrisons at Becherel and Derval, he said, were damaging to him and did not have his support. He sought to explain the other English in the duchy as servants and household officials of the duke and his English duchess. Household officers, however, were not necessarily domestic servants, and John's chief financial officer Thomas Melbourne and several other key officials were English, as Clisson, if not the king, surely knew.[60]

As for Clisson, the duke said that he had proceeded against him "par longues dilations et voie de justice" and would treat him in an appropriate legal fashion.[61] Aside from personal rancor, which evidently grew stronger on both sides over the years, what was the case that John IV had against his former supporter? It seems to have boiled down to two issues. The first was Clisson's agreement to hold Josselin under conditions that placed royal sovereignty ahead of ducal suzerainty and threatened the concept of Breton autonomy that John had been nurturing so carefully. The second issue involved his sense that Clisson had betrayed him. While the intrigues of Charles of Navarre may have aggravated this sense of betrayal, the heart of the matter was John's belief that Clisson had poisoned the king's mind against him, and on this point he was doubtless correct.[62] The mutual grievances of 1370 remained bitter. If Clisson, having sworn a solemn oath attesting to the duke's loyalty, felt dishonored by the growing evidence of John's flirtation with the English, the duke can only have had similar feelings when a man he had trusted to swear on his behalf began to tell the king that John was violating his oath.

In his struggle to maintain some independence, however, the duke of Brittany was making some serious miscalculations. For one thing, he did not make sufficient allowance for Breton hostility to the English, perhaps because he had spent so many years in exile. Breton sailors had been clashing with their English counterparts for generations. More recently, many Breton magnates had supported Charles of Blois, had fought against the English for years, had seen their property ruined or confiscated and given to Englishmen, and had lost friends and relations in battles against them. Most of these lords shared John's vision of Breton autonomy but, as Jones has pointed out, the duke failed to win their support for his foreign policy in the 1370s.[63] The presence of English garrisons in the duchy and Englishmen among the closest ducal advisers cannot have been much to their liking, and they were more disposed to sympathize with Clisson than with their duke.

Although he was one of them, Olivier de Clisson appears to have differed from other members of the Breton aristocracy. It was partly a matter of personality: during his career he displayed a capacity for bearing and sustaining grudges that strikes one as remarkable even by the standards of the medieval nobility. He may also have differed from them on the basic question of what it meant to be Breton. Yvonig Gicquel has argued that Clisson was above everything the head of a Breton faction, that what he really wanted was power in the duchy, and that he would not have made the Josselin transaction if he had seen himself as a French lord rather than a Breton one.[64] The opposing argument, which seems more persuasive in the light of Clisson's career in French politics, is that of Françoise Autrand, who suggests that he made a fundamental choice, casting his lot with the monarchy and rejecting provincial loyalties.[65] The brutal experience of his childhood and long years in exile engendered a certain rootlessness in a man who now, in his early thirties, had acquired great riches and a capacity for independence that few men in any age are able to achieve. In 1379, when hostility to England was not a decisive issue and the Breton lords faced a choice between an autonomous duchy of Brittany and direct royal control, it was Clisson who would miscalculate, failing to realize that most of his compatriots did not share his royalist loyalties.

When the duke of Brittany sent his next mission to the court of Charles V, it was probably around the end of 1371 or the beginning of 1372.[66] In the interim, John's negotiations with England had produced the rather unsatisfactory proposals mentioned above.[67] While John planned his next move in dealing with England, a demand that Edward return his honor of Richmond,[68] he also made demands of the king of France, calling for Charles to deliver to him lands his ancestors had held in Normandy and Burgundy, to relinquish Le Collet, to revoke letters of safeguard granted to Breton subjects, and to quash the canonization proceedings.[69]

Some time later (but before the first of April 1372), John approached the king once more, complaining again about the failure to return lands claimed in other parts of France (from the revenues of which he was supposed to provide the annual income promised to Jeanne de Penthièvre). By now the value of the lands in question had become an important issue, for the continuing crisis of seigneurial revenues was making it impossible to collect amounts based on estimates from earlier periods. Finally, the duke complained that the continued French occupation of Le Collet was damaging to him.[70] By this time (March 1372), Anglo-Breton negotiations had produced a new draft treaty, and during the spring the English were preparing a force of troops to send to Brittany.[71] Yet John IV continued to negotiate with Charles V, receiving an embassy consisting of the counts of Tancarville and Braine. The duke secured satisfaction from them on a good many points he had raised earlier—promises to return Le Collet, to cancel royal safeguards, and to acquit the duke of his obligation to provide ten thousand pounds in income to Jeanne de Penthièvre.[72]

John IV gained these concessions at a time when he was putting the finishing touches on an offensive and defensive alliance with Edward III that his representatives concluded at Westminster on 19 July 1372.[73] His duplicity throughout 1372 is hardly a matter for debate. The issue is whether he kept negotiating with both sides in order to strike the best deal possible under difficult circumstances or whether he was committed to England all along and kept negotiating with Charles V merely to "mask his perjury," as La Borderie put it.[74] Whatever John was really up to, his dealings with the king of France in this period have been worth examining because they identify issues that would be points of contention for a generation. John was clearly committed to the English by July, and any mystery about it was removed when the English troops finally landed in October.[75]

The duke of Brittany, who was still expressing grievances to Charles V in September,[76] nearly two months after his secret treaty with England, now had to feel the outrage of his own nobility as well as Charles V. Hugues de Montrelais, bishop of Saint-Brieuc, the ducal chancellor who had joined Clisson in swearing the loyalty oath of 1370, now defected, offering his loyalty to the duke of Anjou and agreeing to support the canonization of Charles of Blois.[77] John IV claimed that the troops were not to be used against France but only to compel the obedience of rebellious vassals, specifically Olivier de Clisson.[78] This argument, however, was unlikely to mollify Charles V and could easily be taken as a threat by the anti-English Breton baronage. In rejecting it publicly, Charles wrote directly to the lords of Brittany on 24 November, announcing that he had sent a French army to the duchy to expel the English.[79] In effect, the royal dukes, the constable, and the lord of Clisson had interrupted their campaigning in Poitou in October to make a brief but imposing military demonstration. The duke of Burgundy's itinerary shows him (and probably the others) at Clisson on 23 October and at Angers a few days later. After two weeks on the eastern frontier of Brittany, Philip headed back to Angers and then to Saumur, where he was joined by Du Guesclin and Clisson on 22 November.[80]

On that very date John IV, at Brest, confirmed his treaty with England, adding the proviso that he would not have to render homage if Edward III became king of France.[81] His response to the French king in December was a defiant one. No longer trying to excuse himself, he complained bitterly that his enemy, the lord of Clisson, had been permitted to enter his duchy with troops.[82] A copy of the Anglo-Breton treaty found its way into the French royal archives. According to one widely cited, but rather garbled, chronicler, the French acquired this document during their brief campaign in the fall of 1372 when they happened to intercept the duchess of Brittany and found it in her baggage. Delachenal, who considered this chronicler utterly unreliable, rejected the story and argued convincingly that they did not lay hands on the document until they reentered Brittany in force the following spring.[83] The English landing alone was enough to provoke royal action and damage the duke in the eyes of his baronage. French knowledge of the treaty, however, surely must have influenced the rapid collapse of the duke's position in 1373.

The Breton demonstration in November was only a brief interlude in the principal French campaign of 1372, which continued to be the reconquest of Poitou. Du Guesclin and Clisson were soon back in that region, accepting the surrender of Thouars.[84] This place was one of a trio of fortresses west of Poitiers that claimed the attention of the French in the winter of 1372–73, the other two being Niort and La Roche-sur-Yon, which offered more stubborn resistance. Du Guesclin finally took Niort on 27 March 1373, a week or so after defeating the English in an engagement outside Chizé, while Clisson besieged La Roche-sur-Yon.[85] This fortress, which occupied a key position near Clisson's own lordships, held out until well into the summer. Payments to messengers from the duke of Berry suggest that Clisson was at La Roche-sur-Yon in early May, late June, and late July,[86] but a chronicler indicates that he was in Brittany for part of this period, and Louis of Anjou wrote to him at Vannes on 24 July.[87]

Bertrand du Guesclin was able to leave Poitou after the fall of Niort and turn his attention to Brittany. He assembled a large force at Angers and invaded the duchy,[88] probably around mid-April, and he quickly gained the support of the Breton aristocracy. The duke, whose treaty with the English was surely common knowledge by this time, found himself so isolated that he fled to England, embarking on 28 April 1373.[89] Three weeks later, Charles V gave Olivier de Clisson the land of Guillac, a dependency of Josselin, in a document that announced the confiscation of John IV's possessions in France because he was guilty of *lèse majesté*.[90] This confiscation clearly applied to Breton lands held by Englishmen, but it is not so clear what ducal possessions were subject to it. Charles had thoughts of confiscating the ducal title itself, bringing the matter before the Parlement in Paris on 11 August. Either his advisers urged him to use caution or Charles was diverted by the next English attack, for no further action occurred at this time. Charles continued to use language indicating his assumption that John IV had forfeited the duchy and was no longer duke.[91] Later in August, when John IV sent the king a formal defiance renouncing his homage and fealty, he was back on French soil with an English invading army.[92]

Following the duke's flight, most of Brittany fell into French hands quickly. Du Guesclin secured the surrender of Rennes on 20 May.[93] By 24 June, only Brest, Auray, Becherel, and Derval were holding out, and the constable had been besieging Brest since the beginning of that month.[94] While Robert Knolles was defending Brest for the English, he had a lieutenant holding his own fortress of Derval, which Clisson now began to besiege. A week into July, Knolles was ready to surrender Brest if a relief expedition did not arrive by a certain date. This kind of arrangement, provided for in the law of arms and already employed several times in the Poitevin campaign, entailed a relaxation of the siege and a giving of hostages to the besiegers as a guarantee of the garrison's good faith. In this case, the agreement broke down when the earl of Salisbury arrived off Brest with a fleet. Salisbury neither relieved the fortress nor gave battle to the French besiegers, but Knolles took advantage of the occasion to repudiate his promise to surrender, and Brest would remain in English hands for another twenty-four years.[95]

The captain of Derval made a similar agreement with Olivier de Clisson, promising to capitulate on 29 September if no relief arrived. The surrender was to be received by Louis of Anjou, the son-in-law of Jeanne de Penthièvre and nominally the royal lieutenant in Brittany.[96] Hearing of this agreement, Knolles overruled his lieutenant and repudiated it.[97] Lefranc's account of these sieges, heavily dependent on chroniclers and somewhat confused chronologically, repeats their stories of Clisson's rage and brutality towards English hostages and captives at Derval and Quimperlé.[98] Despite the many inaccuracies of these narrative sources, it is evident that Clisson had acquired a reputation for conspicuous brutality towards the English.

The flight of John IV created problems for his English allies, who had planned an invasion of France to be led by the duke of Lancaster. John of Gaunt's indenture of 1 March 1373 provided for him to serve in France for a year beginning on 1 May. His plan was to sail from Plymouth, evidently bound for Brittany, but the quick French successes in the duchy forced the expedition to change its destination to Calais and embark from Dover and Sandwich.[99] The duke of Brittany accompanied Lancaster's forces, which reached Calais in July.[100] If John IV believed this invasion was designed to reassert his control over Brittany, he was disappointed, for after his destination became Calais, John of Gaunt did not even attempt to head for Brittany as Knolles had done three years before, and he may have had a different agenda.[101] His arrival, however, did force the French to divert their military resources once again to the north of the kingdom, leaving their subjugation of Brittany incomplete. As in 1369, Lancaster's opponent was Philip of Burgundy, who kept the French army on John's right flank, with the evident intention of ensuring that this English raid did not approach the environs of Paris as those of 1360 and 1370 had done.[102] This strategy may have influenced Lancaster's campaign, which turned out to be a highly destructive raid into the heart of France.

Burning and pillaging as they went, the English passed through Artois and Vermandois,[103] with the French harrying their flank and inflicting damage on parties detached from the main body. On 9 September, at Oulchy-le-Château in the Soissonais, Jean de Vienne and two other leading French commanders overwhelmed one such force commanded by Walter Huet, who was killed in the encounter.[104] Proceeding ever farther south, Lancaster's army remained vulnerable to attacks of this sort. Olivier de Clisson, who had joined Burgundy's army by 13 September,[105] subsequently inflicted considerable damage in a minor engagement near Sens.[106] Eventually, Lancaster did turn west, passing through the Bourbonnais, La Marche, Limousin, and Périgord, then descending the Dordogne en route to Bordeaux.[107] It was well into December before he reached this destination, having lost a considerable number of his men and most of his horses. In the final stages of this march, the English occupied a few towns, and their now-depleted army had inflicted enormous damage on the French rural economy. Yet they had not been able to impair the French military capability.[108]

To formulate his response to this invasion, Charles V convened a "great council" at Paris, almost certainly on 10 September 1373. His three brothers were there, as were Bertrand du Guesclin and Olivier de Clisson. The situation was very different from that of 1370, for France had achieved important military successes in the intervening period, including that at Oulchy the day before (if, indeed, the news of this encounter had reached Paris). These successes strengthened the hand of those who favored a battle and thought it shameful that a large enemy army should be allowed to pass through the French kingdom with impunity.[109] Ever the proponent of a defensive strategy, Olivier de Clisson opposed this position once again and now, for the first time, Du Guesclin was present to support his argument. So also, apparently, did Louis of Anjou. The two Breton lords and the king's oldest brother joined in advocating the approach that Clisson had taken previously—that it was better to suffer a ravaged countryside than to risk permanent loss of territory in a pitched battle.[110] Charles V's personal inclinations seem to have favored this policy, and so it was adopted—the French avoiding major engagements for the rest of Lancaster's campaign.

Modern French historians have agreed with Charles V. Most recently, Favier has observed that the policy gained him no glory but enabled him to recover his kingdom.[111] The kingdom, however, did have to pay a considerable price. The years 1373 and 1374 were a time of great misery for France.[112] The king's "ordinary" revenues, a partial indicator of rural economic conditions, amounted to just over 47,000 pounds in 1374, about 10 percent of their value forty-five years earlier,[113] and this time may mark the fourteenth-century low point for seigneurial revenues and the kingdom's population.[114] Well aware of the damage troops could cause, the royal government, in January 1374, made the first concerted attempt to impose order on the kingdom's military forces. A royal ordinance required that a company consist of one hundred men-at-arms. It made the appointment of military commanders a royal monopoly and established rules holding captains responsible for the misdeeds of their troops.[115] Both sides in the war were now ready for a respite, and Du Guesclin made a truce with John of Gaunt that was to run until 21 May. Another great council, convened on 9 March 1374, advised against ratifying it,[116] but the level of warfare in the west declined anyway.

The devastation inflicted by Lancaster's expedition had not affected Normandy, which now had to support serious military measures against the fortress of Saint-Sauveur, which had served as a base for destructive enemy operations in lower Normandy for nearly twenty years. After the death of Chandos at the beginning of 1370, Edward III had given custody of the stronghold to Lord Latimer.[117] To deliver themselves from the scourge of this garrison, the Normans had been holding assemblies and raising money since the summer of 1372 with the expectation that the king would send Du Guesclin to lead an attack on the town.[118] The constable, however, could not be spared because Brittany became a higher priority once John IV's English sympathies had become evident. Charles V, however, had found another gifted commander in the person of Jean de Vienne, whom he had named admiral of France at the end of 1373. The king made Vienne his royal lieutenant in lower Normandy on 18 August 1374.[119] Vienne laid siege to Saint-Sauveur, and several assemblies of the Norman Estates bowed to the necessity of granting special taxes to support the operation.[120] In January 1375, the government in Paris took additional measures to support the project,[121] and a fragmentary chronicle for 1375 placed Du Guesclin and Clisson at the siege.[122]

The French made use of artillery at Saint-Sauveur, and by the spring of 1375 had done considerable damage. At length, Latimer's captain of the fortress agreed on 21 May to evacuate it if he were not relieved by 3 July (six weeks later), provided that the French paid him and his men a substantial sum. This agreement was not affected when England and France concluded a two-year truce at Bruges at the beginning of July, and the evacuation of Saint-Sauveur took place on schedule.[123] In mid-June the Norman Estates agreed to a loan to raise the money needed to buy off the departing garrison.[124]

The recovery of Saint-Sauveur and the Anglo-French truce came at a time when important changes were underway at the French court, specifically in the personnel of the royal council. These changes gave a more visible role to a group of royal advisers who were linked to Olivier de Clisson. The interpretation of these changes has become a matter of historical controversy concerning the very nature of Charles V's government.

5

Political Society at Court:
Emergence of the Marmousets

THE POLITICAL CHANGES OF THE YEARS 1374 and 1375 involved the gradual departure of several longtime members of the royal council and greater prominence for a group of royal advisers, later called the Marmousets, with whom Olivier de Clisson was closely associated. These changes ended fifteen years of unusual stability in the royal council, the dominant members of which had served since John II returned from captivity in 1360. The principal historian of the council, Raymond Cazelles, concluded that this body of inherited councillors had kept Charles V in tutelage for the first ten years of his reign and that the king's personal rule began only with the changes of 1374–75. Any discussion of political society in this period must address the Cazelles thesis, for it amounts to a radical reinterpretation of what has been regarded as one of the most important reigns in French medieval history.

During its years of unusual stability, the council was dominated by two families with roots in eastern France—the Dormans and the Melun.[1] The leading figure, Guillaume de Melun, was archbishop of Sens from 1345 to 1376, and his authority after 1360 led Cazelles to call him "the Richelieu of the fourteenth century."[2] He was the most important of those royal henchmen who served John II in his captivity, the *français de Londres*, who distrusted Charles because he seemed reluctant to support treaties for his father's release that entailed dismembering the realm. They made every effort to curtail the dauphin's authority while they negotiated the treaty of Brétigny, and their behavior after John's death in 1364 led Cazelles to conclude that Charles V was "elected" king because no suitable alternative was available.[3] Can we concur that Charles V was, in some sense, the prisoner of advisers he could not overrule?

Aside from the long stability of the council, Cazelles was struck by two other characteristics of the royal government in the first decade of Charles V's reign: (1) the limitation of the king's direct action to a fairly restricted area while large parts of the kingdom were ruled by powerful royal lieutenants with virtually vice-regal authority,[4] and (2) the remarkable power wielded by the "counsellors-general of the aids," a small group of men who supervised and administered the system of regular taxation that came into effect in 1360–63 and who had the authority to act in the king's name without his prior approval.[5] Both of these phenomena, however, are comprehensible in the light of French fiscal history. The kings had found it difficult to collect taxes before 1356 because their subjects believed that taxes were justified only by military emergencies defined in local or regional terms.[6] Then John II's captivity and its consequences revolutionized royal finances by forcing people to adopt a new attitude towards taxation.[7] The monarchy finally acquired adequate regular resources thanks to the indirect taxes enacted in 1360 to pay the king's ransom and the direct taxes granted in 1363 to finance measures to suppress the *routiers*. The fiscal revolution required lengthy debate, during which the crown made important concessions to reformers who demanded more local control over the form and collection of taxes and collection machinery and accounting procedures that would bypass the traditional royal officers and ensure that the proceeds were not embezzled by corrupt officials.

In coming to terms with these concerns, the royal government, between 1345 and 1360, worked out the system of *élus* and *généraux* that would characterize its tax collecting process in future generations.[8] The system was still quite novel and not envisioned as permanent. Those who administered it were still feeling their way. Their most urgent need was to overcome the chronic suspicion of royal officials and ensure that money reached the war treasurers in time for troops to be paid promptly. Such factors dictated the extraordinary authority that the counsellors-general exercised during the first decade or so of the new fiscal regime. Meanwhile, the crisis caused by the *routiers* in the 1360s made it necessary to leave more fiscal and military responsibility in local and regional hands, decentralizing governmental activity through the use of princely *apanages* and powerful regional commanders who often proved very effective.[9] Once recovery was well underway in the middle 1370s, it was possible and perhaps desirable to eliminate some aspects of the decentralization of the 1360s and gradually to redefine the role of the counsellors-general in a way that placed primary emphasis on their auditing responsibilities.[10] The expedients of the early 1360s, gradually reversed in the more victorious 1370s, were creative responses to very serious problems. When viewed in the context of defeat, brigandage, and urgent fiscal necessity, the decentralization of royal power and the authority wielded by the counsellors-general are not good evidence that the king was in tutelage.

The heart of the problem, therefore, remains the royal council, led since the winter of 1359–60 by John II's companions in exile who negotiated his release from captivity. It was made up of nobles and prelates determined to run the kingdom according to the principles of "reform" advocated by their social class. At the outset, it contained no Parisians, bourgeois, or lawyers,[11] and its composition reflected the process by which the crown embraced the nobility, distancing itself from the bourgeois radicalism of the 1350s and managing to "marginalize" the erratic and rebellious king of Navarre. This accommodation took place over the last six years of John II's reign, beginning under the dauphin's leadership but remaining "fragile and conditional"[12] until the Melun brothers took charge of matters, shunting Charles aside, and sealing the pact with the nobility by issuing the great ordinance on currency and taxes in December 1360.[13]

This major accomplishment was fundamental to the revival of the French monarchy, but John's councillors faced an unexpected crisis when the king, who had returned to England for further negotiations, died there in the spring of 1364. Until John's body was returned and buried, Charles V could not exercise full royal authority, and the council seems to have delayed the process as long as possible in order to negotiate with him. The Melun brothers and their friends wanted to retain their positions on the council and to ensure that their work would not be undone by a young king they distrusted.[14] To say that they "elected" the new king is a serious overstatement, but to win their support Charles may well have accepted an arrangement that would explain the subsequent stability of this council.

If the young king did agree to leave intact the core of his father's council, he (and the council) thereby abandoned the earlier Valois practice of altering its membership to reflect changing political circumstances.[15] If Charles was being kept in tutelage, one would expect to find some evidence of a royalist faction of the king's friends trying to force their way onto the council. The absence of such evidence raises several questions: (1) Was the council in fact a single-minded body of men imposed on Charles by his predecessor? (2) did the council still reflect the larger political society? and (3) did political debate and decision-making still occur primarily within the council?

On the first of these questions, Autrand has chided Cazelles for unduly emphasizing the influence of the Melun brothers and seeing their clients everywhere. She argues that Jean and Guillaume de Dormans were not their clients but were associated with Charles when he was dauphin and favored a government based on the legal/judicial traditions of the Parlement, to which John II and Guillaume de Melun were indifferent.[16] Autrand considers the council to have been balanced between the men of John II and those loyal to his son.[17] Some very important advisers of Charles V remained outside the council until the reign was well advanced. To argue that the king's personal rule began only when these men became councillors[18] requires one to accept the questionable premise that only people sitting on the council could exercise decisive political influence.

The council that Charles V inherited bore the heavy imprint of the noble reform party of 1356–57,[19] when it was still closely associated with Charles the Bad and the radical bourgeois leaders in Paris. While these un-savory connections were gone by 1360, Charles could hardly forget his difficult political apprenticeship, when he had been bullied and intimidated by critics of the crown, and a council of fifty members, forced upon him by the Estates General in March 1357, did indeed try to place him in tutelage.[20] With experiences quite different from those of his predecessors, Charles could be expected to abandon some of their political practices, especially if circumstances compelled him to retain his father's councillors when he became king.

Charles V broke with the tradition of using a small group of coun-cillors as the appropriate forum for political debate and decision-making. He had shown his hand as early as 1359, when the Melun brothers brought from England a draft treaty that would have purchased his father's release by ceding to England sovereignty over a large part of France. He convened the three Estates to discuss this document, which they duly rejected, and the *français de Londres* never forgave him for doing so.[21] Unlike his father, who preferred reaching important decisions in camera, Charles V always preferred to consult larger bodies, before whom he could explain and jus-tify the actions he was considering.[22] He summoned the Estates occasion-ally, but had good reasons not to be overly fond of those assemblies. His preferred method was to convene several dozen additional advisers, cre-ating a "great council" of forty to seventy-five people, in which the ap-pointed councillors he had inherited would amount to a small minority. He summoned such ad hoc bodies whenever he faced a critical decision, such as the Gascon appeals in 1368–69, the appointment of Du Guesclin as constable in 1370, the tactics to employ against Lancaster in 1373, and how to deal with the duchy of Brittany in 1373 and 1378.[23] He frequently convened these meetings in the Parlement, which was then experiencing a strong renascence after being eclipsed during the final years of his father's reign.[24] While he had no thought of reversing the alliance with the nobility orchestrated by Guillaume de Melun, he was evidently committed to a concept of "reform" that gave a far greater role to the law and its practitioners.[25] These larger bodies gave Charles access to advice from elements of political society not represented on the now-stable small council.

The council's revolving membership in previous decades had reflected the relative influence of various princes and great lords as well as governmental institutions like the counsellors-general of the aids, the Parlement, or the Chamber of Accounts. In the reign of Charles V, two new sources of political power grew sharply in influence and began to rival the older elements of political society. One of these was the royal household and the other was the military leadership. The household had always had political importance, as the office of "master of requests" had been a stepping stone to power and wealth for the upwardly mobile. Now, however, we find a growing number of nobles, including some important ones, serving as royal chamberlains and enjoying the king's proximity and confidence. Writing about the next reign, Autrand has called attention to the significance of the royal household as a center for the making of governmental policy,[26] and the grand master of the royal household became a figure of such influence that he would come to rank as one of the "great officers" of the crown.[27]

Many of the chamberlains were also members of "military society" —the leading commanders in a newly professionalized army. The old nobility, as a political and military elite owing service to the king, had no separately distinguishable military component before 1360, but years of warfare and the crisis of the rural lordship were bringing changes. The emergence of the *routiers* not only made necessary the fiscal, military, and administrative decentralization alluded to above, but also hastened the developmment of a more stable royal army financed by the taxes adopted in December 1363 to combat the domestic violence.[28] Charles V now could afford several thousand regularly paid troops, and to command them the crown enlisted and cemented ties with nobles from the north and west, often from formerly dissident families and associated with the old Navarrese party in Normandy or the Montfortist party in Brittany.[29] These commanders produced victories and earned rewards, including positions in royal and princely households. They were evolving into a small, specialized military elite within the nobility as a whole. The bitter Anglo-French war of 1369–89 enhanced the importance of this military establishment, making it a newly influential element of political society even though its members did not seriously penetrate the royal council until after the death of Charles V.

Even if one treats the statements of Froissart with great caution, the growing influence of men like Olivier de Clisson is difficult to ignore. The most influential member of the royal household, Bureau de la Rivière (who likewise did not sit on the council for many years) developed a close friendship with Clisson that symbolized (and perhaps even stimulated) a growing alliance between the military leaders and the king's most intimate personal advisers. They exercised an influence on royal policy that was not, for a long time, reflected in the membership on the council. When significant changes began to occur in the council around 1375, men who had been serving and advising the king for years began to hold more visible positions of authority, appearing more prominently in governmental enactments, leaving documentary traces formerly associated with councillors.

The old archbishop of Sens made his last public appearance in the government on 21 May 1375. His subsequent departure was related to a quarrel with the inhabitants around Sens, who had sued him for abuse of forest rights and were supported by the king's proctor. The Parlement ruled against him in August, and his brother, the count of Tancarville, soon had to give up his control of the waters and forests administration. Guillaume de Melun himself died in May 1376.[30] For Cazelles, these dates signified the decisive change, after which the rise of new men in the government marked the beginning of Charles V's personal rule. These men, members of a group of royal advisers that became known to posterity as the "Marmousets," were Bureau de la Rivière, Jean le Mercier, Enguerrand de Coucy, Jean de la Grange, Arnaud de Corbie, Pierre de Chevreuse, and Nicholas du Bosc.[31]

For the most part, we cannot really describe these people as "new men." What was new was the increased frequency with which they were mentioned in official royal acts. The lord of La Rivière had entered the dauphin's household (where his brother also served) in 1358, had been a military commander since 1367, and was the nephew of a prominent member of the royal council as well as a friend of Clisson. Le Mercier had also been in royal service since 1358 and had been a war treasurer since 1369. La Grange, one-time abbot of Fécamp and now bishop (later cardinal) of Amiens, was a former partisan of Charles of Navarre, a member of the council in 1369, and a leading figure in the financial administration. Arnaud de Corbie, first president of the Parlement, had served Philip of Burgundy before entering royal service in 1369. Chevreuse had been in royal service since 1361, mainly as a financial officer, but had been on the council in 1364 and 1369. Nicholas du Bosc, one of the commissioners named to negotiate with the English on the matter of Belleville in 1367, was a member of the royal household who became bishop of Beauvais and one of the counsellors-general of the aids in 1375.[32]

Enguerrand VII, lord of Coucy, was something of a special case, being a "new man" from an old and distinguished noble lineage from northern France. As a young man, Coucy had been a Navarrese sympathizer, accompanying Charles the Bad to Paris in 1358. Later sent to England as a hostage, he had won the favor of Edward III and had married one of the English king's daughters. He did not serve the king of France until the truce of 1375 relieved him of having to fight his father-in-law. After Edward's death in 1377, he became a major royal commander and a close friend of Olivier de Clisson.[33]

With the exception of Coucy, the men who now became more visible in the government had served and advised Charles V for years. Their greater prominence in royal enactments and, in some cases, their promotion to new positions in 1374 or 1375, merely gave their influence a more public character. The king named some of these longtime associates to the council as the members he had inherited finally died or retired, but their appearance there does not signify a radical change in royal policies or governmental practice.

One of the more obscure members of the king's circle was a lawyer in the royal household whom he named to the council in the spring of 1374 with instructions to draw up a written compendium of the powers and functions of the royal government. Two years later, this official presented the king with a document entitled the *Somnium Viridarii*. It was a somewhat hasty compilation, organized as a dialogue between a priest and a knight, a literary motif that had been popular for the past century. In 1378, this treatise appeared in a more polished French version, *Le Songe du Vergier*, containing substantial revisions, possibly made under the king's direction.[34] In this form, it represented the political ideology of the Marmousets, a view of government and royal power that broke less sharply with the views of the preceding fifteen years than one might suppose. Recent scholarship has argued persuasively that the author of *Le Songe du Vergier* was Évrart de Trémaugon, a Breton lawyer from the region of Saint-Brieuc whose brother Yvon was a sometime military commander under Du Guesclin and Clisson who also joined groups of Breton *routiers* on foreign expeditions.[35] Trémaugon and other intellectuals, such as the better-known Nicole Oresme, were part of a small circle around the king that Autrand calls the "Club Charles V." This group discussed and debated matters of law, politics, and philosophy, and may be seen as yet another forum for political debate outside the council.[36]

In 1374, the crown promulgated an important group of ordinances, one in August on the royal succession and two in October that provided, respectively, for the tutelage of a minor king and the regency that would rule while he remained a minor. The last two were specific to the people and conditions of 1374, while the first one endeavored to establish general principles.[37] The enactment of 14 August, sometimes called the Edict of the Bois de Vincennes, was registered in the Parlement at Guillaume de Melun's last public appearance as a member of the council, in May 1375. Cazelles considered these ordinances to be the old archbishop's greatest and most enduring achievement, but Autrand suggests that the king himself designed the edict, in partial imitation of the Golden Bull issued by his uncle the emperor in 1356.[38]

The Edict of the Bois de Vincennes gave formal written effect to what had become the accepted rule as a result of the problems surrounding royal successions earlier in the fourteenth century: the oldest son of the deceased king would inherit the throne; women could neither inherit the throne nor transmit a claim to it; if the late king had no sons, the nearest male relative in the male line would inherit the title, without the need for any election and without challenge to his right to be crowned at Reims.[39] The two enactments promulgated in October are of more interest to this study because they dealt with, and failed to solve, problems that would recur throughout the next reign. They stated that the next king, if a minor, would achieve his majority on his thirteenth birthday, and until that time the regent would be the senior prince of the royal blood, Louis of Anjou. Guardianship of the young king would be shared by the queen mother, her brother the duke of Bourbon, and Charles V's brother Philip of Burgundy, assisted by Bureau de la Rivière, who was singled out in this way, and a *conseil de tutelle* to be drawn from a list of nearly fifty prominent royal advisers. This group strongly resembled those "great councils" that Charles V liked to convene when faced with important political decisions. Besides Guillaume de Melun and other appointed councillors, it included prominent members of military society like Clisson, Coucy, Louis de Sancerre, and Jean de Vienne, as well as their allies among the Marmousets — Du Bosc, Le Mercier, Corbie, and La Grange.[40]

These ordinances were important documents because they formalized the French laws of royal inheritance that would still be in force centuries later, but their significance in the immediate context of the fourteenth century should not be exaggerated.[41] Had they been in force when John II died, they would not have altered the political situation prevailing at that time. Nor did they avert difficulties in 1380, when Charles V's brothers nullified some of their provisions. The rules covering regency and guardianship of a royal heir were reenacted in 1393 but canceled ten years later, while in 1420 the treaty of Troyes would even overthrow the edict of August 1374 governing the succession itself. Uncertain or difficult successions and nagging questions about royal legitimacy would continue to plague the unhappy house of Valois.[42]

The departure of the Melun brothers actually brought little change in the conduct of royal policy because Charles V had not built his government around the council they had dominated. If any major principle separated the king from his father's old advisers, it was the issue of whether to surrender sovereignty over territory in order to make peace with England. The Melun brothers were prepared to do so and had agreed to such a dismemberment of the realm at Brétigny in 1360. Charles V rejected the option of surrendering sovereignty, and he and his circle would not accept a rather modest alienation at Boulogne in 1376. Consequently, the truce of Bruges came to an end in June 1377 without any new peace treaty between the monarchies. The French delegation, made up primarily of men associated with the Marmousets—Nicholas du Bosc, Pierre Aycelin (bishop of Laon), La Rivière, Coucy, Nicholas Braque—was in a position of strength, since the Prince of Wales had died in 1376 after a long illness and Edward III had lapsed into senility, leaving the ten-year old Richard II poised to inherit the English throne.[43]

While the truce was in effect and these negotiations were in progress, the French crown concerned itself with two projects: (1) military action aimed at dealing with the problem of the *routiers*, who once again posed a serious threat to public order during the cessation of hostilities; and (2) the rebuilding of the French navy under the able leadership of Jean de Vienne. To deal with the *routiers*, the government chose a stratagem employed several times during the 1360s—an expedition out of the country. Enguerrand de Coucy, a somewhat footloose warrior with a grudge against the duke of Austria, assembled a force of *routiers* in the fall of 1375 and led them into the Habsburg lands in Alsace. There they were defeated at the hands of the Habsburgs' Swiss allies and a large number of these troublesome soldiers were killed.[44] Those who survived were soon back in France, and the accounts of the war treasurer show that Coucy, Olivier de Clisson, and Guillaume des Bordes were commanding troops against them in 1376.[45] As his ties to Charles V grew steadily closer, Coucy served with French commanders on this enterprise during the truce, but not until the death of Edward III in June 1377 did he make the fateful decision to abandon his English lands, wife, and daughter for full-fledged French allegiance.[46] Henceforth he would be one of the most respected military men in the French government.

Another respected military figure who joined Charles V's team in the mid-1370s was Jean de Vienne, the new admiral of France. Like Coucy, he became a friend and ally of Olivier de Clisson and the Marmousets. After his military successes at Oulchy-le-Château and Saint-Sauveur, Vienne spent the two years of the truce modernizing the *Clos des Galées* and rebuilding the French fleet—the project Charles V had dreamed of in 1369 but had never been able to complete.[47] When the truce expired in the last week of June 1377, Vienne was ready to put to sea. On 27 and 28 June, his forces attacked and pillaged Rye, on the southern coast of England, and for most of the next two months he was able to inflict serious damage on the English channel ports.[48]

Well prepared on all fronts for the renewal of hostilities, the French made major advances in the second half of 1377. Clisson took Auray on 15 August, leaving the enemy with Brest and its environs as the only bastion of resistance in Brittany.[49] He then joined Philip of Burgundy, who was assembling a large force to attack Ardres, one of several strongholds in the north that protected the approaches to Calais. Between 4 and 11 September, the French captured all these fortresses and were ready to attack Calais itself, but Vienne's fleet, which had arrived to blockade the port on 10 September, was forced away by stormy weather, saving this critical bastion for the English.[50] In the southwest, meanwhile, Louis of Anjou conducted a successful campaign that left the English with little more than the cities of Bordeaux and Bayonne.[51]

These triumphs, which appeared to leave the French poised for the final expulsion of the English from the continent, made the end of 1377 the high point of Charles V's reign. At the close of the year, and in the first days of 1378, the king received in Paris his uncle, the aging emperor Charles of Luxembourg. The imperial visit was a great spectacle that seemed to reaffirm the majesty of the resurgent Valois monarchy.[52] Ironically, however, the year 1378 would be marred by a series of misguided decisions and reversals of fortune that would tarnish the end of the reign and deny the monarchy the ultimate success that had seemed imminent when the year began.[53]

The first crisis, and the least damaging one, involved Charles II of Navarre, the old Valois adversary whose queen (sister of Charles V) had died in 1373. His military defeat in 1364 had broken the Navarrese threat to Valois authority, but two subsequent treaties, in 1365 and 1371, had left lingering points of contention. In 1376, a dispute over the conduct of their respective officials in Normandy nearly produced a rupture between the kings of France and Navarre, but then in 1377 they were discussing a treaty of mutual support against England. When the French would not restore the Norman lands taken from Charles in previous treaties, he turned again to England.[54] In 1378, he sent his son, the future Charles III, to his Norman lands, and the French subsequently apprehended one of his confidants, Jacques de Rue, who was traveling to join the prince there. According to the chroniclers, Charles V received a warning that Jacques de Rue was carrying documents implicating him and the king of Navarre in a plot against the king of France. By June, Charles V had obtained a confession revealing various treasonable plots on the part of Charles the Bad, and he ordered the confiscation of Norman lands belonging to the Évreux family.[55] French military forces endeavored to secure these possessions, but the critical port of Cherbourg escaped them when the English sent a force to occupy it in December and captured Du Guesclin's brother, while the constable fumed at the failure of the war treasurer to provide adequate pay for the French troops.[56]

By this time, however, Charles V was becoming embroiled in a more serious matter that would have major consequences for the stability of western Christendom itself—the papal election of 1378, in which one of the influential Marmousets, Cardinal Jean de la Grange, would play an important part. For seventy years the popes had been Frenchmen who spent their pontificates north of the Alps, generally at Avignon. Several of them had been men with particularly close connections to the French crown. Gregory XI, the seventh of these popes, had many contacts in France and had corresponded with Olivier de Clisson regarding the marriage of the Breton heiress of Rais.[57] His legate in Italy, Cardinal Robert of Geneva, had ties to the old reform party in France and thus to Marmousets like La Grange,[58] had worked closely with Breton *routier* captains in Italy, including Yvon de Trémaugon, and was on good terms with Clisson.[59]

Under pressure from pious souls who deplored the papacy's close ties to France and thought the popes should reside in Italy, Gregory XI finally relented and returned to Rome in 1377. He died there several months into 1378, at a time when sixteen of the cardinals were with him in Rome, six others were still at Avignon, and La Grange was between these two locations transacting some business while en route to Rome. The conclave to choose Gregory's successor apparently opened in Rome on 6 April,[60] and the cardinals soon found themselves in a very difficult situation, as a vocal and disorderly crowd began demanding that they elect a Roman, or at least an Italian, to be the next pontiff. In an atmosphere that became increasingly intimidating, the conclave soon chose as pope the archbishop of Bari, who was crowned as Urban VI on 8 April 1378.[61] Unfortunately, the new pope was not a man of conciliatory temperament, and he soon fell to squabbling with the cardinals, treating them rudely and even threatening them.[62] Towards the end of the month, Jean de la Grange finally reached Rome and soon had an altercation with Urban VI. It appears that the cardinal of Amiens became the instigator of a rebellion against the pope on the part of those members of the sacred college who were at Rome. They began to slip away from the city and gradually assembled at Anagni where, on 9 August, most of the cardinals who had elected Urban VI pronounced an anathema against him and declared his election invalid.[63]

The death of Gregory XI did not become known in Paris until after the election of Urban VI, and it occurred to nobody to contest the election. It was not until June that the French court received any communication from the new pope, and it appears that the messenger who brought it also intimated to the French government that the election had taken place under peculiar circumstances.[64] More time passed, and then in August a former confessor to the queen of France reached Paris and told Charles V enough to persuade him that the validity of Urban's election was highly questionable. He then received a letter from the cardinals, indicating that virtually the entire college now rejected Urban VI.[65]

The king convened a council of prelates and theologians who met in Paris on 11 September to hear representatives of the cardinals describe the circumstances of the election in April and request French support for their view that it was invalid.[66] The assembled clerics urged the king to avoid taking sides on this delicate issue, since it was fairly evident that they did not yet know all the facts. For the moment, Charles V accepted this recommendation as his public position, but privately, it seems, he had concluded that the cardinals were in the right. It is doubtful that they would have proceeded with a new election without some assurance that the action would have the approval of the king of France.[67] It is also unlikely that Charles reached his conclusion and signified his approval purely on the basis of personal conviction. Many of the Marmousets had ties to the ecclesiastical faction formerly led by the cardinal of Boulogne and now associated with La Grange and Robert of Geneva, and the cardinals controlled by this faction manipulated the time required for news to circulate, making it difficult for the king to avoid supporting their position. They went ahead with a new election late in September, choosing Robert of Geneva, who took the name Clement VII when he was installed as pope in Fondi on 31 October 1378.[68] This action inaugurated the Great Schism that divided Catholic Christendom and endlessly complicated French foreign relations for the next generation.

In mid-November, Charles V issued orders to recognize Clement VII as pope.[69] Scotland and the Spanish kingdoms would agree, but most other countries remained Urbanists. The schism could not have occurred without the blessing of the king of France, whose private encouragement to the cardinals in September and quick publication of his decision on 16 November were quite at variance with the prudent counsel urged by the assembled (and divided) French clergy in September.[70] Perhaps recent military successes, crowned by the imperial visit to Paris the previous winter, had persuaded royal advisers that the king of France really could act as the arbiter of Catholic Europe.

While Charles V's hasty decision may have helped launch the schism, his brother, Louis of Anjou, was even more outspoken than the Marmousets in opposing Urban VI and welcoming the election of Clement VII.[71] Louis had acquired Provence from the queen of Naples and hoped to be her successor in the Neapolitan kingdom. She was an opponent of Urban VI. Italy now became a battleground, as thousands of soldiers of fortune fought ruthlessly on behalf of the competing papal factions. Clement VII, who was unable to take Rome, hoped to lure the duke of Anjou and an additional force of *routiers* to come to his assistance in Italy. To this end, he proposed to create an Italian realm for Louis, to be carved out of the northern papal states. This creation, to be known as the kingdom of Adria, would be Clement's bait to dangle before ambitious French princes.[72]

Clement did not persevere very long in Italy waiting for this outside assistance. Military setbacks led him to abandon the peninsula and return to the more hospitable papal enclave at Avignon. He arrived there on 20 June 1379,[73] and henceforth his fortunes and the policies of his supporters in Italy would be tied to schemes that were inherently destabilizing to the prospects for peace in Europe because they entailed some form of French intervention in Italy that would threaten the interests of other powers.

Clement's hopes for an early military solution that would resolve the schism in his favor soon were dashed when the French government encountered new misfortunes. In Languedoc, a decade of heavy royal fiscal exactions provoked rebellion at Montpellier in October 1379. The uprising spread across Languedoc and was not fully suppressed until 1384. Charles V decided to relieve the duke of Anjou as royal lieutenant in the Midi.[74] He had already recalled Louis to the north to help him deal with what had become the worst failure of his reign—the duchy of Brittany.

6

Clisson and the Royal Failure in Brittany

THE ROYAL DEBACLE IN BRITTANY at the end of the 1370s offers a prime example of how personal rancors, in this case those of Olivier de Clisson and Charles V, could interfere with sound political judgment. At the same time, it marked the second time in the decade that political leaderhip failed to understand the mood of the Breton aristocracy. John IV had already made this mistake in 1372 when his increasingly evident support of the English antagonized his nobles.

Their hostility had permitted Bertrand du Guesclin to lead an army into Brittany without serious opposition in April 1373 and John IV to flee to England before the end of the month. Royal forces quickly occupied most of the duchy, but when Robert Knolles retracted his agreement to surrender Brest, he imposed an important setback on the French, who thereafter had to maintain military vigilance against a possible English landing at this port.[1] The problem did not seem serious at the time, but what had appeared to be the imminent conquest of Brittany remained incomplete when the duke of Lancaster landed at Calais in July 1373.

For the next five years, a group of Breton magnates administered the duchy, at first under the general supervision of Du Guesclin. This interim regime imposed a hearth tax (*fouage*) on 20 August 1373 to help finance the remaining sieges of English strongholds.[2] Since campaigns elsewhere required the constable's attention, Charles V found it politic to name as his lieutenant in Brittany Louis of Anjou, the son-in-law of Jeanne de Penthièvre.[3] Until his recall from Languedoc in 1379, however, Louis was but a figurehead who rarely appeared in Brittany. The administration of the duchy remained effectively in the hands of the great Breton lords, led by Olivier de Clisson, who generally exercised authority in the eastern part of the duchy, and Jean, viscount of Rohan, who was in charge of the western, Breton-speaking districts.[4]

In January 1374, the king named Rohan his lieutenant general in Brittany with three hundred men under his command.[5] According to a chronicler, John IV returned to Brittany a few weeks later. Having departed from Lancaster's campaign after it reached Bordeaux, he put in briefly at Auray but found no support and returned to England.[6] The French, meanwhile, besieged and captured Becherel in 1374 and then launched their campaign in lower Normandy against Saint-Sauveur. To respond to these initiatives and relieve pressure on English strongholds, Edward III planned an expedition to the continent that experienced serious delays and never put to sea.[7]

On 24 November, Edward named his son Edmund and John IV of Brittany as his lieutenants in France,[8] but not until April 1375 did they sail to Brittany with four thousand men, landing at Saint-Mathieu near Brest. According to the widely repeated accounts of chroniclers, French commanders besieging Saint-Sauveur detached several hundred troops under Clisson, Rohan, and the lords of Beaumanoir and Laval, who proceeded to Lamballe in order to counter the duke's forces who were approaching Saint-Brieuc.[9] John IV and his English troops came close to taking Saint-Brieuc, but were diverted in June when Clisson and his fellow commanders launched a diversionary attack on a small fortress near Quimperlé from which a freebooter was terrorizing the adjacent region. This diversion saved Saint-Brieuc from capture but it soon placed Olivier de Clisson and his companions in grave peril when they were besieged in Quimperlé. John IV relished the opportunity to capture his hated enemy, and had he done so Clisson might have paid a high price for his notorious past brutality towards English prisoners. Before this could happen, however, messengers arrived reporting the Anglo-French truce just concluded at Bruges.[10] It suspended hostilities for two years, and by mid-July most of the English had left the duchy.[11] John IV remained behind, protected by the walls of Brest and exchanging recriminations with Du Guesclin and Clisson. Each side accused the other of violating the accords and demanded that the other withdraw.[12]

For five years following the duke's flight in 1373, the status of Brittany remained in a kind of limbo, punctuated by short-lived English expeditions and the French reduction of all Breton fortresses other than Brest. Although he was occasionally called upon to fight elsewhere, Olivier de

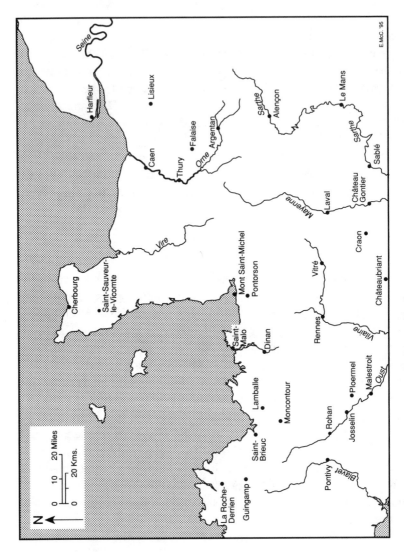

Map 4. Northeastern Brittany and adjacent lands.

Clisson spent a good deal of time in the duchy, intervening on the king's behalf in a dispute at Saint-Malo in 1374,[13] mustering with a large force of men at Vannes in 1376,[14] acting as royal custodian of Nantes,[15] and conducting an inquiry into the possession of Moncontour in 1378.[16] At times he behaved high-handedly, and a dispute over the land of Loyat got him summoned before the Parlement in Paris during the summer of 1377.[17] Clisson also devoted considerable energy and wealth to new defensive works at his principal castles. This process continued into the 1390s, and there is considerable documentation for the work at Blain, where he employed a mason named Guy.[18] It was Josselin, to which he added several massive towers, that became his principal fortress.[19] Clisson became renowned as an expert on fortifications, but at a time when artillery was making Saint-Sauveur untenable, his expertise was becoming outmoded.[20]

Anglo-French negotiations during the truce created some strains between John IV and his English ally, but Charles V did not move to exploit these, and when resumption of the war became imminent in the spring of 1377, John returned to England hoping for more military assistance in regaining his duchy. Assorted vicissitudes, including the weather, ruined the plans for this expedition. The English did put more troops into Brest, which had become their lone foothold in Brittany after Clisson took Auray on 15 August.[21] To strengthen their position, the English government in 1378 acquired title to Brest castle by donating other lands to John IV.[22] In the same year, an English expedition under Lancaster attempted to take Saint-Malo; the effort failed, but it distracted the French who were trying to occupy Cherbourg before it fell into English hands.[23]

This attack on Saint-Malo in 1378 was evidently the last straw for Charles V and his advisers as far as the status of Brittany was concerned. Deciding that it was time to punish the rebellious John IV, who had shown no interest in negotiating a return to royal favor, the crown summoned him to face charges before the Parlement in Paris. Opinions differ as to when he was summoned, nor is it clear whether the summons was directed to a location where John could reasonably be expected to receive it, and there is no evidence that Charles V issued the safe-conduct that was prerequisite for John's personal appearance. We cannot wholly trust sources that are heavily influenced by Breton nationalism, but there remain doubts as to whether the crown adhered fully to proper legal forms in this case.[24] John IV did not appear at the proceedings, nor did he send a legal representative, contrary to his usual practice of sending proctors with lengthy briefs to justify his behavior.

Figure 3. Josselin castle, nineteenth-century restoration. (Photograph by Gwyn Meiron-Jones)

The final date for John to appear at the Parlement was 4 December 1378.[25] Five days later, the king and dauphin made their ceremonial appearance, with Charles V "assis en sa majesté royal en la manière qu'il a accoustumé quant il siet pour Justice." Only three of the lay peers were present, the other six having sent excuses for not attending, but the six ecclesiastical peers did come, along with a dozen other prelates and five barons.[26] The king's attorney set forth the following points: (1) John IV had given Charles his fealty and liege homage through properly empowered representatives, Olivier de Clisson and the bishop of Saint-Brieuc; (2) he had then been guilty of "griefs et exces" against the barons of Brittany, especially Clisson; (3) these lords had appealed to the Parlement, thereby gaining immunity from ducal jurisdiction, but John had continued to abuse them; (4) the duke had treated violently the priest who had brought him the summons to respond to these appeals; (5) when the king learned that the English had entered the duchy, John had written the royal princes promising to get rid of them but had not done so; (6) he had accompanied Lancaster's expedition in 1373–74 and had been involved in various atrocities; and (7) finally, he had turned over Brest and other places to the English and had "fist grans exces" at Saint Malo. The royal prosecutor therefore accused him of felony, perjury, and treason, recommended that he be stripped of his titles, and proposed that the duchy of Brittany be taken into the king's hands ("estre au Roy commise").[27]

Having learned of the royal plan to take action against John IV in the Parlement, Jeanne de Penthièvre had sent a team of six attorneys to Paris, headed by two doctors of law.[28] One of these now addressed the court, pointedly using Jeanne's title of duchess of Brittany and saying that John, rather than being duke, had merely held the duchy. He wished to respond to what the royal lawyer had said, and on the following day the court heard "la cause de Bretaigne en tant qu'il touche la duchesse d'une part et le procureur du Roy dautre part. . . ." The court then deliberated for five full days (11, 13, 15–17 December) before pronouncing judgment.[29]

The charges brought by the royal attorney in this case deserve our scrutiny. The allusion to fealty and liege homage did not refer to the lengthy deliberations that occurred between the treaty of Guérande and the ducal homage of December 1366 because Clisson's fellow envoy in that period had been Latimer.[30] Clisson and the bishop of Saint-Brieuc had represented John IV only in the mission of 1369–70, which culminated in their solemn oath of loyalty on behalf of the duke in January 1370. The duke's "excesses" against Breton barons undoubtedly were part of his effort to consolidate his power (especially in the fiscal sphere) at the expense of the great lords during the period 1365–73. The increasing assertiveness of ducal officers[31] would have provoked the appeals to the king. In this set of charges against John, the crown appeared to single out Clisson as particularly aggrieved. Breton dukes regularly denied the competence of royal courts in such matters, and it is not surprising that this long-running point of contention should occasion accusations of ducal violence against the bearer of a summons. To what date should we assign John's alleged promise to rid the duchy of the English? The allegation seems inconsistent with his defiant stance after the English landing in 1372, and it probably refers to 1369 or 1370, when he was strongly professing loyalty to Charles V. His campaign with Lancaster following his formal defiance in 1373 requires no further comment. His arrangement with the English over Brest and the attack on Saint-Malo in 1378 appear to be the actions that finally provoked the king's judicial response.

What is strikingly absent from these charges is any explicit reference

to the action that had actually triggered the royal occupation of Brittany—
John's evident collusion with England in 1372 while he was portraying
himself as a faithful, if aggrieved, vassal in negotiations with Charles V. We
are presented, in fact, with two different sets of charges: the overt military actions of 1373 and 1378, which occurred after John's open defiance
of Charles V and also after the king had originally sought to confiscate
the duchy,[32] and a group of earlier offenses that clearly revolved around
Olivier de Clisson. The charges relating to these earlier offenses remind us
immediately of the issues leading up to the Josselin transaction and Clisson's definitive break with John IV—the solemn nature of the oath taken
in January 1370 and the presence of the English in the duchy, so resented
by Clisson and (as I have argued) perceived by him as a violation of the
oath.[33] The nature of the charges brought against John IV strongly suggest
the influence of Clisson in the whole proceeding, and his close ties with
the Marmousets further support the view that he was the government's
principal source of advice on Breton policy.

The records of the Parlement do not furnish comparable details on
the position taken by Jeanne de Penthièvre's lawyer, yet the court devoted
a day to hearing them and then took five additional days of deliberation
before it could pronounce judgment. The case against John IV as a defiant
and unrepentant rebel was too clear and well documented to require such
long discussion, so the deliberations must have concentrated on a different matter, the fate of the duchy itself. It was surely this issue that Jeanne
de Penthièvre wished to address. She had important rights at stake, for the
treaty of Guérande identified her male children as the heirs to the still childless John IV. If John were deprived of his titles without confiscation of the
duchy, Brittany ought to pass to the house of Blois/Penthièvre. It appears,
however, that Jeanne did not invoke the treaty as the basis for her claims.
Lacking official records, we must look for her arguments in the *Songe du
Vergier*, written several months earlier by a Breton who had originated in
her lands. In this document, the words of the priest, expressing the position that the crown wished to oppose, probably reflect the position subsequently taken by Jeanne's attorneys. According to this argument, John IV
had no right to the duchy, since the renunciations made by Jeanne in the
treaty of Guérande were rendered invalid by John's failure to carry out the
provisions of the treaty. The king, therefore, was holding the duchy un-
justly and to the prejudice of Jeanne's rights.[34]

The Breton historiographical tradition of Montfortist chronicles, his-
tories based on them, and their interpretation by Dom Lobineau, have

heavily influenced modern writers. These historians understood the confiscation of Brittany to mean its incorporation into the royal domain and the extinction of the ducal title. According to Lobineau, the countess of Penthièvre argued that such an annexation could occur only in the case of a fief or apanage created by a dismemberment of royal territory. Brittany, having never been royal territory, could not be absorbed into a royal domain of which it had never been a part.[35] It is not clear that placing the duchy in the hands of the king meant anything this drastic, but Bretons apparently believed that it did. Lobineau possessed a strong sense of Breton identity, and two chronicles that he published were written only a few years after these events by propagandists for the ducal house who preached a doctrine of Breton distinctiveness and the integrity of the duchy, beliefs that already had deep roots in Breton history. Whether or not Jeanne's representative actually made the arguments Lobineau described, they were compatible with Breton thinking and royal courts had been hearing arguments for Brittany's autonomy since the 1330s.[36] After lengthy deliberations, to which we shall return, the court rendered its judgment on 18 December, not only declaring John IV guilty but also ordering confiscation of the duchy of Brittany.[37]

The serious political consequences of this decision were not immediately obvious, for Charles V waited until April 1379 to put the judgment into effect. Then he named four men of great political and military stature to act as commissioners empowered to occupy Brittany in his name: Louis, duke of Bourbon; Louis de Sancerre, marshal of France; Jean de Vienne, admiral of France; and Bureau de la Rivière, the king's first chamberlain. These commanders assembled troops but did not immediately cross the frontier.[38] To appropriate the ducal domain, the king named the four Breton lords on the scene who had been exercising authority for him in Brittany—Rohan, Laval, Du Guesclin, and Clisson. Clisson, the incorrigible enemy of John IV, complied willingly enough. Laval was very reticent and circumspect, clearly not wanting to be part of a bad business. Rohan was even less willing, while the constable maintained a very low profile.[39] Du Guesclin's limited role may be attributable in part to suspicions on the part of Marmousets like La Rivière, who never cared for him and may not have wanted him to have too much authority in a sensitive operation involving the future of Brittany.[40] In this case, the suspicions were justified, for Du Guesclin seems to have been far more of a Breton patriot than Clisson,[41] and the large contingent of Breton nobles who had served him for years and were still prominently represented among his troops at Saint-

Malo in the fall of 1378, were opposed to royal confiscation of the duchy.[42]

The evident uneasiness of men like Du Guesclin, Laval, and Rohan is understandable in the light of what happened in the last week of April 1379, when a group of nearly forty great Breton lords, seconded by many others of lesser standing, formed a league to oppose the invasion or confiscation of the duchy. They named four of their number as "governors" and levied a tax on their lands to finance any military effort they would have to make.[43] Whether an invader were French or English, their intention was to use force if necessary to preserve the autonomous duchy of Brittany. The original impetus to establish the league came, significantly, from Jeanne de Penthièvre and her followers who had been the French-backed party during the war of succession.[44] The Parlement's failure to support her claims in December was now causing the planned confiscation to fall apart.

The league's four governors had all served the king on occasion and had collaborated with Du Guesclin in governing the duchy since 1373. One of them, Clisson's friend Jean de Beaumanoir, had been an active commander in the armies of Charles V, as had two other members of the league, Olivier de Montauban and Robert de Guitté (the latter having been Du Guesclin's marshal).[45] Such a roster of names could hardly be called pro-English or anti-French, yet the league was determined to prevent the French confiscation, and after a brief overture to John of Blois, it sent a message to John IV in May, inviting him to return to Brittany. John needed some convincing that the request was sincere, and he did not leave England until the end of July.[46] Du Guesclin, had he moved quickly, could have blocked him, but he did not do so, and John IV was able to land unopposed on the north coast of Brittany early in August.[47] Thus the duke, whose dealings with England had literally driven him from his duchy when his leading subjects deserted him, was now back in Brittany, not backed by English troops but at the invitation of those who had rejected him six years before. The royal attempt to confiscate the duchy had backfired disastrously, and there is a broad consensus that it was the worst political blunder of Charles V's reign.[48]

A miscalculation of this magnitude by a king known as "the Wise" demands some explanation. Cazelles believed that the king, finally in full control of the government and surrounded by men of his own choosing (the Marmousets), was reverting to an earlier Valois policy of cracking down on the great feudatories and overly powerful regional governors. Thus the action against Charles of Navarre, the Breton confiscation, and the removal of Louis of Anjou from his southern command were all examples of a single policy.[49] Yet each of these actions was the product of particular circumstances and it is difficult to build a convincing case for associating them together as part of a single policy. Perhaps the leaders of the Melun-Dormans council had opposed drastic action with regard to Brittany in 1373, but many things had happened in the ensuing five years: the duke's formal defiance and overt military action against the crown, a new round of French victories, and the death of Edward III, all of which were arguably more important than changes in the royal council.

If we are to explain the crown's miscalculation in Brittany, we must first return to the deliberations that preceded the judgment in the Parlement. Without direct evidence of the arguments presented during the discussions, we must begin with the viewpoint of the Marmousets expressed earlier in 1378—the arguments of the knight in the *Songe du Vergier*. Those relating to the felonies of John IV and his mistreatment of Clisson closely resemble the charges actually presented in the Parlement to demonstrate John's treason.[50] When we turn to the claims of Jeanne de Penthièvre, we find the knight arguing as follows: the Montfort claim to Brittany was superior to that of Blois-Penthièvre; John IV was fully entitled to the duchy until his felony made it forfeit to the king who was, at present, the true duke of Brittany; Jeanne could not reclaim the duchy on the basis of the treaty of Guérande because all that document guaranteed her was possession of the lands she held before the treaty.[51] These arguments represented a stunning reversal of the position taken by the Valois monarchy throughout the disputed succession in Brittany. In the context of 1378, they have the look of casuistry—a rather lame attempt to justify a legal action that the crown had already decided to take when the opportunity presented itself. It is small wonder that the countess of Penthièvre and her followers felt affronted and betrayed.

How were such arguments received by the royal advisers assembled in the Parlement? The length of the deliberations suggests considerable disagreement, and one can point to a number of other considerations that may have influenced the proceedings. The most avid proponents of royal sovereignty may have hoped for a decisive victory over claims of Breton autonomy, while others may have feared the effects of the royal arguments on a Breton aristocracy that had served the crown faithfully against John IV and the English since 1370. Perhaps Jeanne de Penthièvre was out of favor at court and lacked influential supporters for her claims at this point. The most serious political obstacle to Jeanne's claims remained the fact that her two oldest sons were still captives in England, where they had been sent as hostages nearly twenty-five years earlier. If the crown dispossessed John IV and gave his duchy to John of Blois, there would again be two claimants, both of them in the hands of Richard II's government, which could then offer its backing to the highest bidder. Replacing the ousted duke with his captive cousin, far from liquidating the Breton problem, could merely make it worse. These considerations would have made it hard to resist the Marmousets, who had already decided what they wanted.

One suspects, indeed, that the serious political setback occasioned by the confiscation of Brittany could not have been averted by a different decision in the Parlement. Charles V and his most trusted advisers had lost their patience and had decided to terminate the ambivalent situation that had prevailed in Brittany since 1373. The crown passed the point of no return when it summoned John IV before the court without first securing the release of John of Blois. With the duke's guilt beyond dispute and the alternative duke in English hands, the only feasible action at that point was to take the duchy into royal hands. We have no evidence of any French effort to secure the return of John of Blois. The crown's political mistake thus had three components: the formal charges brought against John IV, the failure to appreciate Breton noble sentiment, and above all the reversal of its traditional support for the claims of Blois/Penthièvre. In each of these three areas we can detect the hand of Olivier de Clisson, and he must bear a good part of the blame for the ensuing debacle.

The charges brought against John IV strongly suggest Clisson's influence. Moreover, the commanders sent to occupy the duchy happened to be his friends.[52] If Autrand is correct in thinking that he had committed himself to the supremacy of monarchy over provincial loyalties,[53] then Clisson may also have misled the Marmousets on the likely reaction of the Breton nobles. His years of exile in England and many subsequent military and diplomatic activities outside Brittany had left him little opportunity to develop roots in the duchy until he began work on his castles there in the 1370s. Years of campaigning together had given him ties to many of his peers among the Breton aristocracy, but it is doubtful that he shared, or even fully grasped, their sense of the special status of Brittany.[54] They did not share his strong personal hatred for John IV, but he had imparted it to Charles V.

Finally, the standing of Jeanne de Penthièvre with the royal government at this critical time may have been damaged by a squabble with Clisson over money. Years before, he had served as her lieutenant while acting on her behalf in financial matters,[55] but this assistance with her finances had made him her creditor, and Clisson was not a forgiving creditor. To the end of his life, he kept a careful accounting of sums owing to him, including debts of very long duration.[56] Although Jeanne did pay off part of her debt in September 1378.[57] she still owed Clisson a much larger sum (over nine thousand pounds). We do not know about their relations while her attorneys were presenting her position to the Parlement in Paris, but it is probable that Clisson did not let her forget her debt to him. Once she and her followers supported the Breton league against royal confiscation in April 1379, Clisson responded in a characteristically vindictive manner, obtaining ecclesiastical sanctions against her as well as a summons to the secular courts.[58] It is possible that ill feeling between her and Clisson encouraged her to pursue a rapprochement with her exiled cousin rather than trusting a royal government that turned to her aggressive creditor for advice on Breton matters.[59] In any case, the nobles of her party reacted to the Parlement's judgment as though the survival of Brittany had been put into question.

The French crown got wind of the trouble rather quickly. Jean le Mercier had left Paris for Brittany with Louis de Sancerre on 13 April 1379, evidently to confer with Clisson and with other Breton leaders. Before reaching Paris again on 3 May, he had surely learned of the formation of the league and could have observed the assembly that drew up the pact. Having reported to the government in Paris, Le Mercier left again for Brittany on 15 May, this time accompanied by Bureau de la Rivière. Negotiations continued for the rest of the month,[60] and it may have been at this time that the crown put forth a new proposal, reported by a chronicler, that the duchy be conferred on the lone son of Jeanne de Penthièvre who was not a captive in England—her third, and youngest, Henry of Blois. The suggestion met with rejection,[61] perhaps because it had come too late, perhaps because the Breton aristocracy was unwilling to countenance such a violation of primogeniture. If, however, the candidacy of Henry was indeed suggested, it provides further evidence that the captivity of his older brothers was a major concern in the Parlement's deliberations in December.

With the Breton political situation continuing to deteriorate, the crown decided in June that its commanders should not cross the frontier to take possession of the duchy with their non-Breton troops.[62] It was now that Charles V turned to his brother, Louis of Anjou, whom he had hastily summoned from Languedoc. If he hoped that Louis and his mother-in-law could reach an accommodation that would undermine John IV, he was too late. Anjou assembled troops near the Breton frontier during July and

August 1379 but preferred to negotiate.[63] So also did Bertrand du Guesclin, who had served the house of Valois faithfully for more than twenty years but faced a serious conflict of loyalties in the present situation and did not wish to fight against his compatriots and recent companions in arms.[64] John IV was in no position to abuse his new-found support and also was prepared to negotiate. In October, he named four important lords, Beaumanoir, Montafilant, Laval, and Rohan, along with his cousin the count of Flanders, to represent his interests in negotiations with Louis of Anjou and Charles V.[65] A truce was soon concluded and Anjou returned to Paris.[66]

This truce terminated the French king's effort to confiscate the duchy but only temporarily halted the hostilities. It was probably the best that anybody could hope for while Charles V lived, for the king's attitude towards John IV was now as unyielding as Clisson's and he was little disposed to compromise. The duke, for his part, resumed his practice of simultaneous negotiations with the English. He had made a preliminary agreement with them before returning to Brittany,[67] and by September the English government was preparing an expedition at Southampton.[68] In January 1380, John IV named envoys to negotiate anew with the English government and with the duke of Lancaster.[69]

Olivier de Clisson remained on active campaign as the principal royal commander in the duchy. In May of 1380, he was leading a retinue of 119 knights and squires, and he kept a strong force in the field most of the summer,[70] having personally advanced salaries to three hundred men-at-arms in Brittany according to a document in which the king subsequently acknowledged that the treasury owed him the staggering sum of eighty thousand francs.[71] Even allowing for the possibility that some of this money represented his salary for his first few months as constable, he had apparently paid out of his own pocket for military salaries a sum that exceeded by more than 50 percent the entire ordinary revenues of the crown in 1374.[72] Once again, one is struck by the magnitude of his wealth.

The crisis of 1379 created some major shifts in allegiance among the Breton nobility.[73] The viscount of Rohan, whose son was soon to marry Clisson's older daughter, had been prominent governing the duchy during the duke's exile and was one of those named by the king to secure the ducal lands in 1379. We have mentioned his reluctance to carry out this last assignment, and after a lifetime of opposition to the Montfort party in Brittany, he now was drawn into the ducal camp.[74] As early as 26 September 1379, the duke rewarded him for good services,[75] and the following April John gave Rohan the confiscated castle of La Roche-Moisan, which he had bestowed on Clisson twenty-three years before.[76] Rohan swore an oath of allegiance to the duke, agreeing to support him against everybody, especially Olivier de Clisson.[77] In another repercussion of the crisis, Bertrand du Guesclin, whose reluctance to fight against his fellow Bretons in 1379 gave new ammunition to his enemies at court, was reassigned to campaign against *routiers* in the Cevennes. The royal government, having apparently lost confidence in the constable, may have been planning to replace him, but Du Guesclin, who was nearly sixty, died in the summer of 1380.[78]

A final consequence of the Breton debacle was a new English invasion. John IV's embassy concluded an alliance on 1 March 1380.[79] When summer came, the English dispatched to the continent the twenty-five-year-old earl of Buckingham, Thomas of Woodstock, the youngest son of Edward III and future duke of Gloucester.[80] Buckingham reached Calais with several thousand men on 19 July.[81] Passing through Artois, like several previous English expeditions, Buckingham's forces crossed the Somme into Picardy, while the French, as always under orders not to give battle, trailed them at a distance. As in the past, Philip of Burgundy commanded the French army, and in the absence of a constable he carried the grand title of captain general. Buckingham did not immediately turn towards Brittany but raided Champagne first. By September, however, he was moving westward, south of Paris. Philip of Burgundy, following but not engaging him, had reached the vicinity of Chartres on 14 September, when he received news that Charles V was dying and promptly left for Paris.[82] During the final stages of Buckingham's campaign, the task of shadowing him fell to Olivier de Clisson and a modest force of 420 men.[83] At length, Buckingham settled down for a long siege of Nantes, which was held by a strong French garrison.

By this time, however, events in Paris had overtaken those in Brittany, for the death of Charles V had improved the prospects for a peaceful settlement.[84] As we shall see, however, the turbulent beginning of the new reign produced results that might be called mixed from the Breton point of view. Louis of Anjou, the anticipated regent, was married to Marie of Blois and was not a friend of John IV, but Louis failed to retain the regency, and the real power at court fell to Philip of Burgundy, whose wife, Marguerite of Flanders, was a cousin of John's and is generally credited with influencing Burgundy's Montfortist sentiments. The bad news, from John IV's point of view, was that Olivier de Clisson was Du Guesclin's successor as constable of France.[85] As Jones has pointed out, Clisson's long feud with the duke and his growing rivalry with the royal uncles at court would form the dominant theme of the 1380s in French and Breton politics.[86]

John IV needed a settlement with the French crown to wipe out the judgment of confiscation and to give him once again a clear title to his duchy, but he was not very enthusiastic about the prospect of negotiating and wished to mollify the English if they learned he was doing so. He had a document drawn up stating that he was treating with the French only out of fear and not from a desire to betray his English allies.[87] His alliance with England, however, had brought him little but exile and disappointment in the 1370s. English expeditions to the continent had been of negligible help to John. In the latest such venture, Buckingham had not hastened to Brittany but had spent weeks raiding far to the east.[88] Now that Philip of Burgundy was in charge of the French government and anxious to end the Breton crisis with a new settlement, the prospects for fruitful negotiations seemed very much brighter, and on 19 November, John IV named an embassy that included the lords of Laval, Montafilant, and Acérac as proctors empowered to negotiate a treaty with France.[89]

The ensuing negotiations took place without the knowledge of the English,[90] as Buckingham's forces were completely occupied with the siege of Nantes, which was held for the French by the constable's first cousin, Amaury de Clisson.[91] By 15 January 1381, the negotiators had drafted a second treaty of Guérande.[92] The king and the uncles ratified this document almost immediately,[93] and on 23 February Olivier de Clisson added his own endorsement.[94] John IV ratified it on 6 April,[95] and four days later he announced it to his subjects and ordered them to swear to uphold it.[96] Finally, Jeanne de Penthièvre added her endorsement on 2 May 1381.[97]

The treaty required the duke to seek and receive a royal pardon and to do homage in the manner of his predecessors. The French promised to return his county of Montfort. John was to have no Englishmen serving on his council or acting as captains of fortresses in Brittany. He was to pay the French crown an indemnity of two hundred thousand francs, due in three installments by Christmas 1382. He was to ally himself with the king of France against the kings of England and Navarre and "all others," and Brittany was to be included in any Anglo-French peace. The Breton magnates were to swear to uphold the treaty and keep the peace.[98] There may have been a secret agreement that his alliance with France would not require him actually to take arms against England. The Breton magnates, in promising to support John against the king if the latter broke the treaty, specified that this exemption from fighting the English be put in writing.[99]

Disclosure of the second treaty of Guérande was a great shock for the English, especially Buckingham, whose troops were still engaged in besieging Nantes. Purchasing their withdrawal cost John IV twenty thousand francs. They returned to England in time to be used there against the Peasants' Revolt of 1381.[100] The treaty was a triumph for John IV, who now controlled his duchy again without the sort of English aid he had relied upon when winning Brittany in the 1360s.[101] Yet the settlement was also a victory for a French government that was increasingly dominated by the duke of Burgundy. It had extricated France from the difficult situation created by the attempted confiscation of Brittany.[102] With John IV no longer beholden to the English, and the latter angered by the conclusion of the treaty, it seemed far less likely that Brittany would be used as a base for English operations against France.[103]

The treaty could not, however, bring real stability to the crown's relations with Brittany because the duke's feud with Olivier de Clisson was as bitter as ever. Clisson and the Marmousets, who had been deeply involved with Charles V's Breton policy, were still a force to be reckoned with. Including Clisson in the second treaty of Guérande was appropriate and even necessary under the circumstances, for no definitive settlement could ignore him. But as Jones has pointed out, this inclusion made him appear as the duke's equal rather than as his subject. Allied to the former king's leading officials and leader of the French military establishment, he was a potential rival of the royal uncles, on whose continuing power and influence John IV's security now depended.[104]

By early May 1381, when all the interested parties had ratified the second treaty of Guérande, John IV concluded a treaty of alliance with Louis of Anjou, a prince whose strategically located *apanage* and whose connections to Clisson and the Penthièvre family made him potentially dangerous to the duke of Brittany. Anjou agreed to support John against all enemies except the king and the royal princes.[105] Attached to this treaty was a second document that is now apparently lost, by which Louis agreed to assist the duke against all enemies and especially against Olivier de Clisson.[106] This wording that specifically targeted Clisson had appeared a year earlier in the oath taken by the viscount of Rohan and should not be taken as evidence of an offensive alliance but rather as part of a ducal effort to protect himself with assurances of support from two of Clisson's longtime friends, should the new constable threaten him in the future. Louis of Anjou may have become annoyed at Clisson for pressing Jeanne de Penthièvre about her debts to him, but it is more likely that his special assurances to John IV regarding Clisson were tied to a second transaction, concluded a month later. On 12 June, Louis agreed to assume responsibility for two thousand

pounds of the income John was supposed to pay the countess of Penthièvre, in return for which Louis regained the strategic castle of Champtoceaux.[107]

Having secured his alliance with the duke of Anjou, John IV now
proceeded to a formal reconciliation with Clisson, who had been relieved
of the castles he had been holding for the king in Brittany.[108] He and John
now agreed to an alliance by which they were to support each other against
everybody except the king of France, the duke of Anjou, and the count
of Flanders. Clisson's affirmation of this document left out Louis of Flanders, whether by accident or design.[109] The following February, John IV
issued a short document swearing to protect the constable's life, lands, and
privileges.[110] After more than a decade, Clisson was again the duke's "dear
and faithful cousin." The reconciliation would not last for long, but for the
moment a serious conflict had been resolved. Shortly after his agreement
with Clisson, the duke granted pardons to his opponents in the duchy, as
provided for by the treaty,[111] and early in June the king required Clisson
and other royal officers to allow the duke unimpeded access to the lands
and revenues that the treaty had restored to him.[112]

John IV was now ready for his final act in his execution of the treaty—
his homage to the king of France. It was a complicated process that began
on 14 July 1381 with royal letters promising him safe-conduct to come before the king and offering him some important hostages as a guarantee.[113]
Then the safe-conduct had to receive the specific adherence of the princes.
Anjou subscribed to it by 20 July,[114] and Burgundy on the twenty-sixth.[115]
These precautions suggest that John IV still nursed strong feelings of suspicion and fear in his dealings with the French government. At length,
on 27 September 1381, John IV formally executed the second treaty of
Guérande, receiving the royal pardon and rendering homage.[116] Two days
later, the king reissued the treaty with a pointed reaffirmation of the duke's
obligation to oppose the kings of England and Navarre.[117] Charles gave
the duke an extension of the deadline on the installment of the indemnity
that was due at Christmas,[118] and he ordered his financial officers to inves-
tigate the value of those troublesome lands in Nevers and Rethel that were
still claimed by the duke.[119]

7

Royal Minority: The Uncles and the Marmousets

THE ROYAL FAILURE TO CONFISCATE Brittany was but one of the set-backs that brought a disappointing end to the reign of Charles V. Soon after the death of the queen in 1378, the king's own health began to de-teriorate, and with it his ability to exercise firm leadership. The eclipse and death of Bertrand du Guesclin left a void in military society at the same time. To fill the office of constable, the dying king apparently preferred Enguerrand de Coucy, to whom he had become very close,[1] but Coucy and Bureau de la Rivière had recommended their friend, Olivier de Clis-son.[2] The dukes of Berry and Burgundy appear to have preferred Louis de Sancerre.[3] The king's ill health and the crown's recent reversals made con-sensus difficult, and the office remained vacant.

Divisions among the princes became evident soon after the death of Charles V on 16 September 1380. His son and successor, Charles VI, was not yet twelve years old, and the ordinances of 1374, which were supposed to take effect in this situation,[4] soon fell victim to the political rivalries of the royal uncles who competed for control of the government. The oldest of the late king's brothers, Louis of Anjou, had been friendly with Clis-son and like him was connected by marriage to the Breton ducal house. Anjou was the designated regent for the young king, but his fiscal ex-actions as Charles V's lieutenant in Languedoc made him unpopular, and some feared that he would draw on French royal taxes to further his Ital-ian ambitions. The youngest brother, Philip the Bold, duke of Burgundy, stood to acquire, through his wife's inheritance, the lands of the count of Flanders and of the latter's aged mother. Like Anjou, he hoped to draw upon the resources of France to advance his foreign ambitions. The differ-ent geographical orientations of their personal ambitions gave these two dukes different, and sometimes conflicting, perspectives on such major issues as the Anglo-French war and the papal schism. Both men were very able, Louis having earned his reputation as a warrior and an effective, if fiscally ruthless, royal lieutenant in Languedoc, while Philip, now thirty-eight years old, was soon to establish himself as the foremost French statesman and diplomat of his generation.

The duke of Burgundy enlisted the support of the other two royal uncles, John of Berry and Louis of Bourbon, in modifying the arrangements of Charles V and diluting Anjou's authority. At the beginning of October, the royal council declared that Charles VI would be crowned king and would reign with the advice of his uncles.[5] This arrangement left the military administration under the young king, that is, under the dukes of Berry and Burgundy who had custody of Charles VI. Neither duke was a good soldier, and so they wished to choose a constable. The appointment, however, required "multas disceptaciones verbales."[6] Although he had been on good terms with one of the candidates (Clisson), Louis of Anjou favored leaving the office vacant.[7] Lehoux concluded that he must not have been much concerned about the perils of the Anglo-French conflict.[8] With his first priority now an Italian kingdom, Louis may have felt that a reduced French commitment to war with England would leave more money available for his projects. However, Michel Pintoin, the monk of Saint-Denis who wrote what has come to be regarded as the official history of Charles VI's reign,[9] noted that the acting head of the army in the absence of a constable was the royal standard-bearer (*Porte-Oriflamme*), who happened to be one of Anjou's supporters.[10]

With Coucy and Sancerre unwilling to take the post, the dukes had to compromise with the Marmousets and finally agreed to appoint Olivier de Clisson, the good friend of Coucy and La Rivière (not to mention Anjou).[11] On 21 October 1380, the forty-four-year-old Breton warrior took his solemn oath as constable to defend the king against all enemies.[12] The royal coronation took place at Reims on 4 November, and some weeks later, on the twenty-eighth, Charles VI issued the formal letters of appointment to the office.[13] The dukes of Berry and Burgundy would come to regret this appointment. They were well aware of Clisson's ties to the house of Anjou and to Bureau de la Rivière, whom they disliked, while he was, of course, also the implacable enemy of the duke of Brittany, with whom they were both friendly. Clisson, however, was greatly respected in the French military establishment, and historians have suggested two other factors that helped make him constable. One of these was the esteem of the young king, who had formed strong opinions about certain royal officials and had a weakness for successful warriors and military parades.[14] The other factor was Clisson's wealth. His proven willingness to pay troops out of his own pocket when royal resources were not available won him strong support, and not long after his appointment he made a loan of ten thousand francs to the always prodigal John of Berry (30 October).[15]

While the uncles accommodated them on the appointment of the constable, the Marmousets found their influence diluted by other changes at court. The uncles appointed a new chancellor from the Dormans family of eastern France.[16] One highly visible Marmouset, the financial expert Jean de la Grange, found it prudent to leave court, in part because the young king disliked him. The cardinal took up residence at the court of Clement VII,[17] where he lived until 1402 and continued to play some role in French ecclesiastical policy. The uncles also very nearly rid themselves of La Rivière, who underwent a brief disgrace after the return from exile of Waleran de Luxembourg, a friend of Burgundy's who blamed him for an earlier banishment. Clisson, however, had enough influence to protect La Rivière and restore him to an important place at court.[18]

What made it so urgent to reach an accommodation with the duke of Brittany and secure the removal of Buckingham's troops was the fact that the French government soon found itself facing a serious domestic crisis. Although the Marmousets included many people associated with the financial administration, one of the policies they had come to advocate was a reduction of the enormous fiscal burden assumed by the French population in the 1370s. Their intellectual mentors, Oresme and Trémaugon, had expressed concern about the justice of taxation,[19] which probably influenced Charles V, and the king may also have worried about the cupidity of his brothers and the nobility's dislike of direct taxation. In this context, Charles V on his deathbed announced cancellation of the *fouage*,[20] a tax that had supplied most of the revenue for the war treasurers who paid the French army. Opposition to taxes had already taken a violent turn in Languedoc, but if the dying king hoped to head off further trouble, his action failed to do so.

The uncles convened the Estates General to meet in Paris a week after the coronation in November, and Louis of Anjou (known for his foreign ambitions and his fiscal exactions in Languedoc) requested new taxes. The reaction was highly negative and there were disturbances in Paris and elsewhere, as people agitated for the cancellation of the indirect taxes (*aides et gabelles*) as well.[21] The uncles had to bow to this demand and agree to cancel all extraordinary taxes levied in the kingdom since the reign of Philip IV.[22]

Then they tried to obtain grants from regional assemblies, but none wished to commit itself without knowing what the others would do.[23] That setback forced the uncles to reconvene the Estates General of Languedoil on 20 December for a general airing of grievances. In January 1381, the government reaffirmed the cancellation of taxes and confirmed the rights and privileges of the past.[24] Then at last it was possible to go to the Estates in various regions and obtain grants of money.[25]

These levies were being collected by the summer of 1381, but they neither provided the government with adequate funds nor defused the general opposition to taxation. In January 1382, the government reimposed the *aides*.[26] The result was an immediate hostile reaction, as towns throughout northern France, led by Paris and Rouen, rose in spontaneous revolt. The crown suppressed these with a mixture of conciliation and force and augmented revenues by levying heavy fines, while curtailing municipal privileges.[27] All this violent opposition to taxation in the towns of Languedoil coincided with major uprisings elsewhere. In Flanders, an extended rebellion led by the city of Ghent had begun in 1379 and would lead to the devastation of the county over the next five years.[28] This violence and disorder was of particular concern to the duke of Burgundy because the county of Flanders had been the most valuable part of the extensive territory that his wife was due to inherit.

In Languedoc, the rebellion that had led to the recall of Louis of Anjou in 1379 opened a period of unrest that would not be put down completely until 1384. With all his faults, Anjou had provided the kind of stern rule that had relieved the Midi from the worst excesses of freelance soldiers, but stability in the region suffered from a feud even more long-lived than that between Clisson and the duke of Brittany. This one was between the successive counts of Armagnac, who were tightly aligned with the duke of Berry by marriage, and Gaston Phoebus, count of Foix (r. 1343–91). Charles V and the Marmousets had kept Berry out of Languedoc, but the duke greatly desired to succeed Anjou as royal lieutenant there. On 19 November 1380, he received the appointment he coveted.[29] As royal lieutenant in Languedoc for the rest of the 1380s, Berry would frequently be absent from the Midi, leaving the count of Armagnac or some other henchman to represent him. To pacify the Tuchin uprising then in progress, he employed Guillaume de Beaufort, viscount of Turenne, a man who was essentially a *routier* captain, although his brother had been pope. Berry's decade in charge of Languedoc would bring this unfortunate region endless factional strife, public violence, and corrupt, extortionate government.[30]

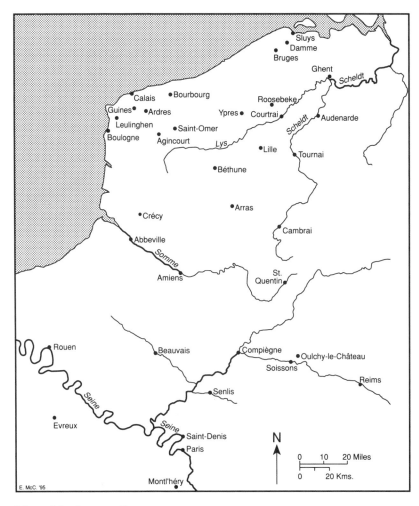

Map 5. Northeastern France.

With Berry having received his diversion, Louis of Anjou began to pursue his own project to win the throne of Naples. Late in July 1381, the royal council agreed to give him some financial support. Two months later, he announced his intention to leave for Italy. Early in 1382 he was still trying to raise more money and was growing irritated at the lukewarm support of the French royal council (which in turn wanted the pope to offer more support). By mid-March 1382, Louis was at Avignon, en route to Italy where he would meet an early death two years later.[31]

With both his brothers involved elsewhere, Philip of Burgundy was now the prince who controlled the government in Paris, while Olivier de Clisson, for all practical purposes, had become the head of the Marmouset faction and that part of the nobility belonging to the anti-Burgundian tradition in French politics. Although Philip was no less ambitious than his brothers, his personal interests were far more compatible with those of the French monarchy. They were based upon his impending inheritance of Flanders and they amounted to an extension of French influence into an area that had long been linked with England. It was possible for Philip to pursue these interests while remaining devoted to the crown of France, and one can credit him with providing the first-rate leadership needed in this difficult time. With the Breton crisis resolved by the new treaty, the aids restored, and the urban uprisings quelled, Philip was now able to direct his attention to the north. His father-in-law, Louis II of Flanders, had appealed for help against the rebels. The English government hoped to disrupt the impending Burgundian succession to Flanders and tried to exploit the uprising. Spies reported to Louis that there was talk of having young Richard II assume the title of count of Flanders, thereby legitimizing the rebellion and providing a legal basis for resisting the count and his son-in-law.[32]

With Burgundy at its helm, the French government agreed to come to the count's rescue. The crown could send against the Flemings an army that, for once, was not diverted by Breton, English, or Navarrese hostilities, but it did lack that core of Breton lords which had contributed much to its success in the 1370s. Although the ensuing expedition was Burgundy's project and Charles VI was nominally leading it, the real military command was vested in the constable. The Flemings made his task easier by failing to use the strategy that had proven successful to their ancestors in defeating French cavalry in 1302. When the royal army entered Flanders in the fall of 1382, cold and rainy conditions and the absence of abundant fodder could have caused it real hardship, but instead of taking a strong defensive position and letting the elements weaken the French, the Flemings sought a battle and took the offensive. Although the French also made errors that could have been costly, their military superiority prevailed against the Flemings at Westrozebeke on 27 November, and they achieved the decisive victory in a pitched battle that so often eluded them in the fourteenth century.[33]

The battle of Roosebeke, as it is known in French history, was perhaps Olivier de Clisson's greatest military victory, certainly in the eyes of those biographers who depended heavily on French chroniclers and did not notice the errors of the Flemings. These writers remind us of one point that is easy to neglect: the impression Clisson made upon the king, a boy not yet fourteen years old. Young Charles, already fond of military display, had now witnessed his first great battle and was filled with admiration for his rough, one-eyed constable. His feelings may have provoked some jealousy on the part of his less warlike uncles, Berry and Burgundy.[34] In any event, Clisson would derive important political advantage from the royal esteem in future years. He probably also added considerably to his wealth, thanks to his share of the booty won on this campaign.[35] The victory did not end the revolt in Flanders, but it did establish Philip the Bold as a dominant figure in the county and was thus an important milestone in what Palmer called the "war of the Burgundian succession."[36]

Military triumph in Flanders greatly strengthened the hand of the royal government, which now systematically and ruthlessly set about extinguishing the last embers of the earlier uprisings in the major French towns.[37] The royal uncles are said to have favored punishing the Parisians by letting the troops pillage the city, while Clisson argued against this advice and succeeded in disarming the rebels and protecting the populace against savage reprisals. According to this story, the grateful inhabitants gave the constable land that enabled him to expand his impressive town house.[38] The royal government had survived the crisis of the great tax revolt, and the *aides et gabelles*, along with the counsellors-general to administer them, were now fully back in force. Although the hearth tax, never popular with the nobility, remained canceled, it was at this point, according to Maurice Rey, that the king's right to tax was finally established beyond dispute.[39]

In Flanders, meanwhile, the rebels (who had lost their leader and were largely restricted to Ghent) appealed to England for help. Henry Despenser, bishop of Norwich, agreed to come to their aid, and his expedition (under the guise of an Urbanist "crusade" against the French supporters of Clement VII) sailed in May of 1383. The early success of the new English landing required another northern campaign on the part of the French army.[40] On this occasion the duke of Brittany and his lords participated on the French side. It was an excellent opportunity for John IV to demonstrate his independence of England and provide evidence of his sincerity in accepting the obligations of a French vassal. He was closely related to Louis of Flanders and probably felt more keenly the obligation to come to his aid than to assist the king of France. The expedition also served the purposes of Philip of Burgundy, whose friendship was crucial to the duke of Brittany. Finally, John IV found that the campaign in Flanders afforded him an opportunity to be rid of his obligation to pay Charles VI an indemnity of two hundred thousand francs. The king had been granting him extensions of the deadline for paying installments of this sum,[41] and he had paid at least 12,500 francs[42] but perhaps no more than that. Following the campaign, the king would discharge him of the remainder of his obligation because of the military service he had rendered.[43]

Before joining the French army, John IV secured royal letters of non-prejudice promising that his attendance would not affect any of his rights in the future.[44] He received royal authorization for the Breton currency to circulate legally elsewhere in France while he was on the campaign but gave the king letters of non-prejudice for this special permission.[45] Leaving Guy de Laval as regent in the duchy,[46] John then came with his men to the royal army. Interestingly, most of those who had been notable royal commanders under Du Guesclin and Clisson in the previous decade served under Clisson's banner on this occasion as well.[47] Clisson, as constable, was once again the principal French commander.[48] Because his salary continued to be seriously in arrears, the king continued to reward him with revenues and gifts such as the grant of all English possessions seized in Flanders.[49] He already was holding and receiving the income from Pontorson in lower Normandy to discharge debts incurred by the king previously.[50] When the crown granted him custody of the important castle of Montl'héry near Paris in March 1383, he had to swear that he would not try to retain this royal stronghold as surety for unpaid salary.[51] It also appears that a fleet was being readied to serve under his command.[52]

The expedition of 1383 did not entail much fighting. The French quickly reversed the English gains, thwarted their effort to aid the Flemish rebels, and bottled them up in Bourbourg. At this point, the French chose to negotiate a truce that would permit the withdrawal of Despenser and his men for a price. The royal uncles had a preference for diplomacy over combat, but it was the duke of Brittany who particularly sought a negotiated settlement. It is very possible that the dukes wished to avoid another great military triumph for Clisson. In any event the English left Bourbourg with their booty on 15 September.[53] Having twice made successful military demonstrations in Flanders, the French government, led by Philip the Bold, now hoped to negotiate a peace that would end English efforts to disrupt the Flemish succession.

The crown entrusted the negotiations to the duke of Berry, who was attended by a large suite and was already collecting a military salary and five thousand francs per month for travel expenses. He now received the enormous sum of one hundred thousand francs to meet at Boulogne with an English embassy headed by the duke of Lancaster.[54] Berry had received over sixty thousand by 5 November,[55] and continued to receive large sums for the rest of the year.[56] After meeting at Boulogne, the two embassies retired to the smaller community of Leulinghen, where they failed to produce a treaty but did conclude a longer truce on 26 January 1384 that was to last until the end of September.[57] Further negotiations occurred through much of 1384 (for which the dukes of Berry and Burgundy were handsomely paid),[58] but the end result was merely an extension of the truce for another eight months.[59]

John of Berry offers an excellent example of what Maurice Rey meant when he characterized the reign of Charles VI as a time when the "the great personages of France decided that they had rights to the financial resources of the state."[60] While Anjou and Burgundy sought to finance political projects outside the realm, Berry was more inclined to indulge extravagant personal tastes that left him perpetually short of money. In 1383 he repaid with interest the ten thousand francs that Clisson had lent him previously, and the constable returned the castle of Fontenay-le-Comte, which he had been holding as security.[61] The extravagant duke, who received such large sums from the royal treasury but always seemed to be short of funds, differed sharply from the constable, whose enormous wealth and much more modest tastes enabled him to advance money to kings, princes, and even the pope.[62] Such differences between the two men impaired their relations, which faced further strains arising from the feudal status of the vast Belleville inheritance.

In his *apanage* of Poitou, the duke of Berry was Clisson's direct lord for some of his possessions and his overlord for other lands that the constable held from the viscount of Thouars. The king had granted Clisson the right to oversee collection of royal taxes in his lands and to retain a portion of them, but he had also given his brother the royal tax receipts in Poitou. The constable did not have any royal taxes collected in his lands, perhaps because the crown perpetually owed him large sums, perhaps because he realized that his lands would be enriched by the immigration of merchants attracted by an apparent tax-free zone.[63] In preventing these collections, however, he was diminishing the total from Poitou that Berry was to receive, and the duke resented it.[64]

The duke also objected that Clisson had failed to pay the inheritance fee, or *rachat*, that he owed to the viscount of Thouars for fiefs recently inherited from his half-sister, Louise de Chateaubriant. Claiming that he alone, as overlord, could authorize such a payment to be waived, Berry must have had a financial incentive to insist on this point. Eventually, royal pressure induced him and Clisson to settle some of their differences. On 20 July 1384, the Parlement recorded an agreement between Clisson and Thouars that ratified an arrangement made with the duke of Berry on the eleventh over the question of *rachat*.[65] On 14 July, Charles VI gave Clisson a letter of non-prejudice for the levy of the aids in his lands.[66] On the fifteenth, he assigned the constable eighty thousand francs on the receipts of the kingdom's salt warehouses, to compensate him for arrears of salary and for the money he had advanced to his troops.[67]

The crown had every reason to desire a reconciliation between Clisson and the duke of Berry, for friction among important figures at court was placing strains on the French government. Already an enemy of the duke of Brittany, the constable had increasingly antagonistic relations with the king's paternal uncles. In February 1384, Berry and Burgundy had expressed solidarity with Brittany, joining John IV in an offensive and defensive alliance. The document did not specify against whom the alliance was directed,[68] but it could be perceived as a gesture of hostility towards Clisson. The constable, however, maintained proper relations with John IV and was with him in Nantes witnessing an oath of fealty in March.[69] To behave with such propriety in the face of a hostile alliance was not a typical characteristic of Clisson's personality, and it is possible that the alliance of the three dukes had a different purpose. John IV was embroiled in disputes with other important people and would have valued a display of support from the king's powerful uncles.

The duke of Brittany had recently dispatched one of his periodic letters of complaint to the royal government, and while he included his familiar demands about the lands he claimed elsewhere in France, his real purpose was to combat royal jurisdictional claims.[70] The duke had been involved in a squabble with another Valois prince, his neighbor, the count of Alençon, who had appealed to the crown after a negative decision by the ducal court at Rennes. John IV bitterly contested the right of the Parlement to hear appeals from his court, but royal judges were as protective of their jurisdictional claims as the duke was of "Breton liberties," and they could hardly ignore an appeal from a prince of the blood.[71] John had also been involved in a bitter dispute with Josselin de Rohan, bishop of Saint-Malo, who had denounced the behavior of ducal officers.[72] When the two sides sought to arrange an arbitrated settlement in which the duke would pardon the bishop, the royal court intervened, insisting that only the king had the right to pardon someone accused of *lèse majesté*.[73] Such confrontations over issues of jurisdiction and sovereignty inevitably marred relations between the duke of Brittany and the strongly royalist Marmousets. An alliance with Berry and Burgundy was one way to keep Breton relations with the crown from deteriorating further.

In England, Michael de la Pole and the party of peace directed the policies of Richard II's government between 1383 and 1386, treating the French with what Palmer has described disparagingly as a policy of appeasement and failing to enlist potential allies in the Low Countries who might frustrate the projects of Philip of Burgundy.[74] The deaths of the countess dowager of Flanders in 1382 and of Count Louis early in 1384 brought to Marguerite, duchess of Burgundy, the long-awaited inheritance that made Philip the Bold one of Europe's most powerful princes. Philip had to do some bargaining to gain entry into Ghent, the remaining stronghold of the Flemish rebels, in 1385, but there seems little doubt that he was able to secure the Flemish inheritance more easily than would have been the case if England had energetically supported his opponents in the years immediately preceding.[75]

The duke and duchess of Burgundy now moved quickly to establish a strong position in the Low Countries, arranging for two of their children to marry into the Wittelsbach family that ruled the neighboring counties of Hainault, Holland, and Zeeland. They were also instrumental in arranging for Charles VI to marry Isabeau, a fifteen-year old princess of the senior (Bavarian) line of the Wittelsbachs.[76] On the other hand, Philip may have damaged his standing with the young king by refusing to return to his royal nephew the lands of Walloon Flanders. Philip IV had taken this region (notably the towns of Lille, Douai, and Orchies) from the count of Flanders early in the century, but Count Louis II had made recovery of these lands a condition for approving his daughter's marriage to Philip the Bold in 1369. The crown had expected Philip to return the territory after he gained control of Flanders.[77]

The relative speed with which the duke of Burgundy attained his goals in the Netherlands enabled him and the French government to give serious thought to an invasion across the channel that might bring a victorious end to the Anglo-French conflict. In each of the next three years, at great expense, they organized projects that seemed to have considerable promise of success, only to be abandoned when unforeseen factors disrupted the preparations.[78] Among the obstacles were the personal animosities of

Olivier de Clisson, who as constable had major responsibility for organizing the expeditions. The dukes of Berry and Brittany appeared to lack
enthusiasm for projects organized under Clisson's leadership.[79] In Berry's
case, however, historians may have relied too heavily on Froissart,[80] who
had a poor opinion of the duke and showed particular inaccuracy in treating matters involving him.[81]

There is no doubt, of course, about the duke of Brittany's simmering
feud with Clisson, which began to acquire a new dimension as the question of John IV's successor became more urgent. The Breton succession
was affected by three other important deaths during the year 1384—those
of the duchess of Brittany, the countess of Penthièvre, and the duke of
Anjou. The death of Joan Holland, John's duchess, after a childless marriage of eighteen years, broke an important tie with England and has been
associated with John's more independent stance in dealing with England
in 1385 and 1386, when he did give at least nominal support to the French
invasion plans.[82]

John quickly began exploring opportunities for a new marriage, for
the first treaty of Guérande had provided that if he failed to have a son the
duchy would pass to the oldest son of Charles of Blois and Jeanne de Penthièvre, whose release from captivity in England John IV had promised
to secure. The duke seems to have made no effort to honor this promise, and we have seen that the Breton nobles were unwilling to accept
the captive's youngest brother as heir.[83] Meanwhile, the English had been
thoroughly annoyed by the second treaty of Guérande in 1381 and some
people in Richard II's government had talked of releasing John of Blois.[84]
Their thirty-year custody of this prince not only had reduced the options of
Charles V in attempting to confiscate the duchy, but also gave the English
a means of threatening John IV.

At the same time, his heir's captivity strengthened the duke's hand
inside the duchy. The old countess of Penthièvre died early in September
1384, and Olivier de Clisson, to whom she doubtless still owed money,
was one of the Breton nobles who participated in the inventory of her
movables.[85] John of Blois now owed John IV homage and *rachat* for the
county of Penthièvre but, being in captivity, he could not perform feudal
duties in person. The duke sent men to seize the county and its principal strongholds pending the settlement of this obligation.[86] The captive's
sister, Marie of Blois, duchess of Anjou, promptly sent a mission to the
duke to discuss the homage, but her envoys returned with the news that
John IV was not willing to receive homage until all the fortresses were in

his hands.[87] The duke's response suggests that his occupation of the county was not, as he had tried to imply, a purely pro forma action associated with a fief's changing hands, but bore more resemblance to a confiscation.[88] It is most unlikely that John IV would have acted in this way if Louis of Anjou were still on the scene, but Louis had died in Italy earlier in the year, leaving Marie a widow with minor children. She turned for assistance to her brothers-in-law, especially the duke of Berry.[89] Discussions began in November and continued for several weeks until, by mid-December, it was believed at the Angevin court that Berry was about to meet with John IV, pressure him to receive homage for Penthièvre, and arrange for extending royal safeguard to the strongholds in that county. Nothing came of this, however, as the uncles stayed away from Paris and the government did not dare to impose a royal safeguard without their authorization.[90] Meanwhile, a disturbing new rumor was circulating to the effect that the duke of Lancaster was considering marrying his daughter to John of Blois.[91]

At this point, Olivier de Clisson intervened, sending his own envoy to John of Blois with an offer to raise and pay his ransom. Clisson intended to demand a quid pro quo and may have done so on this first communication—a marriage between the Breton heir and his own young daughter, Marguerite. If this proposal was discussed at this early date, it seems not to have become general knowledge for a year or more. In any event, the mission to the captive in England produced immediate results. At Gloucester, on 6 January 1385, Blois named Clisson his lieutenant and governor in all his lands.[92] Armed with this authority, the constable seems to have had little trouble finding men to recover the strongholds of the Penthièvre family that John IV had occupied, for around midsummer the duke was writing to Charles VI and complaining about "la detencion qu'il fait des terres de Penthevre. . . ."[93]

Meanwhile, there was work to be done if the ransom were to be raised. Clisson's own great wealth made the project financially possible, but the constable, as usual, preferred to treat the money as an advance that would be owed him at a later date. He conferred with Marie of Blois on 18 February,[94] and finances undoubtedly dominated the discussion, for Louis of Anjou's unsuccessful Italian venture had left his family ruined, and no branch of the Valois family would receive less royal largesse during Charles VI's reign.[95] Soon after this meeting, working through one of Clisson's allies in the government, the cardinal of Laon, they secured a royal grant of one hundred thousand francs for young Louis II of Anjou and permission to retain the aids collected in the Angevin lands. Attempts to extract from the duke of Brittany the annuity he had owed to Jeanne de Penthièvre appear to have failed.[96] On 22 March 1385, the duchess of Anjou, who was anxious to leave for Provence, named Olivier de Clisson governor, guardian, and protector of all her lands in the kingdom during her absence.[97]

By becoming involved in the succession to Penthièvre, Clisson caused his feud with John IV to escalate to a new level. It is not clear why he chose to intervene, but he had a number of possible reasons. His action enabled him to succor the widow of Louis of Anjou in her political and financial plight, while simultaneously annoying his enemy John IV and preventing John of Blois from concluding a marriage alliance with the hated English. It was an opportunity for him to use his great wealth to increase his own power and influence in western France and place his future grandchildren in line for the ducal title in Brittany. Finally, the constable's intervention enabled him to right what he surely perceived as a great wrong: the duke's seizure of lands from a captive whose liberty he had failed to procure after promising to do so in a treaty Clisson was sworn to uphold.[98]

Clisson's initiative in seeking Penthièvre's release led to a flurry of diplomatic and political maneuvering and, as Professor Jones has pointed out, to a number of curious ironies. The constable, who was famous for his hostility to the English and was enthusiastic for the invasion being planned in 1385, now would have to deal with those in England who favored a negotiated peace if he wanted to achieve his cousin's release. The duke of Berry, who was the French prince least supportive of the invasion schemes, found himself taking the position of the war party in England, opposing Penthièvre's release because of friendship for the duke and hostility to Clisson. The English war party opposed releasing the prisoner because it hoped to resume cordial relations with John IV and induce him to break with France. The duke, on the other hand, assisted with the invasion plans and even besieged the English garrison that still held Brest, apparently hoping that the English would try harder to woo him by keeping Penthièvre in custody.[99]

The duke of Brittany's most urgent business, however, was his desire to remarry and beget an heir. In writing to Charles VI on this subject, he was unusually moderate in his reference to Clisson, and he took pains to assure the king that his remarriage would not in any way damage the alliance he had made with the French in the second treaty of Guérande.[100] John IV needed to assume this moderate and respectful stance because the alliance in question had required him to oppose the king of Navarre, and it was Charles the Bad's daughter whom he now wished to marry. There may well have been no serious objections at the French court, for young Jeanne of Navarre was the king's first cousin and niece of the royal uncles. She was also the niece of the viscountess of Rohan, so the proposed marriage offered the duke closer ties to the Rohan family and a wife with Valois blood who was surely more acceptable in Paris than his two previous English spouses.[101] Negotiations for this marriage had begun in 1384, when Jeanne was sixteen, but haggling over the dowry delayed it until the fall of 1386. She and John IV were married on 11 September in a chapel near Guérande.[102] The marriage proved as fertile as the duke had hoped. Jeanne's second child, born in Vannes on Christmas Eve 1389, when the duke was about fifty, was the son who would succeed him as John V of Brittany, and there would be seven surviving children in all.[103]

While the duke was negotiating his marriage and Clisson was trying to effect the release of John of Blois, the French government was busy planning its costly project of invading England. The mints were short of bullion, and the king drew once again on the wealth of his constable. In June 1385 Clisson supplied six hundred marks of gold bullion, receiving 68½ *l.t.* per mark.[104] Besides the constable, the admiral of France inevitably had an important role to play in any campaign that involved crossing the water, and this was especially the case in 1385, when Jean de Vienne had the task of leading an advance party to Scotland, where he hoped to collaborate with the Scots in a diversionary maneuver against England from the north. The main French army, to be led by Clisson, planned to land in Kent near the mouth of the Thames. Vienne's forces reached Scotland and the main army under Clisson was assembling in the Scheldt estuary when Flemish rebels under Francis Ackermann seized Damme in August. From this vantage point they were in position to disrupt the French preparations, so the place had to be besieged and retaken. By the time that Damme was again in French hands, it was too late to launch the invasion of England, and Vienne had to withdraw from Scotland under pressure from a large English force in the north.[105]

The French began to organize an even larger invasion project in the spring of 1386. Jean de Sempy was in charge of assembling troops in Artois and Picardy, while Vienne and Guy de la Trémoille were doing the same in Normandy. Jean de Blaisy and Morelet de Montmor were recruiting in Brittany and Érart de Dinteville in Saintonge. The count of Armagnac was to bring troops from the southwest,[106] and the channel ports were alive with activity. There were special taxes in both royal and Burgundian lands.[107] Numerous military musters from May to November indicate the level of activity and reveal that, as in 1383, the Breton lords again were serving the crown.[108]

These magnificent preparations failed in the end to produce a result, for the invasion force never got under way. Contrary winds appear to have been a problem, at least to the extent of delaying the ships that had to proceed to Flanders from other ports. All the princes were rather slow in arriving in Flanders, especially Armagnac and Berry. John Palmer, who sharply criticizes Froissart's view that Berry was to blame, argues that the real reasons for disbanding the expedition were that the government had run out of money, the troops were beginning to pillage, and there was fear that the Flemings would revolt again when the French forces left.[109] His reasoning is sound, but Froissart should not be dismissed as a chronic prevaricator, despite his curious penchant for misrepresenting the duke of Berry. It was common knowledge that Berry disliked Clisson and opposed the invasion, and Jean Juvenal des Ursins also reported that people blamed the duke for his tardiness. Froissart's informants may well have suspected him of sabotaging the operation.[110] In fact, Berry's most serious offense was the misgovernance of Languedoc, where he was royal lieutenant. He had left John III of Armagnac in charge there, but when Armagnac himself came north with his troops he left Languedoc in the hands of subordinates incompetent to govern. In a violent world dominated by encounters with *routiers*, an ineffective truce could deliver large amounts of territory into the hands of the English, and this was precisely what happened in 1386.[111]

The setbacks of 1386, including the frustration of a second consecutive plan to invade England, left the French short of money but still in possession of a sizable fleet. Many of the ships and seamen, however, were from the county of Flanders, and in the winter of 1386–87, these seafaring people reverted to their more habitual role as transporters of merchandise. One fleet sailed for La Rochelle early in 1387 to unload goods and bring a shipment of wine back to Flanders. By this time, however, the war party had regained control of the English government for the moment, and one of its leading members, the earl of Arundel, was assembling a fleet with which to resist any future French invasion scheme. In March, Arundel intercepted the Flemish fleet returning from La Rochelle and defeated it severely as it approached the ports of Flanders. He proceeded to Flanders, where he hoped to arouse the populace against the French, but apparently failed to move quickly enough. Philip of Burgundy was more fully in control than the English had realized and was able to organize adequate defenses more rapidly than exepcted. Unable to undermine Philip's authority in Flanders, Arundel turned back with his fleet and headed towards Brittany, where the English garrison at Brest needed relief.[112]

The victory of the war party in England and the approach of Arundel's fleet coincided with a new volte-face on the part of the duke of Brittany, who launched a dramatic stroke against Olivier de Clisson that destroyed the final French project for invading England and had profound repercussions for the political society surrounding the king of France.

8

The Crisis of 1387 and the
Triumph of the Marmousets

DESPITE LOSING MOST OF THE FLEET they had hoped to use against England, the French doggedly went ahead with plans for a naval expedition in 1387. Recruitment seems to have been confined largely to western France, under the direction of Jean de Blaisy and Morelet de Montmor.[1] The proposed campaign of 1387 was probably more limited in scope than the efforts of the two previous years, with the fleet intending to conduct the destructive coastal raids at which the French excelled, rather than attempting to put ashore large numbers of French troops. It was also very much the personal project of the constable, who refused to accept the recent setbacks and went ahead with preparations despite the misgivings of the princes and the menacing proximity of Arundel's fleet.[2]

The duke of Brittany, who had lent support to the invasion plan of 1386 and had even besieged the English at Brest, was distinctly cool towards the French plan in 1387, largely because of Clisson and his efforts on behalf of John of Blois. Representing the interests of the house of Anjou in France while the duchess was in Provence, the constable had been in frequent communication with Marie on a number of projects.[3] Obtaining her brother's release was one of these, and the chances of success had improved considerably since 1384. In March 1386, Richard II had assigned the potentially lucrative captive to his favorite, Robert de Vere, who was prepared to cash in on his prisoner despite the bitter opposition of the English war party, led by Arundel and Gloucester, the allies of John IV. De Vere's negotiations with Clisson's representatives seemed to promise an early agreement on the release of John of Blois.[4] Towards the end of August 1386, Clement VII acceded to the wishes of the duchess of Anjou and granted a dispensation for her brother to marry Marguerite de Clisson.[5]

Although he was surely kept informed of developments in England, it is not certain when John IV learned of the papal dispensation, but it must have enraged him. The newly remarried duke was in his late forties and still childless. His heir remained the captive cousin who now was planning to become the son-in-law of his hated enemy. He was fortunate to have had a friend in the person of the duke of Berry, who was still squabbling with Clisson over tax collections in Poitou and remained opposed to any military expedition against England. Pressed by the duchess of Anjou to support the release of her brother and more royal assistance to her family, Berry kept rebuffing the pleas of his sister-in-law.[6] Then, in the spring of 1387, he concluded what Lefranc called a secret alliance with John IV.[7] In a document recorded on 8 May 1387, the two dukes stated explicitly that their alliance was directed against John of Blois, Olivier de Clisson, and Berry's longtime adversary, the count of Foix.[8] A second version of the treaty, issued two days later by Berry alone, may have been the one intended for public consumption. It dropped the names of those against whom the alliance was directed and substituted vaguer language.[9] The duke of Burgundy, who had joined the others in an alliance three years before, was not a party to the one concluded in 1387, perhaps because he needed Clisson's military support for unfinished business in the Low Countries and had no real quarrel with the men against whom the alliance was directed. Lefranc, however, followed Froissart in thinking that Burgundy shared his wife's hostility towards Clisson.[10]

With Arundel's victorious fleet still cruising the channel and the English now actively cultivating him, John IV may have been ready to cooperate with Arundel against the naval plans being made by the French. He was well situated to do so because Olivier de Clisson was in Brittany early that summer, organizing naval preparations at Tréguier. The duke convened an assembly of Breton magnates to meet at Vannes late in June. Clisson was expected to attend this meeting and at some point the duke decided on a bold stroke against him that would be a favor to the English as much as an act of personal vengeance.[11] This action was to precipitate a crisis that would have results quite different from what the duke intended. About a year later, Jean Froissart made the acquaintance of Guillaume d'Ancenis, a Breton lord with a first-hand knowledge of the assembly at Vannes, who was well acquainted with the leading participants.[12] Based on his information, Froissart produced an unusually detailed account of the events there.[13] Despite the chronicler's well-deserved reputation for inaccuracy, this story must be our starting point for considering the crisis.

Responding to the ducal summons, Clisson attended the assembly of

Breton nobles at Vannes. To call him naive for doing so[14] is absurd, since it was a large meeting attended by many of his friends and it would have been highly inappropriate to refuse such a summons from his lord and provoke a fight with a duke who had loyally supported the French invasion plans of the previous year. Clisson's mistake, however, was in letting the duke lure him to the nearby castle of Ermine after the meeting. There John IV had him arrested and clapped in irons on 25 June 1387. According to Froissart, the duke was planning from the first to kill him, thinking to please the English by disrupting the invasion scheme, and believing that the French government would consider it the settlement of a personal feud and not a disloyal act against the king. Before he ordered the execution, however, Guy de Laval spent most of the night arguing that it would do the duke grave damage to execute a person of such stature without any judicial proceeding and after seizing him by trickery. John finally relented and settled for a less drastic course of action, forcing Clisson to sign a humiliating treaty on 27 June to obtain his liberty. The constable promised to pay a ransom of one hundred thousand francs and surrender to the duke more than a dozen strongholds, including the ancestral castles of Clisson and Blain, the fortress at Josselin, and most of those in northern Brittany that Clisson was holding in the name of John of Blois.[15]

Because of these castles, John Palmer has concluded that the duke had hatched a masterful plan, for their retention in his hands "would have ruined the Blois party forever, and would have given the duke a stranglehold on the northern half of the duchy where his own possessions were sparse."[16] The treaty also provided that Clisson would break his connection with the Blois-Penthièvre family and abandon efforts on behalf of the release and marriage of the captive. The constable's ratification was dated a week later, after his release, but may well have been drafted when he was still a captive at Ermine.[17] Those who credit the duke with a cleverly conceived plan tend to ignore or dismiss the Froissart's view that the duke wanted above all to kill Clisson and was talked out of it only with great difficulty. They are no doubt more comfortable with Pintoin's suggestion that John threatened Clisson with death in order to force the surrender of the castles.[18] Was Froissart's account of the duke's murderous intentions and Laval's remonstrances nothing but a fabrication (either by the chronicler or by Guillaume d'Ancenis) intended to give the tale greater dramatic impact? It is possible, but we shall need to return to this matter because it bears upon the question of what priorities lay behind the duke's action and whether it was well-planned or spontaneous.

The arrest and humiliation of the constable had one immediate and predictable result: it wrecked the French military preparations. According to Pintoin, when they learned what happened, the assembled French forces left the coasts, while messengers went to the king to apprise him of events.[19] Clisson, meanwhile, met the ducal demands and gained his freedom in just one week (another indication of the substantial wealth at his disposal), then hastened to the royal court.[20] The king's uncles, and especially John of Berry, doubtless felt a certain pleasure at his misfortune, and they are said to have reproached him for falling into a trap that spoiled the plan for an attack on England.[21] Except for the dukes, however, the royal court reacted with shock and outrage at the events in Brittany. Clisson's immediate effectiveness as constable was seriously impaired, but the king rejected his offer to resign the office.[22] He received expressions of sympathy and assurances of vengeance from three of the most prestigious members of French military society—Enguerrand de Coucy, Jean de Vienne, and Waleran de Luxembourg.[23] The first two of these, of course, were the constable's old friends, but the count of Saint-Pol's support was noteworthy, for he was a Burgundian partisan and an old enemy of La Rivière. It would seem that leaders of the military aristocracy, even if sometimes opposed to each other on a given political issue, could not react with indifference to such an overt attack on the constable of France and were prepared to close ranks on this issue. In Froissart's narrative, it was precisely this consideration that Guy de Laval was stressing in his lengthy argument with John IV against killing the constable.

What might not have been as readily anticipated was the reaction of the young king of France. Charles VI, now eighteen years old, had been manipulated by his uncles for the seven years of his reign. His younger brother Louis, duke of Touraine, was fifteen years old and apparently more intelligent and precocious than the king. Both had conceived a great attachment to the constable. Some years ago, I suggested that these young princes, who were orphaned in childhood, may have grown impatient with the tutelage of their uncles, while admiring the battle-scarred veteran soldier who remained a link to the military successes and other fading memories of their father's reign.[24] More recently, Françoise Autrand has put the matter far more elegantly, drawing an analogy from courtly romances. In these tales, it was not the father who guided the youth through the chivalric adventures of adolescence that led to manhood, but rather the uncle who played this role. In the youth of Charles VI, she believes, Philip of Burgundy was the father figure, while Olivier de Clisson played the part of the uncle.[25] With this analogy, she has captured marvelously the personal relationships that played such an important role in French politics in the later 1380s. It is perhaps an exaggeration to say, as did Françoise Lehoux, that Clisson had an "immense ascendancy" over the king,[26] but it is clear that Charles and Louis were outraged at the constable's humiliation, and their feelings doubtless received encouragement from the Marmousets. The uncles quickly found that John IV's coup had weakened, not strengthened, their position at court, and they had to exercise considerable diplomatic skill to head off the king's strong desire for drastic action against Brittany.

Under these circumstances, we need to reexamine the question of whether the duke's stroke against Clisson was indeed a brilliant plan. If he acted only to wreck the invasion plans (thus pleasing the English) and humiliate his hated enemy, he succeeded, and subsequent developments, although they forced John to pay a price, did not reverse that success. If, however, John IV's true objective was to secure the castles, then the plan was miserably conceived and executed. We find no evidence of any forethought, of any provisions calculated to guarantee the execution of the treaty he extorted from Clisson. There is no evidence that John brought charges, even trumped-up charges, against the constable, no pretense of a judicial proceeding,[27] no self-justifying letters to the royal uncles describing his grievances and explaining that he was acting against Clisson in his private, not public capacity. The duke of Brittany normally was very adept at this sort of thing. Why did he not keep Clisson in prison, solidifying his hold on the castles, dragging out the legal proceedings, and negotiating busily with the uncles? All such actions would have conformed perfectly to the practices of this period and the temperament of the duke.

The absence of any of these actions make it very difficult to accept Palmer's view that the duke had a well-conceived plan to acquire the castles and that it misfired in the end because it "gave rise to suspicion" that he was conspiring with England to disrupt the French naval expedition.[28] We are left with a sense that there was a good deal of spontaneity in the behavior of John IV. Clisson was taken and the expedition aborted, to the ultimate satisfaction of those who were opposed to it. But what to do next? Without evidence to suggest a carefully laid plan, we must consider the possibility that Froissart did not stray far from the truth in this instance, that the duke really did want to kill his enemy, that Laval really did persuade him that it would be a bad idea to do so. The treaty that he then improvised was indeed brilliant in its possiblities, but the duke threw his chance away by releasing Clisson so promptly. Perhaps he was astonished at the enormous wealth that permitted Clisson to raise the money with such ease and speed. Perhaps he merely wanted to be rid of this man, the enemy he did not quite dare to kill but from whom he had extracted remarkable concessions. Events would prove that the duke made some bad decisions, but they appear to have been hasty decisions, not flaws in a brilliant plan.

In their bid to defuse the situation and head off demands for violent vengeance on Brittany, the uncles had to move quickly and deftly. The first step was to resolve the disputes between Berry and Clisson and then to dissolve Berry's now-embarrassing alliance with John IV. By any standard, the constable had been an arrogant and difficult vassal in Poitou. His people had committed outrages against various neighbors that would have brought severe judicial penalties against a man of lesser stature.[29] What had doubtless drawn the dukes of Berry and Brittany together was their common frustration over not being able to treat Clisson as an ordinary vassal and enforce upon him an appropriate standard of behavior. Berry's main conflict with Clisson, however, continued to be financial in nature. The constable was still obstructing the collection of the royal aids in his lands, thereby denying Berry some of the income he expected to receive.[30] If his humiliation in Brittany was to be redressed without a major war, Clisson would have to give ground in Poitou, where he was in the wrong from the government's point of view. On 30 July, Charles VI handed down a ruling against him,[31] and three days later Clisson agreed to comply.[32] These actions must have followed some hard negotiating, for while Berry gained his point on the financial issue, he agreed to abandon the alliance he had made with Brittany in May.[33]

Somewhat more surprisingly, the uncles finally agreed to lend some support to Clisson's effort to secure the release of John of Blois. The constable had advanced half the money (sixty thousand francs), but he had been soliciting help from others in raising the remaining half. Early in October, the dukes of Berry and Burgundy headed a list of people (most of them prominent military commanders) who agreed to guarantee certain sums for the count of Penthièvre's ransom. Jones believes that Clisson contributed to this process by adopting a more accommodating policy towards England, thereby gratifying the duke of Berry and helping to speed the deliverance of his prospective son-in-law.[34] The duchess of Anjou decided she could pay twenty thousand francs, but had to mortgage some of her lands, mostly to Clisson, who received the castellanies of Mayenne and Champtoceaux.[35] By 19 November, well over half the ransom had reached Calais, and in two weeks' time John of Blois was a free man after thirty-four years in England. He married Marguerite de Clisson on 20 January 1388.[36]

The treaty that John IV had extorted from the constable was soon a dead letter except for the money that had changed hands. Once he had made his peace with the crown and the duke of Berry over the issues in Poitou, Clisson could turn his attention to recovering the surrendered fortresses in Brittany. As early as 4 September 1387, commissioners sent by the duke to secure their custody had reported running into opposition.[37] Some weeks later, Clisson's partisans who had taken up arms succeeded in retaking from the duke a number of important places in the county of Penthièvre—Guingamp, Lamballe, Châteaulaudren, Châteaulin—and on 10 October ducal officers were surprised at Saint-Malo, freeing the bishop to resume his anti-Montfortist politics.[38] These successes of the duke's opponents may reflect a strong residual loyalty to the house of Blois-Penthièvre such as that displayed in 1384–85, but it may also indicate that John IV, once again, had alienated the leading nobles of Brittany. If they perceived the seizure of Clisson in June as a violation of safe conduct and hospitality,[39] then their duke had seriously transgressed their social and ethical code.

The evident erosion of John IV's position by the early autumn made it slightly less difficult for the uncles to achieve the negotiated settlement they so desired. Previously, John had felt strong enough to resist concessions, and a royal embassy headed by Bernard de la Tour, bishop of Langres, and Guillaume, viscount of Melun, spent much of August and September in Brittany without apparent result.[40] By November, however, it was clear that John of Blois would soon be released and the duke had lost control of many of the castles in the county of Penthièvre. The crown moderated its demands, restrained Clisson from launching a personal campaign, and dispatched a second embassy to Brittany. It too was headed by the bishop of Langres, and it included three of Clisson's friends from among the military leadership—Jean de Bueil, Hervé le Coich, and Jean de Vienne.[41] Before receiving these emissaries, John IV sought to keep his options open by declaring in writing that anything he agreed to would be done out of fear.[42] According to chroniclers, the duke now told the royal embassy what he might have said with more telling effect when he had Clisson in his hands several months earlier—that he should have killed Clisson but spared him only because of the dignity of his office,[43] and that he acted against him as his vassal, not as constable of France.[44] At length, late in December, John IV conceded defeat, pending a royal inquiry and the king's judgment, which was scheduled to be given at Orléans on Easter (29 March) 1388. He cancelled the treaty he had extorted from Clisson the previous summer, and then agreed in a memorandum to La Tour that he would return to Clisson the hundred thousand francs and put into the king's hands the fortresses that he still controlled.[45]

The duke's defeat was not final, because the war party in England was busily hatching a plan that called for a three-pronged attack on France in 1388. His attempt on Clisson having boomeranged, John IV was ready enough for a new English alliance, but to take such a risk he had to have strong military forces to assist him. Until he could be absolutely sure of English protection, he remained very dependent on the goodwill of the royal uncles, especially Philip of Burgundy. Philip, however, with his expanding interests in the Low Countries, was an enemy of William, duke of Guelders, who was now an ally of the English. William had issued a public defiance to Charles VI and Burgundy was eager to launch a punitive expedition against him. Now that the English had finally found a way to challenge Burgundy's vital interests in the Low Countries, John of Brittany could neither embrace an English alliance nor delay further in accepting judgment on the Clisson affair without compromising his vital relationship with Burgundy.[46] The French were effectively in possession of Saint-Malo, and Clisson at Pontorson had an army ready to enter Brittany.[47] Without English troops on the scene to back him up, the duke would be lost if Burgundy deserted him now.

As usual, the English promised the necessary aid which was, in any case, part of their grand military design for 1388. In the spring, John felt confident enough to ignore the scheduled Easter meeting with Charles VI. The king waited in vain at Orléans for most of April, while John IV, who had put himself in a most delicate position by failing to attend the king, began to realize that the English had let him down once again.[48] Arundel's fleet was not even scheduled to leave Southampton until mid-May, and he would in fact be delayed for nearly another month.[49] Meanwhile, the threat of an attack on Brittany had intensified, as Olivier de Clisson issued a defiance of the duke when he failed to come to Orléans.[50]

Increasingly impatient, the French royal council decided around 12 May to dispatch a third embassy to Brittany, consisting of three of the most prestigious military leaders in France—Coucy, La Rivière, and Vienne, all of them friends of the constable and associated with the Marmouset faction.[51] Froissart was informed (probably correctly) that the uncles briefed them carefully on their mission. They were to approach John IV in a cordial and conciliatory manner but were to persuade him of the absolute necessity of coming to the French court for a resolution of current differences. If he did not wish to go directly to Paris, he would at least have to meet with the king's uncles at Blois.[52] This embassy reached Vannes shortly after mid-May, and with no sign of any English forces to help him, John had no choice but to agree to what the envoys demanded.[53]

As he prepared to meet the uncles at Blois, the duke of Brittany at least had the consolation of knowing that his new duchess was fertile and that he finally had reason to hope for a son to succeed him. The knowledge that he was capable of having direct heirs surely moderated his indignation at the proposed Clisson-Penthièvre marriage.[54] John IV joined the dukes of Berry and Burgundy at Blois towards the beginning of June, and the three dukes proceeded on to Paris for what promised to be a most difficult meeting with the king and the Marmousets.[55]

The mediation of his friends, the uncles, had saved John from the wrath of Clisson and the king when he failed to appear at Orléans, but he had to make a complete, if insincere, submission. Whether or not he would have ruled differently at Orléans in the spring, Charles VI announced a decision on 20 July 1388 that was entirely favorable to his constable. John IV was to give back the hundred thousand francs and all but one of the strongholds he had seized.[56] Having accepted this verdict and returned to his duchy, he named commissioners to receive back certain lands that Guy de Laval had been holding pending a settlement of the dispute.[57] He also resumed discussions with the English about the proposed alliance (Arundel having finally put into Brest after the duke had left for the royal court),[58] but the intense Anglo-French conflict of 1369–89 was slowly coming to an end and the declining military importance of Brittany gradually reduced the duke's leverage.

The king's verdict in favor of Clisson can hardly come as much of a surprise,[59] since he and most of his advisers had displayed strong feelings about the incident of June 1387 as soon as they heard about it. The royal uncles could intervene to promote a peaceful settlement instead of a punitive expedition, but only at the cost of John's complete submission. Perhaps they considered themselves still influential enough to secure a more moderate decision from Charles VI, but John IV cannot have harbored any illusions about the outcome after a year of receiving royal embassies and observing the support for Clisson. One thing seems evident: the dukes of Berry and Burgundy were losing their influence over the king, who increasingly demonstrated an inclination to heed the advice of the Marmousets. As recently as two years before, it would have been unthinkable for the king to pronounce so forcefully against a great magnate who enjoyed Burgundy's friendship. The humiliation of Clisson in 1387 not only backfired on the duke of Brittany directly but also weakened the royal uncles, to the ultimate benefit of the Marmousets.[60]

John IV of Brittany was not the only potential English ally on the continent who was left without military support and had to come to terms with France. William of Guelders would now have a similar experience. This prince, whose defiance of Charles VI occurred shortly after John IV's seizure of Clisson in the summer of 1387, had been threatening Brabant, an important territory that Philip the Bold hoped to absorb one day through inheritance.[61] One must assume that William's purpose was to provoke the French into a military expedition to the Low Countries, where Guelders would have support not only from English troops but also from one of those uprisings against Burgundian influence that the English always seemed to count upon.[62] The French government, meanwhile, took measures to curtail unnecessary expenses and raise new taxes for the campaign.[63]

Philip of Burgundy was eager enough for a campaign to punish Guelders and intimidate other potential enemies in the Low Countries, and his strenuous effort to settle the Breton dispute was tied to his desire to focus French attention on the Netherlands. Led by the king, duke, and constable, the royal army set out towards the beginning of September. Within six weeks, William of Guelders sought a negotiated peace since the allies he had hoped for did not materialize.[64] He duly submitted to Charles VI, being escorted into the royal presence by Olivier de Clisson and the king's first chamberlain, Hutin d'Aumont, with a troop of six hundred men.[65] Having achieved this objective, the French army returned home again. It was late October, and the weather was not good. The troops experienced harrassment from hostile "Germans" and finally suffered a good many losses trying to ford a rain-swollen river. The monk of Saint-Denis thought the return trip was a disaster (*dampnoso reditu*), but by the first of November the king and his advisers had reached Reims.[66]

There, in the royal coronation city, the king held a meeting of his council, probably according to some plan, since there was no obvious reason for convening the council before reaching Paris. At this council, the cardinal of Laon, Pierre Aycelin de Montagu, made a short speech expressing the view that the king had reached the age when he no longer had any need of tutors and should take over direction of affairs himself. The proposal was not expected by the uncles; when they heard it, they realized that the suggestion had probably not been planted by the king himself but had originated with the Marmousets (of whom Aycelin was one). When others who were present supported Aycelin's proposal, Charles VI, who was now nearly twenty years old, agreed to it and thanked the dukes of Berry and Burgundy for their services. The dukes tried to persuade Charles to change his mind on the way back to Paris, but he would not do so, and they had to retire from the council.[67]

If the uncles had suspicions about the source of the cardinal's proposal, these were confirmed a year or so later, when they learned that Clisson had told an emissary of the duke of Lancaster that "I made him king and lord in his [own] kingdom and removed him from the government and hands of his uncles."[68] In slightly more than sixteen months, the political fortunes of Olivier de Clisson had experienced some extraordinary changes. At the end of June 1387, he had been humiliated by his most bitter enemy and forced to surrender his Breton castles and pay a large ransom. He may have been lucky to escape with his life. From this extraordinary misfortune, he had rebounded with astonishing success. The king had nullified the transaction, the uncles had been induced to contribute to the ransom of John of Blois, and the latter had married Clisson's daughter. Now the uncles had been forced to leave the government, the Marmousets were in control of policy, and Clisson was not afraid to claim credit for the coup that brought this about. Less fortunate was the cardinal of Laon, who had first advanced the proposal in the royal council. In a few days, Aycelin died suddenly, amid rumors that the uncles had him poisoned.[69]

When placed within the tradition of late medieval French politics, the ouster of the dukes from the royal council was an extraordinary occurrence. Charles VI was surely discontented with the tutelage of his uncles and could be opinionated, but he was not a strong and decisive individual who would have taken control of affairs by himself without assistance. Nor was any rival prince of the lilies involved. Louis of Anjou was dead; Louis of Bourbon remained carefully aloof from factional struggles. Louis of Touraine, the king's sixteen-year-old brother, began to achieve political prominence after the coup but only gradually. He was in no position to engineer the political changes of 1388 nor, for that matter, to obstruct those that occurred four years later.

In other political crises of fourteenth-century France, there was no precedent for the ouster of powerful princes by a party that lacked a leader of comparable rank. Early in the century, the accession of new kings had accompanied political change. Later, in 1332, the fall of Robert of Artois had been engineered in part by the duke of Burgundy and the count of Flanders. Opposition parties in 1347 and 1355 had used the heir to the throne, and subsequently Charles of Navarre had provided opponents of the crown with a prince of the blood around whom to rally.[70] Now, however, the powerful and prestigious Philip the Bold, supported by the dukes of Berry and Brittany, found himself ousted from power by a party whose most visible member was a Breton nobleman with powerful enemies, a man who appeared to be ruined just sixteen months before.

The triumph of the Marmousets was therefore not a routine shuffle of the council but a political coup without clear historical precedents. The closest analogy to earlier changes in political society may be found in the events of 1347 and 1355 when the heir to the throne had become associated with political malcontents at a time of military or financial setbacks and had asserted some independence from his father. Here again, the insights of Autrand are instructive: Charles VI was asserting his independence from Philip the Bold, who had become the substitute for a father in his life.[71] The argument is persuasive because friction between the king and his older son was a pervasive characteristic of the Valois monarchy in France. The distinctive features of 1388 were the dichotomy in political and social stature between supporters of the "son" and those of the "father" and the emphatic triumph of the former.[72] It is probable that the political environment for the coup was afforded by the succession of heavy special taxes for military expeditions that failed to yield positive results. The expedition against Guelders was not a failure, but the inglorious nature of the return march was surely a catalyst in the ouster of the uncles.

The Marmousets, that element of French political society mentioned so frequently in these pages, now effectively controlled the royal government. It is appropriate to treat them as a party, a coherent political bloc that can be defined and described in some way. When Froissart alluded to "les marmousets du roy et du duc de Touraine,"[73] what did he mean? Autrand has speculated that the term may have meant a grotesque figure or gargoyle, that Marmouset was linked to Mahomet and associated with idols, hence some sort of favorite with intimate access to the king.[74] This reasoning seems a bit obscure, but a translator of Froissart did in fact render the term into English as "favorite."[75] Lefranc considered the word a term of opprobrium, associating it with the verb *marmouser*, meaning to move ones lips in the manner of a monkey.[76] Standard French reference works have tended to follow a similar line, saying that "marmousets" meant "little boys," hence persons of no account, or upstarts,[77] and this word seems to be a better English rendering of the term than "favorites." Historians at least as far back as Michelet have treated the Marmousets in this way. Autrand is correct in objecting to the implication that they were *petits gens*, but she notes that they were not princes who were "born to govern," and that fact made it possible for those who found their influence in some sense unnatural or improper to dismiss them as upstarts.[78]

It is not too difficult to identify those who were prominent among the Marmousets in 1388 and the years immediately following. Since many of these men had long careers, I have used the term to refer to them in other periods. Some of them served Charles V while he was still dauphin;[79] some were recruited to royal service from the ranks of dissidents who had followed Charles of Navarre in the 1350s. They held various positions in church and state, but were most heavily concentrated in those two areas of political society that acquired expanding influence in the 1360s outside the royal council—the royal household and the military leadership. Like some members of the council, certain of the Marmousets had ties to an important former adviser to John II—the cardinal Guy de Boulogne (d. 1373), whose nephew had become pope Clement VII.[80] Their visibility and influence expanded further after 1375 when the eclipse of the Melun brothers (archbishop of Sens and count of Tancarville respectively) brought an end to that long period of stability in the council. Only two of the Marmousets were part of the power structure recognized by Cazelles during the period 1360–75, and both were cardinals—Pierre Aycelin (who served on the Melun-Dormans council for years) and Jean de la Grange (who was prominent in the financial service).[81] Ironically, neither of these men figured in the period of Marmouset rule after 1388, La Grange having left the court in 1380 and Aycelin having died suddenly in 1388. It would be a mistake to view the Marmousets as hostile to the group that dominated the council in those years of stability, for the younger Guillaume de Melun, who succeeded his father as count of Tancarville in 1382, was associated with the Marmousets.[82]

Between them, contemporary writers and modern historians have identified six men in particular with the Marmousets. They have come to symbolize this political group and the modest social origins it supposedly represented. Of these six, only Olivier de Clisson came from an old and powerful lineage. Two others—Bureau de la Rivière and Pierre de Villaines, known as "Le Bègue"—had been in the entourage of Charles V well before he became king. They were from the middling nobility and had considerable service as military commanders as well as performing many other duties. The other three—Nicholas du Bosc, Jean le Mercier, and Jean de Montaigu—were all of bourgeois origins. Du Bosc was now bishop of

Bayeux, while Le Mercier and Montaigu, both financial officers, had been ennobled. Two other Marmousets who were less prominent but very active — Pierre de Chevreuse, another ennobled official, and Ferri Cassinel, then bishop of Auxerre—were also *arrivistes* of bourgeois background, and it was the prominence in the government of such persons of undistinguished pedigree that earned the Marmousets the derogatory label bestowed by posterity.[83]

The visibility of these men of modest social origins has tended to obscure the fact that their party did include men of rank and power. A close associate, for instance, was Enguerrand de Coucy, but his late arrival on the French political scene (1375) makes him a special case, and I did not include his name when compiling a list of forty-three certain or probable members of the Marmouset party some years ago.[84] That list did include twenty-one laymen who were members of the middling nobility and eleven who belonged to great lineages. Of these nobles, a substantial number were from northern or western France and active as royal military commanders, and some of them were among those recruited into royal service from families that had opposed the earlier Valois monarchs. In terms of social and political background, Clisson and La Rivière were more typical of the Marmousets generally than were Le Mercier and Montaigu.

The chronicles helped to create the stereotype by saying that the king now made Le Mercier, Montaigu, and La Rivière his principal advisers.[85] Only Montaigu (a nephew of Cassinel whose wife was the niece of Jean de la Grange and two of whose brothers were bishops) was a relative newcomer to the government. The new chancellor, Arnaud de Corbie, was a veteran of the Parlement. Already serving on the royal council in 1388 were, among others, the two marshals of France (Louis de Sancerre and "Mouton" de Blainville), Chevreuse, Du Bosc, Jean de la Personne, and the bishop of Noyon (Philippe du Moulins), not to mention Clisson, La Rivière, and Le Mercier. The king and his younger brother now attended regularly in place of Berry and Burgundy. The duke of Bourbon was the one royal uncle who remained on the council. Joining it in the months after the Marmousets took power were Villaines, Guillaume des Bordes, "Saquet" de Blaru, Guillaume de Melun, and Jean de Vienne (whose office presumably entitled him to sit on the council). Nobles active in military leadership were the preponderant element on this council, perhaps more so than had been the case for decades.[86]

The regime that took control in 1388 was, therefore, primarily a government of military commanders but especially a government of people who had, for the most part, joined the service of Charles V a long time before. The military element offers an important clue to the apparently surprising success of the Marmousets in seizing power. The leading commanders had reacted with immediate and overwhelming indignation to Clisson's treatment by the duke of Brittany in 1387. He had maintained a large and coherent following among the Breton aristocracy even after 1379. When one adds the fact that he was named constable in 1380 despite the misgivings of the princes, one cannot escape the conclusion that Clisson was the acknowledged leader of the military aristocracy, both in Brittany, where it fought a rearguard action against the consolidation of ducal authority, and in the French government, where it had consistently benefited from the policies of Charles V. With his unusual degree of commitment to the monarchical state, his distinguished military career, and his regional connections, he typified in many respects the kind of noble that Charles V's government had been cultivating.

The closely interrelated aristocracy of the north and west cannot be described as a coherent and unified political force since there were old feuds and other divergent interests lurking in the background at all times. Yet these people did have certain broad common interests of class, region, and status, and many of them, like the nonmilitary component of the Marmousets, had roots in the old reformist opposition of the 1340s and 1350s. Nobles of old lineages and royal officers of undistinguished birth had worked together for a long time, but what appears to have linked these two groups together effectively was the tight partnership between Clisson and La Rivière, with Clisson being the partner with the broader and more powerful constituency. When the constable's enemies next tried to do away with him, Froissart said that the act was expected to finish the Marmousets as well.[87] There is no reason to disbelieve him.

The chronicler usually considered to be best informed about the French court in this period, Michel Pintoin, said that the Marmousets took an oath to sustain each other and to act as one,[88] and subsequent historians have remarked on the solidarity of these men, their relatives, and their clienteles.[89] This solidarity, however, should not be overemphasized, because the Marmousets also were political survivors, and in the crisis of 1392, survival would overcome solidarity. Autrand's generally excellent assessment of the Marmousets as a coherent party includes a statement that the years after their rise to power marked a time of "total" change, with peace, economy, and persuasion replacing war, heavy taxes, and coercion in the policies of the government.[90] Here again, there is danger of overstating the case, for the political agenda of a powerful individual still counted for a great deal. Among such individuals a consensus had emerged favoring the liquidation of the Anglo-French conflict that had raged so fiercely since 1369. Berry, who was not an enthusiastic military man, seems to have lost interest in the war after regaining his Poitevin *apanage* fifteen years before. For Burgundy, peace held out the hope for an end to English intrigue in the Low Countries and the restoration of English trade with his ravaged county of Flanders. Clisson, whose feud with John IV continually affected French foreign policy, seems to have abandoned, or at least moderated, his bellicosity towards England once he grasped the opportunity to make John of Blois his son-in-law.

Autrand was very much on target when she mentioned the kingdom's need for a new internal policy, an area that was not of great interest to princes schooled in war, diplomacy, and dynastic ambitions.[91] The government established in the final years of John II's reign, which Cazelles associated with the leadership of the Melun family, marked the crown's recovery from the crisis of the 1350s and the establishment of political, fiscal, and military institutions that were to make possible the recovery of French royal power. This government had needed to confront the desperate problems of internal disorder, military defeat, and bankruptcy, but by 1389 a generation had passed, and the solution of these old problems left exposed other problems that had not been able to claim attention. One of the earliest concerns of the Marmousets had been for the heavy sacrifices made by the French population, particularly the oppressive burden of taxation. Although economic and demographic conditions seem to have begun their slow but steady improvement after the terrible year of 1374, the crown's concern about these financial burdens had grown during the final years of Charles V's reign.[92] Now the Marmousets began to address the problem systematically.

The government embarked on a series of reforms that inaugurated a period of frugal administration and careful management of resources, providing the king with adequate revenues without having recourse to crushing new taxes.[93] To finance the largely abortive military schemes of the middle 1380s, the crown had levied special *tailles* that were calculated as surtaxes on the aids and therefore bore more heavily on commerce than on noble fortunes. The most recent of these was levied in the winter of 1387–88 to finance the campaign against Guelders.[94] It was to produce revenue equal to 50 percent of the aids, and the uncles converted it to an apportioned direct tax. To minimize opposition from the nobles, they exempted persons of noble lineage who pursued the military profession,[95] but their opponents were not distracted from their belief that the kingdom was burdened with heavy taxes that produced disappointing results. The Marmousets were determined to avoid such taxes, and in May 1389 they concluded a three-year truce with England, the first in a series of agreements that replaced twenty years of warfare with a period of Anglo-French peace that would last more than fifteen years.[96]

The truce naturally permitted a reduction of military costs, but it was preceded by half a year of energetic governmental reform that was intended, among other things, to reduce both taxes and nonmilitary costs. Throughout these months, Olivier de Clisson remained at Paris, very much a part of the reforming regime.[97] In December 1388, the crown reduced indirect taxes.[98] In February 1389, there were ordinances on the Parlement[99] and the royal household.[100] Enactments in March were devoted to the waters and forests administration[101] and the management of the *aides*.[102] An ordinance in early April dealt with the operations of the Chamber of Accounts.[103] In the midst of these specific enactments, Charles VI's government, at the end of February 1389, ordered a general reform of the kingdom. For the first time since the 1350s, royal *réformateurs* were to traverse the entire realm.[104]

The Marmousets also addressed the governance of the city of Paris, replacing the royal *prévôt* (Audoin Chauvernon, a henchman of the duke of Berry) in January 1389 and charging him with wrongful exactions.[105] In a further gesture of goodwill, they undertook to restore some measure of government to the Parisian bourgeoisie, who had lost their mayor (*prévôt des marchands*) and city council (*échevins*) following the suppression of their uprising in 1382. The government now instituted a royal official who would exercise many of the functions formerly carried out by the *prévôt des marchands*. Selected for this post was an ambitious young man from Champagne, Jean Jouvenal, a client of La Rivière's who married a niece of Jean le Mercier.[106] All this activity, coming on top of the earlier reduction in salaries and pensions, gradually made government more efficient and less expensive, and by 1390 there were signs that the changes were yielding positive results for the royal budget.[107]

These policies were not merely a pragmatic attempt to resolve problems by ad hoc measures of the sort that had characterized French royal practice since the beginning of the century. They were part of a more coherent vision of a well-run monarchical state. The intellectual godfather of the Marmousets was Philippe de Mézières, the old crusader and writer who had political ties similar to those of many of the Marmousets. Mézières had been the tutor of young Charles VI, to whom he had communicated many of the views of his father's inner circle. Autrand has argued that Mézières's *Le Songe du vieil pelerin* provided a theoretical basis for the political program that the Marmousets were trying to carry out, stressing principles like reduced taxes and public expenses, restoration of the royal domain, and government officials chosen for their competence.[108]

Guided by such ideas, the Marmousets developed a concept of the state that differed from longstanding medieval tradition. The royal officer was both a public person and a private one. While acting in his public function, he could not be sued or attacked by others, but the crown could take measures against him without waiting for the complaints of those whom he administered. A greater number of officers were to be chosen by "election," and younger men, committed to the Marmousets' vision of public service, entered the government, replacing those who had been creatures of the princes.[109] This new sense of the public function of royal officers who placed the monarchical state ahead of particular interests coincided with the attitude that divided Olivier de Clisson from so many of his fellow Breton lords. It was probably what drew him and Bureau de la Rivière together at an early date. The ideas and the esprit de corps of French officialdom under the Marmousets were not totally new, and much of what they created came to grief for a time during the fifteenth-century civil war between the Armagnacs and the Burgundians. Rarely, however, did such a close-knit group of royal advisers have such an unfettered opportunity to put into practice their vision of a royal bureaucracy, and they made the years 1388–92 a watershed in the early history of public administration in France.

Many of the new measures threatened vested interests, and the Marmousets made a dangerous enemy when they tried to curtail the privileges of the University of Paris.[110] Their administrative reforms included measures for selecting members of the Parlement and the bailiffs and seneschals who represented the king in the various administrative districts of the kingdom. The requirement that the royal council should choose the bailiffs and seneschals would mean in practice that whoever controlled the council also controlled these appointments. All that was intended was that the king should get appropriate advice in appointing his officers in the field.[111] The peculiar circumstances attending the subsequent years of Charles VI's reign would make control of the council a more important matter than in other periods and lead to abuses of this appointment process that could

not have been foreseen in 1389. There were now sixteen senior government officials who can be called "great officers of the crown."[112] Besides
these, the entire central government consisted of only about two hundred
people, of whom half were associated with the parlement and its essentially
judicial functions. France did not yet suffer from an overgrown bureaucracy.[113] Although these people were well rewarded during the period of
the Marmousets' ascendancy, Maurice Rey found that suspicions of avari-
cious royal officers were actually much exaggerated.[114]

The most spectacular manifestation of the Marmousets' desire to reform the governance of the kingdom was in Languedoc, where the duke of
Berry's administration had come under fire for numerous abuses. Like his
older brother, Louis of Anjou, Berry attracted resentment in Languedoc
for his fiscal exactions. Unlike Anjou, however, Berry did not give evidence
of employing the funds for the benefit of the region. He spent little time in
the Midi personally, leaving most of the governing to his nephew, John III
of Armagnac, and to officials who were more successful at enriching themselves than in maintaining public order. The Armagnacs continued their
long feud with the count of Foix, and much of the southwest was infested
with hostile soldiery. Not surprisingly, a rising tide of complaints was
reaching the royal court. Charles VI had left his uncle undisturbed in his
southern lieutenancy when he withdrew from the council, but in 1389 the
king decided to make a personal tour of the region. He sent ahead a team
of six *réformateurs*; among others, the group included two key Marmousets—Cassinel and Chevreuse—and the marshal, Louis de Sancerre. Their
investigations soon uncovered serious charges of corruption.[115]

Charles VI's journey to Languedoc was a carefully planned ritual of
royal sovereignty. Clisson and La Rivière accompanied the king, and while
the ultimate objective of the trip was Toulouse, Charles took a circuitous
route, making staged ceremonial entries at Lyon, Montpellier, and Béziers
to put the royal majesty on display. Autrand has described these events as a
"royal festival on the model of a religious festival," and a classic example of
the style of the Marmousets.[116] Of the many officials charged with abuses,
the most notorious villain seems to have been Berry's trusted henchman
Bétizac, the *viguier* of Béziers, who was actually executed for heresy after
some trickery by the king's men.[117] To deal with the disastrous lack of public order arising from the incapacities of the count of Armagnac and his
feud with Foix, the king sent Jean de Blaisy to raise money and pay off *routiers* to evacuate a number of fortresses. Then his representatives reached

an accord with Gaston of Foix that terminated the old count's thirty-year feud with the Armagnacs.[118]

The reform of Languedoc clearly required that the duke of Berry be removed from his post. The king tried to soften the blow as much as possible, telling him that he no longer needed a lieutenant in Languedoc because he was going there in person.[119] He also promised that neither Berry nor his heirs would be prosecuted for misuse of tax revenues from Languedoc in the 1380s, and he canceled certain debts that Berry owed the crown.[120] The chronicler of Saint-Denis, however, wrote that Berry received the news of his impending removal from Jean Harpedenne, a nephew of Olivier de Clisson, and that he blamed the constable and his friends, conceiving an implacable hatred against them.[121] In blaming the Marmousets, the duke of Berry was certainly correct, but in this case one can hardly say that they were motivated by personal rancor. After issuing orders for the reform of the financial abuses uncovered in Languedoc (late January 1390),[122] Charles VI began his return to Paris. In March, the duke and duchess of Burgundy received the royal party magnificently at Dijon, bestowing gifts on the duke of Bourbon, the bishop of Poitiers, and such Marmousets as Clisson, Coucy, La Rivière, Sancerre, Pierre de Craon, and Jean de Bueil.[123]

If the rise of the Marmousets accompanied the political eclipse of the king's paternal uncles, it also led to increased royal support for the house of Anjou and to the growing political influence of the king's younger brother Louis, duke of Touraine. Like Charles VI, Louis was very fond of the constable, and as they came to power, the Marmousets continued to cultivate his friendship. Louis and Charles had been educated together and were very close, but Louis was supported by an *apanage* much smaller than those of the uncles. According to Autrand, the Marmousets considered Louis an ideal prince because he did not have vast lands and was dependent on the king. Unfortunately, he maintained the life-style of a prince and soon set about building up his landed possessions. The king always seemed willing to confer wealth and power on his brother, and Louis would come to be known for a cupidity rivalling that of his uncles.[124]

As already pointed out, it would be a mistake to credit young Louis with engineering the coup of 1388 or to call him the real power behind the throne in these years.[125] Born in 1372, he was not politically mature enough to challenge his uncles until well into the 1390s, but he was already old enough and influential enough to attract clients and favorites. Increasingly, we find members of his entourage or people on his payroll who were associated with the Marmouset party or were important nobles from the north and west where the Marmousets drew their greatest strength. Louis began to sit regularly on the council in 1389.[126] A scholar who has studied the political struggles of Louis's later years remarked that many key royal officials were his men. We should not suppose that Louis was systematically placing his supporters in important positions during the years when he was in his late teens and early twenties. It is rather that people already in important positions were becoming aligned with him.[127]

In 1389, the king's brother made a generous gift to Bureau de la Riviere and numbered among his chamberlains Jean de Garencières (a Norman lord long associated with the Marmousets), Pierre de Craon, lord of La Ferté-Bernard (Clisson's second cousin), and the important Jean le Mercier.[128] In the 1390s, other important military families of the north and west would become linked with Louis.[129] Just as Olivier de Clisson and this regional nobility had become the political heirs of Louis of Anjou in opposition to Philip the Bold, so the younger Louis would gradually inherit the leadership of this party from Clisson after 1392. The young duke of Touraine married Valentina Visconti, daughter of the duke of Milan, in 1389,[130] and used some of her dowry in 1391 to purchase the counties of Blois and Dunois from the childless Guy de Châtillon.[131] In June 1392, Louis exchanged Touraine for the larger and richer *apanage* of Orléans, and Charles VI granted him an additional annuity of four thousand pounds. We shall refer to him henceforth as the duke of Orléans.[132]

9

The Frustrations of the Marmousets

ALTHOUGH THE REGIME OF THE Marmousets was a reaction against the government of the dukes of Burgundy and Berry and their closest followers, this generalization does not readily apply to foreign policy, where there was an element of consensus that contrasted strikingly with earlier and later periods. In the early years of Charles VI's reign, Philip of Burgundy and Louis of Anjou had divergent foreign ambitions, while the Marmousets and the royal uncles had different policies towards Brittany, and it was thought that the duke of Berry opposed the aggressive policies towards England favored by others in the government. A decade later, the dukes of Burgundy and Orléans were bitterly divided over issues of foreign policy. Under the Marmousets, by contrast, "the princes sank their differences and combined their interests to the mutual advantage of all concerned."[1] The Marmousets and the military leadership were as much a part of this consensus as were the princes.

The crucial elements of the consensus were: (1) peace with England, (2) a Breton policy that was firm but conciliatory, and (3) an Italian policy that sought to accommodate the ambitions of certain princes, the desire to end the schism, and the need to deal with the problem of the *routiers* that always seemed to reappear when Anglo-French hostilities were suspended. The truce concluded with England in June of 1389 was to be followed by negotiations aiming at a permanent peace. Philip of Burgundy, hoping to consolidate his position in the Low Countries and mindful of the economic interests of his new subjects there, played an active role in working for a settlement. His brother, the duke of Berry, was the prince who had been least supportive of the war with England and was becoming the one most committed to ending the papal schism.[2] The Marmousets required peace if they were to achieve their two potentially incompatible objectives of relieving the burden on the taxpayers while building up the resources in the royal coffers. They also wanted French fighting forces to be available for use in Italy.[3]

Did the military aristocracy, on whom the power of the Marmousets ultimately rested, also favor a peace between the two monarchies? The answer is probably affirmative. The destructive effects of warfare on seigneurial capital and the manorial economy were evident everywhere. Literature on warfare and chivalry, designed for noble consumption, now addressed questions of discipline and public order, a notable shift of emphasis away from the right of private war and the pursuit of honor and glory that had characterized writers like Geoffroi de Charny forty years earlier.[4] People at the royal court frequently heard the sermons of an aggressively reform-minded intellectual circle that deplored the barbarities of warriors against peasants.[5] The nobles had every reason to support a reduction in royal expenditures that might alleviate the fiscal burden on their tenants and minimize the risk of inflationary manipulations of the currency.

The most obvious economic interest of the nobility, of course, was the regularly salaried force of men-at-arms that had proven its value to both crown and nobles since its establishment at the beginning of 1364. An Anglo-French peace, however, was not likely to jeopardize this force, thanks to the very conditions that had called it into being in the first place—the depredations of *routiers*. Warriors of many nationalities, employed by both combatants in the war of 1369–89, were left without means of support after the truce of 1389, and almost immediately the danger they posed to Languedoc led to plans for a foreign expedition to lure them out of the kingdom.[6] The need to restore domestic order and the projects for campaigns abroad both left little doubt that a royal army would be needed even after an Anglo-French peace.

Besides the evident need to rid the country of brigands, a number of considerations underlay projects for a foreign campaign. The twenty-two-year-old king, so different from his father, pictured himself as a military leader with a Christian mission.[7] The traditional outlet for Christian knighthood was a crusade against the Muslims. Such an expedition always found supporters, and an important one was the king's former tutor Philippe de Mézières. Years of bitter Anglo-French conflict had damaged whatever solidarity the international chivalric class had formerly possessed, and a collaborative effort on behalf of Christendom might heal these wounds and further promote the cause of peace within Europe.[8] The most powerful and aggressive Muslims, the Ottoman Turks, seemed geographically remote, were consolidating their position under a new ruler, and did not appear to threaten the central Danube valley as they would a few years later. Consequently, in 1389–90, prospective crusaders eyed a nearer and potentially less difficult target in North Africa, encouraged by Genoa, whose possessions suffered at the hands of Barbary pirates. The duke of Bourbon undertook to lead an expedition there in 1390, with the crudaders to be assembled at Marseille by the first of July. The Genoese, who had their own agenda, provided transportation, but after an ineffectual campaign of several months they accepted a deal to withdraw their fleet in return for payment, and the crusaders had no choice but to retire with them.[9] Returning to France in disappointment during the fall, they found the government engrossed with plans for a different sort of campaign.

A few weeks after Louis of Bourbon had departed for North Africa, his nephew, Louis II of Anjou, had left for Naples to pursue his father's claims at the expense of Ladislas of Durazzo, who represented the older house of Anjou in Naples. The project had strong backing from Clisson in the royal council, and Louis enjoyed some temporary successes, but his position remained precarious without either a pope sympathetic to France or a French military presence in the peninsula.[10] These difficulties were to be remedied by a major royal expedition to Italy.

Besides the Angevin branch of the Valois family, the king's brother Louis of Orléans had strong Italian ambitions, nurtured since his childhood by various projects for potential marriages. For a time, his ambitions conflicted with those of his Angevin cousins, but his recent marriage alliance with the ducal house of Milan had brought him the town of Asti, and by 1390 his major project was to carve out a kingdom from the northern part of the papal states.[11]

For the king, of course, the desire to perform great military feats on behalf of Christendom required an end to the schism, which itself might require the use of force. There were, indeed, many who found it troubling to contemplate a crusade or any other large project on behalf of Christendom when the leadership of Catholic Christianity was divided by the papal schism.[12] Although the English and their allies supported the Roman obedience, Urban VI was not a popular figure, and his backers appeared so lukewarm that the Marmousets seem to have thought that the arrival of a French army in Italy would be enough to overthrow the Urbanists and install Clement VII in Rome.[13] With this in mind as well as the ambitions of the princes, the French had been making plans to intervene militarily in Italy since before their truce with England. The plans had now progressed to the point where a huge French army was scheduled to muster at Lyon on 15 March 1391 and proceed to Italy with the active support of Giangaleazzo Visconti's Milan.[14]

What the Marmousets may have been slow to recognize, however, was the impact of Urban VI's death in the fall of 1389. The quick election of Boniface IX to succeed him was, from the French point of view, an unfortunate act that perpetuated the schism and deserved to be repudiated if not punished. For those who had denied the validity of Clement VII's election, however, that of Boniface revitalized their ardor for the Roman obedience by replacing the unpopular Urban with a pope they could support more readily.[15] If, as it appears, the Marmousets misread this situation, it may explain why they also miscalculated the vigor of the English response. Boniface IX appealed to Richard II not to conclude peace with Charles VI without a promise that the French would stay out of Italy. Richard agreed and then engaged in a flurry of diplomatic activity aimed at frustrating the French design. Finally, in February 1391, as the French force was about to assemble, an English embassy warned that an attack on the Roman pope would violate the Anglo-French truce, and Charles VI brought the plan to an immediate halt.[16]

A complicating factor in all these activities was the problem of the *routiers*, which was rapidly becoming serious. John III of Armagnac collected a large force of unemployed soldiers from Gascony late in October 1390 and set out to pass through Provence and across the Alps into Italy, where the two warring states of Milan and Florence each hoped to obtain their services.[17] Armagnac's sister, however, was married to a member of the Visconti family exiled by Giangaleazzo and now fighting for Florence. This republic won the services of Armagnac's troops, a blow to French policy (and perhaps a victory for English diplomacy) because Florence supported Boniface IX, while Milan was Charles VI's main ally against him. The departing *routiers*, therefore, were held up in Provence, where they did considerable damage in the last months of 1390.[18]

It was, in short, no easy task to achieve a complex set of objectives—peace with England, an end to the schism, employment of *routiers* outside the realm, and fulfillment of the king's desire to lead some grand enterprise on behalf of Christendom. The powerful position of Olivier de Clisson in the French government did little to further these objectives; if anything, it made the task more difficult. Notwithstanding his earlier experience on diplomatic missions in the 1360s, Clisson did not possess the personal traits of a skilled negotiator. He was arrogant, quick to take offense, highly sensitive to what he considered his rights and prerogatives, and unable to forgive gracefully anything he perceived as an affront. Such qualities, by no means uncommon among the nobles of late medieval France, seem to have become more pronounced in Clisson as he grew older, wealthier, and more powerful. For a man whose position in the government afforded opportunities for statesmanship, they were serious liabilities.

Clisson wanted to be treated in a manner befitting his position in the royal government, while his enemy, the duke of Brittany, regarded him as an overmighty subject whose power in the French government made him dangerous. Their feud was more than ever a personal matter after 1389. The end of Anglo-French hostilities sharply reduced the danger of Brittany as a tactical bastion for English military power, while John's third wife began producing heirs for the duchy, thus eliminating the possibility of a Penthièvre succession.[19] John IV, however, was determined to strengthen ducal power at the expense of lords whose relative autonomy in the past was incompatible with John's conception of his ducal rights and role. He also sought to strengthen his own autonomy vis-à-vis the monarchy. Autrand has argued that the Marmousets were determined to force him to recognize royal sovereignty, something he was determined to avoid.[20] This more confrontational approach, in which one can surely see the hand of Clisson, replaced a policy that was willing to tolerate silence on the issue of sovereignty as long as John was a faithful vassal and abided by his treaty obligations.

It would be a mistake, however, to exaggerate the change in French policy, for one can argue that prior to 1392 the Marmousets showed surprising restraint in the face of Breton provocations. As critics of the regime of the uncles, Clisson and his friends were unmistakable "hard-liners" towards Brittany. Now with roles reversed and the various factions generally united in their foreign policies and determined not to let the Breton question upset things, the other Marmousets kept Clisson under greater restraint while the dukes did the same with John IV. While we should not underestimate the problem presented by Clisson's difficult personality and the degree to which the duke felt threatened by him, John IV was also to blame for the continuing tensions. Although his financial position seems to have been reasonably strong in this period,[21] he repaid very little of the hundred thousand francs extorted from Clisson in 1387. Clisson, in return, chose not to return several ducal strongholds he had taken.[22]

In January 1389, just six months after the king had ruled against him in the dispute arising from his arrest of Clisson, John IV presented to an assembly of Breton magnates a list of his grievances against Clisson and John of Blois. They included differences over interpretation of the treaty of 1365, failure to observe fully the settlement of 1388, disputes over the limits of ducal and seigneurial jurisdiction—a litany of aggravations typical of what could damage the relations between a late medieval prince and an overmighty vassal.[23] Three months later, John named an embassy to address the king about compensation for lands that could not be returned to him as required by the treaty of Brétigny, now nearly thirty years old.[24] The king was making at least some effort to provide this compensation, ordering financial officials to be prompt in paying some Norman revenues assigned to the duke.[25]

The fact remained, however, that relations between Brittany and the French crown, like the more personal ones between John IV and the Clisson-Penthièvre camp, were encumbered by a generation of truces, treaties, reconciliations, and promises that had not been executed faithfully in all details. There were enough violations, delays, and disputes to provide endless grounds for accusations, litigation, and mistrust. The crown suspected John of being chronically disloyal in view of his long double game between France and England. The French maintained fortifications in the Breton marches and retained possession of Saint-Malo. Feeling threatened and encroached upon, the duke did what he could to make his position more secure. In January 1390, he reached an amicable agreement with his friend the duke of Berry over problems along the border between Brittany and Poitou involving the infringement of rights by each other's officers.[26] These were the sorts of problems that troubled his relations with Clisson and the count of Penthièvre, but it was far easier to settle differences with a friend and equal than with an enemy and subject.

A series of transactions in the spring of 1390 aggravated relations between the royal government and the duke of Brittany. On 7 March, to help pay off the large arrears of his salary, Charles VI gave Olivier de Clisson the stronghold of Pontorson, on the Norman-Breton border.[27] Then, on 20 April John IV undertook to neutralize some potentially hostile enclaves within the duchy by forcing Olivier du Guesclin to sell him the fortresses of La Guerche and Châteaulin for thirty-seven thousand francs.[28] Four days later, the ever-impecunious duke of Anjou sold Clisson the castellany of Champtoceaux, another key fortress on the border of Brittany.[29] Du Guesclin was sufficiently angry at having to sell his castles that he appealed to the Parlement of Paris. When the court agreed to take the case, John responded in June with the argument that acceptance of royal jurisdiction in the matter was a violation of ducal rights secured by earlier treaties.[30] John IV then responded to Clisson's acquisition of Champtoceaux by besieging and capturing the stronghold in the fall of 1390.[31]

Not surprisingly, the French government reacted angrily to this situation, dispatching an embassy in December that expressed the king's strong displeasure, and threatened John IV with another summons before the royal court. This response settled nothing and threatened to turn the incident into a full-blown crisis.[32] At this point, the duke of Berry intervened in the dispute, persuading the king to let him negotiate with Brittany over Champtoceaux.[33] Since a rupture with Brittany could seriously threaten both the peace negotiations with England and the king's Italian plans, Clisson and the Marmousets appear to have been more than usually willing for an accommodation, once Berry persuaded John IV to back down over Champtoceaux. The duke of Bourbon would take custody of the castle, and on 7 February 1391 Charles VI ordered payment for Philibert de Digoine, commander of the troops ordered to hold the place pending Bourbon's assumption of control.[34] John IV now negotiated an alliance with the count of Armagnac, providing for the marriage of the young Breton heir to Béatrix of Armagnac. Since the house of Armagnac had been tightly aligned with the duke of Berry, this arrangement may be seen as an effort to strengthen the ties between Brittany and Berry, but it has also been seen as a triumph of English diplomacy, linking Brittany to a Gascon prince whose sympathies were with Florence against Milan.[35]

The duke of Brittany had, in effect, escaped chastisement because of the French crown's desire not to disrupt projects that were fundamental to royal foreign policy. As Michael Jones has pointed out, John's ability to imperil these projects was one way that "Brittany could make its independence felt in international affairs," and the duke was skillful in glossing over his own faults while pursuing his demands to the French.[36] These demands boiled down to two main issues: (1) revenues promised to the duke of Brittany in compensation for lands he claimed outside the duchy, and (2) the conflict between John's understanding of Breton liberties and the jurisdictional claims of the Parlement of Paris. The first issue concerned primarily those lands in the counties of Nevers and Rethel that were supposed to have been his mother's dowry. Years of bickering over the value of these lands had prevented full implementation of either treaty of Guérande. After receiving arguments as to their value in 1383, Charles VI had ordered his counsellors in the Parlement to evaluate the property,[37] but the duke's representatives had objected to the evaluation in July 1383.[38] In the summer of 1384, Charles VI had called for a new evaluation.[39] In January 1385, the duke had sent representatives to request return of the lands themselves,[40] but the real debate was over the alleged appreciation in their value.[41] Now, at the end of July 1391, John IV sent the king a new delegation to press this issue[42] and to try to justify to the king the more controversial recent actions of the duke, who claimed that he had given the king satisfaction by relinquishing Champtoceaux and had done much to accommodate Clisson and Penthièvre.[43]

Their dislike of the Marmousets must have made it difficult for the royal uncles to persevere in supporting the Anglo-French peace talks while restraining the duke of Brittany. If peace were concluded while they were in power, the Marmousets would be able to claim an achievement that had eluded French governments for many years. Yet their own interests generally favored peace with England.[44] Such military commanders as Coucy, Waleran de Luxembourg, and Guy de la Trémoille are said to have urged the uncles to restrain John IV lest he provoke a confrontation that would ruin the peace negotiations with England, but there is no reason to believe that Berry and Burgundy were secretly egging John on.[45] They appear to have needed no urging to press John IV into a more conciliatory stance, and personal animosities seem to have had less effect on their judgment than was the case with Clisson and John IV.

With the Italian expedition now canceled in order not to imperil the negotiations with England, the government was in no mood to permit the festering Breton question to do comparable damage. The king summoned John IV to meet with him at Tours in November. To insure his attendance, John was to be placed under royal safeguard, and letters to that effect were delivered by an impressive balanced delegation consisting of such Marmousets as Villaines, Chevreuse, and Bernard de la Tour, but also the chancellor of Burgundy and Pierre de Navarre, John IV's brother-in-law.[46] When the king arrived, the duke did not appear, and it required an urgent visit to Brittany by the duke of Berry in December to persuade him to honor the summons and appear at Tours in January, when the uncles, with their sympathies for him, would be in attendance.[47]

Whereas in 1388 the king had sat in judgment on John IV for actions that he and the Marmousets considered an outrage, the tone in 1392 was one of conciliation. The purpose of the meeting at Tours was to produce a definitive Franco-Breton settlement. Charles offered a marriage alliance involving two infants, his daughter and the duke's son (the latter having been recently affianced to the daughter of the count of Armagnac). The king proposed a dowry of 150,000 francs, but John countered by demanding land as well as money for the dowry. This proposal so offended the king and council that Burgundy said he dared not intercede to support the duke's position. According to Philip, the marriage was the key to a permanent settlement and it could not go forward if John persisted in his demands. In the document of 20 January in which the duke summarized these discussions, he indicated that he would prefer another marriage for his son and that if he acquiesced in the royal proposal he would do so only out of fear for the consequences of refusal.[48] Four days later, when the contract had been accepted, John IV repeated that he was acting out of fear and did not consider himself bound by the agreement.[49]

Hard negotiating continued between John IV and the king's representatives. The main disagreements were over the nature of ducal homage for Brittany, the appellate jurisdiction of the Parlement of Paris over Breton cases, and the question of who had what rights over the church in Brittany. On these questions, John was a vassal taking a stand against his lord's encroachments. On the other hand, when asked to make an accommodation with the Clisson-Penthièvre faction, he was in an opposite position, resisting concessions that would prevent him from upholding his conception of ducal prerogatives in dealing with subjects. The dukes of Berry and Burgundy busily acted as intermediaries, while John IV, finally agreeing to a settlement on 26 January, stated once more that concessions made out of fear did not have to be honored.[50]

When a great council assembled in the castle of Tours on 26 January, Philip of Burgundy summarized six main points of contention between Charles VI and John IV. Three involved the church—provision of ecclesiastical benefices, the royal right to collect clerical tenths, and the *regale* of the bishops (a right claimed by both duke and king). The fourth had to do with the appellate jurisdiction of the royal court, which the duke claimed was strictly limited to specific classes of cases. The fifth concerned the homage that the duke required from his subjects. Since he held Brittany from the king, his subjects were to promise him loyal service against everybody but the king of France. If he required of them unconditional oaths of loyalty, he would be in a position to charge with treason any who refused to help him against the king. Finally, the uncles said that John was striking coins he was not authorized to mint, and John replied that he could produce documents authorizing him to strike these coins.[51]

This text, with its six points of contention between king and duke, is, in one respect, a typical example of the issues that could divide a monarch and a great territorial lord in this period. In its immediate context, however, the document is most interesting for what it does not mention: (1) lands (or revenue in lieu of them) that should have been returned to John by treaty thirty years before but had remained a matter of dispute; (2) the duke's continuing use of English troops; (3) French encroachments on Breton soil and fortification of the marches; and (4) the large sum that the duke had extorted from Clisson and had failed to return as the king had ordered in 1388. Of the six items covered in the document, the fourth was indeed an important issue between the king and duke, while the fifth was of central importance in John's relations with the constable, but the absence of other longstanding causes of friction suggests that considerable progress had been made.

Several other documents of the same date indicate the areas of hard-won agreement. The marriage contract between the duke's young son and the king's daughter had numerous provisions about how the young couple would be endowed and how things would be handled if the marriage were not consummated or failed to produce heirs, but it did not augment the dowry originally proposed by the king.[52] Then there were treaties between John IV and the count of Penthièvre[53] and Olivier de Clisson respectively. Clisson had to renounce all appeals he had lodged against the duke and his officers, while the duke agreed to pay him the eighty thousand francs still owing to him from the canceled extortion of 1387, raising the money via a hearth tax on Breton lands other than Clisson's. The constable, however, was to receive his money immediately, as nineteen great lords of Brittany were required to deposit designated sums with his agents at Rieux. These involuntary guarantors of ducal integrity were the ones to be reimbursed from the proceeds of the hearth tax. They would receive very little of this money.[54] John of Blois and Clisson then rendered homage to the duke.[55] To comply at last with the earlier treaties of Guérande, the duke was to provide revenues to the count of Penthièvre (now eight thousand francs). John of Blois would receive custody of nine Breton castellanies to guarantee this income.[56]

The government of Charles VI, apparently giving ground on the matter of appellate jurisdiction, agreed that its courts could accept litigation from Brittany only in the traditional cases of denial of law or false judgment, as the duke had argued.[57] John IV, for his part, ordered his seneschal of Rennes to conduct an inquiry into the form of homage previously required of ducal subjects and the rights of the duke concerning the striking of coins.[58] In short, the many documents produced by these arduous negotiations gave the appearance of a comprehensive settlement, and it is probable that the king and his uncles thought they had accomplished just that. One might even argue that the duke of Brittany, as the weaker party, had everything to gain from such a settlement and had scored something of a coup in securing a royal princess for his son.[59] Nevertheless, this apparent settlement would break down more quickly than any previous one, and while it is difficult to assess responsibility for the incident that triggered its collapse, evidence suggests that John IV felt unable to reach an enduring accord with either the French government or Olivier de Clisson as long as they were so tightly linked together.

Less than two weeks after the negotiations at Tours were concluded, the queen gave birth to a son.[60] With the resulting hope that the succession was secured, and with the Breton problem seemingly resolved, Charles and his advisers moved confidently ahead towards their next important piece of unfinished business—establishing a permanent peace with England. In March, Charles VI and the princes were scheduled to be at Amiens for major negotiations with the duke of Lancaster. Since Charles did not leave Paris until the middle of the month, the actual meeting must have taken place near the end of March. Amid the festivities that normally attended such gatherings, the two sides exchanged demands and concessions that still fell short of a major agreement. By early April, the English had departed and Philip of Burgundy had gone to his own lands. At about the same time, an outbreak of what appears to have been typhoid fever disrupted the plans of the court. The king, the duke of Berry, and other prominent people were afflicted by the disease. Taken to Beauvais early in April, Charles VI remained convalescent for some time and was probably not back in Paris until the final week of May.[61] By that date, the Breton settlement was about to unravel in the greatest crisis of the king's reign.

It had been clear from the outset that John of Brittany did not wish to go to Tours to negotiate with the crown, and as we have seen, he stated repeatedly that he did not feel obliged to comply with arrangements he felt he had been coerced into making. Jones considers the settlement to be a temporary reversal for Breton policy, after which John soon resumed discussions with the English.[62] The duke seems not to have desired any international accommodation that would deprive him of the opportunity to play off the two monarchies against each other. New disputes with Clisson were always cropping up, and within a few months John was ordering the constable to appear at the ducal court to answer charges brought by a convent that claimed he had not paid certain revenues that he owed.[63]

After Tours, thought Alfred Coville, John wanted vengeance on Clisson more than ever, and soon found the instrument for that vengeance in the constable's fugitive cousin, Pierre de Craon, lord of La Ferté-Bernard.[64]

The younger son of the viscount of Châteaudun, Pierre de Craon was born in 1350 and, like the rest of the Craon lineage, was widely connected with the aristocracy of the north and west. His father Guillaume was a first cousin of Olivier III de Clisson and brother to an archbishop of Reims. His mother was closely related to the counts of Flanders, and he himself, at thirteen years of age, married Jeanne de Châtillon, whose paternal lineage had great distinction and whose mother was a Coucy.[65] As a lord with holdings in Anjou and Maine, he had served Louis I of Anjou and his wife, Marie of Blois, especially during the duke's unsuccessful quest for the Neapolitan throne in 1382–84. He had become familiar with Italian politics and the Visconti family, and had moved into the service of Louis of Touraine (later Orléans) in 1389.[66] His geographical and family associations and his service with princes who tended to oppose the duke of Burgundy entitle us to place him in the Marmouset camp.

The career of Pierre de Craon had been marred by incidents that marked him as an unsavory character. He had been pardoned for killing the brother of a personal enemy in 1379 and had played a self-interested and probably dishonest role in dealings between Louis of Anjou and Isabelle de Roucy at about the same time.[67] While on a mission for Louis of Anjou he had been imprisoned by the rival Neapolitan house at Ragusa, and following his release in the spring of 1385 he had become involved in a dispute with the duchess of Anjou over money. He claimed that she owed him twenty-two thousand francs, and she finally made a settlement involving a smaller sum.[68] The duke of Berry, her brother-in-law, criticized this settlement and accused Craon of having betrayed Louis of Anjou. He was out of favor with the royal uncles and suspected of having misappropriated a large sum intended to support Anjou's military operations.[69] As a quarrelsome and litigious individual, Pierre was a worthy equal of his second cousin, the constable, and he was embroiled in a succession of cases before the Parlement, one of them against Clisson himself.[70]

Lord of La Ferté-Bernard since 1388, Pierre had found a new position of influence in the household of the king's brother and soon was in high favor with Charles VI as well as Louis. Like his cousin, Olivier de Clisson, he was able to use his wealth to capitalize on the financial troubles of the house of Anjou, and in 1390 he bought from Marie the fortress of Sablé, which Louis of Anjou had acquired from Craon's cousin in the 1370s.[71] In

1391, however, Craon fell from favor and was banished from court. The reasons for his disgrace remain unclear, as none of the suggested explanations are altogether convincing. There were rumors that young Louis of Orléans liked the company of those who dabbled in sorcery and spells. Pintoin, later followed partially by Juvenal des Ursins, reported Craon's story that he had warned Louis against such involvements, thus irritating the prince and causing his fall from favor; but Craon's own explanation was doubtless self-serving.[72]

Froissart heard that Craon had committed the unpardonable indiscretion of telling the duchess of Orléans about one of her husband's amorous adventures and that Louis had gotten the king to banish him for this betrayal of confidence.[73] Another chronicler reported that many at court (the duke of Berry in particular) blamed him for betraying the interests of the duke and duchess of Anjou in the early 1380s,[74] and Barthélemy Pocquet thought that Clisson, with his strong ties to the Penthièvre family, was particularly resentful.[75] According to Froissart, it was La Rivière and Le Mercier who informed Craon of his banishment from court.[76] It might have been more appropriate for Pierre's cousin, the constable, to perform this delicate mission. Craon may have hoped that Clisson could intervene effectively on his behalf, but perhaps Clisson had acquiesced in the banishment and had sent his two friends to break the news.

Pierre de Craon himself may not have been certain as to why he was disgraced, but it certainly caused him to harbor strong resentments. At first he retired to Sablé, but after a time, he went to Brittany and visited John IV at Suscinio.[77] There, according to Froissart, the duke told him that his banishment was Clisson's doing.[78] That much is believable enough, since John was prepared to blame Clisson for almost anything and was eager to discredit him, but did Craon have any particular reason to credit the story and seek revenge on the constable? Autrand suggests that Clisson "a failli mourir" because he had achieved a position of influence with the king that Craon had failed to achieve with Louis of Orléans.[79] Pierre would testify five years later that Clisson had shown him nothing but hatred and had never ceased to damage him.[80] A chronicler to whom Pierre may have had access said that Craon knew "that he owed his disgrace to the suggestions of messire Olivier de Clisson," that he resolved to seek vengeance and sent him written threats.[81] Significantly, perhaps, this account does not mention the duke of Brittany, but it brings us no closer to an understanding of when and why Craon decided Clisson was to blame.

Having conceived a bitter hatred towards Clisson, Craon now re-

solved to kill him. By May of 1392, if not earlier, he sold his recently acquired castle of Sablé to the duke of Brittany for fifty thousand francs.[82]
Since the king's men later found a substantial sum of money at La Ferté-
Bernard,[83] Craon was not in serious financial distress. Why, then, did he
decide to sell Sablé to John IV, or to put it another way, who was the principal beneficiary of this transaction? If Craon needed ready cash and the
duke was prepared to help him, the sale provided John with a mechanism
for doing so. At the same time, possession of Sablé would strengthen the
duke's defensive position on his eastern frontier and he may have exploited
Craon's banishment and political isolation to gain possession of a strategic
castle. In neither case does the transaction prove that the duke was Craon's
accomplice in plotting against Clisson, but it does implicate him somewhat in the events that followed. John IV was, moreover, again in contact
with the English at the time that Craon was hatching his plot.[84]

Once Craon was out of favor at court, the duchess of Anjou again took
up her old grievance against him, and on 10 June 1392 he was represented
before the Parlement by a lawyer who claimed that Pierre could not attend
in person (presumably because of his banishment). Marie of Anjou's lawyer responded that Craon had been in Paris for six days and was fully able
to appear.[85] In fact, some time earlier, Pierre had assembled a band of confederates in his castle of Porchefontaine and had been bringing them into
Paris stealthily. On the night of 13 June, when Clisson was returning home
with a small escort after dining with the king, Craon and his men waylaid
him and attacked him with swords. Covered with blood, the constable was
knocked through the unlocked door of a shop and his attackers fled, thinking they had killed him. It turned out that they had only wounded him
superficially. By tumbling into the shop, he escaped additional blows that
might have been fatal. He recovered fully within a matter of weeks.[86]

10

Clisson at Bay:
War in Brittany and in the Courts

THE ATTACK ON CLISSON produced an immediate and strong reaction at court. Charles VI, of course, was outraged. As in 1387, he viewed an attack on his constable as an act of treason, but the particular circumstances of Craon's attack, which occurred in Paris itself immediately after the victim had been a royal guest, made the event appear as a direct, personal assault on the king's majesty that could not go unpunished lest similar attacks in the future be encouraged. He immediately ordered Craon's arrest and sent people to pursue him.[1] But while some of the confederates were caught and executed, the lord of La Ferté-Bernard made good his escape and reached Brittany. Angry at Craon's successful evasion, Charles VI ordered the seizure of his property and the destruction of some of his houses in and around Paris.[2] Not until late August did the government complete formal judicial action condemning Craon to perpetual banishment and ordering confiscation of his property,[3] but on 18 July Charles VI assigned the revenues from Craon's estates to his brother Louis,[4] whom he had just made duke of Orléans and showered with favors.[5]

The assassination attempt effectively disrupted the French government, as the sort of restraint displayed after John's attack on Champtoceaux was swept away by the emotions unleashed on the night of 13–14 June. The absence of any influential voice for moderation is extremely striking. It suggests that the posture of the duke of Berry, and indeed his very whereabouts, are essential to any understanding of the critical summer of 1392. According to Froissart, Berry was in Paris throughout the events of June, had prior warning of Craon's plot and could have thwarted it, and even assented to the king's proposed military response while concealing his true thoughts.[6] It is extremely difficult to believe such a tale. Berry was not a popular figure with Froissart's informants, but despite his resentment of the Marmousets he had worked tirelessly to defuse earlier confrontations with Brittany and had no reason on this occasion to act as Froissart described. It is much more likely that the duke, who was recovering from his own illness in April and May and was increasingly preoccupied with other political issues, like the schism and the succession to the county of Foix, merely assumed that the attack on Clisson was Craon's private vendetta. Berry would have known that an attack of this sort could not go unpunished, even though he had no love for Clisson, could understand why the constable might have mortal enemies, and probably would have welcomed any event that might force his retirement.

The government took no further action until July, when Clisson was able to ride again. Early in that month, Berry left for Avignon on a diplomatic mission relating to the unsettled circumstances in the southwest following the death of Gaston of Foix. Despite the impression given by some chroniclers, he would not be back until September and it is likely that he left Paris without expecting the Marmousets to attack Brittany.[7] If we are to look for a culprit among the princes, the behavior of Philip the Bold seems considerably more suspicious, for his men were in extended communication with John IV during May and June of 1392.[8] If the duke of Brittany was implicated in Craon's plans, it is possible that Burgundy also knew that something was afoot.

Olivier de Clisson, of course, had no trouble believing that John IV was behind the attack, and it soon became known at the royal court that Craon had fled to Brittany. On this occasion the duke had the good sense not to harbor the dangerous fugitive, and Craon was soon on his way to Spain.[9] The king believed him to be in Brittany and demanded that John deliver up the culprit. According to the chronicler of Saint-Denis, John admitted having seen and even received Pierre, but insisted that he was no longer in the duchy.[10] Breton chroniclers reported that the king and his brother thought the duke's reponse reasonable but that the council (that is, Clisson and the Marmousets) argued that Craon would never have dared such an act without the support of John IV, who was thereby guilty of an attack on the king's majesty.[11] If Pintoin is correct, the situation was aggravated when men sent by the king to secure Sablé found the castle defended in the name of the duke of Brittany.[12] Whatever the real truth, the royal government became convinced, almost to the point of fixation, that it was John IV who should be punished for Craon's crime. Clisson's feud with the duke had now become the king's feud.

When Clisson was well again (by mid-July), the king convened a council to discuss action against Brittany.[13] This discussion must have taken place after the duke of Berry left Paris, for it is at this point that we perceive, most clearly (and tragically), the lack of a voice of reason at court. The excitable young king, wishing for military glory, devoted to Clisson, and only lately recovered from his illness, refused to believe the duke, and, doubtless egged on by the constable, he called for an attack on Brittany. Louis of Orléans and the Marmousets seem to have supported the decision without dissent, but for the king to lead in person a punitive expedition of this kind without obtaining the counsel of all the princes was a momentous and possibly unprecedented action.[14]

The king's uncles considered it an insult that they had not been consulted,[15] but as the royal army began to assemble in July, Burgundy responded reluctantly to the summons. It appears that there was limited enthusiasm for the expedition among the northwestern nobles who had formed the backbone of the military leadership and the Marmousets' government. The accounts of the war treasurer for this campaign reveal a smaller number of the leading commanders of recent years and indicate many small contingents led by simple squires who had not been prominent as commanders in previous campaigns.[16] One has the impression that many had concluded that Pierre de Craon was no longer in Brittany. Charles VI, however, resisted all contrary advice and displayed a stubborn and almost obsessive attitude worthy of the constable himself. He is said to have been nervous and not sleeping well, urged by his doctors not to go on the campaign, and finally, by early August, exhibiting bizarre behavior.[17] The uncles (actually just Burgundy, since Berry was not present) are said to have kept in contact with John IV in case the mission could be terminated.[18]

The expedition duly proceeded, and on 5 August Charles VI led his forces out of Le Mans en route to Sablé, the former possession of Pierre de Craon that now, to the intense anger of the Marmouset government, was being held by the duke of Brittany.[19] Behind the Breton borders, John IV, again deserted by much of his nobility, was frantically shoring up his defenses and appealing for English aid, but it appeared that his luck had finally run out. In fact, however, his fortune was better than ever. In the forest outside Le Mans, the king of France, apparently succumbing to heat and excitement, went raving mad and killed several people before he could be restrained.[20] Brittany once again had escaped royal wrath, for Philip of Burgundy quickly took charge of matters, canceled the campaign, and quickly sent Enguerrand de Coucy and Guy de la Trémoille to inform John IV.[21]

Jacques d'Avout was not exaggerating when he called the onset of the king's mental illness "the essential event of French history in the last years of the fourteenth century."[22] One could argue that Charles VI was an unstable person who would have suffered a mental breakdown eventually and that nobody could have suppressed the princely feuds that would bedevil France in the coming decades. Nevertheless, the king's illness did appear first in August 1392 and nothing was the same thereafter. Charles actually recovered from this first attack by the fall, but subsequent bouts of serious mental illness or diminished capacity would increase in frequency and duration. Careful scholarship permits the historian to identify the king's periods of greater lucidity and more active participation in government, but it has recently been shown that the king's illness affected his reactions to people and events even when Charles was at his best.[23] Although the king's malady would have a disastrous effect on the French kingdom, it did not diminish the monarchy as an institution and symbol. As Autrand has noted, a population that had experienced half a century of afflictions found in Charles a beloved figure whose sufferings appeared to mirror their own.[24] As long as the king lived, everything had to be done in his name, and people were perhaps too quick to welcome his periods of apparent lucidity.

The surviving sources are not very helpful in establishing a precise sequence of events for the months that followed. For the moment, at least, the rule of the Marmousets was doomed. In his quick resumption of power, Philip the Bold easily brushed aside the twenty-year-old Louis of Orléans, and in doing so he may have inaugurated the celebrated hostility between uncle and nephew.[25] Louis appeared unwilling or unable to assert himself in defense of the regime he had lately supported. Philip's biographer has said that the "frivolity and impetuosity" of the duke of Orléans impeded him in any contest with his politically experienced uncle.[26] Applied to the early 1390s, this charge may be accurate, but Louis gradually acquired the self-confidence he lacked in 1392, and he could afford to bide his time, since his growing clientele included many lesser members of the old coalition, on whose loyalty he could depend in the future. It is possible that Philip acted immediately to remove Clisson from the government,[27] but aside from canceling the Breton expedition and attending to Charles VI, he appears to have deferred other important actions until the duke of Berry returned north in September. On the twenty-fifth of that month, the two dukes established a commission to review recent royal gifts and pensions.[28]

When the uncles did proceed against the Marmousets, they took selective action against a few leading figures who could be punished for advocating the Breton expedition. They were surely not alone in blaming this expedition for the king's mental illness and in questioning a major military decision that bypassed the princes and jeopardized the hard-won diplomatic achievements of recent months. The first prominent Marmouset actually to be arrested was Jean le Mercier, since La Rivière, Montaigu, and Villaines all left court when it appeared that the dukes were back in control.[29] The uncles pursued and arrested La Rivière, after which Villaines gave himself up.[30] In October, the crown halted the salaries and pensions of five Marmousets whom the uncles especially wished to punish—Olivier de Clisson, Pierre de Villaines, Jean le Mercier, Jean de Montaigu, and Jehannet d'Estouteville.[31]

Olivier de Clisson was a special case, for in addition to instigating the Breton expedition he was vulnerable to a second charge, that of corruption. Following his brush with death at the hands of Pierre de Craon, the constable had made a will. This document seems not to have survived, but it was widely reported that Clisson listed assets of 1.7 million francs in movables alone. Few could believe that he had come by such a sum honestly, and the uncles, who were always eager to get their hands on more money, were outraged that he possessed such wealth.[32] Chroniclers report an ugly confrontation with Philip of Burgundy after which the constable retired to the castle at Montl'héry. There he learned that a force had been sent to arrest him, so he departed hastily for his Breton stronghold of Josselin.[33] These events must have occurred while the duke of Berry was still absent, for a document places Clisson at Josselin on 13 September, just as Berry was returning to the Ile-de-France.[34] When royal emissaries arrived at Josselin, Clisson refused their summons to return and answer to charges before the king. On 19 December, in the royal presence, the Parlement stripped him of the office of constable, fined him one hundred thousand francs, and declared him banished.[35]

In the end, only three Marmousets—Clisson, La Rivière, and Le Mercier—remained permanently excluded from royal service. Villaines, Estouteville, and Montaigu all would reappear and even serve on the royal council.[36] Montaigu and Arnaud de Corbie would become the victims of another duke of Burgundy many years later when factional strife had become much more violent. Many of the reforms instituted by the Marmousets were allowed to remain in effect and many less visible Marmousets remained in office.[37] Although angry at their loss of power in 1388 and at the Breton expedition in 1392, the uncles had been able to work fairly effectively with the regime of 1388–92, especially in the diplomatic sphere.

They were not disinterested, but in contrast to Clisson's tenacious pursuit of personal grudges, they displayed enough common sense to place other considerations ahead of personal bitterness.

One modern historian has attributed the relatively light punishment of the Marmousets to the moderation of Philip the Bold.[38] Philip was indeed more moderate than his son would prove to be, but his actions in 1392 reflected political good sense rather than any innate capacity for moderation. He could not ignore the possibility that the coalition that had opposed him in 1387 and 1388 might recover from its disarray and coalesce once more into a formidable party. He could ill afford to create martyrs at a time when uncertainty about the king's health and future made it extremely difficult to know when a political decision would prove to be wise or hazardous. This uncertainty dominated the politics of late 1392. Would Charles VI recover, or die, or remain incoherent for a long time? Would events suddenly propel Louis of Orléans to the throne or regency? Some of the questions would be resolved by the summer of 1393, but it would be years before the uncertainty would be dispelled completely.

After spending several weeks at Le Mans, the king had been moved to Creil, north of Paris, where he spent the month of September under the care of various physicians.[39] Charles VI continued to recover and was back in Paris early in October.[40] It appears, however, that he showed no eagerness to dismiss the uncles or recall old advisers or get back to the serious business of government. His energy for politics seems to have been sapped, and he preferred to leave things as he found them, while enjoying himself at a succession of celebrations and balls.[41] The king would have another, more prolonged, psychotic episode between June 1393 and January 1394, but during the eight months preceding it he seemed fully recovered.[42] No outraged anti-Burgundian party arose to prod him back into a more active role, perhaps because of Burgundy's wisdom in proceeding against only a few isolated individuals. After the Parlement pronounced against Clisson on 19 December, Philippe d'Artois, count of Eu, became constable of France.[43]

In some of their major objectives—definitive peace with England, the ending of the schism, and a crusade—the government of the Marmousets had failed. Those among them who were ostentatious social climbers and suspiciously rich aroused a good deal of resentment. Yet they had given France a period of good government, particularly in the financial sphere, providing the king with reserves of money without burdening the populace with heavy *tailles*. As Autrand put it, they knew how to make the state supportable.[44] In their long years of service,[45] they were, in a real sense, the architects of the French state. Their fall from power returned authority to the princes who were the king's "natural" advisers and collaborators, and thus was less surprising than their triumph in 1388. Yet the dismissals were not reversed when the king recovered his senses in the autumn, and this fact invites further scrutiny.

The Marmousets had conducted affairs without much regard for special intersts, offending whomever they pleased and appearing to feel totally secure in their power. Yet most of them were not men who could afford to act arrogantly. They had two reasons for their sense of security: first, the support of a young, popular, and apparently healthy king and his brother who was heir to the throne until the queen bore sons; second, the cohesion of a regional nobility that provided most of the country's military leadership and had been able to topple the princes in 1388 with little active support from Charles VI or Louis. The summer of 1392 had dealt them two devastating blows. Obviously, the illness of the king, for which nobody was prepared, temporarily deprived them of their most valuable asset—the support of the monarch. Yet Louis of Orléans, as first prince of the blood the obvious person to take charge, might have resisted the uncles with the vigorous and concerted backing of Clisson and the military commanders. One finds no trace of any attempt at such resistance, and it is not enough merely to dismiss Louis as immature and frivolous. What was missing was that self-confident cohesion that had bound the military commanders and the rest of the Marmousets together in a politically significant bloc. This brings us to the other serious blow they received in 1392, the attack on Clisson and the government's response to it.

The previous attack on Clisson, his capture in 1387 by John IV, had been a clear-cut act by a magnate with a reputation for disloyalty whose action ruined a military campaign and directly challenged the monarchy and its military security. The action of Pierre de Craon, in some ways an even greater affront to the monarch, came from within the family, so to speak. Craon was Clisson's own cousin, related to many other members of the regional nobility that had sustained the Marmousets, and until quite recently a person of great influence at court and in the affairs of the princely houses (Anjou and Orléans) most closely associated with the northwestern aristocracy. A powerful hatred had triggered Craon's plot. Can the duke of Brittany have been his only friend and supporter, or was his bitterness towards the constable indicative of other divisions that weakened the cohesion of the northwestern nobility? Even if his attack has the totally unexpected action of an isolated individual, it can only have thrown this nobility into disarray.

What made things worse was the government's insistence that John of Brittany had to be punished. The January accords at Tours had been achieved with great difficulty and people surely expected them to resolve, or at least cool down, long-standing disputes that had divided Brittany for a generation, threatened the peace talks with England, and placed serious strains on society in northwestern France. Was the duke of Brittany clearly culpable as in 1387? Despite the council's suspicions, many must have doubted it. When respected figures raised strenuous objections to the campaign and the king and constable refused to listen to these opposing views, it was difficult to generate mass enthusiasm for the proposed punitive expedition. Such support was present in 1387–88, when the uncles with difficulty managed to avert it. The situation in 1392, however, could only raise the specter of 1379, when the stubbornly pursued royal policy towards Brittany had caused the Breton magnates to desert to the exiled duke. To overthrow the January accords was not a decision to be taken lightly when the duke's culpability was far from clear. The proposed expedition threatened to divide the regional aristocracy, and this political environment left no room for cohesive action to preserve or reinstate the authority of the Marmousets against Philip of Burgundy in the fall of 1392. Olivier de Clisson, who had kept the coalition together previously, was now an obstacle to cohesion because of the intensity of his feud with the Breton duke. The expedition so rudely interrupted at Le Mans was in a very real sense, his expedition,[46] and that he made no attempt to rally support against Philip suggests strongly that he knew his support was, on this occasion, rather slim.

For the first time since 1370, Olivier de Clisson was no longer a central figure in French political society. In the remaining fifteen years of his life, however, he remained a potent force in Breton politics. When the king's first psychotic episode led to his fall from power, the duke of Brittany seems to have acted very cautiously. Although Pintoin said that John made an unsuccessful attempt to arrest him when he first fled to Brittany,[47] we may doubt it. To guarantee payment of the eighty thousand francs he still owed Clisson, various ducal hostages were being held at Angers in accordance with the treaty of Tours. Clisson had received part of the money in July, at the very height of the recent crisis.[48] On 13 September 1392, he was negotiating with ducal representatives at Josselin over the completion of the payments and the release of the hostages.[49] In November Clisson's representatives and those of the duke were meeting again on this subject and discussing the hearth tax, to be managed by the Breton magnates, that was intended to raise the rest of the money owed to Clisson.[50] The details of this arrangement were announced on 6 February 1393.[51] Meanwhile, during the fall of 1392, the duke was also negotiating with representatives of Clisson's son-in-law, the count of Penthièvre, over the arrangements made at Tours to regulate their financial relations.[52]

Thus throughout the autumn we do not find an atmosphere of bitter conflict but rather one in which the parties seem to have been making an effort to implement the accords of Tours. The duke had reason to be cautious, for he had had a narrow escape. Now that the uncles were back in power, it was important to accommodate them. It was necessary for him to relinquish Sablé castle by reselling it to Marie of Blois, who clearly did not want him holding such a fortress in the heart of her county of Maine. John IV expressed his willingness to sell it on 26 October 1392,[53] but the transaction did not take place until 1394, when Marie empowered proctors to represent her in the spring,[54] while the duke acknowledged receiving payments in September and December.[55] With Clisson no longer constable, and at Josselin rather than in Paris or Pontorson, the duke no longer had the same use for Sablé. The threat of French invasion during the summer had also led John to pursue some hasty negotiations with England, this time with the possibility that he might sell his Breton rights to Richard II and retire to his estates in England.[56] When the king's madness saved him from the invasion, he was able to take a harder line with England, but he had to be sure that the improving health of Charles VI would not bring a return of the Marmousets.

When, in December, the Parlement acted against Clisson in the presence of an apparently recovered king, John IV could finally believe that his bitter enemy was finished as a leading royal adviser. By February of 1393, he was at war with Clisson and Penthièvre. John's supporters included some Breton lords who had served prominently in royal armies at an earlier time, but many nobles refused to help him, and his adversaries boasted considerable military and pecuniary resources.[57] Froissart reported that John IV shut himself up in Vannes and did not venture abroad for fear of being ambushed,[58] but his estimate of Clisson's popularity and the duke's unpopularity is clearly an exaggeration. The chronicler's evident sympathy for Clisson in this quarrel may be attributable to the influence of Clisson's good friend Enguerrand de Coucy, a longtime friend and informant of Froissart's.[59] There is, however, no reason to doubt that both sides were aided by outside supporters—the duchess of Burgundy sending assistance to John IV while Louis of Orléans supported the former constable.[60]

This seemingly interminable feud could still threaten, or at least complicate, the ongoing Anglo-French peace negotiations despite the changes in power at the French court in 1392. Towards the end of April, Philip of Burgundy wrote a revealing letter to the duke of Brittany, informing him of the progress in the negotiations and expressing his concern about rumors that John was planning to make a marriage alliance with the duke of Lancaster, who was the chief English negotiator at the peace talks. What really irritated Philip was that "especially for love of you and to please you, my said lord [king] discharged the lord of Clisson from the office of constable." According to Philip, John IV's representatives had assured him that if Clisson were removed Brittany would join in opposition to England.[61] It seems evident that the uncles had believed Clisson's feud with John IV to be the main reason for the duke's many dalliances with England and that the ouster of Clisson from the government would remove John's incentive to invite English intervention and thus eliminate an obstacle to peace. Now they were beginning to suspect what the Marmousets had been saying for years—that John IV was unreliable and that there was more to his flirtations with England than Clisson's influence at court.

The new Breton civil war featured raids, ambushes, and sieges, much like the earlier war of succession during which older men like Clisson had learned their military tactics, and contemporaries thought it particularly bloody and destructive.[62] John IV initiated the conflict in February and employed the recently returned Pierre de Craon in an engagement that he hoped might end it quickly—a surprise attack on Josselin castle. Having been warned, Clisson foiled the duke by slipping away to Moncontour, but he left his wife at Josselin. Her brother, the viscount of Rohan, intervened and got help from the duchess of Brittany in promoting a truce that would spare the fortress from capture.[63] In April 1393, the antagonists met and negotiated this truce, which required major concessions from Clisson and was to last for no more than two weeks.[64] It appears that Clisson evaded some of the provisions, and the war continued, reaching something of a stalemate. During the summer, the duke was complaining about Clisson's "damnable" military preparations,[65] and the former constable proceeded on nonmilitary fronts as well, bringing an action against John IV in the royal courts for violating the treaty of Tours. In September 1393, he was given until 2 February 1394 to get his case before the Parlement.[66]

In the first week of 1394, the contestants proclaimed another truce (explicitly excluding Pierre de Craon) that was to last for two months.[67] The king had now emerged from his second psychotic episode and felt well enough to make a pilgrimmage to Mont-Saint-Michel, close to the Breton border. He dispatched an embassy to John IV, composed of Bernard de la Tour, Hervé le Coich, and Louis Blanchet, a royal secretary. The duke treated these envoys rudely until some of his advisers prevailed upon him to moderate his tone.[68] He agreed to take advantage of the current truce and attempt to negotiate, naming proctors on 22 January who were empowered to discuss a number of specific issues with Clisson on the basis of the accords reached at Tours two years before.[69]

The duke of Brittany's position was beginning to erode in 1394. Having been denied the quick victory he expected when he first attacked Clisson at Josselin, he had hardly endeared himself to the French government with his harsh words for its envoys. One chronicler reported that the duke of Berry, long hostile to Clisson, now welcomed him back into his good graces,[70] but this claim is disputed.[71] In any case, the king canceled the judicial actions taken against Clisson thirteen months before[72] and also ordered that Le Mercier and La Rivière be released from prison.[73] When, in April, the uncles opened a second action against them,[74] it did not proceed, owing to organized support for the defendants, led in part by the duchess of Berry.[75] Besides these indications that his enemies were evading disgrace, John IV experienced another reversal when he lost possession of the often rebellious town of Saint-Malo, authority over which Clement VII conferred on the king of France in June.[76]

Having made no progress towards a peaceful settlement, the two sides resumed fighting. Months of bitter fighting in 1394 left neither side with significant gains, but left a trail of destruction and brutality.[77] At one point, Clisson captured and executed men who had been his jailers at the duke's castle seventeen years before.[78] John IV shifted his attacks to the county of Penthièvre, destroying La Roche-Derrien and fortifying the cathedral of Saint-Brieuc.[79] Having established his base at Moncontour, southeast of the town, Clisson invested Saint-Brieuc towards the end of June and used artillery to bombard the cathedral. Saint-Brieuc fell in about two weeks.[80] The duke then hastened to besiege the outnumbered Clisson, but Saint-Brieuc offered access to the sea. At this point the royal government intervened.[81]

Having obtained so little satisfaction from its earlier embassy to the duke, and now being determined to put an end to the strife in Brittany, the crown decided to turn to a royal prince.[82] On 2 July 1394, Charles VI placed Philip of Burgundy in charge of resolving the conflict, telling him to assemble John IV, John of Blois, and Olivier de Clisson and obtain a settlement that would address the concerns of the crown.[83] A month later, Philip ordered troops to Brittany to reinforce his position in dealing with the belligerents.[84] The royal complaints against him became known to John IV, whose first response was reminiscent of his conduct on other occasions: he said at the end of August that if he accepted any conditions that were contrary to his rights and liberties, it would be out of fear of the king and he would not be bound by the agreement.[85] He may have communicated these feelings to his old friend the duke of Berry, who wrote him a cautionary letter late in September, urging him to listen carefully to what Burgundy had to say.[86]

The crown's complaints against John IV (including many that were rather familiar) may be summarized as follows: the duke's failure to respond in Parlement to charges by the lady of Rais (as he had promised at Tours to do); his requirement of unconditional homage from the Breton magnates, to the prejudice of the king; the striking of unauthorized coinage by the duke; violation of the royal safeguard over Saint-Malo and royal sovereignty over Breton cathedral churches; wrongful Breton seizure of a royal sergeant carrying out a mission under the seal of the Châtelet of Paris; the seizure of Champtoceaux from Clisson in direct violation of the accord of 1388 and attacks on the possessions of Penthièvre in violation of the Tours accords of 1392; the assertion, by ducal representatives at Avignon, that Brittany was not part of the kingdom of France; the harboring in Brittany of fugitives from royal justice; the pillaging of the duke of Berry's subjects in Poitou; and the seizure of a royal officer bringing letters to Clisson and Penthièvre.[87]

In replying to these complaints on 3 October, John IV invoked the sovereignty and ancient customs of Brittany on all issues involving jurisdiction and the protection of churches. He claimed that some of his aggressive actions were justified, and he demanded the return of former Breton possessions in eastern France as well as Saint James de Beuvron in Normandy.[88] This entire exchange bore a resemblance to earlier exchanges of grievances in 1388 and 1392. What was different now was that John was dealing with a French government in which Olivier de Clisson did not play a role, and he no longer could argue that he was being victimized by the rancor of Clisson and the Marmousets. Philip of Burgundy was not merely the chief French negotiator in 1394; he was the dominant figure in the royal government that presented the grievances against the duke and also a longtime friend whose goodwill John could not afford to lose. Having spent most of October at Angers, Philip put additional pressure on the duke by advancing to Brittany.[89] From Ancenis, on 12 November, he sent John IV a safe conduct to come and negotiate with him.[90] After another exchange of views,[91] John finally agreed, on 24 November, to accept Philip as the mediator of his long dispute with Clisson and Penthièvre, "pour la grant confiance que nous avons en son grant sens, loyaute, et preudomie."[92] Three weeks later, he named proctors to represent him before the duke of Burgundy.[93]

Clisson and Penthièvre, for their part, told Philip that John IV had committed various violations of the Tours accords for which they wanted reparations and that they had appealed to the Parlement because litigants there were exempt from ducal jurisdiction and under royal safeguard. Specifically, the duke had seized without reasonable cause some of the lands set aside to provide the 8,000 *l.t.* promised to Penthièvre by the treaties of Guérande and Tours, for which the count had rendered homage as required by the king. The duke had rejected peaceful recourse to the king as required by the treaty of Tours, had taken La Roche-Derrien, besieged its castle, and refused to obey a royal embassy sent to halt his military actions. Clisson spoke of the large force sent against Josselin and the fact that he had been able to collect only around fourteen thousand francs from a hearth tax that was supposed to provide twenty thousand towards the unpaid portion of the hundred thousand francs the duke had been required to reimburse him since 1388. Never one to miss a chance to acquire mone money, the former constable also demanded reparations for the three hundred thousand francs' worth of damage he claimed the duke's forces had done in his lands and the three hundred thousand francs that it had cost him to maintain troops in the field for a four-month period.[94]

Burgundy expected to make his ruling by Christmas, but he postponed the date until 2 February because the king and council wanted to discuss the matter back in Paris.[95] Early in January 1395, Philip reported to the royal council, which debated the responses to the king that John IV had submitted in the fall.[96] It was on 24 January 1395 that Philip the Bold handed down his judgment. He ruled that John IV must stop impeding the count of Penthièvre's use and enjoyment of those properties assigned to him because of the 8,000 *l.t.* in revenues that were owed under the treaty of Guérande. One of these properties, La Guerche, would remain in the duke of Burgundy's custody at the expense of John IV, and both sides would appoint impartial commissioners to assess the value and revenues of the disputed lands. Another impartial commission would determine how much the duke still owed Clisson of the sum he had extorted in 1387. All ports and harbors in the lands of Clisson and Penthièvre would enjoy the same rights and ancient customs as in the past. All crimes and offenses committed by all parties during the recent war were pardoned and all legal actions canceled. All lands and prisoners were to be returned without ransom. On the issue of reparations, Burgundy ordered that a *fouage* of thirty *sols* per hearth be levied by his own appointees throughout Brittany, except in the lands set aside to furnish the eight thousand pounds to Penthièvre. The proceeds of this tax, payable in two installments, would be divided between the two parties. Clisson and John of Blois would henceforth obey the duke with their persons and their property without any appeals to the Parlement, where any current actions were to be quashed. Clisson would, however, be able to bring criminal charges against the duke or his officers by proctor. The accused would be exempt from responding in person for a specified number of years. In general, the treaties of Guérande and Tours were to be observed strictly; the contestants and their barons would swear an oath to this effect; and any future disagreements would come under royal jurisdiction.[97]

Two weeks after this judgment, John IV published the terms of the settlement and told the officers of the ducal administration that hostilities had ceased.[98] By mid-February his commanders were certifying the announcement of peace locally.[99] By the end of April, the two sides were arranging the exchange of prisoners.[100] During the month of May, John IV and the count of Penthièvre were discussing the transfer of lands that were to guarantee the count his promised income,[101] and early in June Clisson returned some lands that he had seized during the conflict.[102]

In spite of all these steps towards the implementation of Burgundy's judgment, more than four more months would pass before John IV and Olivier de Clisson concluded the agreement that really ended the conflict. The delay may have been caused by the work of those who were determining the revenues of various estates and ascertaining how much the duke still owed Clisson, but historians have tended to follow Froissart in describing a continuing guerrilla warfare. According to this narrative, the greater nobles still largely supported Clisson, the duke finally offered to send his son and heir to Josselin as a hostage, and Clisson was so moved by the gesture that he sent the boy back and became reconciled with John IV.[103] Whatever one makes of this story, the duke was at Redon on 19 October 1395 empowering representatives to treat with Clisson and John of Blois over the castellanies that would provide the count with the revenue of 8,000 *l.t.* that had been such a point of contention in the past.[104]

This action was merely a legal formality, for an agreement drawn up that very day in nearby Aucfer embodied the settlement of these matters.

According to this arrangement, the duke would not give up La Guerche and two other places that were to have been surrendered but offered the castellany of Châteaulin-sur-Treff and some additional revenue as substitutes. All parties also agreed on reciprocal pardons for acts of war and the return of lands taken during the conflict, while Clisson agreed that any litigation he undertook would be through proctors only.[105] This agreement at Aucfer thus went beyond the question of how to secure revenues for John of Blois and constituted an explicit acceptance by all parties of major provisions of the arbitration handed down by the duke of Burgundy nearly nine months earlier. Formal ratification of this settlement took place a week later, on 26 October,[106] and on that date Blois named and empowered a representative to take possession of Châteaulin.[107] The entire transaction was complete by the twenty-eighth,[108] and the long struggle was finally at an end.

As the final, military phase of his long feud with the duke of Brittany was coming to an end with the settlement of 1395, Olivier de Clisson's feud with Pierre de Craon, conducted in the royal courts, began to enter an intense new phase. In the last years of his life, the former constable would prove to be a tireless litigant. Having apparently fought against Clisson on behalf of John IV in 1393 and having been excluded from the truce of January 1394,[109] Craon had left Brittany at some point, but his whereabouts are uncertain for nearly two years. Later testimony in court indicated that he had made a pilgrimage to the Holy Sepulcher, possibly as a precondition for seeking a royal pardon.[110] In the fall of 1395, Craon received a royal safe-conduct for four months, which he spent at the abbey of Saint-Denis.[111] At the expiration of this period, on 26 January 1396, the king granted him a new safe-conduct that was to last for six months and be valid anywhere in the kingdom except Brittany, in order to give him an opportunity to reach an accord with Clisson.[112] Then on 4 March, the Parlement concluded the lengthy case brought against Craon by the duchess of Anjou five years earlier by declaring that he was guilty of embezzling money as Marie had charged. The duchess was empowered to recover the funds from his property holdings and he was condemned to perpetual banishment and the confiscation of his possessions.[113]

Having already been condemned to banishment and confiscation in 1392 for his attack on Clisson, Pierre de Craon now stood convicted of two serious crimes. The way was now clear for him to seek a royal pardon for these offenses, and one may suspect that work was proceeding on the pardon even before the second judgment against him. On 15 March, at a session of the royal council from which Louis of Orléans absented himself, the crown issued a letter of pardon for both crimes, treating the attack on Clisson as a private matter and not as a treasonous attack upon the holder of a major royal office. Noting that Clisson had not been killed or mutilated in the attack and that Craon had suffered considerable punishment already, the king pardoned him and lifted the banishments, subject, however, to a fine that the council would determine, plus whatever civil compensation might be adjudicated to the injured parties.[114]

A week later, on 22 March, Craon presented this letter to the Parlement to be recorded. He was joined by several of his accomplices in the attack on Clisson. Some important royal counsellors from the military aristocracy, such as Enguerrand de Coucy, Louis de Sancerre, the lord of Albret, and the baron of Ivry, were guarantors of his good behavior.[115] At this point, however, things began to go wrong for Craon, suggesting that another party was influencing the court. On 29 March, his distinguished guarantors asked to be relieved of their responsibilities and although Craon still had a valid royal safe-conduct, he and his accomplices were arrested and imprisoned. The king immediately ordered their release, but the court questioned the validity of the order and sent people to him to learn his true intentions.[116] Charles VI, who had experienced a psychotic episode between November and February but would not have another until February 1397,[117] asserted that he and his council had indeed commanded the release of the prisoners, and so the Parlement accepted the order but required that they remain in Paris.[118] Then, on 4 April, the court ordered them to appear for judgment.[119]

At this point, the king decided to visit the court in person, and on 10 April 1396, accompanied by the princes and the leading members of the council, Charles held a *lit de justice*—the ceremonial appearance of a king in his Parlement. Its purpose was to establish the fine that should be paid to the king in accordance with the letters of pardon, but after hearing various speakers, Charles agreed that the decision should be deferred until "justice soit bien informées" and the interested parties should have a chance to testify on "la verification de la dicte remission."[120] One of those present, Jean de Poupaincourt, would be Clisson's principal attorney.[121] Some months passed, doubtless so that the parties could prepare their cases. Then, on 17 August, they presented their positions to the court.[122]

The ensuing litigation revolved around the question of whether the letter of pardon should be accepted by the Parlement. After receiving testimony on several days in August and September,[123] the Parlement may have adjourned or granted a continuance, for nothing more was done until December, when the court heard considerable testimony and argument during the first three weeks of the month.[124] The lawyers representing Clisson and Marie of Blois argued that the royal pardon did not show reasonable cause and that important facts about Craon's plots had been wrongfully concealed from the king. They alleged further that his infidelity more than a dozen years before had caused the death of the duke of Anjou in Italy.[125] There was some question as to whether Craon had to respond in person to these allegations, but after granting him a brief delay the Parlement decided that he should do so. When he failed to appear, the court ordered him to surrender as a prisoner at the Châtelet within the hour or risk losing the benefits of his letter of remission.[126] He evidently did not comply with this order but still had powerful protectors. In May 1397 he was back before the Parlement with a new royal safe-conduct.[127]

Stymied in the French courts by the tenacious legal maneuvering of his enemies, Pierre de Craon turned to the king of England, who accepted his homage and granted him a pension in October 1398.[128] The case was decided to Clisson's satisfaction on 7 June 1399, when the Parlement ruled that Craon and his accomplices were guilty of *lèse majesté*, could not receive a royal pardon, and had to pay damages of 100,000 *l.t.* to Clisson and 200,000 *l.t.* to the duchess of Anjou.[129] Twice more, in November 1399[130] and February 1400,[131] the king issued him letters of pardon, but they were never accepted by the court. Although Craon lived on until 1409, without further punishment or imprisonment, Olivier de Clisson, having pursued the case with great tenacity, had achieved his goal of assuring that his attacker owed him reparations and never received a valid royal pardon.[132]

II

From Marmousets to Orleanists

THE EVENTS OF 1392 REMOVED Olivier de Clisson from the center to the periphery of French political society, but many of his associates in the Marmouset government remained influential. Clisson's ties to the duke of Orléans and the northwestern military elite, while weaker after 1392, were far from being obliterated. The political rivalries that continued to plague the monarchy of Charles VI had deep roots, and the emerging struggle between the dukes of Orleans and Burgundy was very much a legacy of the political society in which Clisson had played a central role. His disgrace had weakened the link between the two elements that had sustained the Marmouset regime—the military commanders and the legal/financial officers, but both played a role in the princely rivalries, at least until the political scenery underwent changes in the last three years of Clisson's life.

The French political conflicts between 1392 and 1407 extended far beyond the borders of France and our purpose here is not to attempt a comprehensive analysis of the issues, but to suggest how the Orleanist party drew upon the legacy of the Marmousets and yet evolved into something quite different. One issue of paramount importance for contemporaries will receive only brief treatment here—the effort to resolve the Great Schism in the church. The schism continually preoccupied the king, the princes, and especially the prelates, the University of Paris, and the ecclesiastical chroniclers of the period. Yet the Marmousets, who bore considerable responsibility for the schism, did not display great interest in resolving it except on terms completely satisfactory to Clement VII and in conjunction with other projects. Clisson and his fellow military commanders seemed interested in the problem of the schism only when a military solution was contemplated. Our focus will be on those other issues that had been of interest to the Marmousets and would continue to create deep divisions in French political society. These issues were military, financial, and diplomatic in character. In a general sense, they bore upon the nature of royal power and the emerging French state, but as in previous years they would be defined to a large extent by the ambitions and animosities of a few powerful individuals.

Of these important players, the one who occupied the role of a color-less, if greedy, moderate was John, duke of Berry, now in his mid-fifties and the man most involved in the regular operations of government because of his fairly continuous residence in the Ile-de-France [1] while his brother and nephew performed on a larger political stage. Philip of Burgundy was the more powerful figure when he was present, but his commitments elsewhere often kept him away from court. The most controversial figure among the royal princes was Charles VI's brother Louis, the duke of Orléans. Eight years old at the death of Charles V, Louis was sixteen when the Marmou-sets took control of the government and, as we have seen, his political career gradually took shape from that point onward. Like his brother, Louis had been close to the constable, but we have seen that he did not try to rally support for the Marmousets against the uncles in the crisis of 1392, probably because the events of that year damaged the cohesion that would have been necessary for the northwestern military class to unite under his leadership.[2] Louis confined himself to modest military aid in Brittany and to symbolic acts such as refusing to attend the Parlement that rendered judgment against Clisson in December 1392 or the meeting of the council that approved the letter of pardon for Pierre de Craon in 1396.[3]

The duke of Orléans has been compared to his uncle, Louis I of Anjou,[4] who was able, intelligent, and consumed by ambitions in Italy, while unpopular in France because he was associated with heavy taxation. The younger Louis was all of these things and also had a reputation for fri-volity and the pursuit of pleasure.[5] One must be wary of placing too much trust in the portrayal of the duke of Orléans by the chroniclers, who tended to have Burgundian sympathies and give Louis "bad press" for various rea-sons. One reason for his negative image was that his strong support for the popes at Avignon, especially Clement VII, while consistent with the poli-cies of the Marmousets, made him appear to be the prince least interested in ending the schism. He acquired a bad reputation in influential clerical circles, especially among theologians at the University of Paris, whom the dukes of Burgundy generally tried to cultivate.

A much more serious factor in his unfavorable image turned out to be his marriage to Valentina Visconti in 1389. This talented and culti-vated young woman had a strong sense of her rank,[6] and to some impor-tant personages at court she represented the wrong branch of the ruthless

TABLE 2.   The Valois Princes and the Counts of Armagnac.

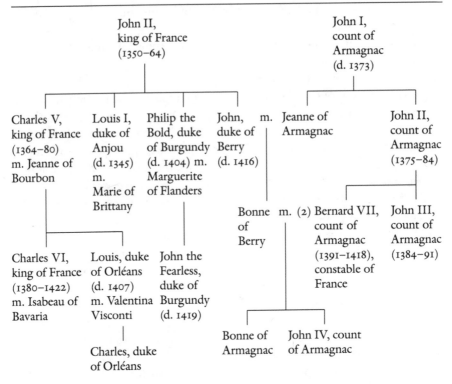

ruling family of Milan. Her father, Giangaleazzo, had gained undisputed authority there by murdering his uncle, Bernabo, whose children had married into such important families as the Wittelsbachs in the Empire and the Armagnacs in southwestern France. Giangaleazzo was a brother-in-law of the dukes of Berry and Burgundy, but two of Burgundy's children had married into the Holland-Hainault branch of the Wittelsbachs. Queen Isabeau came from the Bavarian branch of the same family, and her marriage to Charles VI owed a good deal to Burgundian encouragement. This influential Bavarian family, and those of the Valois who were connected to it, tended to maintain a strong hostility towards Giangaleazzo Visconti, his aggressive policies in Italy, and his daughter who had married a French prince. While Giangaleazzo might well have come into conflict with the pope had there been no schism, the fact that he was the principal enemy of the Roman popes inside Italy made him a potential ally of those supporting the Avignon obedience or wishing to acquire papal lands in Italy. The ambitions of Louis of Orléans, when they led to policies of cooperation with his father-in-law, were bound to find opponents at the French court.[7] Aside from the dynastic factor, the duke's Milanese marriage gave rise to hostile sentiments of a more xenophobic character. Valentina would not be the last Italian princess to have a high position at the French court and be suspected of having a baleful influence there. The rulers of Renaissance Italy had a reputation for ruthlessness and cruelty towards rivals and enemies and were believed to include in their arsenals such techniques as poisoning and the use of magic spells. The fourteenth century had been a time of many calamities including a good many instances of sudden (and sometimes unexplained) illness and death among prominent persons. Rumors of poisoning often circulated when royalty or other important people died suddenly. People often attributed misfortunes to satanic conspiracies or magic spells. There were stories associating Giangaleazzo and his daughter with such sinister practices. It did not require much imagination to suspect the workings of sorcery in the mental affliction of the king and to associate Louis of Orléans with the casting of spells. This was another way in which his Italian marriage had a negative effect on his image.[8]

Charles VI and Louis of Orléans had been very close as they grew up together. The king loved his brother and found it hard to refuse him anything, but the relationship had a sinister aspect in that when Charles had his first attack he made an attempt to kill Louis and apparently feared that his brother wished to kill him.[9] When he had recovered in October 1392, those close to the king evidently thought that it would help him to be diverted from affairs of state by balls and celebrations. Perhaps this idea was well-intentioned, but it has been attributed to the frivolous, pleasure-seeking natures of the duke of Orléans and the queen. Such behavior by people in high places generally earned the criticism of moralists, but a sensational and nearly tragic event late in January 1393 brought considerable blame and criticism upon Orléans. This was the incident of the *Bal des Ardents*, when the king and several young friends dressed as savages and covered themselves with a flammable substance that was ignited by a torch. Four people died in the ensuing fire and the king barely escaped.[10]

In November 1392, after recovering from his first psychotic attack, Charles VI had formally confirmed his father's ordinance of August 1374 regarding the royal succession and majority age.[11] His narrow escape in January now led him to make specific arrangements for the care of his children and the regency of the kingdom,[12] and these measures also recalled those of Charles V in 1374. The regency would fall to Louis of Orléans, subject to certain limitations on his authority, much as Charles V in 1374 had established Louis of Anjou as regent in the ordinance overthrown by Burgundy and the other uncles after the king's death in 1380. Perhaps Charles VI hoped to secure the agreement of all the princes in order to forestall a repetition of what had happened in 1380.[13] Michael Nordberg has suggested that the struggle for power between Burgundy and Orléans originated in this provision for a regent if the king should die leaving minor heirs. Louis could use the document as a basis for exercising power during the king's incapacity as well, making it easier for him to appoint his partisans to office.[14]

Nordberg's analysis is not entirely satisfactory. For one thing, the duke was joined by the queen and the three uncles in governing the realm when the king was incapacitated,[15] so the real power depended on who happened to be present when the king was unable to act. Moreover, the undeniable preponderance of Orleanists in governmental positions,[16] which persisted until after the death of the duke of Orléans, can be explained in a different way. During the period of Marmouset rule, Louis had enlarged his household, granting positions, often ceremonial in nature, to many of the Marmousets and northwestern military commanders. He and the king heaped gifts and honors upon royal officials.[17] In effect, Louis had acquired ties to many of the more experienced people in the administration, men who were already in royal service. They formed the core of his following, not people that Louis planted in key positions. Had Philip the Bold wished to purge the government of Orleanists, as his son would later attempt to do, he would have had to dismiss scores of the king's most loyal, trusted, and experienced officials, something he was in no position to do in the 1390s and was doubtless too politic to attempt. Yet insofar as the royal administration was staffed by people loyal to the earlier tradition of the Marmousets and now linked to Orléans, we can understand why some historians have found the seeds of the future power struggle in the overthrow of the Marmousets in 1392.[18] Personal animosities also remained politically important, just as they had been during Olivier de Clisson's years in power. The duchesses of Burgundy and Orléans squabbled over precedence at court,[19] and neither the queen nor the duchess of Burgundy could conceal their hostility for Valentina's branch of the Visconti.

For a few brief years during the ascendancy of the Marmousets, before the English blocked the planned Italian expedition of 1391, French foreign policy had the support of all parties because it addressed the ambitions of the princes and accommodated other objectives as well.[20] Having once decided against intervention in Italy, however, the crown could no longer harnass princely ambitions together in a common policy. Philip of Burgundy remained, as always, largely concerned with solidifying his base in the Netherlands. That Louis of Orléans had ambitions in Italy did not bother him at all,[21] unless it conflicted with French royal policy on the schism, hurt the interests of his Flemish subjects, or entailed collaborations with Giangaleazzo that made the ire of his Bavarian allies impossible to ignore. In the middle 1390s, Philip was far too concerned with getting peace with England and peace in Brittany to be seriously concerned about the Italian schemes of his nephew.

For a few years, therefore, Orleanist Italian adventures can be seen as a sort of sideshow, keeping busy many former supporters of the Marmousets without jeopardizing the interests Philip considered vital. The duke of Orléans had a foothold in Italy in the county of Asti, which had come to him as Valentina's dowry. He would need Milanese cooperation if he were to pursue the dream of winning an Italian kingdom of Adria, the bait that Clement VII still dangled to attract military support from a French prince. Louis found a pretext for intervening in Italy when a disputed election for the doge of Genoa in 1392 was followed by a revolt of Savona against the Genoese. The king of France received an invitation to extend his suzerainty over Genoa.[22]

Charles VI agreed to this proposal,[23] but it was Louis of Orléans who first intervened there, in June 1393. Historians differ as to whether it was his initiative after Charles VI refused to go further, or whether Louis was acting on the king's behalf during the king's psychotic episode, but in any case his possession of Asti gave him a convenient vantage point for action.[24] The following months were filled with complicated maneuvering among the Genoese factions (who wished either to crush their rivals or to achieve civic stability), the pope (who hoped French forces could finally install him at Rome), Giangaleazzo Visconti (who hoped French arms might break the power of those who opposed his expansion in Italy), and Orléans, who still dreamed of an Italian kingdom. In February 1394, Louis sent two of his chamberlains, Jean de Garencières and Jean de Fontaines, to Italy with a small force.[25] By May they reached an alliance with one of the Genoese factions,[26] and in June Garencières was back in Paris to report on the situation.[27] Louis then appointed another old Marmouset, Enguerrand de Coucy, his lieutenant in Italy on 8 July.[28] Coucy left Avignon on 4 September, reached Asti on the twenty-second, and gained some dubious reinforcements from the remnants of the *routiers* who had accompanied the count of Armagnac to Italy three years before. He secured the submission of Savona and then proceeded against the hostile faction in Genoa.[29] The Florentines, who were understandably wary of all this activity by the agents of Giangaleazzo's son-in-law, indicated that they would not oppose French action against Genoa.[30]

This intervention in Italy had been discouraged or encouraged by the French government in accordance with current royal policy on the schism, which in turn was influenced by the state of the Anglo-French peace talks. Having tended to support the use of force to bring Clement VII to Rome, Charles VI's government changed course early in 1394, when peace with England appeared imminent, and established a commission to study all possible ways to end the schism. In the summer of 1394, when Coucy and his troops were dispatched to Italy, the English peace talks had collapsed and the crown had resumed its old policy on the schism. In September, however, events occurred that caused the French government to give up, once and for all, the policy of using force to gain victory for the Avignon obedience. Clement VII died and the cardinals at Avignon elected Pedro de Luna pope as Benedict XIII, to the consternation of the French court.[31]

The death of Clement, coming at the very beginning of Coucy's expedition, effectively ended the scheme for an Italian kingdom of Adria for Louis of Orléans.[32] There remained the possibility of carving out a principality along the Ligurian coast, but Avout has suggested that Genoese commercial ties with Burgundy's Flemish subjects made Philip the Bold oppose any plan that would place Orléans in control of that city.[33] This view presupposes the existence of a significant rivalry between Louis and his uncle by this date. Nordberg, by contrast, has insisted that there was as yet no evidence of any antagonism between the two dukes and that the Genoese project was, from the first, a royal one.[34] In some respects, Nordberg is correct, but in reacting against the orientation of Avout he has surely overstated his case. For years Louis had been on good terms with Burgundy's opponents; his ties with Giangaleazzo were resented by people close to Philip; and his position as potential regent of France made him a threat. While the intervention in Genoa nominally may have been a royal project, it cost Louis a great deal of money. The crown had furnished him with two thousand francs in 1393,[35] then, in March 1394, granted (or regranted) him some properties taken from Pierre de Craon,[36] and finally added the county of Angoulême and another four thousand francs in income in October 1394.[37] Yet his finances were so strained by the Italian campaign[38] that by early 1395 he had to pawn his valuables to support

Coucy's expedition. He extricated himself financially only by ceding to the crown his interests in Genoa for three hundred thousand francs.[39]

His nephew's interest in Italy had served Philip well, diverting Louis from other projects that the uncles deemed important and wanted to control. It provided distant employment for Coucy and other military men who had buttressed the Marmouset regime and had close ties to Olivier de Clisson. Philip the Bold's settlement in Brittany and the closely related peace negotiations with England could be managed with little interference from the Marmousets. As it was, these projects were difficult enough, as we have seen in the case of Brittany. Philip continued to draw handsome stipends for his services as chief negotiator with England,[40] and in June of 1393 he managed to conclude a provisional treaty. It was to have been sealed at a personal meeting between the two kings, but Charles VI's second psychotic attack forced a postponement, and it would last for seven months. In March 1394, the dukes of Berry, Burgundy, Lancaster, and York resumed negotiations that lasted for two months and, once again, were to culminate in a meeting of Charles and Richard to conclude the treaty. The proposed settlement was based on a principle that had been under discussion for nearly twenty years—the political separation of Aquitaine from England. The plan, in this case, was for Aquitaine to become the duke of Lancaster's hereditary duchy.[41]

This time, the proposed treaty was scuttled by a revolt in Gascony, where there was little enthusiasm for an Anglo-French peace and strong opposition to the idea of a resident duke. While John of Gaunt prepared an expedition to assert his control of the duchy, Richard II embarked on a campaign in Ireland.[42] It was in this context that the French crown abandoned its recent conciliatory position on the schism and endorsed Coucy's expedition to Italy. In Aquitaine Lancaster had to accept a settlement that failed to achieve the separation from England required by the Anglo-French agreement. Meanwhile, the death of Richard II's queen had produced another complication, leaving him at least temporarily without the prospect of an heir and causing him to begin shopping for a wife. He cast his eye on Spain, where the English already had established marital connections, and decided to pursue the hand of Yolanda of Aragon, the fiancée of Louis II of Anjou. The French were much disturbed at the possible consequences of such a union, and in April 1395 they sent an embassy to Richard in Ireland, offering him a daughter of Charles VI. He immediately halted his campaign, returned to England, and responded to the French in July by making exorbitant demands to drive up the price of a settlement. His ambassadors returned to Paris in January 1396, and on 9 March the bargain was struck—not a treaty of peace, but a twenty-eight-year extension of the current truce, to last until September 1426. Richard II agreed to marry Charles VI's young daughter Isabelle, and he did so on 4 November.[43] The long-awaited peace had been achieved at last. Despite the lack of a definitive settlement, the extended truce was expected to last for a generation, and the marriage bound together two kings who had considerable goodwill towards one another.

Having secured the best that could be hoped for in negotiations with England, the royal government moved quickly to undercut Louis of Orléans, assuming a royal protectorate over Genoa[44] and making treaties with Florence against his father-in-law, the duke of Milan.[45] Valentina, the duchess of Orléans, was forced to leave the royal court, and while Louis received more financial concessions,[46] it seems clear that his opponents had been waiting only for an arrangement with England before exerting their power against him.

One strong advocate of the Anglo-French peace and the marriage alliance that made it possible was Philippe de Mézières. This former tutor of Charles VI had exerted an important influence on the Marmousets and was a respected figure known as a longtime advocate of a crusade against the Muslims.[47] As the Ottoman Turks advanced in the Balkans during the 1390s, crusading talk had grown in intensity and had become a part of the Anglo-French peace negotiations. After the talks had broken down in 1394–95, the crusading plans still went ahead. The original plan had been for the dukes of Burgundy, Lancaster, and Orléans to lead an expedition to assist the king of Hungary, Sigismund of Luxembourg. When various delays precluded a campaign in 1395, it appears that Sigismund himself was at fault.[48] When the fateful campaign took place in 1396, it lacked the seasoned princely leadership that had been discussed previously. Leader of the now largely French crusade was Philip of Burgundy's son, John, count of Nevers, a young man in his mid-twenties with little experience as a warrior. He was accompanied by some of the most distinguished military commanders of the previous generation, men like Enguerrand de Coucy, Jean de Vienne, and the constable Philippe d'Artois. Many of these veterans had been central figures in the successful campaigns of Charles V's reign and were part of that military establishment, led by Olivier de Clisson, which had supported the Marmousets. The count of Nevers was more ready to listen to the younger knights who placed glory ahead of caution. As is well known, the crusaders refused to accept the tactical suggestions of Sigismund, allowed themselves to be led into an ambush, and suffered defeat and massacre in the battle of Nicopolis on 25 September 1396.[49]

The battle of Nicopolis was a disastrous blow for the old Marmouset party in that it wiped out an important group of Charles V's veteran leaders. Coming in the same year as the humiliations of Orléans and his wife described above, it can be seen as something of a turning point in the process whereby the remaining Marmousets became Orleanists and the Orleanists became a party actively opposed to the policies of Philip of Burgundy. One part of the process was a renewal of ties between Louis of Orléans and Olivier de Clisson. For several years after 1392 we have little evidence of contacts between the two men. Louis had sent a small force to fight on his side in Brittany,[50] and in February 1395 the duke sent horses as gifts to Clisson and his friend the lord of Beaumanoir.[51] In 1397, when collections of military pay orders and receipts show a sharp increase in activity on the part of Louis of Orléans,[52] the duke paid a trusted member of his household, Enguerrand de Marcoignet, for taking a message to Clisson in Brittany during February.[53] By 18 October, he and the former constable had concluded a pact of mutual support against all enemies except the king and dauphin.[54]

The carnage at Nicopolis made necessary changes in the royal military administration, and the veteran Louis de Sancerre, who got along with all factions, was promoted to constable.[55] The factions were becoming more evident in 1397, as the increasingly open rivalry between the duke of Burgundy and the Orléans-Marmouset party grew in intensity. Looking ahead to the violent hostilities that occurred after Philip's death, Pocquet has said that their mutual courtesy kept Louis and Philip from letting their rivalry get out of control.[56] Nevertheless, the differences escalated after 1396 for a number of possible reasons. Increasingly, the princes were in competition for royal revenues that may have been insufficient to satisfy them both.[57] Another factor must have been the rude treatment of the duke and duchess of Orléans by the anti-Visconti faction in 1396. Then too, the decimation of the veteran military leaders at Nicopolis had weakened the party that had previously opposed Philip, perhaps persuading the duke of Burgundy that he could proceed against his opponents with less moderation than he had employed in 1392. Of great importance, however, was the reorientation of the foreign ambitions of the duke of Orléans. Now thwarted in Italy, Louis turned his attention towards the northeast, a region that Burgundy considered his own sphere of influence.[58]

Why should Louis have provoked his uncle by challenging him in this

geographical region? It was an opportunity to strike back at the Wittelsbachs, whose influence at the French court was responsible for the hostility
to Milan and the banishment of Valentina. In March 1398, Orléans made
an alliance with the emperor Wenceslas that was directed against the duke
of Burgundy and the house of Bavaria.[59] He had spent much of 1397 negotiating with Wenceslas,[60] and the treaty had followed a meeting between
the emperor and Charles VI at Reims.[61] Louis was dominant at the French
court in these first months of 1398 when Burgundy was absent in his own
lands.[62] The official purpose of the royal summit conference was to co-
ordinate efforts to end the schism by getting both popes to resign, but
the meeting had its tragicomic aspects: at a time when Europe required
outstanding leadership to bring an end to the schism, the emperor was
a notorious alcoholic and the king of France mentally ill. Their meeting
at Reims could not produce a decisive breakthrough in dealing with the
schism.

By May 1398, Philip of Burgundy was back at the royal court, where
he would remain for nearly a year.[63] His presence curtailed the influence
of Orléans and enabled the duke of Berry to push for more aggressive actions to deal with the schism. During the summer, the French government
took the controversial and unilateral action of announcing the "subtraction
of obedience," removing the French church from the authority of Benedict XIII in hopes of forcing him to accept the concept of mutual resigna-
tions to end the Schism. Louis of Orléans neither participated in this action
nor supported it.[64] The policy had its flaws and would not achieved the
hoped-for results, but one has the impression that Orléans was not terribly
interested in the religious issues and was more concerned with frustrating
his uncles than in promoting another constructive solution to the Schism.

A series of events in 1399 and 1400 continued to punctuate the esca-
lating ducal rivalry. Louis made an alliance with Henry of Lancaster, the
exiled first cousin of Richard II. This treaty was to have force only while
England and France were at peace and it was not directed against either
king, but it could only be perceived by Richard II as an unfriendly act.[65]
It helped to destabilize his regime and, when Henry shortly returned to
England and overthrew Richard, the Anglo-French peace so laboriously
negotiated by the uncles earlier in the 1390s was placed in grave jeopardy.
Charles VI's daughter no longer was queen of England. Another important event of 1399 was the death of John IV of Brittany at the beginning
of November.[66] Philip of Burgundy was in nearby Normandy during that
autumn,[67] so there was no opportunity for Orléans and Clisson to exploit

the Breton situation for profit, despite rumors in Brittany that they were up to something.[68] The duke of Orléans then received a serious setback in August 1400 when the princes of the empire deposed his ally Wenceslas and replaced him with Rupert of Bavaria, a member of the Wittelsbach family. The Luxembourg-Wittelsbach rivalry in the empire was far from over and would continue to parallel that of Orléans and Burgundy in France.[69]

In virtually every political situation that came up after 1396, the dukes of Orléans and Burgundy were on opposing sides. Philip, who was accustomed to a leading role in the royal government, did not neglect his interests in the Low Countries, of course, but he still attempted to maintain a set of coherent royal policies geared to the needs of the kingdom. Louis, however, appears to have been largely reactive when he was in the ascendancy at court, seeking primarily to obstruct the projects of his rivals as he did in opposing the subtraction of obedience in 1398. The behavior of the duke of Orléans at the level of royal policy bears some resemblance to that of Olivier de Clisson in the royal courts during the same period, when Clisson's primary objective was to prevent Pierre de Craon from receiving a valid pardon. One would like to know a great deal more about the relations between Orléans and Clisson after their alliance of October 1397. The aging Breton warrior had been the young duke's boyhood hero. Was he now becoming a true role model? Clisson's most striking characteristics had been his unrelenting persistence in bearing grudges and his equally persistent approach to the accumulation of wealth. Louis of Orléans had shown signs of possessing the first of these traits in his reaction against the anti-Visconti influences at court. Now he began to display the second trait as well, and his acquisitiveness would assume such proportions as to draw the princes to the brink of war.

Louis did not possess a very prosperous *apanage*. He seems to have been in some financial difficulty from the time of his Italian project in 1394–95, and he had found it necessary to borrow twenty thousand francs from his friend Clisson.[70] In June of 1399, after Philip of Burgundy had left the royal court for five months,[71] Louis secured from the king a declaration that he and his heirs would hold all their lands in France as peerages in the same manner as they held the *apanage* of Orléans.[72] The king subsequently granted Louis the town of Château-Thierry (1400) and the county of Dreux (1401).[73]

To achieve major improvements in his financial situation, however, Louis of Orleans required access to the royal fiscal structure. The Marmousets, it will be recalled, had achieved important gains in the sphere of royal

finance, reducing expenditures and avoiding the imposition of extraordinary *tailles*. The uncles had not immediately returned to the unpopular
policies of the past, but the marriage of the king's daughter with a large
dowry in 1396 justified a traditional feudal aid, and the crown imposed
a *taille* for this purpose. It was this tax that Orléans was allowed to retain when it was collected in his own lands.[74] A year later, there had been
another *taille* for the "needs of Christendom."[75] The resumption of these
extraordinary taxes and the apparently growing expenses of royal and ducal
households gave a renewed importance to those officials who administered
the king's revenues from taxation—the counsellors-general of the aids. It
was this body of three to six men that had exerted great authority in the
reign of Charles V when tax revenues were the vital cog in the French war
effort.[76]

Louis of Orléans now resolved to exert as much influence as possible
on the counsellors-general. The financial administration, always something
of a Marmouset stronghold, doubtless had some ties to the duke in years
past, but these increased towards the end of the century. Charles VI appointed four new counsellors-general in 1399[77] and another fourteen over
the next eight years. Nordberg concluded that eleven of these eighteen
appointees were Orleanists and only four were identified Burgundian sym-
pathizers.[78] In October 1401, Charles VI created an unfortunate precedent
by appointing his cousin Charles, lord of Albret, to the new position of
president of the counsellors-general.[79] Albret was an Orleanist, as were
two other important royal appointees—Jean de Montaigu (grand master
of the royal household) and Guillaume de Tignonville (provost of Paris).[80]
The duke of Burgundy had been absent from court since late June,[81] and
Louis enjoyed preponderant influence. At the beginning of August he had
interfered in the effort to put pressure on Benedict XIII and had gotten
the king to give him the *garde* of the Pope.[82]

It was, however, the evidence of Orleanist influence over the counsellors-general that seems to have triggered the aggressive Burgundian
response of 1401. Philip wrote a letter to the Parlement in late October, im-
plying that the kingdom's resources were being mismanaged.[83] He began
to make military preparations and Orléans responded by summoning his
own supporters, who included a number of important northwestern military commanders.[84] Early in December, Burgundy marched on Paris with a
force of more than six hundred men. A civil war seemed imminent, but the
other two royal uncles moved hastily to negotiate a settlement and secured
a truce early in January 1402.[85] This reconciliation, in which the queen and

the duke of Anjou also participated, took place in the presence of a royal council that was about half Orleanist in composition.[86]

Neither the Burgundian military demonstration nor the subsequent reconciliation deflected Louis of Orléans from his quest for greater financial resources. In February 1402, he prevailed upon the king to launch an inquiry into whether his *apanage* was inferior to those of the uncles.[87] Then, when Burgundy returned to his own lands for several weeks in the spring, Louis got himself appointed sovereign governor of the aids, a position that gave him authority over the counsellors-general.[88] He promptly ordered the levy of a very large *taille* that was to be levied on the clergy as well as the laity. This action, which could not be justified by some special royal need like previous taxes of this sort and was consequently very unpopular, brought Burgundy back to the vicinity of Paris, where he was able to pose as a defender of the fiscally oppressed.[89] Charles VI responded in June by granting Philip the same status as Louis, making him co-sovereign of the aids. It was not an action calculated to halt princely plundering of royal resources, but the king, who may have perceived that his uncle could be mollified by a share of the proceeds, did achieve a new reconciliation between the rival dukes.[90] As late as October, Charles d'Albret also continued to have a role in the financial administration,[91] but after the death of Louis de Sancerre he was named constable of France on 6 February 1403, so another key position was staffed by an Orleanist.[92]

No royal action was able to bring about an enduring reconciliation. Louis had consistently tried to undermine the uncles' policy on the schism as the subtraction of obedience became less popular, and he would eventually induce the king to abandon this strategy.[93] In August 1402, he issued a defiance to Henry IV of England in hopes of attracting to his following the anti-English element in France.[94] Around the same time, he escalated the conflict with Philip by purchasing Luxembourg from Jost of Moravia, the brother of Wenceslas. The cost was paid largely out of French royal taxes.[95] Louis now had a northeastern bastion close to Burgundy's Netherland possessions, but it was vulnerable to attack by Rupert. The princely conflict now returned to Brittany, whose dowager duchess concluded a proxy marriage with Henry IV and prepared to leave for England. It was imperative that her young sons not accompany her and highly desirable that they be placed under the tutelage of a regent acceptable to the French government. Louis induced Charles VI to nominate Olivier de Clisson as regent of Brittany, but as we shall see, Philip the Bold's political maneuvering led the Bretons to reject Clisson and accept Burgundy himself as regent.[96] This political success, however, entailed a rather substantial expenditure of Burgundian resources,[97] which may have increased his sensitivity to the question of royal finances.

Thwarted in his hopes of having an Orleanist control Brittany, Louis faced another challenge when his father-in-law died (also in 1402). Fearing that Rupert might attack Milan, Orléans began making preparations in the spring of 1403 for his own expedition to Italy.[98] In May 1403, he won a political success when the royal government agreed to return to the obedience of the Avignon pope, Benedict XIII.[99] The five-year experiment with refusing obedience had created hardship and discontent within the French church without forcing Benedict to resign. Having become reconciled with Benedict, Charles VI asked Louis to meet with him, and the duke and pope held extensive discussions at Tarascon late in the year. As the Orleanist army was assembling in the vicinity for its march on Italy, there were rumors that Louis was reviving the old French plan for ending the schism by force and perhaps even pursuing the imperial crown.[100] In fact, he never did cross the Alps with his forces, and he did induce Benedict to withdraw his stated objections to ending the schism by the *voie de cession* and to agree in principle to convening a general council to reunify the Church.[101]

While Louis had prevailed over the uncles on the issue of French royal policy towards the schism, his position at court suffered damage during the spring of 1403. New royal ordinances overthrew the rules for a regency set up in 1393 and declared that in the event of the king's death the heir would be crowned immediately and no individual of the royal lineage would have custody of the kingdom in his name, while during the king's "absences" (psychotic episodes), the queen, the dukes, the constable, and the chancellor would govern jointly.[102] These enactments left Louis without any basis for asserting his role as first prince of the blood when the king was incapacitated. Since this royal action closely resembled what the uncles had done in 1380 to the rules for a regency set up by Charles V in 1374, it is easy to believe, as Nordberg did, that the uncles were behind the action.[103] R. C. Famiglietti, however, questions their involvement and believes it was the king's own idea to make the change.[104] Adding insult to injury, Philip of Burgundy got the king to agree to marriages of royal children to members of the Burgundian family rather than the house of Orléans.[105] What is not at all clear, of course, is how much real standing any of these actions had. The king's mental illness had now reached the point at which he might issue conflicting orders within a few days of each other according to who had access to him.[106]

What does remain certain is that Louis of Orléans still had a strong power base. The military commanders who were under his banner in the fall of 1403 included names that had been prominent in royal service for many years—Mornay, Harcourt, Gaucourt, Mauny, Garencières, and Le Bouteiller.[107] Such men had been a force in French politics since the days of the Marmousets, and Louis had comparable support in such bodies as the counsellors-general and the Chamber of Accounts. Whether or not the new ordinances on the succession remained in force, it seems clear that Burgundy had not succeeded in dislodging Orléans from his position of influence.[108]

In any event, Philip the Bold died in April 1404. His successor, John the Fearless, was considerably less popular with the queen and the duke of Berry, and except for a few days at court in September and three weeks the following February, he was occupied in the Burgundian lands until mid-August 1405.[109] Orléans was at last the unchallenged princely influence at the royal court, and he gained vast authority in the financial sphere, an authority that many thought he abused.[110] While Louis had the charm, talent, and influence to prevail at court, his rival, who lacked the attributes prized by courtly society, was far more adept at reading the mood of the clergy, intellectuals, and bourgeoisie.[111] In August 1405, John and his brothers assembled an army, sent the king a protest over the mismanagement of the kingdom,[112] then marched on Paris and entered the city in triumph. Orléans and the queen had left the city, but Burgundy sent troops to force the return of the young dauphin who had attempted to follow them.[113] This aggressive Burgundian action quickly elevated the princely rivalry to a new level of hostility. Peace was not restored until October,[114] but when it occurred it left Orléans as before in control of the king's finances and in a position to enrich himself considerably while cutting off most of the royal funds going to John the Fearless.[115] Burgundian demands for reform found support from the University, and in November Jean Gerson gave his famous oration *Vivat Rex*, attacking the government.[116] Writings criticizing the court or describing the ideal ruler became more common in the first two decades of the fifteenth century, as other prominent intellectuals besides Gerson contributed to the "mirror of princes" tradition in political literature.[117]

Despite their growing support from reformers, successive dukes of Burgundy had now failed twice to achieve lasting results with military demonstrations against Louis of Orléans. In January 1406 Charles VI did substitute John's name for that of his late father in those ordinances governing the death or "absence" of the king,[118] but this gain for Burgundy did not affect the fact that Orleanists remained well-entrenched in the royal council, particularly among its ex officio members (the great officers of the crown). This unwieldy body had more than fifty appointed members in 1406, twenty-five of them being confirmed Orleanists. Of the rest, about half were Burgundian supporters. In the spring of 1407, when John the Fearless was absent, a reorganization of the council cut his strength even further. The new, streamlined council had twenty-six appointed members, no less than twenty of whom were Orleanists.[119] Feeling shut out of power at the royal court and threatened financially by the strength of the Orleanists, John the Fearless was not one to emulate his father's tact and diplomatic skill in dealing with political enemies. He decided to have his cousin killed, and after some delay his agents accomplished the deed on the night of 23 November 1407.[120]

The murder of the duke of Orléans in Paris was curiously reminiscent of Pierre de Craon's attempt to assassinate Clisson more than fifteen years before. It accelerated the disintegration of French political society and inaugurated a civil war that would not be resolved for a generation and would bring ruin upon France. Only thirty-five years old, Louis of Orléans had outlived his old friend Olivier de Clisson by just six months. Events in Brittany during the final years of the old constable's life would also have political reverberations well into the fifteenth century.

12

Clisson's Final Years: The Legacy of a Long Feud

THE DUKE OF BRITTANY had made peace with Olivier de Clisson under terms that were, essentially, dictated by the royal government and might have been unacceptable to John IV at an earlier date. By the fall of 1395, however, it was becoming increasingly clear that England and France again were engaged in serious peace negotiations, conclusion of which would leave John IV without much of his former political leverage. He remained extremely anxious to recover Brest and the county of Richmond from the English, and the French did not object to his continuing negotiations with the duke of Lancaster.[1] Only a month after his settlement with Clisson, John IV concluded an agreement whereby his daughter would marry Lancaster's grandson.[2]

As it happened, this alliance came too late to be of use to Brittany. The Gascon revolt and Lancaster's disappointing resolution of it had frustrated the earlier peace talks, and Richard II, who was now negotiating his own marriage alliance with France, disapproved of the Breton scheme. John IV's ability to exploit the marriage market was now limited and defined by the availability of royal princesses and the marital policies of the royal government.[3] The English, having concluded their long truce with France, were prepared to evacuate Brest for a price, and after considerable negotiation during the first half of 1397 the parties settled on a payment of 120,000 francs and named representatives who completed the transaction by the end of June.[4] The duke, as on similar occasions in the past, raised the money by means of a hearth tax, to which John of Blois contributed twelve thousand francs.[5]

Meanwhile, after the failure of his proposed marriage alliance with Lancaster, the duke did not have to search long for a new husband for his daughter Marie. Isabelle of France, now to be the bride of Richard II, had

been intended for John, count of Perche, the son of the count of Alençon and the holder of lands near the eastern frontier of Brittany. With the
count of Perche and Marie of Brittany having both become available, it
was not long before their fathers had arranged a contract for their marriage
(June 1396).[6] Another important marriage on the agenda of the aging duke
was that of his oldest son and heir, the future John V, who was seven years
old in 1396. With some display of reluctance, the duke had agreed at Tours
in 1392 to the betrothal of his son to another child, Charles VI's daughter
Jeanne. This promise had not inhibited him from dangling his son before
the English in subsequent negotiations with Richard II, but this game
could work two ways and the English had displayed interest in a marriage
involving Jeanne.[7] In the changed political atmosphere of 1396, marrying
his son to a daughter of France was the most attractive option available to
John IV, and a second betrothal took place in December 1396, followed by
the wedding in July 1397.[8]

Having completed these important alliances, John IV moved to liq-
uidate his other outstanding problems and secure the future of his duchy.
By the end of 1397, he had finally resolved the long dispute with the
crown over restitution of his ancestral lands in the counties of Nevers
and Rethel and was soon receiving royal payments as compensation for
these lands.[9] In August 1398, he concluded a treaty of alliance with his
brother-in-law, Charles III of Navarre, another prince whose political importance and capacity for independent action were diminished by the
Anglo-French peace.[10] In April 1399, another arbitration by the duke of
Burgundy helped settle the litigation arising from John IV's long dispute
with Jeanne Chabot, lady of Rais.[11] When the duke of Brittany died on
1 November 1399,[12] he had resolved many of the problems that had beset
his thirty-five-year reign and had left his duchy as secure as it could be,
given the limitations imposed by the minority of his sons.

There remained one major source of friction and acrimony in Brittany
—the behavior of ducal officers and their alleged violations of the rights of
other jurisdictions. Zealous officials committed to ducal sovereignty had
antagonized neighboring lords like the duke of Berry in Poitou and especially those Breton barons who opposed the steady growth of ducal power
at their expense. At Saint-Malo, the duke's officials had pushed the hostile bishop into a virtual rebellion that culminated in the transfer of this
strategic port city to the crown. The royal presence there, and the resul-
tant friction, created a new threat to John IV's claims to jurisdictional autonomy. When the bishop complained to the duke's court at Ploermel in

the spring of 1397, John IV ordered his seneschal there to make an inquiry into the truth of the bishop's allegations.[13] The bishop then complained to the king, and the government responded with a royal letter ordering the duke to restrain his officers.[14] Nobody was less likely to tolerate alleged excesses by ducal officers than Olivier de Clisson. It will be recalled that Philip of Burgundy, when he arbitrated the duke's quarrel with Clisson, had left the latter free to bring criminal charges in the royal courts against the duke's officials. Never one to shrink from an opportunity for profitable litigation, Clisson was soon bringing such charges. In this action he was joined not only by the count of Penthièvre but also by his other son-in-law, Alain de Rohan.

Jean I, the old viscount of Rohan, whose marriage connections to both Clisson and the duchess of Brittany had enabled him to maintain enough neutrality to be an occasional mediator in Breton disputes, had died at La Chèze late in 1395.[15] His son and successor, Alain VIII, having married Béatrix de Clisson, had become the constable's partisan, being one of the few Breton lords to march with the French in 1392.[16] In the spring of 1396, Alain negotiated with the duke a composition of three thousand francs in lieu of the traditional *droit de rachat*, along with a statement that this payment would not compromise Clisson's rights as count of Porhoët.[17] Under Alain, the important Rohan lordship became attached to Clisson's party and its legal maneuverings. In the winter of 1397–98, he entered complaints about ducal officers in the court of general pleas at Ploermel.[18] He took his grievances to the duke on 19 July[19] and 27 August 1398.[20] Then, in September, he appealed to the crown on grounds of denial of justice.[21] Perhaps this action followed the meeting of the Breton Estates at Rennes (9–17 September), although Rohan is not listed as one of those who were present.[22] Clisson, Penthièvre, and Rohan joined in an action against the duke in the Parlement of Paris, beginning the process on 20 March 1399, but with most of the serious pleading occurring on 10 and 11 April.[23] Their complaints covered a range of issues, but the bulk of them concerned the levy of various taxes by ducal officers.[24] On 4 September 1399, royal letters removed the three lords from ducal jurisdiction and declared that the Parlement would hear their appeal.[25]

It was this situation that confronted Jeanne of Navarre, John IV's widow, in November 1399. Jeanne had her own lawyer at the Parlement to respond to the appellants.[26] The barons of Brittany may have had their own differences with ducal officers and surely wished to avoid another royal intervention in the duchy. They urged Jeanne to reach an accommodation with Clisson and his powerful sons-in-law. The agreement was concluded on 3 January 1400 [27] and accepted by the Parlement three weeks later, bringing an end to the legal actions brought by the opposing parties. [28] Now that John IV had been succeeded by a ten-year-old heir, the issue of excesses by ducal officers receded in importance as Bretons had to concern themselves with the potential threat to the autonomy of the duchy. The royal government obliged the duchess by giving her several postponements of the homage she would have to render on behalf of the young John V, [29] but the intentions of both the Penthièvre party and the royal government were the subject of rumor and speculation.

The most intriguing story, from a later chronicler of generally Montfortist sympathies, concerned Clisson's daughter Marguerite, who supposedly asked her father to take advantage of the situation and advance the claims of her own children over those of young John V. The old constable is said to have rebuffed her so angrily that she fled from his presence and broke a leg falling down the stairs at Josselin castle. [30] Marguerite's subsequent behavior makes this tale plausible. With her husband now in his late fifties, her hopes and ambitions had come to reside in her young sons, for whose advantage she was quite prepared to reopen the family feud with the house of Montfort. Her sixty-three-year-old father, on the other hand, was now at last the duchy's most prestigious and powerful figure, with no good reason to desert the young duke and his mother, through whom he might exert great influence.

Another chronicler, whose sentiments most closely reflected those of the late duke's entourage, accused Clisson of plotting with Louis of Orléans to bring the duchy under royal control. [31] Several chroniclers said that Louis had assembled troops at Pontorson in hopes of escorting the young Breton princes back to Paris, but the barons of Brittany wanted to retain custody of young John V. [32] In fact, the French royal court was at this time in some disarray, having traveled to Normandy to escape an epidemic, and then having learned that Richard II, Charles VI's son-in-law, had lost his English throne. Louis of Orléans went to Pontorson (apparently without many troops) not to subvert Breton autonomy, but hoping to safeguard the young duke against possible English action in the duchy. [33] He and Clisson could not have executed a bold stroke in 1399 because Philip of Burgundy was alert to the situation and ready to prevent it. [34] Moreover, the evidence for this period points to entirely cordial relations between Clisson and the duchess of Brittany. They were in the process of negotiating the settlement of litigation that they concluded early in January. Later in 1400, Jeanne paid Clisson a sum that was owing to him from the proceeds of the *fouage* of thirty *sols* established in the settlement of 1395.[35] Just as Clisson now seemed fully prepared to cooperate with Jeanne, the duchess had a good reason for cultivating the loyalty of the former constable. She wished to get her son fully established as duke so that she could leave for England, where momentous developments had altered the international situation.

The old duke of Lancaster, John of Gaunt, the friend and almost exact contemporary of John IV, had died early in 1399. His son Henry, exiled from England by Richard II, had found support in France (from the Orleanists) and had visited Brittany to recruit men and vessels for a return to England. He received a warm welcome from the duke and the thirty-one-year-old duchess, who was a celebrated beauty.[36] Henry, a widower, probably noticed both the failing health of John IV and the beauty of his wife. In any case, he was back in England by July and within two months had deposed his cousin and seized the throne as Henry IV, to the consternation of the French court. Once established on the throne, Henry expressed an interest in marrying the recently widowed duchess of Brittany. Jeanne of Navarre welcomed the opportunity to become queen of England and was anxious to stabilize affairs in the duchy so that she could depart. On 3 April 1402, she and Henry were married by proxy in England.[37]

In preparation for her departure, Jeanne arranged for her son to make a formal entry into Rennes, where he was installed as duke on 23 March, just three months past his twelfth birthday. Not only were Olivier de Clisson and his sons-in-law present at this event, but it was the elderly former constable who had the honor of knighting John V and his nine-year-old brother, Arthur de Richemont (who in 1425 would become the next Breton to serve as constable of France).[38] Clisson was now cast in the role of elder statesman, the only man in Brittany with the prestige and influence to exercise the government in the minority of the young duke. He doubtless relished the possibility of becoming the effective ruler of the duchy after his long and contentious career, but there were serious obstacles to his achieving this authority. More than any other group in Brittany, the officials who had loyally served John IV distrusted Clisson and (in view of his tenacity in bearing grudges) feared his reprisals if he became their master. It was unthinkable to them that John IV's old foe should become the guardian of John's successor.[39] They had maintained close contact with the duke of Burgundy, who had dined with Breton envoys in May 1400[40] and had been in frequent communication with Jeanne of Navarre and her officers thereafter.[41]

Notwithstanding these Breton-Burgundian contacts, it appears that the court of France did not become aware of Jeanne's intention to marry Henry IV until April 1402, by which time the proxy marriage had virtually sealed the transaction. It is possible that Burgundy was aware of the situation and was preparing for it, but did not wish the government as a whole, which was dominated by Orleanists, to have a similar opportunity to prepare. In any event, the news created serious concern in the French government. It is not clear whether Henry IV had political motives for marrying the dowager duchess of Brittany and saw potential advantage in gaining control of her children. The French crown certainly feared this possibility and was determined to prevent the young duke and his brothers from accompanying their mother to England and coming under the effective custody of their new stepfather.[42] It was at this time (April) that Charles VI was apparently lucid, Burgundy absent from court, and Orléans influential enough to get himself put in charge of the financial administration.[43] Louis had no trouble persuading the king that Olivier de Clisson should be given tutelage over the young Breton princes and effective regency of the duchy.[44]

Towards the end of April, however, the king had another attack and would be incapacitated for about six weeks. Burgundy, who returned to court late in May and was in the vicinity for the next few months,[45] could not afford to have Brittany under Clisson's control because it would place this important duchy in the Orleanist camp at a time when the two dukes were increasingly hostile to each other. There was, however, no Breton outside the Clisson camp who had anything like the prestige of the former constable and the authority to manage affairs.[46] It was not until 23 August, two months after the king had supposedly recovered, that Charles issued letters urging the dowager duchess and the Breton lords to accept Clisson as guardian of the boys and regent of Brittany.[47] At first glance, it seems curious that Philip had not talked the king into abandoning the idea of a Clisson regency and did not prevent the letters of 23 August from being dispatched, but the absence of an obvious Breton alternative to Clisson limited his options and forced him to work behind the scenes.

In fact, by August the duke of Burgundy had reason to believe that the king's nomination of Clisson would encounter formidable opposition, perhaps extending well beyond the ducal entourage with whom he had been in contact. It is the contention of Pocquet that virtually Philip's entire itinerary after early May was part of a campaign to line up support for a Breton policy that would exclude Olivier de Clisson from the regency and permit Philip himself to assume that position. Among those whom he entertained and cultivated during the summer months were prominent names associated with the Marmouset-Orléans faction, such as Charles d'Albret, Jean de Montaigu, the widow of Bureau de la Rivière, and Jean d'Estouteville, lord of Villebon.[48]

There is, unfortunately, no persuasive evidence that Burgundy was discussing the Breton situation with all these people. It is equally possible that he was using these meetings to undermine Louis of Orléans in another area—his ambition to oversee the royal financial administration. The king canceled the *taille* and installed Burgundy as co-administrator of finances during the summer, but for these actions to be at all reassuring, people had to become convinced that Louis was a dangerous person to have in charge of the king's revenues. The Marmousets had stood, above all, for frugal finances and against princely plundering of royal resources. The growing acquisitiveness of their longtime princely ally, the duke of Orléans, enabled Philip of Burgundy, in his old age, to assume the unlikely role of defender of the taxpayers and advocate of reform.

Whatever may have been discussed at these meetings and dinners during the summer months, we may surely agree with Pocquet that Philip the Bold was engaged in active politicking. Moreover, his continued contacts with, and generosity towards, influential figures in Breton politics, beginning with Jeanne of Navarre herself, were achieving the desired result. Olivier de Clisson's position, apparently so unassailable in March, had eroded by September 1402, and the king was persuaded that opposition to his regency could not be ignored. He agreed to send the duke of Burgundy to arrange the affairs of Brittany and bring the young princes back to Paris. The matter was by no means a foregone conclusion, but the elderly duke was still a most adept diplomat. He left for Nantes with his sons, arriving there early in October to pursue his delicate mission.[49]

At Nantes, Philip continued his policy of lavish entertainments and generous gifts for the duchess, her sons, and influential Breton nobles and officials. Conspicuously absent from the procedings were Clisson, his sons-in-law, and such major supporters as the lords of Malestroit, Beaumanoir, Derval, and Rostrenen, but Philip did entertain the lords of Laval and La Hunaudaye, who had ties to the Clisson-Penthièvre party.[50] At the Estates of Brittany on 19 October, Philip received custody of John V and his three young brothers.[51] Three days later, Philip's sons, John the Fearless and Antoine, count of Rethel, gave their guarantees to all that their father had promised in assuming the tutelage of the princes.[52] Lest the opposition party challenge the validity of Philip's position, he obtained letters from the king ordering Rohan (and probably others) to obey Burgundy as the official guardian of John V.[53] Perhaps at this time, Philip or the duchess had certain of Clisson's strongholds placed under captains loyal to them.[54] On 15 November, Philip promised the Breton magnates that the young duke and his brothers (who were to accompany him to Paris) would be returned to Brittany the first time the Bretons requested it.[55]

On 18 November 1402, Philip and his sons concluded a treaty with the young princes that amounted to a disguised alliance against the duke of Orléans.[56] The next day, Burgundy ordered the financial officials of the duchy to obey the duchess, to whom they were to deliver their receipts.[57] Having skillfully concluded his business in just seven weeks, Philip the Bold left Brittany with John V and his brothers, arriving in Paris on 10 December,[58] bringing to a close the last, and one of the most brilliant, diplomatic achievements of his long career. Jeanne of Navarre left for England on 13 January 1403, taking only her two youngest daughters.[59]

The Burgundian diplomatic stroke of 1402 ensured that Brittany would not fall under English or Orleanist control at this time, but it did not have a major impact on the internal affairs of the duchy. John V reached his fourteenth birthday on 24 December 1403[60] and rendered homage as duke two weeks later.[61] After Philip the Bold died in April 1404, John began to free himself from Burgundian tutelage and to replace those officials appointed by Philip.[62] On 14 January 1405, John the Fearless agreed to end Burgundian custody of the Breton princes.[63]

Meanwhile, John of Blois died early in January 1404, being succeeded as count of Penthièvre by his oldest son Olivier, named for his maternal grandfather.[64] John V occupied the county to exercise his right of *rachat*, and since the young count was a minor under eleven years old, the duke was also concerned about his guardianship. On 18 May 1404, in a meeting of his council that Olivier de Clisson attended, John V granted Marguerite the tutelage of her children without requiring her to appear in person to take custody.[65] Clisson's last military operation, a victory over English vessels threatening the western coasts of the duchy, occurred early in 1404; his participation in the council of 18 May marked the sixty-eight-year-old warrior's last involvement in Breton politics.[66] His daughter Marguerite, in the name of her son, began to pursue policies of hostility to John V. In this respect she resembled her father during his long feud with John IV, but in doing so she turned her back on Olivier de Clisson's French connections. In the process, she caused a revolution in political alignments while reviving the Montfort-Penthièvre dispute in Brittany with ultimately disastrous results for her family.

Marguerite's dramatic new initiative was an alliance with John the Fearless. Having lived most of her life in an atmosphere of hostility to the house of Montfort, she supported the Penthièvre claims to Brittany and desired a strong protector for her young sons. Clearly, she no longer felt that she could look to her father to play this role. The duke of Burgundy, meanwhile, had to be concerned that his loss of control over the young duke might be exploited by the Orleanists. A possible restraining influence on John the Fearless had been removed early in 1405 by the death of his mother, the longtime advocate of Burgundian support for the Montfort family. It is not clear when and under what precise circumstances Marguerite de Clisson granted Burgundy the guardianship of her son, but the alliance was sealed when Olivier married a daughter of John the Fearless on 7 July 1406. At this date he was still less than thirteen and still a minor. His bride, a child named Isabelle, died a few years later,[67] so the marriage was never consummated. The sixteen-year-old John V reacted immediately and decisively to this rapprochement between the houses of Burgundy and Penthièvre, concluding a treaty of alliance with the duke of Orléans on 29 September.[68] With one stroke, John the Fearless had brought about a result that his father had labored long and skillfully to avoid.

Having retrieved his young sisters from England, John V now arranged political marriages for them. On 30 July 1406 he contracted to marry Blanche of Brittany to Jean, son of the count of Armagnac, that redoubtable Bernard VII who would become the leader of the anti-Burgundian party.[69] In the spring of 1407, John V applied sufficient pressure on the Rohan family to arrange a marriage between his remaining sister, Marguerite, and young Alain (IX) de Rohan, another grandson of Olivier de Clisson.[70] These two marriages took place on the same day—26 June 1407.[71] The marriage between Marguerite of Brittany and the Rohan heir must be seen as part of a ducal attempt to open a breach between the two powerful families represented by Clisson's daughters. As long as the former constable remained active, his daughters and sons-in-law had formed a cohesive political bloc under his leadership, and their collective holdings covered a large and strategic part of Brittany. The relative tranquillity that had prevailed since the death of John IV was now severely threatened by

Marguerite de Clisson. The young duke could not permit her new alignment with Burgundy to extend to her sister's family. If it were possible
to exploit differences between the sisters and draw the Rohan family more
tightly into the ducal orbit, John V had every reason to do so. There seems
no point in supposing that he was trying to detach Rohan from the vener-
able Clisson at this late date.[72]

Olivier de Clisson was preparing for his death in the winter of 1406–7.
His second wife, Marguerite de Rohan, had made her will on 14 December 1406 and was probably dead before the end of the month.[73] Shortly
after Christmas, the Parlement confirmed a transaction she had made with
her husband three years earlier, transferring to him the important Breton
fortress of Moncontour in the county of Penthièvre and in return for his
castle of Montaigu in Poitou.[74] Clisson, who was evidently awaiting this
confirmation, then granted Moncontour to his own daughter Marguerite
on 28 January 1407, but neither he nor the Parlement had adequately considered other parties with an interest in this castle, and the transaction
provoked a new confrontation between Penthièvre and the duke of Brittany.[75] On 4 February 1407, Olivier's daughters signified their agreement
to a provisional division of his huge estate, of which one-third was to go
to Marguerite and two-thirds to her older sister, Béatrix, viscountess of
Rohan.[76] Having worked out the division in this document, the old warrior drew up his will the following day.[77]

The will itself did not mention the extent of Clisson's fortune or how
it would be divided and, if his previous will in 1392 was similar in form, one
is left wondering how it was so widely reported at that time that he was
worth 1.7 million pounds. Among those named as executors in the will of
1407 were the bishop of Saint-Malo and two of Clisson's most faithful lay
supporters, the lords of Beaumanoir and Rieux. One striking feature of the
document is the relatively small amount that a man of such wealth chose to
donate to charity. The specific bequests came to less than twenty-five thousand pounds, and well under half this amount was destined for churches
and the poor.[78] In a separate document, he gave an apparently generous
donation to the canons of Saint-Julien in Le Mans to endow masses for
his soul, but what he actually gave them was an uncollected debt of very
dubious value—the unpaid hundred thousand francs in reparations that
the Parlement had imposed on Pierre de Craon in 1399.[79] He did honor an
earlier promise to found a college of canons at the parish church of Notre
Dame de Clisson,[80] but even at the end of his life Clisson did not display

Figure 4. Tomb of Olivier de Clisson and Marguerite de Rohan, church of Notre-Dame-du-Roncier, Josselin. (Photograph by Michael C. E. Jones)

remarkable generosity, piety, or conscience. He did instruct Beaumanoir to return the constable's sword to the king.[81]

Olivier IV, lord of Clisson and Belleville and count of Porhoët, the most renowned soldier of his time, breathed his last on 23 April 1407, the seventy-first anniversary of his birth, after a long career in which he left his mark on many actions and policies of the French monarchy.[82] As a military man he had been one of the towering figures of his century, at least the equal of Du Guesclin, Chandos, and the Black Prince. His extraordinary wealth had earned him the envy of the royal uncles, had made him the creditor of king and pope, and had enabled him to resuscitate single-handedly the moribund Penthièvre party in Brittany.

The full extent of this fortune may never be known, but Clisson's movable property amounted to a very large sum, especially if one considers 100,000 pounds that the duke would take in lieu of *rachat* and evidence that valuable objects disappeared during his final illness.[83] Marguerite had received 218,000 pounds by July of 1408 and recognized that this amount was somewhat more than her one-third share, leading one to conclude that an amount in the neighborhood of 600,000 pounds had been distributed to the sisters by this time.[84] With more than 700,000 pounds in movables thus accounted for, we should also include among his assets the outstanding sums owed to Clisson by the king and other important personages, debts that the constable carefully recorded. Much of this money was probably not collectible, but the impressive total of 276,216 francs means that his total assets exceeded a million pounds in movables.[85] Items inventoried by his executors, at Josselin alone, amounted to considerable wealth. Besides clothing, weapons, books, documents, and items not given a value, the inventory included: (1) more than 77,000 francs left as surety by various Breton lords to guarantee the duke's repayment of the rest of the sum extorted from him in 1387;[86] (2) gold and silver plate, whose estimated weight in marks suggests a value in currency conservatively reckoned at more than 9,200 *l.t.*;[87] (3) receipts in various currencies collected from some of his lordships amounting to (again, very roughly) more than 5,000 *l.t.*;[88] and (4) bags of cash amounting to more than 56,000 francs.[89]

Two months after drawing up his will, the old constable was still alive but clearly in failing condition. If we are to believe a document relating to subsequent litigation, the duke of Brittany now brought charges against the dying man, accusing him of various crimes. Because of his terminal illness, Clisson could not respond to the summons, and the ducal court condemned him to imprisonment and forfeiture for failing to appear. The document indicates that John V sent a large force of men to Josselin for the purpose of seizing Clisson and his property. The heirs tried to negotiate with the duke, who refused an offer of sixty thousand francs to cancel the action but then agreed to an offer of one hundred thousand francs. The two daughters were to pay this amount, contributing in proportion to what they would inherit from their father, and they had jointly sent men to take sixty thousand francs stored at Blain castle, possibly the sum required by the duke for an initial payment.[90]

Lefranc, finding no mention of this incident in any chronicle and no evidence that the duke raised such a force of troops, dismissed the document as the work of a scribe who had confused several events including the siege of Josselin in 1393.[91] La Borderie and Pocquet, however, thought

Lefranc was vainly trying to explain away a document that found supporting evidence elsewhere, and they questioned only the force of troops that
the duke was said to have dispatched to Josselin.[92] What seems to have
been involved here was not so much a ducal attempt to brutalize an infirm
old man as a series of legal actions and negotiations aimed at extracting
from the heirs the largest possible payment in lieu of *rachat* and an end to
the troublesome appeals to Paris that Clisson had initiated over the years.
Several documents refer to the hundred thousand francs as a payment in
lieu of *rachat*,[93] and we know the duke had the right to a year's revenue
from the lands of the deceased. The enormous size of the payment was justified by Clisson's wealth, but John V had other important objectives—the
quashing of Clisson's outstanding litigation and the political isolation of
his Penthièvre cousins.

By 22 April, Clisson was "more dead than alive," and John V permitted
Alain and Béatrix de Rohan to take over his lands, as a consequence of the
agreement whereby their son would marry the duke's sister.[94] They in turn
announced that they would not pursue the suits and appeals before the
Parlement of Paris that were still pending at the time of Clisson's death and
that they would henceforth be obedient to the duke.[95] John V then granted
a pardon to Clisson for bringing these actions[96] but also obtained a royal
letter requiring the heirs to appear in Parlement to renounce the suits.[97] All
these documents surely deal with a single prearranged transaction worked
out before the marriage contract of 19 April: the ducal threat to seize the
dying constable and his estate, the cancellation of the litigation initiated
by Clisson and his sons-in-law, the negotiation of the payment in lieu of
the *rachat* to which the duke was legally entitled. This last was evidently to
be paid in three annual installments, since only a small amount remained
on the final payment at the end of April 1409.[98]

How much of this was done without Marguerite's knowledge? One
suspects that Béatrix and Alain de Rohan, who were given immediate custody of Clisson's lands when he died, had by this time reached an understanding with the duke. John V's saber-rattling has scandalized historians
who thought it was directed at a dying man, but on closer examination it
has the look of a well-rehearsed drama, staged for the purpose of isolating
the countess of Penthièvre and maneuvering her into accepting arrangements to which the other parties had already agreed. Marguerite de Clisson now became an embattled figure, frequently in court against her sister
and brother-in-law over the division of the paternal inheritance while also
having to defend the county of Penthièvre against the aggressive measures

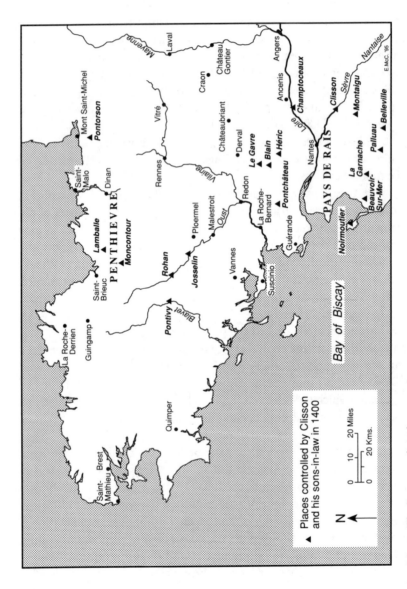

Map 6. The Breton political scene, 1400–1410.

of the duke of Brittany. Unlike her sister, she had been married young to a much older man, had been widowed, and now had to fight for her inheritance and the rights of her children. In the process, she left a "paper trail" far greater than that of Béatrix, whose husband upheld her interests until his death in 1429. The sources documenting Marguerite's career reveal her as aggressive, litigious, acquisitive, and tenacious in bearing grudges—in short, a woman who possessed many of her father's less likable qualities while being denied by her gender the military career that had won him the respect and friendship of influential people.[99]

After agreeing to one division of the Clisson inheritance in their father's lifetime, the sisters reached another accord on 4 May 1407,[100] but many complications remained to be settled. Over the next few years, the division eventually generated nearly thirty documents, details of which need not concern us here.[101] The definitive agreement regarding the principal lordships seems to have been that of May 1409. The ancestral barony of Clisson and the holdings around Montfaucon and Champtoceaux passed to Marguerite and the Penthièvre family, as did Palluau and Chateaumur in the old *terre de Belleville* in Poitou. Béatrix and Alain de Rohan received Clisson's strategic holdings in central Brittany that bordered on their own —Josselin and the county of Porhoët—along with the fortress of Blain and the important Poitevin lordships of Beauvoir-sur-Mer and La Garnache. The two sisters were not the only participants in the division. Other relatives, such as Olivier IV's nephew Jean Harpedenne and his cousin Isabeau de Ramefort, also had interests in the estate.[102]

This agreement was not reached easily, for at the moment of Olivier de Clisson's death we find Alain de Rohan promising to use the revenues from Clisson to endow his son's marriage to the duke's sister,[103] while some weeks later he was rendering homage to Louis II of Anjou for Montfaucon and Champtoceaux.[104] All these lands were destined for Marguerite. Besides the undated litigation already mentioned,[105] the sisters opposed each other in the Parlement of Paris in 1408,[106] and then engaged in another round of litigation before the ducal court at Ploermel in 1413. Marguerite alleged that there were sixty thousand pounds that had not yet been divided, that the Rohans should pay two-thirds of certain debts owed by the estate, that they had wrongly pocketed profits from Clisson's lands since his death, and that the estate included money that Clisson had collected as taxes on the county of Penthièvre.[107] Her sister and brother-in-law responded that Marguerite had not paid her third of the hundred thousand pounds exacted by the duke, that the original division had to be modified because Marguerite had received more than a third of the movables, and that John of Blois had actually owed Clisson large sums for his expenses in defending the county of Penthièvre.[108] The parties agreed to submit some points to arbitration and to empower representatives to make a full accounting and work out final details,[109] but six years of dispute must have left scars.

With Marguerite thus occupied in debate over the division of the inheritance, John V felt free to move against her in the summer of 1407 in order to deny her possession of the fortress of Moncontour, which her father had given her late in January. Her stepmother, Marguerite de Rohan, who had traded it to Clisson, was the widow of Jean de Beaumanoir and had a son-in-law and grandsons with claims to Moncontour. To clear her title to the castle, Marguerite de Clisson reached an agreement with these heirs (Charles, Rolland, and Robert de Dinan) in May 1407, trading them some other property.[110] The duke, however, declared that Moncontour was subject to *rachat* and sent men to occupy strongholds in the county of Penthièvre, forcing Marguerite into an agreement at Redon in September.[111] What John V really wanted, however, was to have Moncontour in friendly hands, and he hoped to give it to his brother Arthur. He prevailed upon one of the heirs, Rolland de Dinan, to accept other lands in return for ceding the castle to Arthur in February 1408,[112] an action that Marguerite de Clisson must have regarded as illegal. Meanwhile, the duke's men began pressing their jurisdiction in the county and Marguerite responded aggressively, so that charges of "excesses" on both sides threatened to escalate the quarrel into the sort of conflict that had consumed the energies of their respective fathers for so many years. John V undertook to isolate Marguerite and her sons by seeking the support of the Estates of Brittany in the summer of 1408. Failing to reach a negotiated settlement, John V was preparing for military action when his mother-in-law, Queen Isabeau, begged him to bring troops to protect Paris against an anticipated attack by John the Fearless.[113] When the duke of Brittany led his forces to Paris, the royal government proclaimed truces in the Breton affair and ordered local officers in Normandy and the marches not to give assistance to either side in Brittany.[114]

Back in the duchy towards the end of the year, John V resumed his quarrel with Marguerite, while maintaining a wary eye on John the Fearless, lest the Burgundian duke decide to assert his protectorate over Penthièvre, as Marguerite doubtless hoped.[115] As the dispute over Moncontour dragged on, it became further complicated by the threat of English

TABLE 3. The Later Lords of Clisson.

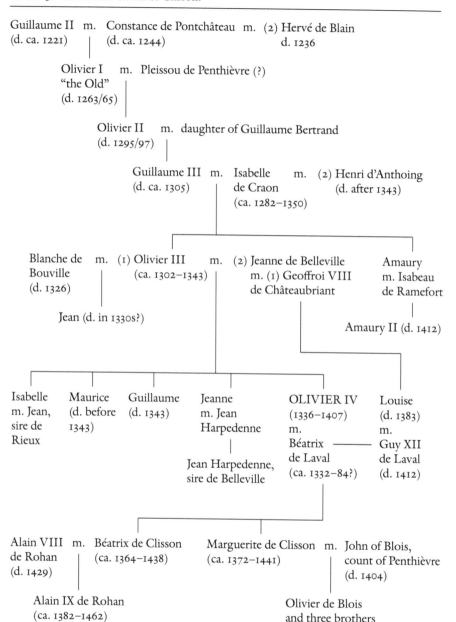

Guillaume II m. Constance de Pontchâteau m. (2) Hervé de Blain
(d. ca. 1221) | (d. ca. 1244)   d. 1236

        Olivier I   m. Pleissou de Penthièvre (?)
        "the Old"
        (d. 1263/65)

                Olivier II   m. daughter of Guillaume Bertrand
                (d. 1295/97)

                        Guillaume III m. Isabelle   m. (2) Henri d'Anthoing
                        (d. ca. 1305)   de Craon   (d. after 1343)
                                           (ca. 1282–1350)

Blanche de   m. (1) Olivier III   m. (2) Jeanne de Belleville   Amaury
Bouville   (ca. 1302–1343)   m. (1) Geoffroi VIII   m. Isabeau
(d. 1326)   de Châteaubriant   de Ramefort

    Jean (d. in 1330s?)   Amaury II (d. 1412)

Isabelle   Maurice   Guillaume   Jeanne   OLIVIER IV   Louise
m. Jean,   (d. before (d. 1343)   m. Jean   (1336–1407)   (d. 1383)
sire de   1343)   Harpedenne   m.   m.
Rieux   Béatrix ——————— Guy XII
                                    Jean Harpedenne, de Laval   de Laval
                                    sire de Belleville (ca. 1332–84?) (d. 1412)

Alain VIII m. Béatrix de Clisson   Marguerite de Clisson m. John of Blois,
de Rohan   (ca. 1364–1438)   (ca. 1372–1441)   count of Penthièvre
(d. 1429)   (d. 1404)

    Alain IX de Rohan   Olivier de Blois
    (ca. 1382–1462)   and three brothers

intervention.[116] By the summer of 1410, the broader crisis of French political society once again facilitated a settlement in Brittany. The princely alliance against Burgundy had to be dissolved,[117] and John V reached an understanding with John the Fearless.[118] Early in August, the duke of Burgundy intervened in his capacity as tutor to the young count Olivier and arranged that Moncontour would be ceded to the duke of Brittany. The latter's uncle, Charles III of Navarre, assigned him lands and revenues to help him compensate the count of Penthièvre and Charles de Dinan for Moncontour.[119] This transaction was ratified by Charles VI on 9 August,[120] by the Parlement in Paris on 4 September,[121] and by Marguerite de Clisson later that month.[122] In December 1410, a new accord produced the duke's withdrawal from the castles he had occupied in the county of Penthièvre,[123] and final ratifications in March of 1411 sealed the whole agreement.[124]

The intermittent political struggles of the four years following the death of Olivier de Clisson had left the duke of Brittany in a stronger position, while the county of Penthièvre, shorn of Moncontour and its former close ties with the house of Rohan, was less able to mount a threat to ducal power. It remained, however, a powerful political and territorial entity within Brittany, and the resources at Marguerite's disposal included, after all, a third of her father's estate. Clisson's younger daughter, understandably wishing to further the ambitions of her sons, also demonstrated her father's capacity to sustain a grudge. After nearly a decade of peace in the duchy, the Penthièvre brothers, egged on by their mother, seized John V unawares in 1420 and held the duke prisoner for several months in a curious reprise of 1387. The result was a disaster for Marguerite and her family, for John V had far greater support than his father had in 1387, and after securing his release he was able to banish his rivals from the duchy and confiscate their lands, putting ducal power in Brittany on a truly secure footing at last.[125] The legacy of Clisson's long feud with the house of Montfort thus proved to be his daughter's folly and the end to any hope of having his descendant sitting on the ducal throne.

Conclusion

MANY DETAILS OF Olivier de Clisson's career will remain a mystery because of gaps in the documentation, but it is clear that he and his family were at the center of some of the most important developments in fourteenth-century French politics.

The Clisson family, with its Breton, Norman, and Angevin lands and ties to powerful neighbors like the Craon, Belleville, and Laval families, was deeply embedded in that northwestern nobility that felt estranged from the first two Valois kings. The harsh measures taken by Philip VI against Olivier III and his wife in 1343 made them a symbol of the tension between the monarchy and this regional aristocracy. Similarly, the French crown's early effort to cultivate Olivier IV and detach him from the English was symbolic of a broader royal effort in the early 1360s to regain the support of these nobles. Whether this rapprochement was attributable to factors outside royal control, or to the skill of the future Charles V, or to a council that imposed it on Charles, the result was highly favorable to the crown and to its military position in the 1370s and 1380s. In the dispute over Belleville, the French restoration of lands to Clisson seems to have outmaneuvered the English.

The influence of Olivier de Clisson on the policies and military successes of Charles V is not proven by archival sources, and those reluctant to cite Froissart have tended to ignore the question. The evidence, however, indicates that the king's most intimate advisers, like Bureau de la Rivière, developed close ties with Clisson, in contrast to their poor relations with Bertrand du Guesclin. Clisson had learned the military trade in England, had fought alongside men like Knolles and Chandos, and had early recognized the tactical value of assuming a defensive posture and letting the enemy take the offensive and make the mistakes. Historians disagree over whether Charles V was wise to avoid pitched battles and allow the English to spread destruction through the kingdom, but in any case it was Clisson, not Du Guesclin, who took the lead in urging this policy upon the king. It is significant that Du Guesclin's first act on becoming constable in 1370 was to form a close alliance with Clisson. This pact made it possible to recruit to the royal army more Breton commanders than Du Guesclin alone could have enlisted. Under Clisson's influence, moreover, Du Guesclin finally learned to avoid the costly pitched battles that had been his undoing in the past.

The pervasive influence of Breton affairs, both for good and for evil, on the political and military fortunes of the French crown, had begun as early as Clisson's childhood, but the continuing significance of Brittany enhanced the importance of Clisson in French governing circles, just as his influence at court made the Breton question more central, more enduring, and more intractable than it might have been otherwise. The Josselin transaction of 1370 could not have been engineered by the king or by Clisson alone. It required their close collaboration, their joint suspicions of the duke's association with the English, and their joint commitment to checkmate John IV's activities in this area.

The king's politically disastrous decision to confiscate Brittany in 1378 bears the mark of Clisson's influence. The failure to give adequate and timely consideration to Jeanne de Penthièvre and her family was the principal mistake, and it is noteworthy that at this critical moment Clisson was embroiled with Jeanne over the payment of her debts. As the royal government's most influential source of advice and information on Brittany, Clisson must bear some of the responsibility for both the successes and the failures of the crown in this duchy. In 1378 and 1392, his personal animosities affected his perception of the situation and lured his king into ill-advised actions. In 1384–85, after the death of Jeanne de Penthièvre, his decisions again demonstrated how his personal Breton projects could impinge upon the greater sphere of French foreign policy, as he became the champion of John of Blois—representing him against John IV in Brittany, raising money for his ransom, and arranging for him to marry Marguerite de Clisson rather than a Plantagenet princess. It is clear that Clisson's personal animosities hindered seriously the French plans for a decisive invasion of England in the 1380s. His sudden capture by the duke of Brittany, which brought an abrupt end to the last of these projects, also set in motion the events that enabled the Marmousets to supplant the king's uncles at the royal court.

Clisson's role as the leader of the Marmousets has long been well-known; the attempt on his life in 1392, the abortive Breton expedition,

Charles VI's psychotic attack, and the fall of the Marmousets are also familiar stories. What has not received adequate attention is Clisson's prestige
among the military nobility of the north and west and the support that this
group gave to the Marmousets for two decades prior to 1392. The military
commanders who supported the Marmousets and the royal officers who
formed the core of the Marmouset faction were the people who in turn
formed the nucleus of the Orleanist party during the last decade of the lives
of Louis of Orléans and Olivier de Clisson. Yet this party had been sorely
weakened at the outset of that decade by the carnage at Nicopolis, one of
those battles that carried off French military leaders of major political importance.

What remains more problematical is the possibility that Clisson may
have had a direct and unfavorable influence on Louis of Orléans himself.
As a boy, the duke had admired the constable. They had common friends
and intermittently cooperated in the years after 1392. Clisson, however,
could be quarrelsome and brutal; he arrogantly flaunted the motto *Pour
ce qu'il me plest*; and he was not an ideal role model for a teenaged prince.
Two traits commonly associated with Clisson—the bearing of grudges and
a strong acquisitive streak—became increasingly noticeable in Louis's personality during the last decade of his life. Whatever one makes of this resemblance, it seems certain that the impact of Olivier de Clisson on French
political and military society did not come to a sudden end in 1392. A more
significant date was 1404, the year when Philip the Bold died and old age
forced Clisson out of the political arena. It may be argued that the passing
of these two old antagonists, even more than the shocking assassination of
Louis of Orléans in 1407, really set the stage for the long civil war of the
so-called "Armagnacs" and "Burgundians."

Our purpose in these pages has been to emphasize the importance
of Clisson as a political and military figure, but we cannot treat him as a
hero, given his many unattractive qualities. With his fits of anger, his bearing of grudges, his litigious nature, and his brutality towards enemies, he
resembled most members of his class, even at times presenting an exaggerated caricature of their worst qualities. His visibility and political influence
made these characteristics striking and important in Clisson's case. In this
respect, he compares unfavorably with Philip of Burgundy, who was so
often his rival. Philip impresses one as a man who managed to rise above
most other members of his social class by keeping some of these qualities
firmly under control. He lacked the military skill and prowess that were the
basis for Clisson's authority but he far exceeded Clisson's skills in diplo-

macy and statesmanship. He skillfully retrieved bad situations in Brittany in 1381 and 1394–95, and in 1392 he managed the ouster of the Marmousets without causing violent dislocations. His negotiating skills had much to do with the Anglo-French peace accords. His talents were on display again in Brittany in 1402, when he secured the duchy for his camp when Clisson might have managed an Orleanist coup there.

Philip's importance became apparent soon after his death, for his son lacked his capacity to restrain violent and brutal impulses, having a temperament that reminds one more of Olivier de Clisson than of his own father. Within a year's time, John the Fearless was injecting into French politics an element of immoderation that antagonized some who had cooperated with his father and thrust him into an isolation from which he could find no escape except through the murder of his cousin of Orléans. In Brittany, when Clisson had passed from the political scene, we find his daughter Marguerite reopening old wounds, antagonizing the duke, and seeking to protect the interests of her sons by making an arrangement with John the Fearless. This action in turn forced John V into the Orleanist camp for a few years and helped to cause a breach between the houses of Rohan and Penthièvre. When he finally died, Olivier de Clisson's legacy proved not to be the relatively accommodating spirit of his last years, but rather the grudges and antagonisms of an earlier time, revitalized by a daughter who resembled him in many ways.

The death of the skilled diplomat Philip the Bold, quickly followed by the eclipse of the aged Clisson, thus meant that Breton and French political society entered a new period of turmoil beginning around 1405. In Brittany it would end with the triumph of the duke and the destruction of the Penthièvre family in 1420, but for France as a whole the ordeal would be greater and longer. What was left of the old military society in France was largely destroyed at Agincourt in 1415 or at Verneuil in 1424. The nobility of the north and west, its lands controlled by the English and its adult males largely gone, could no longer be the bulwark of a successful monarchy as it had been between the mid-1360s and 1392. Yet the importance of this regional aristocracy to the strength of the monarchy was not at an end. When victory finally returned to the Valois, it was another Breton constable, Arthur de Richemont, who led the French army back into Paris in 1436.

Appendix 1.
The Leaders of French Military Society

IN AN APPENDIX TO his massive study of late medieval military society in France, Philippe Contamine listed forty leading commanders during the years 1369–80, the time of the French military recovery under Charles V. These men had been retained by Charles V either for continuous service over a two-year period or in four different years. The list included princes of the royal family and some foreigners.[1]

I have prepared a much longer list that is intended to represent the leading French commanders over a lengthy period, 1360 to 1415, but excludes foreigners and royal princes. The "prominence" of these men is determined either by their military office (including that of bailiff or seneschal in a militarily sensitive district) or by the number of years in which they served. I have decided against continuing to use the formula I proposed in a preliminary article, which combined the number of years of documented royal service and the number of documents recording that service.[2]

In using the records of the royal war treasurers preserved at the Bibliothèque Nationale,[3] I treated as a "commander" only those who had at least five other persons serving under them. The list presented here excludes not only foreigners and princes, but also a few whose geographical origins I have not yet determined, several names that appear with different heraldry and seem to refer to more than one person, and those whose prominence was derived largely from non-military service or who served the crown in less than seven different years.

The 188 men listed in Table A. 1 represent about 12 percent of all who served the crown in positions of command during this period. Because of the exclusions indicated above, a few important names are missing and further research may permit their addition to the list. Such additions would not impose a significant change in the distribution of names by geographical origin. The men listed here were the elite of French military society between the treaty of Brétigny and the death of Olivier de Clisson. A full prosopographical study of them and their families would yield interesting information but require a separate book.

Other than Normandy (Norm.) and Brittany (Brit.), the regions used for "geographical origin" are defined as follows:

North   = Artois, Picardy, Vermandois
IDF   = Paris, Senlis, Vexin, Chartres, Orléans
West   = Anjou, Maine, Touraine, Poitou, Limousin, La Marche
East   = Champagne, Burgundy, Sens, Maconnais, Franche-Comté
Center = Berry, Bourbonnais, Auvergne
South   = Lower Languedoc, Quercy, Rouergue, Agenais

When making generalizations in this book about "nobles of the north and west," I refer not only to the two regions as just defined but to Normandy and Brittany as well. The table understates the importance of Bretons because some lords associated with Brittany are listed under another region if their principal lordship was there, and because some Bretons who were prominent comanders in the 1370s did not serve the crown in as many as seven years. While a few men enjoyed remarkably long careers, many did not, and the roster of royal commanders in 1400 was very different from that of 1369. While the 188 men on the overall list have been analyzed by geographical origin, I have performed the same analysis for four smaller periods, considering, in each case, only those on the larger list who served three or more years in the smaller period. These periods are

1. The 1360s: A time of nominal Anglo-French peace when many nobles owed allegiance to England, with fewer military pay records but considerable activity because of the *routiers*.
2. The 1370s: The "high tide" of the French military recovery, when the army was financed by the *fouage* for the defense of the realm and Du Guesclin was constable.
3. 1380–92: The period when Olivier de Clisson was constable and the French organized three major expeditions to the Low Countries and planned three invasions of England.
4. 1393–1407: The period between the fall of the Marmousets and the deaths of Clisson and Louis of Orléans.

Information for the years after 1407 is not included in Table A.2.

TABLE A.I   Leading French Commanders, 1360–1415: Years of Service and
Political Affiliations.

Symbols for political affiliation:
X = Family supported English, Navarrese, or Breton Montfortists before 1364.
M = Associated with Marmousets, 1380–92.
O = Supported, or received payments from Louis of Touraine/Orléans,
        1389–1407.
O = Family member received payments from Louis of Touraine/Orléans,
        1389–1407.

Name	Origin	Number of years served	Dates of service	Known affiliations
Albret, Arnaud-Amanieu d'	South	13	1368–90	
Albret, Charles d'	South	11	1402–15	O
Angennes, Regnaut d', sire de Rambouillet	IDF	27	1380–1415	
Armagnac, John I, count of	South	8	1355–57, 1368–72	
Artois, Philippe d', count of Eu	Norm.	10	1379–94	
Aubeterre, Jean-Raymond d'	West	13	1378–1406	
Audrehem, Arnoul sire d'	North	14	1338–70	
Aumont, Pierre, dit "Hutin" d'	IDF	29	1368–1413	
Bardoul, Pierre	Norm.	13	1366–79	
Barguètes, Jean de	Norm.	21	1361–91	
Baveux, Guy le, sire de Tillières-sur-Avre	IDF	16	1358–84	*O*
Baveux, Robert le	IDF	13	1364–94	O *O*
Baynac, Gaillart de, sire de Floressas	South	8	1355–80	
Beaujeu, Antoine, sire de	East	7	1364–74	
Beaumanoir, Jean IV, sire de	Brit.	8	1368–76	
Beaumont, Alain de	West	21	1368–1405	O
Besille, Regnaut de	Norm.	15	1368–97	
Besu, Egret de	Norm.	12	1369–87	
Béthisy, Jean de	North	10	1369–93	
Béthune, Robert de, viscount of Meaux	North	17	1373–1405	O

TABLE A.I *(Continued)*

Name	Origin	Number of years served	Dates of service	Known affiliations
Bigot, Jean le, sire de Condé-sur-Risle	Norm.	8	1356–89	
Blainville, Jean de Mauquenchy, dit "Mouton" de	Norm.	24	1358–90	X M
Blaisy, Jean de, sire de Mauvilly	East	16	1370–93	M
Blaru, Guillaume de Saquenville, sire de	Norm.	8	1362–72	X
Blaru, Jean de Saquenville, sire de	Norm.	12	1367–1405	X O
Blequin, Guillaume de	North	11	1378–1400	
Bois, Barthélemy du	Norm.	9	1374–88	
Bois, Huguenin du	Norm.	19	1365–93	
Bois, Jean V du, sire de l'Epinay-le-Tesson	Norm.	17	1365–89	
Bois, Jean VI du, dit "Gascoing", sire de l'Epinay-le-Tesson	Norm.	12	1365–92	
Boissay, Robert, sire de	Norm.	26	1368–1408	O
Boissière, Guillaume de la, sire de Perrigny	Center	21	1373–1405	O
Bordes, Arnauton des, sire de Montguion	IDF	8	1383–94	
Bordes, Guillaume des	IDF	27	1361–96	M
Boucicaut, Jean (le Meingre)	West	15	1349–67	
Boucicaut, Jean le Meingre the younger	West	30	1386–1418	
Boulay, Hue du	IDF	22	1364–92	
Bournel, Hue de, sire de Thiembronne	North	10	1383–97	
Bouteiller, Guillaume II le, sire de Saint-Chartier	Center	25	1377–1413	O
Bouville, Charles, sire de	IDF	8	1364–84	
Braquemont, Guillaume de, dit "Braquet"	Norm.	21	1378–1413	X M O
Briqueville, Guillaume, sire de	Norm.	12	1364–88	X

TABLE A.I   (*Continued*)

Name	Origin	Number of years served	Dates of service	Known affiliations
Bueil, Jean III, sire de	West	22	1368–91	M O
Bueil, Pierre de, sire du Bois	West	27	1375–1411	O
Cailleville, Philippe de	Norm.	14	1361–88	*O*
Calonne, Jean de, sire de Courtebourne	North	14	1375–96	
Carbonnel, Richart, sire du Pont-Satty	Norm.	10	1368–1404	
Chalus, Robert de	South	19	1376–1415	
Chantemerle, Jean "Taupin" de	IDF	31	1370–1400	O O
Charny, Geoffroi de (younger)	East	18	1364–93	X
Châtelain de Beauvais, Guillaume le	Norm.	12	1369–88	
Châtillon, Hue de, sire de Dampierre and Rollancourt	East	13	1357–88	X
Chauvigny, Guy de, viscount of Broce	Center	10	1369–87	
Chiffrevast, Jean de	Norm.	19	1374–96	
Clères, Georges de	Norm.	11	1368–92	X
Clisson, Olivier IV, sire de	Brit.	25	1368–92	X M O
Coich, Hervé le	IDF	24+	1343–95	O O
Colombières, Henri de, sire de La Haye du Puits	Norm.	14	1363–80	
Combray, Fralin de	North	14	1378–1404	O
Coucy, Enguerrand, sire de	North	21	1376–96	X M O
Dammartin, Charles de Trie, count of	IDF	17	1364–93	
Dauphin, Guichard, sire de Jaligny	Center	18	1369–99	
Dinteville, Erart, sire de	East	8	1370–88	
Diquemure, Thierry de	North	8	1375–92	
Épaules, Guillaume aux	Norm.	22	1364–93	
Espagne, Arnaud d'	South	11	1355–83	
Estouteville, Colart d', sire d'Auzebosc	Norm.	12	1364–87	M

TABLE A.1 (*Continued*)

Name	Origin	Number of years served	Dates of service	Known affiliations
Estouteville, Colart d', sire de Torcy	Norm.	38	1364–1412	M O
Estouteville, Jean ("Jehannet") d', sire de Charlemesnil	Norm.	27	1373–1416	M
Estouteville, Jean ("Jehannet") d', sire de Villebon	Norm.	16	1383–1416	M
Estouteville, Robert VI, sire d'	Norm.	14	1367–93	
Eudin, Enguerrand d'	North	14	1367–91	M
Fayel, Guillaume, dit "le Bègue" de,	Norm.	30	1368–1405	O
Ferté-Fresnel, Jean, sire de la	Norm.	28	1352–1410	
Fevrier, Geoffroi	Norm.	13	1368–86	
Fiennes, Jean, dit "Lionnel" de	North	11	1369–98	X
Fiennes, Robert, dit "Moreau" de	North	18	1356–83	X
Gaillonel, Adam ("Adennnet") the younger, sire d'Ancy-le-Franc	IDF	10	1381–1408	
Garencières, Jean de, sire de Croisy	Norm.	18	1379–1415	X M O
Garencières, Yon, sire de	Norm.	31	1356–1407	X M O
Guesclin, Bertrand du, count of Longueville	Brit.	25	1353–80	
Guesclin, Olivier du, sire de la Roche-Tesson	Brit.	15	1371–92	
Guitté, Robert de, sire de Vaucouleurs	Brit.	17	1368–93	
Haie, Jean de la, sire d'Eroudeville	Norm.	16	1364–92	O
Hallay, Jean du	Brit.	11	1364–90	
Hangest, Jean V, sire de	North	13	1366–88	X O
Hangest, Jean de, sire de Heuqueville	North	18	1387–1412	X O O

TABLE A.I   (*Continued*)

Name	Origin	Number of years served	Dates of service	Known affiliations		
Harcourt, Jacques de, sire de Montgommery	Norm.	11	1371–96	X		
Harcourt, Jean VII, count of	Norm.	9	1390–1415	X		
Harenvilliers, Claudin de	Norm.	15	1357–80			O
Heuse, Jean, dit "Le Baudrain" de la	Norm.	30	1355–93			
Hommet, Jean du, sire de Varengières	Norm.	11	1380–90			
Houssaye, Alain de la	Brit.	10	1364–81			
Illes, Regnaut des, sire de Milencourt	Norm	16	1358–79			
Isque, Colart d'	North	14	1369–1410			
Ivry, Charles d'	Norm.	16	1390–1415	X		O
Juch, Jean de	Brit.	8	1370–81			
Laigue, Guillaume de	South	26	1375–99			
Landevy, Jean de	Brit.	11	1374–1405			
Laval, Guy de, dit "Brumor"	West	7	1368–78			
Laval, Guy XII, sire de	West	11	1368–1409			O
Lespinasse, Jean de	Center	10	1378–93			
Lestendart, Jean de	Norm.	19	1362–83			
Lestendart, Simon de	Norm.	8	1368–91			
Linières, Philippe de	Center	15	1368–1407			
Luiserne, Thomas de la	Norm.	17	1365–94			
Luxembourg, Waleran de, count of St. Pol and Ligny	North	13	1373–1413			
Magneville, Guillaume de	Norm.	11	1364–83			
Marche, Jean de Bourbon, count of La	Center	13	1365–92			
Marcilly, Foulques de	West	9	1368–93			O
Mareuil, Guillaume, sire de	West	11	1373–92			
Mareuil, Raymond de, sire de Courtenay and Villeboy	West	19	1369–96			
Martel, Guillaume	Norm.	19	1374–1406	X	M	O
Masuyer, Roger le	Norm.	13	1356–73	X		

TABLE A.1 *(Continued)*

Name	Origin	Number of years served	Dates of service	Known affiliations
Mauny, Alain de	Brit.	10	1371–90	
Mauny, Hervé de, sire de Torigny	Norm.	23	1371–1407	O
Mauny, Olivier de, the elder	Brit.	14	1365–87	
Mauvinet, Guillaume	West	14	1368–92	
Melun, Guillaume de, count of Tancarville	Norm.	36	1369–1414	M
Melun, Jean de, count of Tancarville	Norm.	7	1355–81	
Merle, Guillaume de, sire de Messy	Norm.	15	1358–86	
Merle, Jean de, sire de Messy	Norm.	20	1370–1403	
Mesnil, Robert, dit "Taupin" du	IDF	8	1370–88	O
Meulan, Raoul de, sire de Courseulles	Norm.	13	1366–92	
Moine, Olivier le	Brit.	8	1370–85	
Montagu, Jean de, sire de Sombernon	East	8	1363–87	
Montauban, Olivier, sire de	Brit.	7	1370–78	
Montbron, Jacques, sire de	West	10	1376–94	
Montcavrel, Jean, sire de	North	10	1378–94	M O
Montenay, Jean, sire de	Norm.	9	1378–1415	O
Montjean, Briant de	West	8	1368–88	
Montmor, Jacques de, sire de Briz	IDF	28	1363–99	
Montmor, Morelet de	IDF	19	1372–97	
Morchies, Jean de, dit Galehaut	North	9	1374–90	
Mornay, Pierre de (elder), sire de La Ferté-Nabert	Center	19	1370–1400	M
Mornay, Pierre de (younger), dit "Le Gaulnet"	Center	12	1376–1421	O
Moustier, Étienne de	Norm.	22	1360–87	
Naillac, Guillaume de	Center	20	1369–94	O O

TABLE A.I   (*Continued*)

Name	Origin	Number of years served	Dates of service	Known affiliations		
Nesle, Guy de, sire d'Offémont	North	12	1380–1405	O		
Passac, Gaucher de	West	21	1368–1405	O		
Paume, Georges de la	North	13	1369–1418			
Paynel, Guillaume, sire de Hambie	Norm.	25	1366–94	X	O	O
Paynel, Jean	Norm.	9	1380–91	X		O
Paynel, Nicole	Norm.	18	1374–94	X		O
Personne, Jean de la, viscount of Acy	North	25	1362–99		M	
Poitiers, Guillaume le Bâtard de, sire d'Etrepy	East	19	1366–90	X		O
Pons, Regnaud, sire de	West	22	1368–1416			
Pont, Thibaut du	Brit.	7	1371–77			
Pontailler, Guy de	East	12	1363–91			
Rabastens, Pierre-Raymond de sire de Campagnac	South	25	1352–89			
Raineval, Raoul de, sire de Pierrepont	North	13	1356–91	X		
Raineval, Waleran, sire de	North	9	1368–88			
Rambures, Andrieu de	North	23	1370–1405			
Riboule, Foulques, sire d'Assé-le-Riboule	West	15	1368–95		O	O
Rivière, Bureau de la	East	27	1361–92	M	O	O
Rochechouart, Aimery de, sire de Mortemer	West	14	1373–94			
Rochechouart, Jean de	West	7	1379–1404			
Rohan, Alain VIII, visct of	Brit.	14	1370–93			
Rouville, Pierre Gougeul, dit "Moradas," sire de	IDF	8	1374–98			
Sancerre, Jean III, count of	Center	9	1369–91			
Sancerre, Louis de, sire de Charenton	Center	36	1367–1402			
Savoisy, Philippe de	East	15	1361–92	O		
Sempy, Jean de	North	21	1364–90			
Seneschal [d'Eu], Jean le	Norm.	12	1364–82	O		
Sermoise, Pierre de	East	15	1357–78			

TABLE A.1 (*Continued*)

Name	Origin	Number of years served	Dates of service	Known affiliations	
Taillecol, Alain de, dit "L'abbe de Malpaye"	Brit.	18	1364–91		
Tesson, Raoul	Norm.	10	1368–81	X	
Tesson, Robert	Norm	13	1378–1404	X	O
Thieuville, Henri, sire de	Norm.	12	1355–78		
Tignonville, Guillaume, sire de	IDF	10	1386–1406	M	O
Tournebu, Girart de, sire d'Auvillier	Norm.	9	1366–86	X	
Tournebu, Pierre, sire de	Norm.	11	1356–78	X	
Trémoille, Guillaume de la	West	9	1369–94		
Trémoille, Guy, sire de la	West	17	1364–95		
Tréseguidy, Maurice de	Brit.	24	1361–92		
Trie, Jean de	IDF	8	1376–94	X	O
Trie, Regnaut de	IDF	12	1369–1401	X	O
Trousseau, Pierre	West	20	1368–99		O
Tucé, Guillaume, sire de	West	9	1368–83		
Vé, Jean, sire de	North	13	1378–95		
Vienne, Jean de, sire de Roullans	East	28	1362–96	M	
Villaines, Pierre, dit "le Bègue" de	IDF	25	1360–1406	M	O
Villiers, Guillaume de, sire du Hommet	Norm.	12	1369–86		O
Villiers, Pierre de, sire de L'Isle Adam	Norm.	22	1353–87		O
Vivonne, Regnaut de, sire de Thors	West	7	1364–94		
Warignies, Gilles, sire de	North	12	1376–95		
Warignies, Robert de	Norm.	18	1356–77		
Wissant, Morelet de	North	8	1368–80		

Of the 188 commanders listed above, at least 17 percent were from families known to have been in opposition to the crown before 1364. It will be seen in the table below that the 1370s and 1380s were the periods of greatest documented military activity, but 70 percent (132) of the leading commanders had already served by the end of 1370 and 64 percent (121) served after 1390. Of these last, about one-third are known to have been Orleanists.

TABLE A.2.   Distribution by Geographical Origin.

Origin	1360s	1370s	1380–92	1393–1407	Overall
	A. Distribution by Number				
Norm.	30	50	52	18	67
Brit.	5	16	11	1	17
West	1	15	18	10	24
North	4	15	24	13	28
Subtotal for					
northwestern nobles	40	96	105	42	136
IDF	15	12	17	13	20
East	7	12	10	1	12
Center	1	9	12	6	12
South	2	5	3	3	8
Total	65	134	147	65	188
	B. Distribution by Percentage				
Norm.	46%	37%	35%	28%	35.5%
Brit.	7%	12%	7.5%	1.5%	9%
West	1.5%	11%	12%	15.5%	13%
North	6%	11%	16%	20%	15%
Subtotal for					
northwestern nobles	60.5%	71%	70.5%	65%	72.5%
IDF	23%	7%	12%	20%	11%
East	11%	9%	7%	1.5%	6%
Center	1.5%	7%	8%	9%	6%
South	3%	4%	2%	4.5%	4%

Although more than 72 percent of the leading royal commanders were from the northwestern regions, the preponderance of these regions was less in the 1360s, when much of the west was in English hands, and after 1392, when Bretons were largely absent after Clisson's dismissal from office. Within the northwestern group, we find a steady increase in the importance of commanders from the north and a gradual decline in the relative importance of the Normans.

Appendix 2.
Genealogy and Wealth of the Clisson Family

THE ANCESTRY OF MANY noble families of Brittany cannot be traced back before the mid-fourteenth century, partly because much of the modern Breton nobility rose from social obscurity in this period and partly because few Breton lineages maintained family archives that have survived.[1] It is nonetheless surprising that the Clisson family, which had achieved great stature by the thirteenth century, has lacked an adequate genealogy. Standard reference works such as those of Anselme, La Chesnay-des Bois, and Levot,[2] to which historians turn for genealogical data, contain little information about the family and much of what they do provide is so outlandish as to defy the imagination. The lords of Clisson evidently did not lavishly endow or bury their dead at a single ecclesiastical establishment, and the family has lacked the monastic necrology that has sometimes enlightened historians about other comparable noble dynasties. Since the male line died out early in the fifteenth century, the Clisson lacked descendants who were motivated to concoct a distinguished genealogy. Efforts to reconstruct the family's history must begin with the notes compiled, largely from cartularies, by René Blanchard more than a century ago.[3] I have examined many of the sources he used and have found additional documentation, but there remain curious gaps and uncertainties in the history of this remarkable family.

Many French noble families of subsequent importance emerged from obscurity in the first third of the eleventh century, appearing as commanders of castles who used their positions of power to establish hereditary lordships. The earliest known lord of Clisson may have been the Gaudin (Gualdinus), who was said to have been involved in the foundation of an Angevin priory in the 1040s.[4] The source that mentions him, however, is suspect, and although his forename would appear subsequently in the Clisson family, this first Gaudin cannot be authenticated. We can establish the beginning of the Clisson line only later, with the first authenticated members of this family—Baudry (Baldricus) de Clisson, who appeared in at least eight documents between 1061 and 1084, and Gaudin de Clisson, probably his son, who appeared in six documents between 1091 and 1112.[5]

In the twelfth century, when many dynasties of castellans became established as prominent members of the feudal nobility, documents on the Clisson family suddenly diminish. Several scattered references to the name appear in the period 1109–49, with Giraud being the forename most in evidence,[6] but nothing indicates which, if any, of these people had inherited the castle from Gaudin. The reappearance of the name Gaudin at the end of the twelfth century suggests that the same family continued to hold the castle, but because Clisson was located in the often disputed marches of Brittany, Anjou, and Poitou, the castellans may have been reduced to a struggle for survival that left few opportunities to endow religious houses or witness charters in the first half of the century. After mid-century, we begin to gain firmer ground. In 1152, Aimery (Americus), lord of Clisson, witnessed a donation made by Raoul, lord of Rais, to the abbey of Buzay.[7] Aimery made subsequent appearances during the course of the 1150s,[8] and although we encounter another hiatus in the records of about a generation, he was very probably the ancestor of the later Clissons, since Guillaume, lord of Clisson, who made a donation to Buzay in 1218,[9] had a son named Aimery.[10]

Guillaume, in fact, was the first really prominent member of the family. The name is found in at least nineteen different documents between 1185 and 1217.[11] He witnessed a charter of Geoffrey Plantagenet, count of Brittany, in 1186[12] and one of Count Guy in 1205, which referred to Clisson as a baron.[13] We last hear of this Guillaume in 1218.[14] Given Guillaume's prominence, it is disconcerting to find so little documentation for the previous generation (1158–85). A reference to Eustachie, "lord" of Clisson, evidently refers to a *lady* of Clisson. She appears to have been married to a lord of Clisson named Gaudin and was probably a member of the family that ruled the neighboring lordship of Rais. Her son Gaudin was doubtless Guillaume I's younger brother.[15]

The progeny of Guillaume I, lord of Clisson, pose more problems. He seems to have had four sons and several daughters. One son, Aimery, is mentioned in 1212 and may have predeceased his father, while another, Gaudin, also appears in just one document.[16] Another son, named Garsire, may have been the eldest. Around 1200, Guillaume made a donation to the abbey of Geneston for the souls of his wife Flavie and their son, Garsire.[17] Between 1204 and 1216, lists of Breton knights owing military service indicated the presence of both an older and a younger Guillaume de Clisson.[18] The younger Guillaume, by this time, seems to have been his father's heir. The next clearly identified lord of Clisson, Olivier I, later known as "the Old," seems to have been born in the early years of the thirteenth century. Historians have called him the son of Guillaume,[19] but his father would have had to be the younger Guillaume. We know the identity of Olivier's mother, Constance de Pontchâteau, from a donation she made, long after her husband's death, to the abbey of Blanche Couronne.[20] Since Olivier was called lord of Clisson in 1221 and Constance contracted a second marriage in 1225,[21] it would seem that the younger Guillaume died not long after the elder one if, indeed, he did not predecease him.[22] Olivier I may have been a minor at the time he inherited the title.

The documents leave no doubt that Guillaume I was wealthier and more influential than previous lords of Clisson, perhaps because he had inherited another lordship,[23] but it was his grandson, Olivier I, who became a truly prominent and troublesome political figure, although Blanchard's notes only mention him nine times between 1244 and 1262.[24] The name Olivier came from the Pontchâteau family,[25] a clear indication of the prestige Constance brought to the Clisson family. After becoming a widow, she married Hervé de Blain (d. 1236), by whom she had two sons, but at her death in 1244 it was Olivier de Clisson who inherited Blain, an important castle northwest of Nantes, while his half-brothers received lesser parts of the Pontchâteau inheritance. The location of these lands made Olivier far more important than a marcher lord in the remote southeast. He obtained the homage of his half-brothers and became embroiled in hostilities with Duke John I for apparent violations of Breton feudal custom.[26] This conflict (1254–61) ended in his defeat, and early in 1262 he had to relinquish his lands to his son, Olivier II, who paid an indemnity of four thousand pounds, while the Blain brothers regained their lands from the duke.[27]

Although Olivier the Old lived on for some years, we can assume that subsequent references to Olivier de Clisson in the thirteenth century refer to Olivier II, whose seal has survived in excellent condition on a document of 1267 recording his oath of fealty to the duke of Brittany.[28] Olivier II appeared in various documents over a thirty-year period,[29] among them an important agreement in 1276 between John I and the great lords of Brittany relating to the right of *rachat*.[30] His final appearance was in a document of 1293 in which Olivier II recognized his obligation to provide over three months a year of guard duty at the castle of Montfaucon and an even longer period at Champtoceaux.[31] It is from this text that we learn of his possession of Le Thuit in Normandy and his holdings at Montfaucon and around Champtoceaux. The rebellion and defeat of Olivier I had clearly not been a serious setback to the family's rise to wealth and prominence.

The life and career of Olivier II pose serious problems for those wishing to establish a genealogy for the Clisson family. Having taken over the ancestral lands at the beginning of 1262, he could not have been born much later than 1240 and may have been born earlier. Yet the most prominent genealogical sources state that he married Isabelle de Craon,[32] who was assuredly the mother of Olivier III and another son, Amaury. Isabelle, however, was the third child of a marriage contracted in 1277. She would have been born around 1282. Her elder sister was married in 1299,[33] and it is unlikely that Isabelle was married earlier. Since, however, her son, Olivier III, contracted his first marriage in 1320,[34] Isabelle must have been married soon after her sister.

Since Isabelle was more than forty years younger than Olivier II de Clisson and had barely reached childbearing age at the time of his death (between 1293 and 1298),[35] she could not have been his wife. Buteau concluded plausibly that since Olivier II held Le Thuit in Normandy by 1293, he must have been the Clisson who married a member of the Bertrand family.[36] It was the son of this couple who married Isabelle de Craon. Guillaume III had succeeded his father as lord of Clisson by 1298 when he was still a minor and had died by 1307, leaving a minor heir.[37] Although we know that Isabelle married a lord of Clisson, no trustworthy document gives the first name of her husband. Michèle Buteau and Yvonig Gicquel were so sure that his name was Olivier that they proposed a second son of Olivier II who was named for his father. There is no basis for believing in the existence of such a person.[38] Guillaume was clearly his father's heir and it is not likely that a daughter of the Craon family would have married a cadet. There remains the purely academic question of whether her marriage to Guillaume (around 1300) was arranged in Olivier II's lifetime or by Guillaume's guardian.

In any case, Isabelle de Craon was left a widow with two small children when still in her early twenties and she subsequently remarried, taking as her spouse a knight from Hainault named Henri d'Anthoing, to whom she was still married in 1343 when she was around sixty years of age.[39] The prestige of Isabelle's family is undeniable. Her brother, Amaury III, lord of Craon, sired a number of children, among them his successor, Amaury IV, an archbishop of Reims (Jean de Craon, who helped negotiate the first treaty of Guérande), and Guillaume, viscount of Châteaudun.[40] These nephews were the first cousins of her two sons—Olivier III, lord of Clisson, and Amaury de Clisson, lord of L'Isle Aurillé and Blaudinay.[41] The notorious Pierre de Craon, lord of La Ferté-Bernard, was a son of the viscount of Châteaudun and thus the second cousin of Olivier IV de Clisson, whom he tried to kill in 1392.

Olivier III, who became lord of Clisson by 1307, was probably born around 1302. He was still a minor when he married Blanche de Bouville in 1320.[42] This couple had a son, Jean, before Blanche died in 1326. Jean certainly predeceased his father and may have died before attaining his majority.[43] As we have seen, Olivier III's second wife was Jeanne, daughter and principal heiress of Maurice, lord of Belleville. She had married Geoffroi VII, lord of Châteaubriant and had borne him two children, a son, Geoffroi VIII, who died at La Roche-Derrien in 1347, and a daughter, Louise, who inherited Châteaubriant and part of the Belleville legacy and married Guy XII, lord of Laval.[44] These children were still very small in 1328 when Jeanne de Belleville was widowed. Her marriage to Olivier III de Clisson required a papal dispensation in 1330 and probably occurred in that year.[45] Their two older sons, Maurice and Guillaume, had been born by 1334,[46] but both were dead a decade later, leaving Olivier IV (b. 1336) as the only surviving son.[47] The couple also had two daughters. Isabelle may in fact have been their first child because she was married to Jean de Rieux when he and Olivier III defected to the English at the end of 1342. Jeanne, the younger daughter, probably accompanied her mother and Olivier IV to England. When she married, her spouse was one of Edward III's men, Jean Harpedenne, who became seneschal of Saintonge under the English.[48] Her son of the same name grew up as a French nobleman, became associated with the Marmousets, and eventually was lord of Belleville.[49]

In 1333, Olivier III arranged for his younger brother Amaury to marry Isabeau, daughter and heiress of Maurice, lord of Ramefort.[50] An early supporter of Montfort in the war of succession, Amaury accepted amnesty at the the end of 1344 and died fighting for Charles of Blois at La Roche-Derrien.[51] He and Isabeau had three children. Their son, Amaury II, served the French under his cousin Olivier IV and died in 1412. Their older daughter, Isabeau, lady of Ramefort, married Renaud d'Ancenis, while the younger one, Mahaud, first married Guy de Bauçay and then Savary de Vivonne.[52]

Although Olivier IV de Clisson was one of the most important men in France in the later fourteenth century, there remain surprising uncertainties in the genealogy even for this period, particularly in regard to his wives and daughters. Béatrix of Brittany (1296–1384), daughter of Duke Arthur II and widow of Guy X, lord of Laval, arranged for Clisson to marry her daughter Béatrix in 1362.[53] Olivier IV, then approaching twenty-six years of age, may have been younger than his bride, given the age of the older Béatrix at this time. If so, Béatrix de Laval was married at an older age than was customary for young women of her social class, perhaps because of the Breton war of succession. Not only were numerous potential spouses slaughtered at La Roche-Derrien (1347) and Mauron (1352), but her mother, as Jean de Montfort's sister, may have been less sympathetic than the Lavals to the Blois-Penthièvre cause and therefore anxious to find a more politically acceptable spouse for Béatrix. The older Béatrix delayed the transfer of her daughter's dowry until after the treaty of Guérande ended the succession crisis.[54]

Historians have generally asserted that Olivier de Clisson and Béatrix de Laval were married on 12 February 1362, the date of their marriage contract.[55] Direct evidence is lacking, and the delay in transferring the dowry raises some doubts about the matter. It was, however, rather common for adult marriages to take place soon after formal execution of the contract, and it was not at all uncommon for dowries to be delayed. The couple's first child, another Béatrix, married the son of the viscount of Rohan and their son, the future Alain IX, is said to have been born in 1382.[56] It is therefore reasonable to suppose that Béatrix and Olivier were married in 1362, that their daughter was born a year or so later, and that she was married at the age of seventeen or eighteen.

The sources remain curiously silent about Béatrix de Laval during her marriage. She bore a second daughter, Marguerite, who married John of Blois in 1388 when the latter was nearly forty-three years old. A possible marriage of Marguerite to the lord of Amboise was under discussion as early as 1375,[57] when Marguerite may have been very young. It appears that one of Clisson's children was born in 1372 when Béatrix must have been close to forty.[58] If this child was Marguerite, she would have been fifteen when she was married and only twelve when her father first discussed that marriage with John of Blois. If the two Clisson daughters were in fact eight or nine years apart in age, Béatrix and Olivier may have lost some intervening children.

Given the documentation that Bertrand de Broussillon has assembled for the Laval family, it is curious that we have no clear documentary evidence for the death of Béatrix de Laval or for the date of Clisson's second marriage. His second wife, Marguerite de Rohan, was the sister of Jean I, viscount of Rohan and thus the aunt of Clisson's son-in-law. She was also the widow of Clisson's onetime captor Jean de Beaumanoir and the step-mother of his companions in arms, Jean and Robert de Beaumanoir. When the elder Beaumanoir died in 1366, he and Marguerite had been married for ten years and she had borne him three daughters. She and Olivier were probably about the same age.[59] Some historians have placed her marriage to Clisson in the 1370s,[60] but as late as September 1378 they were still not married to each other.[61] There is, in fact, evidence that Béatrix de Laval was still alive in 1384 when she paid two hundred pounds to establish four masses.[62] This donation suggests that she thought her end was approaching, and we may tentatively place her death in 1384 or 1385. This source, being a later copy, lacks the authority of contemporary handwriting, but there is no real evidence that Clisson married Marguerite de Rohan before the late 1380s and therefore no reason to suppose that Béatrix died at an earlier date.

As the foregoing pages should have made clear, the Clisson family had a long tradition of making advantageous marriages. Olivier IV's two matrimonial alliances with the Rohan family were in keeping with this tradition. Although we lack a precise date for either of them, their approximate timing suggests considerable political shrewdness. Béatrix de Clisson evidently married Alain VIII de Rohan in 1380 or 1381, after John IV's return from exile and at a time when the duke was carefully cultivating Alain's father, Jean I de Rohan.[63] Olivier's marriage to the sister of Jean I followed another ducal overture to the Rohan family, John IV's marriage, in 1386, to Jeanne of Navarre, a niece of the viscountess of Rohan.[64] Clisson's marriage to Marguerite may also be seen as a way of strengthening his Breton connections after his imprisonment by the duke in 1387. Olivier and Marguerite were certainly married by 22 May 1390.[65] They had been good friends for many years, and it seems clear that Olivier had genuine affection for his second wife, with whom he shares a tomb. She appears to have exerted a moderating influence on his often vindictive temperament[66] until her death, at about the age of seventy, just a few months before Olivier.

The succession of advantageous marriages made by members of the Clisson family also had a good deal to do with the fabulous wealth enjoyed by Olivier IV, but we should not overemphasize the inheritances and dowries at the expense of other factors. The last thirty years of his life coincided with the brief upturn in the seigneurial economy between two periods of acute decline, a phenomenon discussed in Chapter 1. Not every lord was in a position to profit from this short-lived revival, but it surely was beneficial to Clisson, who bought up profitable properties when other, less fortunate holders were forced to sell.[67] Clisson differed from the stereotypical medieval nobleman, at least in degree, in that he was less generous in his gifts and considerably more interested in commercial profit than were many others of comparable economic and social standing.[68] Over a period of years, these differences could have considerable impact on one's finances.

Finally, Clisson profited from his twelve years in perhaps the most lucrative position in the royal government, the office of constable. He owed this appointment, at least in part, to his well-earned reputation as a ferocious warrior and able strategist, but his personal wealth was also a consideration. His ability to pay large numbers of troops out of his own pocket when royal funds were lacking, as in 1371 and 1380, added to his attractiveness as a candidate for constable. In this office, he was well positioned to collect a share of the anticipated profits of war (booty and ransoms), and he was entitled to a salary of 2,000 *l.t.* a month in wartime. Since this salary was generally in arrears, he received numerous gifts and concessions from an appreciative monarch while continuing to treat the arrears as a royal debt owing to his estate.

Let us summarize briefly the principal acquisitions of the Clisson family, beginning with Olivier I's inheritance of Blain and Héric, northwest of Nantes, from Constance de Pontchâteau. Other lands of the Blain-Pontchâteau family seem to have come into the hands of the Clisson subsequently. Olivier II added Le Thuit in Normandy and possessions at Montfaucon and Champtoceaux in Anjou, two castellanies that would be in the hands of Olivier IV subsequently. Olivier III's second marriage led to the vast Belleville inheritance. All these lands were confiscated, of course, in 1343, but over the next fifteen years Jeanne de Belleville acquired lands and revenues from Edward III that passed to Olivier IV at the end of 1359.

In 1360–61, Clisson began to reacquire his family's confiscated possessions outside Brittany, and in 1363–65 he regained their Breton holdings while doubtless collecting ransoms and rewards as a result of his service at Auray. In 1365–66, the dowry of his first wife included the lordship of Villenoble near Paris and an annuity of 2,000 *l.t.* on royal receipts in Champagne. In 1370, he exchanged this last income and Le Thuit for Josselin and the county of Porhoët. The duke then confiscated some of his Breton holdings, but Clisson regained most of them when he was helping to govern Brittany during John IV's exile (1373–79), and the king added Guillac to his possessions in 1373. His one enduring loss when Anglo-French hostilities resumed was probably the customs revenues at Bordeaux that Edward III had bestowed on his mother.

Charles V gave Clisson various costly gifts including funds for the construction of the Hôtel de Clisson in Paris. He received rights to ransoms in the Poitevin campaign of 1372, booty from the Flemish campaign in 1382, and virtual control of Pontorson because of arrears in salary. In 1382, he received custody of the castle of Montl'héry near Paris and a salary as its captain.[69] He also received, during the 1380s, effective control over various fortresses and incomes in the county of Penthièvre as a result of his role as lieutenant and principal creditor of his future son-in-law, John of Blois.[70] Meanwhile, the death of his half sister, Louise de Châteaubriant, in 1383, brought him several lordships that had been part of his mother's Belleville inheritance.[71] In 1388, he rendered homage for the Poitevin stronghold of La Roche-sur-Yon, which had come into his hands as a royal gift.[72]

How much wealth did all these possessions generate?[73] In 1392, when John IV was required by the treaty of Tours to pay Clisson the eighty thousand francs still outstanding from the sum extorted from him in 1387, the expense was to be borne by the Breton population through a hearth tax. This tax was not to be levied, however, in lands held by Clisson himself, and an estimate of the taxable hearths in Brittany indicated that Clisson controlled 18,699 out of a total of 98,447, or nearly one-fifth of the entire duchy.[74] When Clisson made the will in 1392 that has not survived, it was believed that he had 1.7 million francs in movables,[75] but the figure represents pure hearsay unless his heirs agreed to a division in another lost document. As we have seen, his death in 1407 was followed by the disappearance of some valuables and a payment of one hundred thousand francs to the duke, while his daughter Marguerite, who was entitled to one-third of the movables after deduction of special bequests, admitted in court in 1408 that the 218,000 francs she had received was somewhat more than a third of the total. The earlier, unsubstantiated, total of 1.7 million francs seems too high for the movables alone in 1407, but far too low to represent the total value of the Clisson estate.[76] This oft-cited and perhaps meaningless figure, if reckoned in actual gold francs, would have the monetary equivalent of nearly six metric tons of gold (the equivalent of around 190,000 troy ounces) according to one calculation.[77] It would be fruitless to pursue further the question of Clisson's precise wealth and purchasing power, but these figures make it evident that Olivier IV was one of the very richest people in Europe, probably the wealthiest man in France who was not of royal or princely rank.[78]

Probable Genealogy of the Early Lords of Clisson.

Generation I	
Baudry de Clisson, fl. 1061–84	lived ca. 1030 to ca. 1085
Generation II	
Gaudin de Clisson, fl. 1091–1112	lived ca. 1060 to ca. 1115?
Generation III	
Giraud?	lived ca. 1090 to ca. 1150?
Generation IV	
Aimery, sire de Clisson, fl. 1152–58	lived ca. 1110/15 to ca. 1160?
Generation V	
Gaudin (II) m. Eustachie (de Rais?)	lived ca. 1135 to ca. 1180?
Generation VI	
Guillaume, fl. 1185–1218, sire de Clisson and La Benâte and baron, m. Flavie	lived ca. 1162 to ca. 1218/20
Generation VII	
Guillaume II, fl. 1204–16, m. Constance de Pontchâteau (d. 1244)	lived ca. 1185 to ca. 1221

Abbreviations

ADCA	Archives Départementales, Côtes d'Armor (Saint-Brieuc)
ADIV	Archives Départementales, Ille-et-Vilaine (Rennes)
ADLA	Archives Départementales, Loire-Atlantique (Nantes)
ADPA	Archives Départementales, Pyrénées-Atlantiques (Pau)
ADS	Archives Départementales, Sarthe (Le Mans)
AESC	*Annales: Economies, Sociétés, Civilisations*
AHM	*Archives historiques du Maine*
AHR	*American Historical Review*
AHP	*Archives historiques de Poitou*
AN	Archives Nationales, Paris
ASAN	*Annales de la Société Académique de Nantes et du Département de la Loire Inférieure*
BÉC	*Bibliothèque de l'École des Chartes*
BIHR	*Bulletin of the Institute of Historical Research* (London)
BMN	Bibliothèque Municipale ("Médiathèque"), Nantes
BN	Bibliothèque Nationale, Paris
CBourg	Collection Bourgogne (Bibliothèque Nationale)
CL	Collection Clairambault (Bibliothèque Nationale)
Doat	Collection Doat (Bibliothèque Nationale)
Foedera	*Foedera, conventiones litterae et cujuscunque generis acta publica inter reges Angliae et alios quosvis imperatores, pontifices, principes vel communitatates.* Comp. T. Rymer, 3d ed., 10 vols., ed. G. Holmes. The Hague, 1739–45.
Frois-B	Jean Froissart. *The Chronicle of Froissart translated by sir John Bourchier, Lord Berners.* 6 vols. London, 1901–3.
Frois-D	Jean Froissart. *Chroniques. Dernière redaction du premier livre. edition du manuscrit de Rome Reg. lat. 869.* Ed. George T. Diller. Paris and Geneva, 1972.
Frois-J	Jean Froissart. *Chronicles of England, France, Spain and the Adjoining Countries . . . by Sir John Froissart.* 2 vols. Trans. Thomas Johnes. London, 1842.
Frois-KL	Jean Froissart. *Oeuvres de Froissart.* 25 vols. in 26. Ed. H. Kervyn de Lettenhove. Bruxelles, 1867–77.
Frois-SHF	Jean Froissart. *Chroniques de J. Froissart* (Société de l'histoire de France). 13 vols. Ed. Siméon Luce, Gaston Raynaud, Leon Mirot, and Albert Mirot. Paris, 1869- .
FR	Manuscrits français (Bibliothèque Nationale)

HL	C. Devic and J. Vaissete. *Histoire générale de Languedoc avec des Notes et les pièces justificatives.* Ed. A. Molinier et al. 16 vols. Toulouse, 1872–1904.
Jones, *DB*	M. Jones. *Ducal Brittany, 1364–1399.* Oxford, 1970.
LAT	Manuscrits latins, Bibliothèque Nationale
Lobineau	G. A. Lobineau. *Histoire de Bretagne, composée sur les titres et les auteurs originaux.* 2 vols. Paris, 1707.
Mandements	L. Delisle, ed. *Mandements et actes divers de Charles V (1364–1380), recueillis dans les collections de la Bibliothèque Nationale.* Paris, 1874.
Morice	H. Morice. *Mémoires pour servir de preuves à l'histoire ecclésiastique et civile de Bretagne.* 3 vols. Paris, 1742–46; repr. 1968.
MSHAB	*Mémoires de la société de l'histoire et d'archéologie de Bretagne.*
NAF	Nouvelles acquisitions françaises (Bibliothèque Nationale).
NAL	Nouvelles acquisitions latines (Bibliothèque Nationale).
ORD	*Ordonnances des roys de France de la troisième race recueillies par ordre chronologique.* 21 vols. Ed. E. J. de Laurière, D. F. Secousse et al. Paris, 1723–1849.
Palmer, *EFC*	J. J. N. Palmer. *England, France, and Christendom, 1377–1399.* London and Chapel Hill, 1972.
P.J.	*Pièces justificatives*
PO	Pièces originales (Bibliothèque Nationale).
RBV	*Revue de Bretagne et de Vendée*
RHAM	*Revue historique et archélogique du Maine*
RJ IV	*Recueil des actes de Jean IV, duc de Bretagne.* 2 vols. Ed. M. Jones. Paris, 1980.
RSD	*Chronique du Religieux de Saint-Denis contenant le règne de Charles VI 1380–1422.* 5 vols. Ed L. Bellaguet. Paris, 1839–40.
RTF 1322–56	J. B. Henneman. *Royal Taxation in Fourteenth Century France: The Development of War Financing, 1322–1356.* Princeton, 1971.
RTF 1356–70	J. B. Henneman. *Royal Taxation in Fourteenth Century France: The Captivity and Ransom of John II, 1356–1370.* Philadelphia, 1976.
Saint-André	G. de Saint-André. *C'est le libvre du bon Jehan, duc de Bretagne.* Ed. E. Charrière (Paris, 1839), in vol. 2 of *Chronique . . . par Cuvelier.*
Soc. Charles	R. Cazelles. *Société politique, noblesse et couronne sous Jean le Bon et Charles V.* Genève, 1982.
Soc. Philippe	R. Cazelles. *La société politique et la crise de la royauté sous Philippe de Valois.* Paris, 1958.
Toudouze, *DCR*	G. G. Toudouze. *Du Guesclin, Clisson, Richemont.* Paris, 1942.

Notes

Chapter 1

1. See Map 2 for some of these possessions.

2. The motto "Pour ce qu'il me plest" appears behind a small equestrian statue of Clisson in the dining room of Josselin castle (see photograph in A. de Rohan, *Le château de Josselin* [Rennes, 1985], p. 2). The engraving in Lobineau 1, facing p. 434, shows the motto as "Pour ce qu'il me plaist."

3. R. Cazelles, "Les Mouvements révolutionnaires du milieu du XIVe siècle et le cycle de l'action politique, *Revue historique* 464 (1962): 279–312, sets forth his basic thesis on the role of the king's small council. It will be seen in Chapter 5 that I disagree with his analysis of the period after 1360 set forth in his later book, *Soc. Charles* (1982).

4. P. Contamine, *Guerre, état, et société à la fin du moyen âge* (Paris, 1971), 163.

5. Many of these documents are indicated in the Bibliography under Bibliothèque Nationale, Collection Clairambault and Pièces Originales. For the process of identifying the prominent commanders, see Appendix 1 and J. B. Henneman, "The Military Class and the French Monarchy in the Late Middle Ages," *AHR* 83 (1978): 952–54 and notes.

6. Henneman, "Military Class," 952–54 and notes, and the tabulations in Appendix 1. For most of the major regions of France, see Map 1.

7. R. Cazelles, *Étienne Marcel: Champion de l'unité française* (Paris, 1984), 233, described a political cleavage in 1358 that placed the west and northwest of the kingdom in opposition to the east and south, and remarked that this division reflected the political battles of the first half of the century that pitted the north and west against Burgundy and Champagne. This important question deserves further study.

8. *Soc. Philippe*, 107–32, 226–35, 433–34.

9. P. Contamine, "The French Nobility and the War," in *The Hundred Years War*, ed. K. Fowler (London, 1971), 138–39.

10. *Soc. Charles*, 64–65. This list is found in BN NAF 7607, fols. 159r–173r.

11. See Appendix 1. For some preliminary remarks about this geographical distribution, see Henneman, "Military Class," 952.

12. Contamine, "French Nobility," 38–39.

13. G. H. Oexle, "Christine et les pauvres," in *The City of Scholars: New Approaches to Christine de Pizan,"* ed. M. Zimmermann and D. De Rentiis (Berlin, 1994), 208.

14. M. Jones, *The Creation of Brittany: A Late Medieval State* (London, 1988), 221; B. Guenée, *Un Meurtre, une société: L'Assassinat du duc d'Orléans, 23 novembre 1407* (Paris, 1992), 38–39. For example, Olivier de Clisson, when he died in 1407, left a fortune in movables alone that was three thousand times as great as the income of a petty noble whose lordship generated two hundred pounds in revenue. When constable of France, Clisson drew a salary that was sixty-six times the salary paid to an ordinary knight.

15. M. Le Mené, *Les campagnes angevines à la fin du moyen âge: étude économique (vers 1350–vers 1550)* (Nantes, 1982), 161; G. Bois, *The Crisis of Feudalism: Economy and Society in Eastern Normandy, c. 1300–1500* (Cambridge and New York: 1984, an English translation of his *Crise de feodalisme* [Paris, 1976]), 219.

16. Bois, *Crisis*, 227; Le Mené, *Compagnes angevines*, 456.

17. Le Mené, *Compagnes angevines*, 447, points out that some of these sources of revenue are hard to classify juridically but arose from the ability to command and the obligation to protect the subjects of a lord.

18. Bois, *Crisis*, 50 ff. The table presented here omits some figures for other years in the 1420s and 1430s that show fluctuations in the fifteenth century.

19. Le Mené, *Campagnes angevines*, 209–10. R. Favreau, *La Ville de Poitiers à la fin du moyen âge: une capitale regionale* (Paris, 1978), 178–79.

20. Bois, *Crisis*, 294–95, mentions the impact of the plague, but seems to regard warfare (discussed below) as the major factor in Normandy after 1357.

21. Among the studies that provide enlightening details on how the plague of 1348 affected the population, see R. Emery, "The Black Death of 1348 in Perpignan," *Speculum* 42 (1967): 611–23; E. Carpentier, "Autour de la peste noire: Famines et épidemies dans l'histoire du XIVe siècle," *AESC* 17 (1962): 1062–92; G. Prat, "Albi et la peste noire," *Annales du Midi* 44 (1952): 15–25.

22. Although Bois, *Crisis*, seems sensitive to charges of excessive "Malthusianism," he leaves no doubt as to where he stands: "the demographic system is the major issue. . . . a regressive trend long since begun" (3).

23. Le Mené, *Campagnes angevines*, passim; Favreau, *Ville de Poitiers*, 178–84.

24. H. Touchard, *Le Commerce maritime breton à la fin du moyen âge* (Paris, 1967), 55. Y. Gicquel, *Olivier de Clisson (1336–1407): Connétable de France ou chef de parti breton?* (Paris, 1981), suggests (208), that the disruption of trade by civil war kept the plague out of the duchy, and even questions (155) whether Brittany experienced any demographic decline, but the region did experience famine in the 1340s, according to J.-P. Leguay and H. Martin, *Fastes et malheurs de la Bretagne ducale 1213–1532* (Rennes, 1982), 104, and economic dislocations there have been noted by M. Buteau, "La Naissance de la fortune de Clisson" (*Mémoire de maîtrise*, University of Vincennes, 1970, deposited at Archives départementales du Morbihan, Vannes), 1. It is also clear from J. Kerhervé, *L'État breton aux 14e et 15e siècles: Les Ducs, l'argent, et les hommes* (Paris, 1987), 549–51, that the number of hearths had declined nearly 50 percent by 1395. What is not clear is when the outdated larger hearth count was first compiled. The Breton Estates granted a hearth tax (*fouage*) to the duke in 1365 (below, Chapter 3), but circumstances may have precluded a new census at that time, forcing the tax to be based on hearth counts used

for earlier *fouages* mentioned by M. Planiol, *Histoire des institutions de la Bretagne* (repr. Paris, 1981) 3: 311.

25. Bois, *Crisis*, 221.

26. Ibid, 220. Favreau, *Ville de Poitiers*, 181, indicates a catastrophic fall in agricultural receipts in Poitou between 1348 and 1378.

27. Le Mené, *Compagnes angevines*, 213–14.

28. Bois, *Crisis*, 94.

29. Ibid., 255–56.

30. Ibid, 316 ff. and 335 ff.

31. Le Mené, *Campagnes angevines*, 220. For the Breton war of succession, see the next chapter.

32. Le Mené, *Campagnes angevines*, 198, 215, 220–23.

33. Ibid., 200–203.

34. Ibid., 206–8.

35. Ibid., 229, and his summary, 501–2. In the early years of the century, the duchy of Anjou avoided the worst effects of the princely civil war in France. The duke's alliance with Brittany and Alençon may have helped (ibid., 224–25).

36. Ibid., 462. Bois, *Crisis*, 230–231.

37. Le Mené, *Compagnes angevines*, 458–60; Bois, *Crisis*, 228–30.

38. Bois, *Crisis*, 229.

39. Ibid., 231–33.

40. Le Mené, *Compagnes angevines*, 454. According to Buteau, "Naissance," 104, the value of justice to a great lord is demonstrated by Olivier de Clisson's constant effort to extend his jurisdiction.

41. Le Mené, *Compagnes angevines*, 464.

42. Ibid., 466; Bois, *Crisis*, p. 235.

43. Bois, *Crisis*, 300 ff. places the recovery in this period, while Le Mené, *Campagnes angevines*, 470, limits it to the first twenty years of the fifteenth century. Neither author gives the recovery much emphasis because of the ensuing crisis. A single shipment of grain at Champtoceaux, authorized by Olivier de Clisson in 1375 (ADLA E 232, no. 2 16), exceeded the total shipments reported for 1355–56 (Touchard, *Commerce*, 38). Additional evidence of some recovery may be adduced from the repairs to castles and churches after 1380 following heavy earlier war damage: BN FR 20686, fols. 10–12, 15–21 (Poitou), 26–41 (Normandy), 42–49, 50–57 (Limousin); and G. Mollat, "Les Désastres de la Guerre de Cent Ans en Bretagne," *Annales de Bretagne* 26 (1910–11): 183–201.

44. Bois, *Crisis*, 300–313, reviews the demographic, military, monetary, and fiscal changes that contributed to better times in the latter part of the century without, however, my emphasis on the lords.

45. For 1328–31, see *RTF 1322–56*, 348; for 1374, A. Vuitry, *Études sur le régime financier de la France avant la Révolution de 1789* (Paris, 1878–83) 2: 654–56. Some of this large decline is attributable to reductions of the domain for the creation of large princely *apanages* in the 1360s. The improvement in the 1380s and 1390s, however (see M. Rey, *Le Domaine du roi et les finances extraordinaire sous Charles VI* [Paris, 1965], pp. 370–77), was not accompanied by significant terri-

torial changes in the domain. The figure for 1460 is taken from C. Petit-Dutaillis, in E. Lavisse, *Histoire de France* (1900–11) 4 pt. 2: 255. Because these authors do not present precisely the same things as "ordinary revenues," I have added or subtracted items to make the figures as comparable as possible, but have not adjusted them for changes in the currency. For a review of medieval royal revenues, see my forthcoming chapter in *Rise of the Fiscal State in Europe, 1200–1815*, ed. R. Bonney (Oxford and New York: 1996).

46. J. B. Henneman, "Taxation of Italians by the French Crown, 1311–1363," *Mediaeval Studies* 31 (1969): 15–43, esp. 26–27, 35–43.

47. *RTF 1322–56*, 331–44.

48. Ibid., 169, 340, 343; R. Cazelles, "Quelques réflexions à propos des mutations de la monnaie royale française (1295–1360)," *Le Moyen Age* 72 (1966): 262–63; E. Bridrey, *La Theorie de la monnaie au XIVe siècle, Nicole Oresme* (Paris, 1906), esp. 45–54, 183–297, 485–88.

49. *RTF 1356–70*, 25–83.

50. Bois, *Crisis*, 236–37.

51. Kerhervé, *État breton*, 737–38, indicates fiefs of some Breton nobles producing less than twenty pounds a year. BN FR 11531, 320–54, a list of *rachats* owed to the duke of Brittany towards the end of the fourteenth century, indicates average payments of thirty pounds. These were supposed to correspond roughly with a year's income but may have been less.

52. BN PO 789 doss. 18,789 Clisson, no. 61.

53. G. Jouve, *Montcontour de Bretagne* (Saint-Brieuc, 1990), 84–85.

54. AN P 594, fols. 1–23v, lists forty-eight fiefs directly dependent on La Garnache and then, fols. 24r–36r, lists fiefs of Beauvoir-sur-Mer, a dependency of La Garnache and some additional holdings in the direct *mouvance* of La Garnache.

55. Le Mené, *Campagnes angevines*, 158–59.

56. G. Bois, "Noblesse et crise des revenus seigneuriaux en France aux XIVe et XVe siècles: essai d'interpretation, *La Noblesse au moyen âge, XIe–XVe siècles: Essais à la mémoire de Robert Boutrouche*, ed. P. Contamine, (Paris, 1976), p. 220.

57. M. G. A. Vale, "Warfare and the Life of the French and Burgundian Nobility in the Late Middle Ages," *Adelige Sachcultur des Spätmittelalters: International Kongress Krenis an der Donau, 22. bis 25. September 1980* (Osterreichische Akademie der Wissenschaften, Wien, 1982), 174.

58. *Ibid.*, pp. 182–86. On the vulnerability of petty lords and lordships to the *routiers*, see also Favreau, *Ville de Poitiers*, 180, 183.

59. Le Mené, *Campagnes angevines*, 488–90.

60. *ORD*, 7: 186–89 (1388), 524–27 (1393).

61. Brittany was exceptional in that a noble could participate in certain local or retail commercial activities without losing status: Touchard, *Commerce*, 356–63.

62. Contamine, "French Nobility," 145.

63. Contamine, *Guerre*, 654–56. Vale, "Warfare," at 192–93, lists many different prices for horses in the late thirteenth and the fourteenth century, ranging from a few pounds to a few hundred. On the importance of the horse, see also Guenée, *Meurtre*, 48–49.

64. *AHM* 5: 161–62, no. 180.

65. Contamine, *Guerre*, p. 641.

66. See above at note 27.

67. Vale, "Warfare," 175. Vale further points out (p. 177) that a noble who could not equip himself properly as a warrior was not in a position to grasp the opportunities afforded by military employment or the profits of war.

68. *Mandements*, no. 154; BN FR 25764, no. 173; BN NAF 7414, fol. 154.

69. Bois, *Crisis*, 259. Vale, "Warfare," 179–80, referring to the nobility, calls royal service "the life-line at which they clutched." In the words of Contamine, "French Nobility," 159, "the budget of the state was to some extent a budget of noble assistance." See also Guenée, *Meurtre*, 39–40. Kerhervé, *État breton*, 723–34, has shown that the duke of Brittany employed many lesser nobles in his financial administration.

70. Guenée, *Meurtre*, 60–61. C. Gauvard, *"De grace especial": Crime, état, et société en France à la fin du moyen âge* (Paris, 1991), places honor at the root of most violent crime and has a lengthy chapter, 705–52, on wounded honor as a factor in crime. She is at pains to point out, however, that "honor" in this sense was not a monopoly of the nobility.

71. *Soc. Charles*, 29; Cazelles, *Étienne Marcel*, 46.

72. *Soc. Philippe*, 288–89; *Soc. Charles*, 61–62; Cazelles, *Étienne Marcel*, 116–17.

73. *Soc. Charles*, 62. Throughout this book, the word "reform," when not otherwise qualified, will refer to this agenda, but from the reign of Charles V it increasingly included another component—an emphasis on law and judicial procedures in the conduct of government.

74. Cazelles, "Mouvements révolutionnaires," 294.

75. *Soc. Philippe*, 137, 140, 146–48.

76. Ibid., 142–45.

77. *Soc. Charles*, 91–92; R. Cazelles, "Le Parti navarrais jusqu'à la mort d'Étienne Marcel," *Bulletin philologique et historique* (1960): 847–49.

78. *Soc. Charles*, 89; Cazelles, *Étienne Marcel*, p. 304; Cazelles, "Parti navarrais," p. 845; *Chronique des règnes de Jean II et de Charles V*, ed. R. Delachenal (Paris, 1910) 1:39, 63.

79. Cazelles, "Parti navarrais," 860–62.

80. S. H. Cuttler, *The Law of Treason and Treason Trials in Later Medieval France* (Cambridge, 1982), 116–17, 142, 145, 150. Gauvard, *De grace especial*, 840–43, points out that expanding royal power not only created more instances of *lèse majesté*, but that the crime itself can be seen as a crime involving wounded honor, in this case the king's.

81. *Soc. Philippe*, 159.

82. *Soc. Charles*, 149–50.

83. *Soc. Philippe*, 248–52.

84. Ibid., 429; *Soc. Charles*, 85 ff.

85. R. Delachenal, *Histoire de Charles V* (Paris, 1909–31) 1:83.

86. *Soc. Charles*, 142–43, 161; Cazelles, *Étienne Marcel*, 120.

87. *Soc. Charles*, 94, 161.

88. Ibid., 138–39, 147, 173 ff., 181.

89. *RTF 1356–70*, 30–35 and notes.

90. *Soc. Charles*, 154, 159.

91. Cazelles, *Étienne Marcel*, 115–16, 253; *Soc. Charles*, 358–60. The issue of whether to dismember the realm by granting Edward III full sovereignty over his French lands was one that would continue to divide the advisers of John II from those of his son Charles (see Chapter 5).

92. *Soc. Charles*, 204, 220–21; Cazelles, *Étienne Marcel*, 130.

93. *Soc. Charles*, 219–21; Cazelles, *Étienne Marcel*, 138.

94. Delachenal, *Charles V* 1:149–157.

95. *Soc. Charles*, 230.

96. Ibid., 270–73. See also *RTF 1356–70*, 44–48 and notes, and the important recent work of F. Autrand, *Charles V le Sage* (Paris, 1994), 266–68.

97. *Soc. Charles*, 290–92; Cazelles, *Étienne Marcel*, 235–39.

98. *Soc. Charles*, 330; Cazelles, *Étienne Marcel*, 268; Delachenal, *Charles V* 1: 356–63; *RTF 1356–70*, 67; Autrand, *Charles V*, 298–330.

99. *Soc. Charles*, 332–33. Cazelles mentioned more than once the king of Navarre's shifting alliances and the ways in which he exasperated his supporters (ibid., 59, 193). On the other hand, in *Étienne Marcel*, 315, he stated that the main reason that nobles rallied to the dauphin was their hope for wealth in salaries or plunder. Payment of royal military salaries in actual gold coin rather than weaker money of account offered increased purchasing power to nobles who served and made royal service more attractive (Contamine, *Guerre*, 98, 116–17).

100. *Soc. Charles*, 332, 402 ff.

101. Ibid., 380–82.

102. *ORD* 3:433–442 (5 December 1360), discussed in *RTF 1356–70*, 117–21, and Autrand, *Charles V*, 426–29. Autrand (ibid., 417) rightly calls this ordinance the keystone of the new pro-noble regime that took power in 1360.

103. The defeat of Charles the Bad's troops at Cocherel in Normandy occurred in the spring of the year. For the battle of Auray in Brittany, see next chapter. An excellent brief summary of Charles V's rapprochement with former dissidents is found in F. Autrand, *Charles VI: La Folie du roi* (Paris, 1986), 174. Autrand's two excellent royal biographies, which are cited frequently in these pages, would be more useful to scholars if they contained notes that cited specific sources.

Chapter 2

1. A. de la Borderie, *Histoire de Bretagne* (continued by B. A. Pocquet du Haut-Jussé; Paris & Rennes, 1896–1914), 3:409; Jones, *Creation*, 26, 34.

2. F. A. A. de la Chesnaye-Des Bois, *Dictionnaire de la noblesse de la France*, 3d. ed. (Paris, 1863–76), 14:401.

3. Ibid. 6:442–43.

4. R. Blanchard, "Cartulaire des sires de Rays," *AHP* 28 (1898): lxxxi–lxxxii. On the Breton marches, consult Map 2 and see the remarks of Planiol, *Institutions* 3: 10–12.

5. See Appendix 2 for details of the Clisson genealogy, for which the major genealogical reference works are utterly inadequate.

6. On the source of the name Olivier, see Buteau, "Naissance," 15. On Blain and the inheritance of Constance, see L. Prevel, "Le Château de Blain: Sa description, son histoire," *ASAN* 40 (1869): 39; F.-L. Bruel, "Inventaire de meubles et de titres trouves au château de Josselin à la mort du connétable de Clisson (1407)," *BÉC* 66 (1905): 211, note 1; C. Gaden-Puchet, "Le Château de Blain" (ADLA, microfilm of unpublished *Mémoire de maîtrise*, University of Paris, 1969), 3–5; M. Buffé, *Blain de la prehistoire à nos jours* (Nantes, 1968), 53.

7. Morice 1, cols. 976, 980–981, and ADLA E 165, no. 1, partly published by Prevel, "Château de Blain," 132–33.

8. On the destruction and reconstruction of Blain castle, see Gaden-Puchet, "Château de Blain," 5, and Buffé, *Blain*, 56–57. For Olivier II's career, marriage, and acquisition of Le Thuit, see Buteau, "Naissance," 18–22. As indicated in Appendix 2, familiar genealogical works have seriously erroneous accounts of him.

9. Blanchard's notes in ADLA 7 JJ 70 document the death of Guillaume by 1307. Isabelle de Craon could not have married Olivier II, as older sources have asserted and must have married Guillaume (again, see Appendix 2).

10. Buteau, "Naissance," 34–38. On the importance of the vast Belleville holdings, see Chapter 3.

11. *AHP* 13 (1883): 111; BN FR 22348, fols. 55r–56r. Maurice (named after Jeanne's father, as often happened with the son of an important heiress) seems to have died young. For more on the offspring of Jeanne and Olivier III, see Appendix 2.

12. La Borderie, *Histoire* 3:382.

13. B. Pocquet du Haut-Jussé, *Deux feodaux: Bourgogne et Bretagne* (Paris, 1935), 24; Lobineau 1: 306; P. Gaillou and M. Jones, *The Bretons* (Oxford, 1991), 218. Squabbles over the dowry were well underway by the 1330s (AN JJ 66, nos. 925, 1422, 1424).

14. Doat 243, fols. 274r–v; ADLA E 165, no. 2; ADCA E 1, 1st liasse; M. Chauvin-Lechaptois, *Les comptes de la châtellenie de Lamballe (1387–1482)* (Paris, 1977), 11; La Borderie, *Histoire* 3:400–410.

15. La Borderie, *Histoire* 3:403–9. The plan to convey the duchy to the king of France is mentioned in *Chronique latine de Guillaume de Nangis . . . continuations*, ed. H. Géraud (Paris, 1843) 2:144–45. In June of 1337, John III had arranged for his niece to marry the five-year-old Charles of Évreux, future king of Navarre (BN FR 22338, fol. 99r). Not only was Charles of Blois close to Jeanne in age, but Philip VI surely favored a marriage to his nephew over the risk that Brittany might pass to the house of Évreux.

16. Gaillou and Jones, *Bretons*, 218.

17. *Chronique de Jean le Bel*, ed. J. Viard and E. Deprez (Paris, 1904–05) 1: 246–59; Frois-D, pp. 462–73; Frois-J 1:87–92; Frois-SHF 2:87–102, 269–305; A. Bouchart, *Grandes chroniques de Bretagne* (Paris, 1986) 2:36–38; *Chronique normande du XIVe siècle*, ed. A. Molinier and E. Molinier (Paris, 1882), 38–39; Lobineau 1: 311–14. Modern writers who have followed this interpretation of the events include F. Plaine, *Histoire du Bienheureux Charles de Blois, duc de Bretagne et*

vicomte de Limoges (Saint-Brieuc, 1921), 493–94; La Borderie, *Histoire* 3:420–29 and J. Sumption, *The Hundred Years War: Trial by Battle* (London, 1990), 374–77.

18. Gaillou and Jones, *Bretons*, 218–20. Cf. Jones in *Froissart, Historian*, ed. J. J. N. Palmer (Woodbridge, 1981), 78. Perhaps the most detailed recent treatment of the events of 1341 and 1342 is that of M. Jones, "Nantes au debut de la guerre civile en Bretagne," *Villes, bonnes villes, cités et capitales: Mélanges offerts à Bernard Chevalier* (Tours, 1989), 108–13.

19. Gaillou and Jones, *Bretons*, 220.

20. BN FR 22338, fols. 117r–154v.

21. Buteau, "Naissance," 40.

22. Morice 1, cols. 1122–23.

23. M. Jones, ed., "Some Documents Relating to the Disputed Succession to the Duchy of Brittany, 1341," *Camden Miscellany* 24 (1972): 15–70.

24. Ibid., 4.

25. Morice 1, cols. 1421–24 (from ADLA E 165, no. 3). Gaillou and Jones, *Bretons*, 220.

26. Gaillou and Jones, *Bretons*, 220–21. For the English concessions to Montfort, see Morice 1, col. 1424, and *Foedera* 2 pt. 4:119.

27. La Borderie, *Histoire* 3:428. Amaury became the guardian of Montfort's son (Lobineau 2, col. 489, and below, note 36).

28. Gaillou and Jones, *Bretons*, 222. A plan of compromise drafted by two bishops is in Morice 1, cols. 1426–28.

29. La Borderie, *Histoire* 3: 421.

30. Jones, *Creation*, 222, 225. See also Kerhervé, *État breton*, 723–38, and above, Chapter 1, note 51.

31. Gaillou and Jones, *Bretons*, 223.

32. Ibid., p. 222; Frois-D, pp. 503–48; Bouchart, *Grandes chroniques* 2: 50; Sumption, *Hundred Years War*, 389–91. The principal Montfortist emissary to the English in this period was Amaury de Clisson. Jones, "Some Documents," 72–74, has published Edward III's confirmation of an indenture with Clisson dated 21 February 1342 and, among other things, identifying Clisson as the tutor and guardian of Montfort's little son. See also *Foedera* 2 pt. 4:120; Morice 1, cols. 1435–36; and M. Jones, "Les Capitaines anglo-bretons et les marches entre la Bretagne et le Poitou de 1342 a 1373," *Actes du 111ᵉ Congrès National des sociétés savantes* (Paris, 1988): 361.

33. Gaillou and Jones, *Bretons*, 223; Sumption, *Hundred Years War*, 406–7; La Borderie, *Histoire* 3: 471–72. Kerhervé, *État breton*, 31, points out that most of the historical ducal lands were near the coasts.

34. *Robertus de Avesbury de gestis mirabilibus regis Edwardi Tertii*, ed. E. M. Thompson (London, 1889), 344–48; Sumption, *Hundred Years War*, 407 ff.; La Borderie, *Histoire* 3:477.

35. *Soc. Philippe*, 151.

36. Buteau, "Naissance," 49–51, gives the authoritative statement of Clisson's holdings at this time, but see also M. Duboueix, "Topographie de la ville de Clisson," *ASAN* 39 (1968): 145–47.

37. A. Lefranc, *Olivier de Clisson, connétable de France* (Paris, 1898), 24; Toudouze, *DCR*, 57.

38. H. Furgeot, ed., *Actes du Parlement de Paris*, vol. 1 (Paris, 1920), no. 3817.

39. Bouchart, *Grandes chroniques* 2:58; A. Mazas, *Vies des grands capitaines francais du moyen âge*, 2d ed. (Paris, 1838), 4:349.

40. La Borderie, *Histoire* 3:474; Jones, "Capitaines," 361. For Edward's letter of 5 December, see Frois-KL 18:199–202, and *Robertus de Avesbury*, 340–42.

41. Lefranc, *Olivier*, 38.

42. Jones, *Creation*, 341.

43. AN U 785, fols. 6v, 124r; Lefranc, *Olivier*, 23–24 and 429–30 (*P.J.* 2, from AN X²ᵃ 4, fol. 186); *Chron. normande*, 60; *Les Grandes Chroniques de France*, ed. J. Viard (Paris, 1920–37) 9: 241–42; La Borderie, *Histoire* 3: 482; *Soc. Philippe*, 153; Cuttler, *Law of Treason*, 147; Gauvard, *De grace especial*, 115–16, 903; M. Langlois and Y. Lanhers, *Confessions et jugements des criminels au Parlement de Paris (1319–1350)* (Paris, 1971), 150–52; Y. Doucet, *Histoire de la vallée de Clisson* (Maulévrier, 1992), 65–66. Documents relating to the confiscation or the judgment are also found in BN FR 22338, fols. 159–164, and ADLA E 103, no. 12. Royal officers apparently seized some lands belonging to Clisson's mother, Isabelle de Craon, as part of her dowry, and these had to be returned: BN FR 10430, p. 296; Fonds Grandville en Bringolo, cabinet 28. Clisson's execution and the early deaths of two of his confederates (Rais and Machecoul) soon broke up Edward's coalition in the marches (Jones, "Capitaines," 362).

44. Bouchart, *Grandes chroniques* 2:63; Saint-André, lines 200 ff.; Lefranc, *Olivier*, 26–27; Doucet, *Vallée*, 66. La Borderie, *Histoire* 3:482, found Clisson's arrest a flagrant violation of the provision in the truce that allowed adherents of both sides to come and go freely.

45. *AHP* 13 (1883):109. The persistent legend that Jeanne was timid and retiring before the execution of her spouse is refuted further by the fact that the Parlement had already summoned her to answer charges of disloyalty: Cuttler, *Law of Treason*, 147. Most recently Doucet has perpetuated her reputation as the "Breton tigress" (*Vallée*, 67–68).

46. On 21 September 1343, the pope acted on French complaints and asked Edward to halt violations of the truce by his supporters: B.-A. Pocquet du Haut-Jussé, *Les Papes et les ducs de Bretagne* (Paris, 1928) 1:277; La Borderie, *Histoire* 3:483. For the condemnation of the lady of Clisson for treason, see Langlois and Lanhers, *Confessions et jugements*, 153–54; BN FR 22338, fol. 164r; Lefranc, *Olivier*, 29, 430; The king's men estimated that the confiscated Clisson-Belleville properties were worth a total of twenty thousand pounds in income (H. Moranvillé, "Rapports à Philippe VI sur l'état de ses finances," *BÉC* 48 [1887]: 388–90). For grants of some of this income to royal followers, *AHP* 13 (1883): 289, 293; *Registres du Trésor des Chartes 3: Règne de Philippe de Valois*, ed. J. Viard and A. Vallée (Paris, 1979) 2: 358–59, 377, 390. Buteau, "Naissance," 44–49, carefully discusses the Clisson-Belleville holdings and their disposition.

47. Small fragments of the story, containing obvious errors, appear in *Chronographia regnum francorum*, ed. H. Moranvillé (Paris, 1893) 2:205–6, and *Chron. Normande*, 60–61, the sources cited by Lefranc, *Olivier*, 26–29, and La Borderie, *Histoire* 3:483. A longer account is that of the often unreliable P. Levot, *Biographie bretonne* (Vannes and Paris, 1852) 1: 360–61. I have drawn here primarily on

O. Biou, "Notice sur Jeanne de Belleville, poème de M. Émile Pehant," *ASAN* 39 (1868): 197–220, but have followed Buteau, "Naissance," 52, in saying that Jeanne reached Hennebont, where the countess of Montfort had been staying. Mazas, *Vies* 4:351, followed Pehant's poem and Levot in saying she reached the less probable destination of Morlaix, and also in treating Guillaume as her younger son, but he departed from these sources is saying that the fortress whose garrison Jeanne massacred was actually Lannion, near Morlaix.

48. The countess of Montfort was not at Hennebont when Jeanne de Belleville arrived. Having probably traveled to England with Edward III in May 1343, she was certainly living in London in August and November and probably did not return to Brittany (La Borderie, *Histoire* 3:486–89; see also below, notes 54–57). Jeanne de Belleville must have conducted her hostile operations in August and early September, and is unlikely to have tarried in Brittany after her property was seized and her income cut off in November–December. Since Jean de Montfort was at Hennebont when he made the grant cited in the next note, it is at least conceivable that Jeanne was still there in 1345, but I find no basis for accepting the view of Gicquel, *Olivier*, 31–32 that she and Olivier did not reach England until the time of the Black Death (1348–49).

49. Morice 1, cols. 1452–53. The gift was confirmed by Edward III nine years later: Morice 1, cols. 1494–95; Lobineau 2, cols. 491–492; G. Peyronnet, "Les Sources documentaires anglaises de l'histoire médiévale de la Bretagne," *Annales de Bretagne et des pays de l'ouest* 96 (1989): 310.

50. Lobineau 2, col. 491. This income had belonged to her family but presumably had not been received since the outbreak of the war. Buteau, "Naissance," 55, considers it an important donation. On Edward's largesse to Jeanne, see also Lefranc, *Olivier*, 32–34.

51. *Foedera* 3 pt. 1:20–22; Pocquet, *Papes* 1:299; *Robertus de Avesbury*, 398; Buteau, "Naissance," 53. F. Plaine, *Jeanne de Penthièvre, duchesse de Bretagne* (Saint-Brieuc, 1873), noted the absence of Jeanne of Flanders from this list.

52. Lobineau 2, col. 491. Mazas, *Vies* 4:354, said that Jeanne did not marry Bentley until 1349, and in fact that is the first year in which his name is mentioned in grants to her.

53. La Borderie, *Histoire* 3:486–89; J. Leland, "Heroine or Lunatic: The Alleged Madness of the Duchess of Brittany" (paper, Bowling Green State University, 1986), 6. For the payment of her expenses in 1344, see *Foedera* 2 pt. 4:164.

54. Leland, "Heroine or Lunatic," passim, but esp. 5–9.

55. Gaillou and Jones, *Bretons*, 224–25; Kerhervé, *État breton*, 583.

56. The Montfortist cause suffered important defections when Philip VI declared an amnesty towards the end of 1344, and the English practices in Brittany could have been a factor. Leland, "Heroine or Lunatic," 9–10, suggests that Jeanne's incarceration may have influenced the defectors, but one of them, Amaury de Clisson, was still carrying out missions for Edward III as late as September (La Borderie, *Histoire* 3:487). Perhaps her supporters did not yet suspect that she was a prisoner.

57. Gicquel, *Olivier*, 39; Toudouze, *DCR*, 61.

58. Mazas, *Vies* 4:354–55; Buteau, "Naissance," 53; Lefranc, *Olivier*, 37–38; Gicquel, *Olivier*, 39–40; J. Roy, *Histoire d'Olivier de Clisson* (Paris, 1872), 30.

59. Toudouze, *DCR*, 61; Buteau, "Naissance," 53; Lefranc, *Olivier*, 37–38.

60. Lefranc, *Olivier*, 38. As Jones, *Creation*, 225–26, points out, the great strains of the civil war led to the failure of traditional feudal ties in Brittany generally.

61. For the amnesty of Amaury de Clisson (AN JJ 75, no. 148) and thirteen others (nos. 149–161), see *Registres du Trésor des Chartes* 3 pt. 2:379–80. Cf. La Borderie, *Histoire* 3: 480, 494.

62. Morice 1, cols. 1442–47; Plaine, *Histoire*, 542–49.

63. La Borderie, *Histoire* 3:498–499.

64. Ibid., 500–505; *Gr. Chron. de France* 9:298–306; Saint-André, lines 405–46; *Cont. Nangis* 2:194; Plaine, *Histoire*, 565–70. Bouchart, *Grandes chroniques* 2:70, lists over a dozen great Breton lords killed in the battle.

65. La Borderie, *Histoire* 3:507.

66. *Foedera* 3 pt. 1:3, 35, 38; Lobineau 2, cols. 491, 492–93; Peyronnet, "Sources documentaires," 310; K. Fowler, *The King's Lieutenant: Henry of Grosmont, First Duke of Lancaster (1310–1361)* (London and New York, 1969), 89.

67. Jones, "Capitaines," 365.

68. Ibid., 365–66; *Gr. chron. de France* 9:326. See documents published in Frois-KL 18: 334–35 and *AHP* 17 (1887): 26–32; also Fowler, *King's Lieutenant*, 390–91; Lefranc, *Olivier*, 33.

69. La Borderie, *Histoire* 3:530–533; Jones, "Capitaines," 366–67; Gaillou and Jones, *Bretons*, 226; *Robertus de Avesbury*, 415–16; Saint-André, lines 470–90; Plaine, *Jeanne*, 21–22. Edward III had appointed Bentley on 8 September 1350 and granted him the revenues of Brittany four days later: *Foedera* 3 pt. 1:57.

70. La Borderie, *Histoire* 3:534–39; Plaine, *Histoire*, 600–601; Gaillou and Jones, *Bretons*, 226; *Foedera* 3 pt. 1: 81, 92; Morice 1, cols. 1486–87.

71. *Foedera* 3 pt. 1:126–28; Morice 1, cols. 1508–11; La Borderie, *Histoire* 3:549.

72. Jones, "Capitaines," 367. Edward named Jean Avenel to be his captain in Brittany on 4 April 1353: *Foedera* 3 pt. 1:84.

73. *Calendar of the Close Rolls Preserved in the Public Record Office: Edward III* (London, 1908), 10:76.

74. Jones, "Capitaines," 367, discovered in ADPA the hitherto unknown evidence of Clisson's trip in 1354. Lefranc, *Olivier*, 39, thought his first verifiable return to France was in 1359.

75. Mazas, *Vies* 4:357–58.

76. E. Perroy *The Hundred Years War*, trans. W. B. Wells (London, 1951), 129–31; Autrand, *Charles V*, 174–220, and above, Chapter 1.

77. Lobineau 2, col. 498; Fowler, *King's Lieutenant*, 161–62; Gaillou and Jones, *Bretons*, 226.

78. Lobineau 2, col. 497; *RJ IV*, no. 1.

79. Jones, "Capitaines," 368. Mazas, *Vies* 4:355, declared that Clisson first gained his reputation as an audacious fighter during this campaign.

80. La Borderie, *Histoire* 3:551–59; Gaillou and Jones, *Bretons*, 226. For Froissart's well-known account of the siege of Rennes, see Frois-B 1:395; Frois-KL 6:21–26.

81. *Soc. Charles*, 94–95, 551–53.

82. Lobineau 1:349; Lefranc, *Olivier*, 36–39. Gicquel, *Olivier*, 10, makes the important point that Clisson was, perhaps especially, a political figure, while Du Guesclin never wanted to be anything but a soldier.

83. The consequences of John II's capture, mentioned in the last chapter, are discussed in more detail in *RTF 1356–70*, 25–122 and (for the freebooters in northern France) 206–46.

84. Fowler, *King's Lieutenant*, 163–64; Gaillou and Jones, *Bretons*, 226; *Foedera* 3 pt. 1: 137 (order of 28 April to raise the siege); J. J. Champollion-Figeac, ed., *Lettres des rois, reines et autres personnages des cours de France et Angleterre* (Paris, 1839–47) 2:113–14 (second order of 4 July). The Anglo-French truce is in *Foedera* 3 pt. 1:133–36.

85. Jones, *DB*, 14–15.

86. G. Demay, *Inventaire des sceaux de la Collection Clairambault à la Bibliothèque Nationale* (Paris, 1885–86) 1:777 (CL 12, p. 715).

87. Autrand, *Charles V*, 278, 359–60, 367, 382–83, 417–19; *Soc. Charles*, 372.

88. Jones, "Capitaines" 368.

89. *CCR Edward III* 10:481. On the same date, Edward ordered ships made ready for Clisson's voyage: Peyronnet, "Sources documentaires," 464; Morice 1, col. 1527.

90. Jones, "Capitaines" 375, citing a document not included in the edition of *Foedera* at my disposal, but listed by Peyronnet, "Sources documentaires," 464.

91. Morice 1, cols. 1529–30; *Foedera* 3 pt. 1:192; Buteau, "Naissance," 57–59; Lefranc, *Olivier*, 40; Toudouze, *DCR*, 88–89; Gicquel, *Olivier*, 41–42. The lands now named as Olivier's inheritance were by no means all his family's former holdings in the marches, but only those parts that Edward had bestowed on the Bentleys in 1349 (see above, note 52) and what he had promised to Raoul de Caours a year earlier (above, note 66).

92. *Foedera* 3 pt. 1:202–9 (treaty of Brétigny); 3 pt. 2:1–7 (treaty ratified at Calais in October); Gaillou and Jones, *Bretons*, 226.

93. *Foedera* 3 pt. 2:5 (article 25 of the treaty). For the French execution of this provision, see Chapter 3.

94. Morice 1, col. 1546; *Foedera* 3 pt. 2:62; La Borderie, *Histoire*, 369; Plaine, *Histoire*, 679–83.

95. Morice 1, cols. 1547–48, 1453–54.

96. Ibid., col. 1556 for the prolongation of the truce; La Borderie, *Histoire* 3:565–66.

97. Saint-André, lines 873–922; La Borderie, *Histoire* 3:576–79; Plaine, *Histoire*, 684–90; Lobineau 1: 361–62; G. Minois, *Du Guesclin* (Paris, 1993), 173–74.

98. ADCA E 1, second liasse; ADLA E 165, no. 5; Morice 1, cols. 1565–66; Lobineau 2, cols. 504–6; Lefranc, *Olivier*, 47; La Borderie, *Histoire* 3:579. Gicquel, *Olivier*, 63–64, and Minois, *Du Guesclin*, 178–79, maintain the traditional view that Jeanne de Penthièvre was responsible for rejecting the plan, but Plaine, *Jeanne*, 24–26, argued against this charge.

99. Saint-André, lines 991–1010.

100. *Anciens mémoire du XIVe siècle sur Bertrand du Guesclin*, in J. F. Michaud,

Nouvelle collection des mémoires . . . (Paris, 1836–39) 1:473–76; Bouchart, *Grandes chroniques* 2:83; Saint-André, lines 1201 ff.; Lobineau 1:371; Toudouze, *DCR*, 99–101; Lefranc, *Olivier*, 50–52.

101. *Anciens mémoire* 1: 476–78; Bouchard, *Grandes chroniques* 2:82–91; Saint-André, lines 1371–1415; Frois-B 2: 128–29, 140; Frois-KL 7: 25–31, 51–52, 60; Lobineau 1: 372–75; Gicquel, *Olivier*, 67–70; Roy, *Histoire*, 40; Mazas, *Vies* 4:358; Toudouze, *DCR*, 102. Cf. *Chron. des règnes* 2: 5–6.

Chapter 3

1. The quoted words here are those of P. Guérin "Recueil de documents concernant le Poitou . . . ," *AHP* 17 (1887): 325, note 1, and are followed by Delachenal, *Charles V* 4:35. Delachenal deserves credit for pointing out that restitution of Clisson's lands in this period was more than a mere execution of the treaty.

2. Frois-SHF 6:lxxvii, note 2.

3. The document Luce cited (AN JJ 87, no. 274) is clearly dated 27 December, not September, as are two other copies in Nantes (BMN 1689/1533, no. 7 and 1696/1540, 8th piece) and BN PO 789 doss. 17,879 (Clisson), no. 38. On the other hand, Thomas Pinchon, bailiff of Caen, reissued with his endorsement (*vidimus*) a document dated 27 September in which the Chamber of Accounts of the duke of Normandy ordered the barony restored to Clisson by virtue of the treaty of peace (BN FR 26271, no. 485). These texts make mention only of Thury, but one must concur with Buteau, "Naissance," 61, that it was a question of Le Thuit (discussed in Chapter 2 at note 8).

4. *Foedera* 3 pt. 2:30. The treaty of Calais did make one very important change from its predecessor, relegating to a separate document the renunciations of French sovereignty and English claims, which were to be delayed until all the transfers of lands from France to England were complete. See the comments of P. Chaplais, "Some Documents Regarding the Fulfillment and Interpretation of the Treaty of Brétigny (1361–1369)," *Camden Miscellany* 19 (1952):6–7.

5. On the extent of Jeanne's holdings, see Delachenal, *Charles V* 4:33–36, and Buteau, "Naissance," 38–39. The most important archival source for these lands is AN P 594.

6. *Chron. des règnes* 1: 289, and footnote, pp. 268–69); *Foedera* 3 pt. 1:202 (Brétigny); 3 pt. 2:18 (Calais).

7. *Foedera* 3 pt. 1:192 (cited in last chapter).

8. Clisson's half-sister, Louise de Châteaubriant, lady of Laval, held Montaigu, Palluau, Châteaumur, and Les Deffens at the time of her death in 1383 (Buteau, "Naissance," 100), while his younger sister, Jeanne, who was married to Edward III's henchman Jean Harpedenne, received property as well, but it is not clear when these women gained possession of the lands.

9. AN JJ 91, no. 208, published by Guérin, *AHP* 17:310–15.

10. *AHP* 17: xlv–xlviii; A. Bardonnet, ed., *Procès-verbal de délivrance à Jean Chandos, commissaire du roi d'Angleterre, des places françaises abandonées par le traité de Brétigny* (Niort, 1869), 3–8, 31 ff.

11. AN JJ 89, no. 698, published by Guérin in *AHP* 17: 324–27; Lefranc, *Olivier*, *P.J.* 4, pp. 431–32; BN FR 22325, p. 814; Morice 1, col. 1621; Chaplais, "Some Documents," 37. See also Delachenal, *Charles V* 4:34–35.

12. In 1344, when Philip VI had given the confiscated lands to his son and heir, John ordered an inventory of all the Belleville holdings. The resulting document, AN P 594, listed dozens of fiefs in "la terre de Belleville en la châtellenie de Garnache" (fols. 1–23v) and similarly invoked "la terre de Belleville" when listing the fiefs at Beauvoir-sur-mer (fol. 23v), Palluau (fol. 29r), and so forth. By January 1362, the English had possession of a document that probably had the same information: "item, le livre des fiez de Belleville." See J. Viard, "Documents français remis au gouvernement anglais à la suite du traité de Brétigny," *BÉC* 58 (1897): 160.

13. Bardonnet, *Procès-verbal*, 68. The detailed French response to the English requests (AN J 641, no. 5) is published in *Chron. des règnes* 3:81–96 (*P.J.* 10) and (from an English manuscript) Chaplais, "Some Documents," 29–38. John II's letter of restitution was appended in response to the eleventh English request, "que il requirent de la terre de Belleville quelle soit rendue au roy Dangleterre, non obstant quelle soit rendue au sire de Clicon."

14. Chaplais, "Some Documents," 41, 50; Delachenal, *Charles V* 4:34–35; Guérin in *AHP* 17:l–li.

15. Delachenal, *Charles V* 4:36–37; Guérin, in *AHP* 17:l–li, 326–27, n. 1.

16. AN J 654, no. 1.

17. AN J 654, no. 2.

18. The treaty is in *Foedera* 3 pt. 2:70–72, with related documents on pp. 74–75, 78–79. See also Chaplais, "Some Documents," 8. John II's principal ambassador during the spring and summer of 1362 was Jacques le Riche: AN J 641, no. 9, published in *Chron. des règnes* 3:96–101 and Chaplais, "Some Documents," 45–48.

19. Lefranc, *Olivier*, 69.

20. Ibid., *P.J.* 5, pp. 432–34. ADIV 1 F 1527, no. 34; Gicquel, *Olivier*, 42. Some old genealogical works say that Clisson's bride was named Catherine, but in contemporary texts she is always called Béatrix, the name of her mother and eldest daughter.

21. Lefranc, *Olivier*, 43; Buteau, "Naissance," 63; Toudouze, *DCR*, 89–90; Levot, *Biographie bretonne*, 362. Although marriages often took place on or soon after the date of the contract, the marriage of Olivier and Béatrix may have been delayed, since Clisson and Laval were on opposite sides in the war of succession. The couple did not receive the dowry until 1366 (below, note 40), but were certainly married before 15 February 1365 (ADIV 1 F 1527, no. 35) and probably well before then (see Appendix 2).

22. Toudouze, *DCR*, 89, believed that the reacquisition of Le Thuit, Champtoceaux, Beauvoir, and La Garnache, when added to the property he already held in 1360, had brought Clisson's annual income up to around forty-five to fifty thousand pounds. The figure seems inflated, especially if it assumes that he was able to collect in full the predicted receipts from all these properties.

23. See above, Chapter 2, sources cited in notes 98 and 99, as well as Lefranc, *Olivier*, 45; *RJ IV*, no. 30; Jones, "Capitaines," 369, note 46.

24. See citations in Chapter 2, note 101. For specific references to Clisson's

valor in Froissart's chronicle, see Frois-B 2:138; Frois-KL 7:48–49, 57, and Frois-J 1:332–33. Referring to the accounts of chroniclers, Lefranc, *Olivier*, 61–62, observed that his conduct in this battle revealed "the violent and terrible instincts, the hard and pitiless character" of a man whose enemies would begin to call a "butcher."

25. Mazas, *Vies* 4:360; Toudouze, *DCR*, 105–6; Gicquel, *Olivier*, 70–71.

26. Lefranc, *Olivier*, 60; Delachenal, *Charles V* 4:457, note 1, and 458.

27. The inquest was undertaken in 1500 in connection with claims made by Clisson's descendant the viscount of Rohan (ADLA E 182, nos. 1, 2, 18). The account reported here is published in Lobineau 2, cols. 536–37, and has been widely repeated. See Lefranc, *Olivier*, 68–69. In the end, Clisson did acquire Le Gavre, probably in the 1370s but possibly not until many years later (Bruel, "Inventaire," pp. 223–24, note 6). More documentation on Le Gavre is found in ADLA E 166, no. 1.

28. Jones, *DB*, 48.

29. Ibid., 48–50; Peyronnet, "Sources documentaires," 466. John IV did return some of the properties given to Knolles (but not Derval), assigning him various other revenues as compensation. See *RJ IV*, no. 60 (8 November 1365). On Huet, see *RJ IV*, nos. 87, 126, and Jones, "Capitaines," 368–69 and notes. On the importance of Le Collet, see Delachenal, *Charles V* 4:458.

30. M. Jones, "The Diplomatic Evidence for Franco-Breton Relations, c. 1370–1372," *English Historical Review* 93 (1978): 308, note 1.

31. Jones, *DB*, 53–54. As late as 1372, Pierre de Craon, lord of La Suze, was complaining about lands of his that had been given to Huet and not returned (ADIV 1 F 626). The crown had similar problems with confiscated properties, having, for instance, bestowed Le Thuit on a supporter after confiscating it from the Clisson, but it had more resources for compensating those who had to return such lands (*Mandements*, nos. 930A, 937A).

32. La Borderie, *Histoire* 3:595–97.

33. Morice 1, cols. 1584–85; Lobineau 2, col. 507; Gaillou and Jones, *Bretons*, 227.

34. Jones, *DB*, 2, 19.

35. Lobineau 2, cols. 508–16; Morice 1, cols. 1588–89 (evidently based on AN J 241 B, no. 45). The treaty and subsequent royal ratifications may also be found in ADLA E 165, no. 6 and E 236, fols. 63r–66v; ADIV 1 E 7, no. 2; ADCA E 1, third liasse. See also *Chron. des règnes* 2:7–8 and Jones, *DB*, 1.

36. See above, Chapter 2, note 13; below, notes 41 and 73, and also Chapters 6, 8, 10.

37. Kerhervé, *État breton*, 81–82, 584, 587–88.

38. The actual wording of the treaty (Lobineau 2, col. 511) was that "ledit M. Jehan de Bretagne comme duc, par la forme de ses predecesseurs Ducs de Bretagne ont accoustumé faire aux Roys de France, & entrer en foy & hommage du Roy de France, dudit Duché et Pairie de France."

39. Morice 2, cols. 1607–8; Lobineau 2, cols. 524–25; BN Dupuy 635, fols. 139r–140r; ADLA E 6, no. 3.

40. Jones, *DB*, 46; Morice 1, cols. 1608–13; Lobineau 2, cols. 525–30; AN J 241 B, nos. 46, 47; ADLA E 165, nos. 18, 19; BN FR 16654, no. 5, fols. 44–53.

The embassy that preceded the ceremony of December 1366 and worked out the arrangements cited in the next note may be the one mentioned in *RJ IV*, no. 93. For Clisson's earlier mission in May, see below at note 51.

41. *RJ IV*, no. 88 (indicating parts of the larger documents cited in the last note, namely Lobineau 2, cols. 529–30; Morice 1: cols. 1612–13). See also *Chron. des règnes* 2:24–25, and Autrand, *Charles V*, 528–29. Soon after the homage and ratification, Charles V confirmed the privileges of Brittany (ADLA E 103, no. 14 and E 236, fols. 14v–15r) and agreed to pay 6,000 *l.t.* of the annuity John owed Jeanne de Penthièvre, since his lands in eastern France had not been restored (Morice 2, cols. 1613–14; Lobineau 2, cols. 530–31; AN J 241 B, no. 49). He had promised to restore these lands when he ratified the treaty in May (ADLA E 108, no. 1; ADIV 1 E 5, no. 12), but those comprising the dowry of Jeanne of Flanders remained an intractable problem.

42. *RJ IV*, nos. 49, 50, 55. As the wrangling continued over Belleville and other disputed points in the Anglo-French treaty, Edward III had created the principality of Aquitaine for his son on 19 July 1362: *Foedera* 3 pt. 2:67–68.

43. Frois-B 2: 149; Frois-SHF 6: 181–82; Frois-KL 7: 73–74, 78 ("reut li sires de Clicon toute sa terre entierement, que li roisa Phelippes jadis li avoit tolue et ostée. . . . Clicon depuis s'acointa dou roy de France si bien que c'estoit fait en France tout ce qu'il voloit et sans lui n'estoit rien fait"). See also Bouchart, *Grandes chroniques* 2:97.

44. ADIV 1 F 1527, no. 35.

45. ADIV 1 F 1527, nos. 36–38; A. Bertrand de Broussillon, *La Maison de Laval, 1020–1605, étude historique* (Paris, 1895–1900) 2:266–67, no. 727. The war of succession surely affected delivery of the dowry. Guy de Laval was a Blois supporter, Clisson a Montfortist, and Laval's mother, Béatrix of Brittany, a sister of the older Jean de Montfort. The revenues from Champagne actually belonged to Béatrix, who donated them as her daughter's dowry, but was the French king willing to receive homage for them from an avowed Montfortist while the war was still in progress?

46. AN AA 60; Bertrand de Broussillon, *Maison de Laval* 2: no. 728. The dowry also included the castle and lordship of Villenoble, near Paris: Buteau, "Naissance," 63; J-L Martin, "Un Grand Seigneur breton en Ile de France: Olivier de Clisson," *Bulletin de la Société d'Émulation des Côtes-du-Nord* 82 (1953): 59–62.

47. Lefranc, *Olivier*, 63. Clisson's oldest daughter, Béatrix, had also probably been born by this time (see Appendix 2).

48. Toudouze, *DCR*, 106.

49. *RJ IV*, no. 50 (ADLA E 119, no. 5), indicating that Clisson and Jean de Beaumanoir represented the duke on 20 June 1365 when Edward confirmed his alliance with John IV (above, note 42).

50. *RJ IV*, no. 87.

51. Morice 1, cols. 1599–1600. Jones, in *RJ IV*, no. 74, has corrected the date of this commission to 22 March 1366. Both Morice and Lobineau 2, cols. 520–21 dated it 22 May 1365, as did BN Dupuy 635, fols. 137r–138v. This error confused Lefranc's discussion of Clisson's homage for the revenues in Champagne (*Olivier*, 64).

52. See above, notes 39 and 46.

53. Lefranc, *Olivier*, 64–65. Autrand, *Charles VI*, 174, notes the French court's interest in his military qualifications.

54. Bouchart, *Grandes chroniques* 2:99, exaggerated the amount of the ransom. Chandos actually demanded forty thousand francs for Du Guesclin's release, and the crown advanced the money in several installments: BN FR 23952, fols. 40r–v; AN J 381, nos. 4–6; of the sixteen documents in J 381, no. 6, a number have been published by Charrière at the end of Cuvelier's chronicle: *Chron. Du Guesclin* 2:393–401.

55. *RTF 1356–70*, 194–97 and notes.

56. On the Najera campaign, see Bouchart, *Grandes chroniques* 2:105–6; Frois-B 2:208–14; Frois-KL 7: 200–217; *Chron. des règnes* 2:30–31; Lefranc, *Olivier*, pp. 70–71; Minois, *Du Guesclin*, 314–18.

57. Minois, *Du Guesclin*, 77. Chroniclers certainly place Clisson with the prince in Bordeaux during Du Guesclin's captivity (*Anciens memoire*, 523–25; Cuvelier, *Chron. Du Guesclin* lines 13410, 13479).

58. Autrand, *Charles V*, 491–518, and also 546, 552, where the return of the companies was a major French grievance against the Prince of Wales. *Chron. des règnes* 2:37–40; Bouchart, *Grandes chroniques* 2:111; Frois-B 2: 277–78; Frois-KL 7: 248–49; Delachenal, *Charles V* 3:441–42, 449–50. In July 1367, Charles V convened an assembly at Chartres to consider measures against the companies: *ORD* 5:14–18.

59. Cuvelier, *Chron. Du Guesclin*, lines 14304–10, said that Du Guesclin was seeking help on his ransom from various Breton lords in 1368. Charrière, Cuvelier's editor, has published most of the relevant documents from AN J 381 (ibid., 2:402–7). At the end of 1367 Du Guesclin agreed to a ransom of 100,000 gold *doubles* (on the ransom, see Minois, *Du Guesclin*, 327–30, who equates the sum to 140,000 *l.t.*), and again the king put up most of the money, with the constable of Bordeaux receiving several large sums on 25 April 1368. After his release, Du Guesclin was called to deal with the *routiers* in Languedoc: Delachenal, *Charles V* 3:459–62.

60. See above, note 18.

61. Chaplais, "Some Documents," 104–5 (Charles V's letter), 105–6 (those of the former hostage princes) and 167 (Edward III's concurrence). Some of these documents are in BN FR 23952, fols. 60–62 and were cited by Delachenal, *Charles V* 4:39.

62. *Foedera* 3 pt. 2:134–35; Guérin, in *AHP* 17: 326–27, note 1.

63. Morice 1, col. 1621; Lobineau 2, col. 532.

64. Frois-SHF 6:lxxvii, note 2.

65. BN PO 789, doss. 17,879 Clisson, no. 2.

66. AN JJ 103, no. 209; JJ 122, no. 150; A. Bertrand de Broussillon, "Documents inédits pour servir à l'histoire du Maine au XIV⁰ siècle," *AHM* 5 (1905): 173–76, 291–92. This campaign is discussed, with various inaccuracies, by Lefranc, *Olivier*, 78–79; Luce, in Frois-SHF 7: xxvii; Mazas, *Vies* 4:363–64; and Toudouze, *DCR*, 123.

67. Large parts of this document, our principal source for the *fouage* of 1368, are published in the notes of Delachenal, *Charles V* 4:58–60.

68. *HL* 10, cols. 1285–91; Autrand, *Charles V*, 554. P. Tucoo-Chala, *Gaston Fébus et la vicomté de Béarn, 1343–1391* (Bordeaux, 1960), 90, indicates that Armagnac had to pay the count of Foix three hundred thousand gold florins.

69. J. Rouquette, *Le Rouergue sous les anglais* (Millau, 1887), 132–34; Delachenal, *Charles V* 4:64–66; *RTF 1356–70*, 247–53.

70. Rouquette, *Le Rouergue*, 133–34, indicating that the offer to Clisson preceded and provoked Armagnac's appeal to the French court in June. Our source for this offer is a subsequent letter from the count of Armagnac in the Millau archives, much of it quoted by Delachenal, *Charles V* 4:73, note 2.

71. Delachenal, *Charles V* 4:73.

72. ADLA E 217, no. 2, membranes 2–4. The total debt came to 70,200 florins, and Jeanne also still owed 25,000 florins to the pope: Pocquet, *Papes*, 354–56. On the ambiguous position of the viscounty of Limoges after 1360, see R. de Chauvernon, *Des Maillotins aux Marmousets: Audoin Chauvernon, prévôt de Paris sous Charles VI* (Paris, 1992), 37.

73. Charles V promised to pay Jeanne 6,000 *l.t.* in December 1366 (Morice 1, cols. 1613–14) and Jeanne issued receipts for this amount during 1367 (BN FR 22319, pp. 295, 296) and received additional sums over the next few years (ADLA E 165, nos. 9–14). In April 1367 she was negotiating with the duke over assignments of income from ducal lands inside Brittany (ADLA E 165, no. 15; BN FR 22319, p. 298). The cycle continued, however. In January 1369 the king again promised John IV to deliver his mother's dowry lands and in the meantime to pay Jeanne 6,000 *l.t.* (ADLA E 108, no. 2; ADIV 1E 6, no. 2), while Jeanne was still trying to obtain her annuity from lands in Brittany in 1370 and 1371 (BN FR 11531, p. 53; BN FR 22319, p. 295).

74. ADLA E 217, no. 2, membranes 1–2.

75. Ibid., membranes 2–8.

76. BN FR 11531, p. 115; ADLA E 217, no. 3; BN FR 22319, p. 523. Spifame had dealt with the French royal family in 1364 (BN FR 20403, no. 2).

77. BMN 1693/1537, no. 19 (1 October 1370) and documents cited in the next note. BMN 1703/1547, no. 5 (23 May 1371) indicates that Jeanne was guaranteeing repayment of some of the money Clisson owed to Spifame.

78. Lobineau 2, cols. 537–538; Morice 1, col. 1631; BN PO 789 doss. 17,879 Clisson, no. 39 (9 May 1369). I was incorrect in supposing that Jeanne appointed Clisson her lieutenant on this date (J. Henneman, "Reassessing the Career of Olivier de Clisson, Constable of France," in *Law, Custom, and the Social Fabric in Medieval Europe: Essays in Honor of Bryce Lyon*, ed. B. Bachrach and D. Nicholas [Kalamazoo, 1990], 217).

79. Lefranc, *Olivier*, 83; Toudouze, *DCR*, 124; Jones, *DB*, 54; and Gicquel, *Olivier*, 84, all treat Clisson's position as Jeanne's lieutenant as part of a pattern of growing hostility towards the duke, whereby Clisson "signified his disapproval" of ducal policies, as Jones put in *Creation*, 259. Buteau, "Naissance," 65, thought that in becoming Jeanne's lieutenant Clisson had become extremely dangerous to the duke.

80. When he regained that castle in 1361, Clisson held it of the duke of Anjou, who had recognized in his marriage contract to Marie of Blois (the daugh-

ter of Jeanne de Penthièvre) in 1360 that the fief belonged to Brittany (Lobineau 2, cols. 499–502; Morice 1, cols. 1534–37). It was returned after the Breton conflict ended, and in 1367 Charles V had given Anjou another castle in compensation. *AHP* 17: 345–47 (publishing AN JJ 97, no. 197); Morice 1, cols. 1615–16; M.-R. Reynaud, "Maison d'Anjou et maison(s) de Bretagne (vers 1360–vers 1434)," *1491: La Bretagne, Terre d'Europe* (Brest, 1992), 179.

81. *RJ IV*, no. 170, citing ADLA E 245, no. 3, fol. 20v.

82. See above, at note 37, for the hearth tax of 1365 which engendered friction with the magnates. Lefranc, *Olivier*, 79, and Toudouze, *DCR*, 124, thought John IV had removed Clisson from command at Champtoceaux, perhaps because he had served Charles V. Jones, "Diplomatic Evidence," 309, spoke of "measures to deprive Clisson of the profits of some of his lordships."

83. Jones, *DB*, 54.

84. Autrand, *Charles V*, 555–63; Delachenal, *Charles V* 4:85–90, 101–6; *Chron. des règnes* 2:46 (notes); Doat 244, fols. 7r–8r; Rouquette, *Le Rouergue*, 140–41; G. Loirette, "Arnaud Amanieu, sire d'Albret, et l'appel des seigneurs gascons en 1368," *Mélanges historiques offerts à M. Charles Bémont* (Paris, 1913), 331–35, 338–40. On the assembly of June 1368, Frois-KL 18: 485–88 (publishing AN J 293, no. 16).

85. AN J 293, no. 18; AN X 1a 1469, fols. 340–42; Autrand, *Charles V*, 564; Delachenal, *Charles V* 4:136–43; E. A. R. Brown and R. C. Famiglietti, *The Lit de Justice: Semantics, Ceremonial, and the Parlement of Paris, 1300–1600* (Sigmaringen, 1994), 23. Before summoning the prince, Charles had consulted with several eminent law faculties on whether he could legally accept the appeals (Chaplais, "Some Documents," pp. 54–55; Christine de Pizan, *Le livre des fais et bonnes moeurs du sage roy Charles V*, ed. S. Solente [Paris, 1936] 2: 203–4).

86. P. E. Russell, *The English Intervention in Spain and Portugal in the Time of Edward III and Richard II* (Oxford, 1955), 138–42, 162–65; Minois, *Du Guesclin*, 339; *Foedera* 3 pt. 2:157–58.

87. Autrand, *Charles V*, 533–34. Important Franco-Flemish agreements reached in April and May 1369 are in AN J 250, nos. 16, 17; French territorial concessions in July are indicated in AN K 49, no. 39.

88. Sumption, *Hundred Years War*, 226–28, 246–49.

89. Delachenal, *Charles V* 4:197.

90. *Mandements*, no. 507; BN FR 26009, no. 972; J. Sherbourne, "John of Gaunt, Edward III's Retinue, and the French Campaign of 1369," in *Kings and Nobles in the Later Middle Ages: A Tribute to Charles Ross*, ed. R. Griffiths and J. Sherbourne (New York, 1986), 44; Delachenal, *Charles V* 4: 198 ff. On 14 July, Charles V wrote that the expenses of the attack on England would be borne by the crown, which would in turn reserve half the prizes taken: Luce, in Frois-SHF 7:lxxii, note 2, citing AN P 2294.

91. R. Favier, *La Guerre de Cent Ans* (Paris, 1980), 333; Sherbourne, "John of Gaunt," 44; Delachenal, *Charles V* 4: 204–5.

92. *Mandements*, nos. 562, 563; A. Coville, *Les états de Normandie, leurs origines et leur developpement au XIVe siècle* (Paris, 1894), 108–9; *RTF 1356–70*, 266–67; Delachenal, *Charles V* 4: 201–3, 226; AN K 49, no. 40.

93. A. Goodman, *John of Gaunt: The Exercise of Princely Power in Fourteenth-Century Europe* (Harlow, Essex, 1992), 229–30.

94. Ibid.; Frois-J 1:429; Favier, Guerre, 333–34; Delachenal, *Charles V* 4: 209–10; Sherbourne, "John of Gaunt," 44.

95. Frois-B 2: 291; Frois-J 1: 419; Frois-KL 7: 415.

96. Favier, *Guerre*, 333.

97. Delachenal, *Charles V* 4:213.

98. Favier, *Guerre*, 334.

99. Palmer, *EFC*, 5–6.

100. Delachenal, *Charles V* 4:200, 209–10. Charles was ordering provisions for ships as late as 19 October (AN K 49, no. 43) and a small raiding party did put to sea in December.

101. *RTF 1356–70*, 266–67.

102. *Chronique des quatre premiers Valois*, ed. S. Luce (Paris, 1862), 202.

103. Delachenal, *Charles V* 4: 204–5, 214.

104. Sherbourne, "John of Gaunt," 44–45. Goodman, *John of Gaunt*, 229–30, agrees, thinking that Gaunt's disruption of the invasion plans was largely inadvertent.

105. Guérin, in *AHP* 19:xxi. The crown subsequently executed the French comander who had surrendered (ibid., 53–57). On Craon's expedition, see Morice 1, col. 1632.

106. C. Samaran, "Pour l'histoire des grandes compagnies. Le videment de Château-Gontier par les anglais (1369)," *Mélanges d'histoire du moyen âge dediées à la mémoire de Louis Halphen* (Paris, 1951), 641–43.

107. Morice 2, col. 1633; L. Delisle, *Histoire du château et des sires de Saint-Sauveur-le-Vicomte* (Valognes, 1867), 151, 153; *Mandements*, no. 570; BN FR 23271, pp. 384–85. Charles V made Craon his lieutenant in lower Normandy early in September (*Mandements*, no. 573).

108. *Chron. des règnes* 2:133–34; Delachenal, *Charles V* 4:219–22. The confiscation ordered against Chandos was for pillaging French subjects (*Mandements*, no. 540 [28 May 1369]).

109. Delachenal, *Charles V* 4:220; Luce, Frois-SHF 7:lxi; P. Charon, "Relations entre les cours de la France et de Navarre en 1376–1377," *BÉC* 150 (1992): 87 and note 9.

110. *Chron. Valois*, 204; Lefranc, *Olivier*, 95.

111. *RJ IV*, no. 187.

112. *RJ IV*, no. 143.

113. For the two points of view, see Jones, *DB*, passim, but esp. 199–204, and La Borderie, *Histoire* 4:13–23.

114. Bouchart, *Grandes chroniques* 2:117; Lobineau 1:393; Roy, *Histoire*, 52–53. The supposed passage of four hundred English troops from Saint-Malo across Brittany to Poitou in the spring of 1369 is accepted by Autrand, *Charles V*, 590, but I have found no documentary proof of the incident.

115. *RJ IV*, no. 145 (AN J 241, no. 50). The mission may have been delayed or interrupted because Clisson was in Nantes on 30 November (ADLA E 56, no. 2).

116. ADLA E 103, no. 15.

117. ADLA E 108, nos. 4 and 5; ADIV 1E 16, no. 1.

118. Morice 1, cols. 1637–38; AN J 240, no. 22; Gicquel, *Olivier*, 78–79.

119. AN J 246, no. 1312, published by Jones in *RJ IV*, no. 154, with the indication that the document could belong to either 1369 or 1370. It fits the context of 1370 better. In 1369, Charles V was preoccupied with the legalities of reopening the war and with the plans for an offensive strike by sea. Unlike 1370, he did not seem to show much concern about Brittany in the spring of 1369.

120. For the background of Porhoët, see L. Rohan-Chabot, "Le Porhoët, la vicomté, le duché de Rohan," *Association bretonnne: Bulletin des comptes rendus* (1976), 43–44. On its strategic location, see also Buteau, "Naissance," 65–66.

121. BN FR 11550, no. 1, fols. 1–2v, published in *Cartulaire du Morbihan*, ed. L. Rosenzweig (extrait de la *Revue historique de l'Ouest*, 1893–97), no. 565.

122. The document published by Morice 1, col. 1639, is dated the same day (14 May). The two counts refer explicitly to an exchange of property with Olivier de Clisson and Béatrix de Laval and make no mention of the Norman lands they will get from the king. BN FR 11550, which is a notebook containing contemporary copies of documents relating to this transaction, contains a letter from the two counts dated 24 May (no. 2, fols. 2v–3v) that treats the transaction as an arrangement with the king. The deal must have required some weeks of negotiating before it was announced in May.

123. BN FR 11550, no. 3 (fols. 3v–4r), published in *Cart. Morbihan*, no. 566; Morice 2, col. 70.

124. Morice 1, col. 1639. On the dowry, see above, notes 44–45.

125. BN FR 11550, nos. 4–8 (fols. 4v–6v) are documents belonging to July and August 1370 and are instructions to, or acknowledgments by, royal officials in lower Normandy. Three more documents in the same notebook (nos. 10–12, fols. 7v–8v) are from later in the year. By this time Alençon was royal lieutenant in lower Normandy.

126. John's objections are mentioned in the document cited in the next note. Lefranc, *Olivier*, 84–85, recognizing the importance of having Josselin held under royal sovereignty, said that the arrangement was contrary to the "feudal law" of Brittany. Doucet, *Vallée*, 73, has made essentially the same point.

127. Manuscripts of this important document are in AN J 400, no. 66 and (in a later hand) BN NAF 7268, fols. 21r–22. It has been published by Morice 1, col. 1640, and Lobineau 2, cols. 539–540. Lefranc, *Olivier*, 84, regrettably chose to call this document a "treaty" with Charles V; the term has caused confusion in the work of some subsequent writers, but not Buteau, "Naissance," 65–66, who clearly saw the connection between John IV's reluctance to turn over Josselin and Clisson's arrangement with the king. In the light of Clisson's subsequent campaigning (see Chapter 4), it is not at all clear that he actually took possession of Josselin in 1370 or 1371.

128. *RJ IV*, no. 170, a document that deals only with Champtoceaux. John IV evidently did not confiscate such major holdings as Clisson and Blain, but it appears from Lobineau 2, cols. 583–585 that the duke did take possession of La Roche-Moisan at some point prior to 1371, possibly at this time.

129. The undated document in Lobineau 2, cols. 583–585, probably drafted

a year or more after the Josselin transaction, seems to identify as a major point of contention between the duke and Clisson the presence of Englishmen on the ducal council. It is likely that the two men had exchanged words over this issue and that Clisson then approached the king with a plan to guard against John's possible disloyalty.

130. Jones, *Creation*, 330–31, discusses treason in a way that is pertinent to the behavior of Clisson and the duke. It was the old-fashioned Germanic view of treason found in the *chansons de geste*—betrayal of the personal ties implicit in the lord-vassal relationship, dealing with the known enemies of ones lord. Clisson's perception of John's dealings with the English and John's perception of Clisson's dealings with Charles V were surely colored by this old view of treason that still figured in the noble mentality.

131. *Chron. des règnes* 2:299–300; Delachenal, *Charles V* 4:356 (also citing AN J 618, no. 7). See also Lefranc, *Olivier*, 116–17; and Levot, *Biographie bretonne*, 1: 364. Mazas, *Vies* 4:375, thought that Charles the Bad told his tale to the duke because he was angry at Clisson for becoming a partisan of Charles V. While the story interested these older authors, it has been virtually ignored by recent historians.

Chapter 4

1. *HL* 9: 802–6; Delachenal, *Charles V* 4:163–88.

2. Du Guesclin received a payment from Louis of Anjou at Moissac on 26 July: BN PO 1433, doss. 32,448 (Du Guesclin), no. 17. On his recall from Spain, see Cuvelier, *Chron. Du Guesclin*, lines 16,884–904; 16,905–28; 17,115–17; 17,220–23.

3. Guérin, *AHP* 19:x. The English had seized La Roche-sur-Yon (above, Chapter 3, note 105) and the French La Roche-Posay, in each case taking fortresses held in violation of the treaty of Brétigny. See Delachenal, *Charles V* 4: 189–90.

4. G. Clément-Simon, *La rupture du traité de Brétigny et ses conséquences en Limousin* (Paris, 1898), 18–19 and note 3. The French finally regained the castle and *ville* of Limoges by negotiation in November 1371 (Doat 244, fols. 63r–69r).

5. AN J 242A, no. 51.

6. Doat 244, fols. 14r–16v; Plaine, *Jeanne*, 44–46 (publishing a document in ADPA E 137). This retrocession was a well-kept secret, for in December 1371 Charles V still spoke of having annexed the castellany of Limoges (Doat 244, fols. 55r–57v) and only at the beginning of 1381 did the crown formally confirm the retrocession of 1369 and order its implementation (fols. 99r–103v).

7. Delachenal *Charles V* 4:258.

8. Ibid., 223–24 (see also 282). The formal act of confiscation (*ORD* 6: 508–10) occurred only in May 1370, and before its enactment the king had men in Limousin rallying people to the Valois cause: Clément-Simon, *Rupture*, 30.

9. Delachenal, *Charles V* 4:287–89.

10. Ibid., 291–97; Clément-Simon, *Rupture*, 37–42.

11. *Chron. des règnes* 1:71–75; F. Lehoux, *Jean de France, duc de Berri, sa vie, son action politique* (Paris, 1966–68) 1:134–35; *RTF 1356–70*, 92, 98, 139.

12. Delachenal, *Charles V* 4:309–17.

13. Ibid., 318.

14. AN KK 251, fols. 39r–v (Berry's letters to Clisson). It is not certain when Clisson actually took possession of Josselin. According to C. Floquet, *Châteaux et manoirs bretons des Rohan* (Loudéac, 1989), 34, he did not do so until 1373 (when the French overran Brittany). This author, who is guilty of a number of errors, may be following a questionable statement by Mazas, *Vies* 4:375, but given his busy military schedule in 1370–72, Clisson may indeed have had to delay his occupation of Josselin.

15. For an account of the campaign and the role attributed to Clisson, see Frois-B 2:347, 352; Frois-J 1:452; Frois-KL 8:15–18, 24–25, 33–35. Favier, *Guerre*, 350, accepts this account.

16. AN K 49, no. 52; *Anciens mémoire*, 566. See Autrand, *Charles V*, 576–80; Delachenal, *Charles V* 4:320–22. His oath as constable, dated 20 October, is published by Charrière, *Chron. Du Guesclin* 2: 407 (*P.J.* 19).

17. *Chron. des règnes* 2:147; Delachenal, *Charles V* 4:321, 328–32; Luce, in Frois-SHF 8:iii–iv, note 1. For the execution of the forced loan, see AN K 49, no. 52; *Mandements*, nos. 728–33. The prose chronicle of Du Guesclin (*Anciens mémoire*, 566) has him urging the king to take money from these *chaperons fourrez*.

18. *Soc. Charles*, 449–52.

19. On the campaigns in the south, see sources cited by *RTF 1356–70*, 194–205, 253–56.

20. Lefranc, *Olivier*, 98.

21. Lobineau 2, cols. 538–59; Morice 1, cols. 1642–43 (partially reprinted, with comments, by Lefranc in *Olivier*, 100–101); C. Du Cange, *Dissertations ou reflexions sur l'histoire de S. Louis du sire de Joinville*, in Petitot, *Collection complète des mémoires rélatifs à l'histoire de France* 3 (Paris, 1819): 363–65. Morice (and perhaps also Du Cange) used a different manuscript from that used by Lobineau, but none seem to have used the copy in BN NAL 2574, no. 12.

22. Luce, in Frois-SHF 8: iii–iv, note 1. Luce did not associate this pact with the larger phenomenon of private alliances that were proliferating in this period (see Guenée, *Meurtre*, 110–11), perhaps because these generally aimed to strengthen existing feudal ties. See P. S. Lewis, "Of Breton Alliances and other Matters," in *War, Literature and Politics in the Later Middle Ages*, ed. C. T. Allmand (Liverpool, 1976), esp. 124–25, 129–31. The alliance between Clisson and Du Guesclin clearly did not have this purpose. See Minois, *Du Guesclin*, 372–73; Doucet, *Vallée*, 74.

23. On the differences between the two men, see above, chapter 2, at note 82, and also Delachenal, *Charles V* 4:463; Roy, *Histoire*, 64; Minois, *Du Guesclin*, 372. Levot, *Biographie bretonne* 1:364, said that Clisson had won Du Guesclin's friendship by his efforts to get him ransomed after his capture at Najera. The pact has also been seen as an example of a certain chivalric tradition of brotherhood-in-arms, an arrangement sometimes adopted to make peace between former enemies (M. Keen, "Brotherhood in Arms," *History* 47 [1962]: 1–17. I am indebted to Professor Elizabeth Brown for calling my attention to this article).

24. Clisson's high standing at the French court at this time is suggested by the generosity of Charles V, who gave him, on 10 November, four thousand pounds

with which to construct a house in Paris and made a similar gift the following August (A. D. de la Fontenelle de Vaudoré, *Histoire d'Olivier de Clisson, connétable de France* [Paris, 1826] 1:256; Buteau, "Naissance," 120).

25. Lefranc, *Olivier*, 205–6, observed that Clisson was a better general and that he deserved some of the credit for Du Guesclin's later victories because he moderated the latter's "impetuous and imprudent" behavior. Favier, *Guerre*, 339, sees Du Guesclin as the French "artisan of reconquest" and Clisson as their expert on the English. Gaden-Puchet, "Château de Blain," 7, speaks of Du Guesclin's impetuosity and ascendancy over the troops, while Clisson brought to the alliance a "consummate military science learned in the English school and a superior intelligence."

26. Luce, in Frois-SHF 6:lxxvii, note 2. On the Breton chiefs who joined Clisson and Du Guesclin after their alliance, see Lobineau 1: 395; Lefranc, *Olivier*, 102; Toudouze, *DCR*, 140–41.

27. Autrand, *Charles V*, 589.

28. For Alençon as royal lieutenant in 1370, see AN K 49, no. 496, BN FR 20372, nos. 1–7, 9–15, 17, 47, 50; BN FR 26009, no. 999; *Mandements*, no. 714; Coville, *États*, 112–13, 387–88.

29. Delachenal, *Charles V* 4:319, 327.

30. See Luce, in Frois-SHF 8, notes to pp. v–vii; and Charrière, in *Chron. Du Guesclin*, 2:377–78. The most successful modern writer in this regard is Minois, *Du Guesclin*, 374–81.

31. Lefranc, *Olivier*, 103–5; *La chronique du bon duc Loys de Bourbon par Jean Cabaret d'Orville*, ed. A. M. Chazaud (Paris, 1876), 25–26; Christine de Pizan, *Livre des fais* 1: 196, 198–99; *Anciens mémoire*, 555–56; *Chronique normande*, 196–97; *Chron. Du Guesclin*, lines 17,994–18,472; Frois-B 2:360–62; Frois-KL 8:47–54.

32. Delachenal, *Charles V* 4:341.

33. *Chronique normande*, 198–99; *Anciens mémoire*, 557–62; *Chron. Du Guesclin*, lines 18,652–64; 18,678–725. For accounts based on these sources, see Lefranc, *Olivier*, 108–10; Levot, *Biographie bretonne* 1:364; Roy, *Histoire*, 73–78. The main problem with these stories is that Clisson's exploit against the English relief force is said to have occurred at Saint-Mathieu (Finisterre) at the western end of Brittany. A more likely location would have been Saint-Malo, or even Saint-Maur-sur-Loire, which Cresswell was forced to evacuate around this time, but the chroniclers are quite specific about the matter.

34. *Anciens mémoire*, 563; *Chron. Du Guesclin*, lines 18,573–602.

35. CL 958, p. 351.

36. Morice 1, col. 1666. This region, located just south of Clisson itself, was of course the location of his mother's lands. Clisson still held this lieutenantcy in the spring of 1372: BN NAF 23634, no. 196.

37. BN PO 1813 doss. 41,909 Malestroit, no. 2.

38. The royal orders to Clisson (26 August) are in Lobineau 2, cols. 570–71. On 5 September, Clisson wrote Jean le Mercier indicating the troops he had raised for this purpose (Morice 1, cols. 1666–67); *AHP* 20:288–89. The action at Moncontour is related badly by *Chronique Cabaret d'Orville*, 88. See Delachenal,

Charles V 4:391–93; Lefranc, *Olivier*, 112–13. Moncontour in Poitou must not be confused with the Breton stronghold of the same name discussed in Chapter 12.

39. Morice 1, cols. 1633–34; Lefranc, *Olivier*, 119–21.

40. Lefranc, *Olivier*, 115 and *P.J.* 7, p. 436; Toudouze, *DCR*, 140.

41. *Anciens mémoire*, 564–65. Charles did express gratitude for the constable's past services by forgiving his debt for a previous ransom paid by the crown: AN J 381, no. 9. D. F. Jamison, *The Life and Times of Bertrand du Guesclin* (Charleston, 1864) 2:207, said that the arrears of salary owed to the constable by the king and the money Du Guesclin owed Charles for paying his ransoms roughly offset each other in early 1373 when both debts were canceled.

42. Delachenal, *Charles V* 4:423. Clisson and Philip of Burgundy had been at Paris together on 21 March 1372 (CBourg 52, fol. 167r).

43. Delachenal, *Charles V* 4: 408–16; *Anciens mémoire*, 566–67.

44. On this campaign, see Lefranc, *Olivier*, 135; Delachenal, *Charles V* 4: 422–23, and Lehoux, *Jean de France* 1:282–88.

45. *Chron. Du Guesclin*, lines 19,640–49; Lefranc, *Olivier*, 121–29; Delachenal, *Charles V* 4:424–25; Jones, "Capitaines," 370–71. Near Soubise in August, the French took two important prisoners, Thomas Percy, the English seneschal of Poitou, and Jean de Grailly, captal of Buch.

46. *Chron. Du Guesclin*, lines 21,713–74, 21,836–53; Lefranc, *Olivier*, 124, 131–33; Levot, *Biographie bretonne* 1:365. On the capture of Benon, see also Lehoux, *Jean de France* 1:290–91, and *ORD* 5:606.

47. Luce, in Fois-SHF 8:xlviii, note. 2.

48. E. Petit, *Itinéraires de Philippe le Hardi et Jean sans Peur, ducs de Bourgogne* (Paris, 1888), 85; AN P 1334¹ no. 6, fols. 23r–24r; Delachenal, *Charles V* 4:436. Autrand, *Charles V*, 589. The royal ratification of this treaty in 15 December is found in BN FR 22339, fols. 58r–61r; BN FR 3910, no. 63 (fols. 111r–119v); and AN JJ 103, no. 361 (published in *AHP* 19:176 ff.).

49. Delachenal, *Charles V* 4:430.

50. Jones, "Capitaines," 371–72.

51. Lefranc, *Olivier*, 112.

52. *Foedera* 3 pt. 2:187–88; Morice 1, cols. 1672–75; Jones, *DB*, 67; Delachenal, *Charles V* 4:463–64; La Borderie *Histoire* 4: 17.

53. Jones, *DB*, 70–71; Minois, *Du Guesclin*, 399.

54. Pocquet, *Papes*, 358; Minois, *Du Guesclin*, 398; Gicquel, *Olivier*, 55.

55. Jones, in *RJ IV*, p. 170 at no. 127; Pocquet, *Papes*, 359.

56. Pocquet, *Papes*, 360; Jones, in *RJ IV* pp. 191 (at no. 163A) and 213 (at no. 200A); Gicquel, *Olivier*, 56–57; La Borderie, *Histoire* 4:17. Some of the testimony on the canonization is published in Morice 1, cols. 1–33. The full compendium is that of F. Plaine, *Monuments du procès de canonisation du bienheureux Charles de Blois, duc de Bretagne, 1320–1364* (Saint-Brieuc, 1921).

57. Jones, "Diplomatic Evidence," 303–12.

58. Lobineau 2, cols. 583–85; Morice 2, cols. 36–37.

59. This is the most likely time inferred from Jones's analysis cited in note 57.

60. Lobineau 2, cols. 581–83. Jones, *DB*, 38–39 (on John IV's English ad-

visers, but playing down their significance) and 32 (on Melbourne). Some French historians accept the view that more than 20 percent of the ducal council were English: Minois, *Du Guesclin*, 396–97; Leguay and Martin, *Fastes et Malheurs*, 122.

61. Lobineau 2, cols. 581–83.

62. On Charles the Bad, see Chapter 3 at note 131. Doucet, *Vallée*, 72–73, follows the view that the king showed Clisson evidence of ducal deception (during his mission to Paris in January 1370). I take the opposite position, being convinced that Clisson knew more about the Breton situation than the king and was relaying his suspicions to Charles V's government.

63. Jones, *DB*, 61, 70.

64. Gicquel, *Olivier*, 59, 151–52.

65. Autrand, *Charles VI*, 175.

66. Jones, as cited above, note 57.

67. See above at note 52.

68. *RJ IV*, no. 192; Jones, *DB*, 68–69. Having granted Richmond to John IV's father at the beginning of the succession crisis (see Chapter 2), Edward III periodically repossessed the earldom and granted it to others. For most of John IV's reign as duke, Richmond was not in his hands.

69. *RJ IV*, no. 211, published previously by Jones in "Diplomatic Evidence," 312–16.

70. *RJ IV*, no. 195, published previously in "Diplomatic Evidence," 316–18.

71. La Borderie, *Histoire* 4:18–19; Jones, *DB*, 68–69. In *RJ IV*, no. 190, John IV established a commercial agreement between Brittany and the duchy of Guyenne (21 February) in which he already referred to an alliance with England.

72. *RJ IV*, no. 196, published previously in "Diplomatic Evidence," 318–19; Jones, *DB*, 69–72.

73. *Foedera* 3 pt. 2:202–3; Morice 2, cols. 40–45. On 20 June Edward granted John authority over the English strongholds in the marches of Poitou and Brittany (Morice 2, cols. 39, 47; ADLA E 186, no. 2). This grant soon lost its significance when the English suffered naval defeat off La Rochelle, but in December Edward granted John all lands he could conquer in France (Champollion-Figeac, *Lettres* 2:188–89).

74. La Borderie, *Histoire* 4:20.

75. Jones, *DB*, 72.

76. *RJ IV*, no. 203, in which John seemed to be winning a favorable resolution of some of his complaints.

77. Morice 2, cols. 50–51. Montrelais, who had ambitions, became a cardinal in 1375: Pocquet, *Papes*, 361.

78. *RJ IV*, no. 206, indicating part of AN J 246, no. 133, published in *Chron. des règnes* 3:178–83. See also Delachenal, *Charles V* 4:466; and La Borderie, *Histoire* 4:21, 23.

79. *RJ IV*, no. 207, indicating other parts of AN J 246, no. 133 (see previous note). According to Bouchart, *Grandes chroniques* 2:120–21, important Breton lords like Rohan and Laval had warned the duke they would abandon him if he favored the English but John encouraged the English to send him troops secretly.

80. Petit, *Itinéraires*, 87–88.

81. *Foedera* 3 pt. 2:206–8; *RJ IV*, no. 205; Lobineau 2, cols. 585–88; Morice 2, cols. 53–57. Lefranc, *Olivier*, 145, said that with this document John IV made himself into a "veritable English subject," evidently not recognizing that John had actually inserted a provision that pointed in the opposite direction.

82. *RJ IV*, no. 208. Clisson had for some months been maintaining a garrison of Spanish crossbowmen at Blain castle, according to pay receipts in BMN 1684/1528, no. 2.

83. *Chronique Cabaret d'Orville*, 38–39; Delachenal, *Charles V* 4:468–69. La Borderie (*Histoire* 4:22) is among those supporting this tale.

84. Lehoux, *Jean de France* 1:296–97.

85. Bouchart, *Grandes chroniques* 2:121; Delachenal, *Charles V* 4:439–40; Minois, *Du Guesclin*, pp. 405–9; Guérin, in *AHP* 19:xl–liv.

86. AN KK 251, fols. 94v, 126r, 127r. Of course the recipient of a message would not necessarily be at the same place on the date the messenger was paid. On this siege see also Luce, in Frois-SHF 8: lxxv, note 1. La Roche-sur-Yon probably fell around the end of July: Lehoux, *Jean de France* 1:308, 313; Guérin in *AHP* 19:lv.

87. Bouchart, *Grandes chroniques* 2:124; for Anjou's letter, a note of Blanchard from an account in AM Angers, ADLA 7 JJ 70. Anjou, in fact, may have been the one who actually oversaw the siege and surrender of La Roche-sur-Yon: Jamison, *Life and Times* 2:222–24.

88. Bouchart, *Grandes chroniques* 2:122.

89. Jones, *DB*, 73–74 gives an excellent brief account of the disaffection of the Breton lords. On the campaign and the duke's flight, see *Chron. des règnes* 2:169; Lobineau 2, cols. 718, 838; Delachenal, *Charles V* 4:468–69; J. Bréjon de Lavergnée, "La confiscation du duché de Bretagne en 1378," *MSHAB* 59 (1982): 330–31.

90. AN JJ 104, fol. 115, no. 270, published by Lefranc, *Olivier*, P.J. 8. A Breton copy of this document is published in *Cart. Morbihan* no. 577. Guillac in fact had been held by a succession of Englishmen, most recently Thomas Melbourne (ibid., nos. 557, 568; Kerhervé, *État breton* 882).

91. B. Pocquet du Haut-Jussé, "La Dernière Phase de la vie de Du Guesclin: L'affaire de Bretagne," *BÉC* 125 (1967): 152–53. Charles convened in the Parlement a great council of seventy lords and prelates to consider the confiscation of Brittany (AN X ^{1a} 1470, fol. 50v, partly published in Bréjon de Lavergnée, "Confiscation," 340). Minois, *Du Guesclin*, 433, thinks that the project stood a greater chance of success in 1373, when hostility to John IV was at its height, than when it was revived in 1378–79 (see Chapter 6).

92. *RJ IV*, no. 225, where Jones gives the document a later date than that assigned by Morice 2, col. 67 and Fois-KL 8:451.

93. Bouchart, Grandes chroniques 2:123; Delachenal, *Charles V* 4:475.

94. Delachenal, *Charles V*, 475–77 for the campaign and 477 for the siege of Brest; *Chron. des règnes* 2:169. Cf. Luce in Frois-SHF 8:lxxv–lxxvi and notes.

95. Delachenal, *Charles V* 4:478; Luce, in Frois-SHF 8:lxxxi, note 1.

96. *Mandements*, no. 984; Luce, in Frois-SHF 8:xciii, note 1.

97. AN J 642, nos. 21 and 22. See the discussion of Delachenal, *Charles V* 4:479.

98. Lefranc, *Olivier*, 147–50.

99. Goodman, *John of Gaunt*, 232.

100. Luce, in Frois-SHF 8:lxxxiii, note 1.

101. Delachenal, *Charles V* 4:480–82.

102. Ibid., 491.

103. Frois-SHF 8:149–50, with corrections and citations by Luce, p. lxxxiv and notes.

104. Delachenal, *Charles V* 4:492.

105. Petit, *Itinéraires*, 98; BN CBourg 52, fols. 169v–170r.

106. Doucet, *Vallée*, 76; *Chronique Cabaret d'Orville*, 54–55; Frois-SHF 8:169, and comments of Luce, p. xcix, note 1.

107. One can plot some of Lancaster's movements by following those of Philip of Burgundy: Petit, *Itinéraires*, 98 (September), 98–99 (October), 99–100 (November). Philip was at Troyes in Champagne after the middle of September, reached Auxerre towards the end of the month and Rouannes in the county of Forez on 11 October, crossing the Loire there and proceeding to Auvergne, arriving at Clermont on 5 November. He was at Bourges 17–18 November, and then (apparently no longer considering Lancaster a serious threat) was back at Sens with his wife late in the month before returning to Paris on 2 December. For the later stages of the campaign, see Delachenal, *Charles V* 4:496–97.

108. A. Coville, *Les Premiers Valois et la guerre de Cent Ans (Histoire de France*, ed. E. Lavisse, Paris, 1900–11, 4 pt. 1), 243; Delachenal, *Charles V* 4:498–500. Goodman, *John of Gaunt*, 223, says that his army "seems to have come near to collapse" in the winter of 1373–74. Lancaster was back in England late in April (ibid., p. 53).

109. Frois-SHF 8:161–163, and the helpful accompanying analysis by Luce on p. xciv and note 1.

110. Ibid.; Lefranc, *Olivier*, 154–57. The one modern writer to emphasize Clisson's role in the royal strategy (Autrand, *Charles V*, 600–601) believes that Clisson, because of his higher social position and because he was more *pensante*, felt more comfortable than Du Guesclin did in speaking up before the royal council. Minois, *Du Guesclin*, 416, emphasizes the resentment this policy engendered among the peasants.

111. Favier, *Guerre*, 339. Another French scholar called Lancaster's expedition "very unwise but now customary" (E. Perroy, "The Anglo-French negotiations at Bruges, 1374–1377," *Camden Miscellany* 19 [1952]: xiii).

112. Autrand, *Charles V*, 592; Delachenal, *Charles V* 4:502–3.

113. Vuitry, *Régime financier* 2:654–56, for the receipts of 1374. See Chapter 1, note 45.

114. On the rural economy in the fourteenth century, see Chapter 1. The population index compiled by Bois for upper Normandy showed a sharp decline from seventy in 1357 to forty-three in 1380, but this region escaped the raid of 1373 and its population may actually have been growing when it attained the index

number of forty-three around 1380. Conditions elsewhere in France in the mid-1370s were surely more desperate than in Normandy.

115. *ORD* 5:558–61; Contamine, *Guerre*, 142–44. On the need to regulate the army in order to maintain peace and order, see C. T. Allmand, "Changing Views of the Soldier in Late Medieval France," *Guerre et société en France, en Angleterre, et en Bourgogne, XIVe-XVe siècle*, ed. P. Contamine, C. Giry-Deloison, M. Keen (Lille, 1991), esp. 183–84.

116. AN X^1a 1470, fols. 110r–v. Perroy, "Anglo-French Negotiations," pp. xiv–xv, shows that Delachenal, *Charles V* 4:501, was wrong about the dates of the Anglo-French negotiations and therefore misunderstood the recommendation of this council.

117. Delachenal, *Charles V*, 522.

118. Coville, *États*, 113–15; AN K 49^B, no. 69.

119. BN FR 22451, no. 5, partly published in Delisle, *Saint-Sauveur*; Coville, *États*, 115–16; Delachenal, *Charles V*, 524. A summary of Vienne's career is found in Delachenal, *Charles V* 5:19–20, and is based largely on the first fifty pages of H. Terrier de Loray, *Jean de Vienne, amiral de France (1341–96)* (Paris, 1877). According to BN NAF 3653, no. 289, Robert Knolles brought a large force of troops to Saint-Sauveur in June 1374.

120. Delachenal, *Charles V* 4:524–25; Coville, *États*, 113–19; Terrier de Loray, *Jean de Vienne*, P.J. 23, 145.

121. Delachenal, *Charles V* 4:525.

122. Delisle, *Saint-Sauveur*, 274.

123. Delachenal, *Charles V* 4:527–29.

124. Delisle, *Saint-Sauveur*, 255–57; BN FR 26012, nos. 1636, 1637, 1640, 1641, 1645, 1647, 1652, 1659.

Chapter 5

1. *Soc. Charles*, 466–68, 473–74.

2. Ibid., 577. Cf Autrand, *Charles V*, 416.

3. *Soc. Charles*, 455–63. See also Autrand, *Charles V*, 359, 367–69, 382–83, 421–23, 456–60.

4. Autrand, *Charles V*, 495–503.

5. Ibid., 481–93.

6. Above, Chapter 1.

7. In effect, the circumstances of the 1360s set French finances on the road to what Kerhervé, *État breton*, 589, has called "normalization," the "acceptation du fait fiscal par la mentalité collective."

8. *RTF 1322–56*, passim, but esp. 185–88, 230–33, 285–86, 291–96, 328–29; *RTF 1356–70*, passim and esp. 291–92 (conclusions).

9. On the circumstances that compelled local and regional fiscal initiatives, see *RTF 1356–70*, 133–225. After the accession of Charles V, his brother, Louis of Anjou, wielded great authority as royal lieutenant in Languedoc, and governmental effectiveness there showed improvement soon after his arrival. The greater effi-

ciency of this decentralization has been recognized clearly by Autrand, *Charles V*, 433, 523.

    10. On 13 November 1372, Charles V issued new instructions on the counsellors-general (*ORD* 5:645), and Cazelles saw a decline in their role by 1374 (*Soc. Charles*, 542–43). The ordinance in fact probably owed a good deal to the influence of Jean le Mercier, an influential adviser of Charles V long before he appeared on the royal council. See H. Moranvillé, *Étude sur la vie de Jean le Mercier* (Paris, 1888), 36–40.

    11. Autrand, *Charles V*, 417. On the agenda of the noble reformers, see above, chapter 1, at note 73.

    12. Autrand, *Charles V*, 360.

    13. Ibid., 689, and above, Chapter 1, at note 102.

    14. Autrand, *Charles V*, 457–60.

    15. For a detailed examination of the earlier practice, see *Soc. Philippe*, 75–261; *Soc. Charles*, 119–452; and Cazelles, "Mouvements révolutionnaires, 279–312.

    16. Autrand, *Charles V*, 424–26, 689–90, 702–6, 711–12. As dauphin, Charles had been developing his own circle of trusted advisers since the summer of 1357 (ibid., 271, 704).

    17. Ibid., 692. Using the terminology of the Fifth Republic, she describes this situation as "cohabitation."

    18. *Soc. Charles* 542–49.

    19. Ibid., 418–21.

    20. For the council of 1357, ibid., 265–71, and Autrand, *Charles V*, 266 ff. For a survey of the crisis faced by the dauphin during his father's captivity, see *RTF 1356-70*, 37–83, and Autrand, *Charles V*, 221–380.

    21. Autrand, *Charles V*, 366–69.

    22. Ibid., 455.

    23. AN J 293, no. 16 (30 June 1368); AN K 49, no. 52 (Oct 1370); Lefranc, *Olivier*, 154–57 (1373); AN X^{1a} 1471, fol. 134v (December 1378). For other references to "great councils" of this sort, see Autrand, *Charles V*, 560–64, 576–80, 627–28, 834, and *Soc. Charles*, 467.

    24. Autrand, *Charles V*, 424–26.

    25. Ibid., 370, 558, 702.

    26. Autrand, *Charles VI*, 203. Guenée, *Meurtre*, 40–41, emphasizes the influence of the nobles around Charles V, whose household and court became "the theater of royal magnificence" (p. 131). On the role of the chamberlains, see also Autrand, *Charles V*, 701–702. On the household specifically, see M. Rey, *Les finances royales sous Charles VI: les causes du déficit 1388-1413* (Paris, 1965), 23 ff.

    27. Rey, *Finances*, 34–42, on the grand master; also Guenée, *Meurtre*, 40–41.

    28. *RTF 1356-70*, 225–31. For the fiscal and administrative impact of the *routiers*, see above at notes 8 and 9.

    29. The authoritative work on the evolution of the French army in this period is Contamine, *Guerre*, esp. 135–233. For a list of the most prominent royal commanders, see Appendix I.

    30. *Soc. Charles*, 544–45; Autrand, *Charles V*, 688–89.

    31. *Soc. Charles*, 545–49. Of those mentioned by Cazelles, only two (Coucy

and La Rivière) were military commanders. Autrand, *Charles V*, 690–91, 695–98, adds the important name of Philippe de Mézières, who joined the council in 1373. In her discussion, she tends to associate the term "Marmouset" only with the period after 1388 and thus to see the years 1375–80 as a transitional period following the withdrawl of the Melun brothers.

32. J. B. Henneman, "Who Were the Marmousets?" *Medieval Prosopography* 5 (1984): 19–63. See also (on Chevreuse in 1364) BN FR 20402, no. 54; (on Du Bosc) Perroy, "Anglo-French Negotiations," 9, note 3, and BN FR 20880, nos. 42–48, 50–66; (on La Grange) Autrand, *Charles V*, 538–39, 693–95; (on La Rivière) BN PO 2496 doss. 56,094 Rivière, and Autrand, *Charles V*, 699–702; and (on Le Mercier) Moranvillé, *Jean le Mercier*, 5–8, and *Soc. Charles*, 75.

33. The most recent work that gives extensive coverage to Coucy and his career is that of B. Tuchman, *A Distant Mirror: The Calamitous Fourteenth Century* (New York, 1978).

34. M. Schnerbe-Lièvre, editor's introduction to *Le Songe du Vergier* (Paris, 1982) 1: lxix; *Soc. Charles*, 555; J. Quillet, *La philosophie politique du Songe du Vergier (1378): Sources doctrinales* (Paris, 1977), 10, 20; Autrand, *Charles V*, 736–37.

35. Schnerbe-Lièvre, *Songe* 1: lxxxv–lxxxviii; A. Coville, *Évrart de Trémaugon et le Songe du Vergier* (Paris, 1933), 12–14, 22. Documents on the career of Yvon de Trémaugon include BN PO 2876 doss. 68,376 Trémagon, nos. 5, 6, 42; BN NAF 7414, fol. 232r; BN NAF 8604, no. 12; BN NAL 184, fol. 156v; Morice 1, cols. 1643–44.

36. Autrand, *Charles V*, 728–42.

37. Ibid., 635; *Soc. Charles*, 579–80.

38. Autrand, *Charles V*, 627–28; *Soc. Charles*, 581; Brown and Famiglietti, *Lit de justice*, 24; *ORD* 6:30–31

39. AN K 51, no. 1; *ORD* 6:26–30.

40. N. Valois, *Le conseil du roi aux XIVe, XVe, et XVIe siècles* (Paris, 1888), 75–76; AN K 50, no. 10; *ORD* 6:45–54. In March 1375, Louis of Anjou gave the king a formal oath of loyalty in connection with being designated regent: BN FR 3910, fols. 137r–139v.

41. In *Soc. Charles*, 579–81, Cazelles considered them the most enduring legacy of the Melun-Dormans council, in part, however, because he was convinced that Charles V had been "elected" rather than inheriting the throne automatically. They were certainly significant to the Marmousets, and Trémaugon presented them forcefully: *Songe* 1:127–29 (chap. 78) and 248–57 (chap. 142).

42. Many years ago, I had a conversation with the late professor Robert Fawtier, in which he stressed his conviction that the Valois kings, at least through Louis XI, suffered from a strong sense of insecurity because of uncertainties as to whether they truly were the legitimate successors of St. Louis.

43. On the peace negotiations, see Autrand, *Charles V*, 616–25, and Delachenal, *Charles V* 5:3–4.

44. Tuchman, *Distant Mirror*, 269–79.

45. BN NAF 7414, fols. 241v and following. For another indication that Coucy and Clisson were active in eastern France in 1376, see Petit, *Itinéraires*, 503.

46. Tuchman, *Distant Mirror*, 301–4.

47. Delachenal, *Charles V* 5:23–24.

48. Autrand, *Charles V*, 781–82; Delachenal, *Charles V* 5:27–34.

49. *Chron. des règnes* 2:192. Charles V demonstrated his high regard for Clisson in 1377 by giving him more than two thousand francs to purchase gold vessels: BN PO 789 doss. 17,879 Clisson, nos. 3 (21 October 1377) and 4 (25 March 1378).

50. Delachenal, *Charles V* 5:34–35. Christine de Pizan, *Livre des fais* 1:233. For Froissart's report of the French commanders present for this campaign, see Frois-B 2:464 and Frois-KL 8:405–6.

51. Delachenal, *Charles V* 5:49–59.

52. Ibid., 62–68; Christine de Pizan, *Livre des fais* 2:89–129; *Chron. des règnes* 2:285 and notes; Moranvillé, *Jean le Mercier*, 59–60, and especially Autrand, *Charles V*, 780, 786–803, who considers the imperial visit and the Valois-Luxembourg alliance very important.

53. The death of his queen early in 1378 was taken hard by Charles and may mark the beginning of his disappointing final years. See Christine de Pizan, *Livre des fais* 2:133–36; Autrand, *Charles V*, 808–9; Delachenal, *Charles V* 5: 120–22. Autrand points out, however (Charles V, 806–7), that the evolving European state ran into opposition and difficulty in various countries at about the same time.

54. Charon, "Relations," 93–102.

55. D.-F. Secousse, *Recueil de pièces servent de preuves aux memoires sur les troubles excités en France par Charles II dit le Mauvais* (Paris, 1758), 373–437; *Chron. des règnes* 2:285 and notes, and *P.J.* (v. 3): 208–13; Delachenal, *Charles V* 5:184–218; Autrand, *Charles V*, 810–16; Moranvillé, *Jean le Mercier*, 63; Coville, *États*, 119–20. More documents on this campaign (including destruction of captured Navarrese castles) are in AN K 51, nos. 32, 34, 37, 38.

56. Minois, *Du Guesclin*, 429; Delachenal, *Charles V* 5:220–23; C. Given-Wilson, "The Ransom of Olivier du Guesclin," *BIHR* 129 (1981): 17. For the forces assembled by La Rivière against Cherbourg, see Delisle, *Saint-Sauveur*, 315–16.

57. Pocquet, *Papes*, pp. 369–72.

58. Robert of Geneva was related to a pro-Navarrese reforming French cardinal of the previous generation, Guy de Boulogne (Autrand, *Charles VI*, 193).

59. J.-C. Cassard, "Les *Gestes des Bretons* en Italie ou le voyage sans la découverte," *1491: La Bretagne, Terre d'Europe* (Brest, 1992), 107. On Robert's connection with Clisson, see Bruel, "Inventaire," p. 206, note 5.

60. Delachenal, *Charles V* 5:127–29.

61. N. Valois, *La France et le grand schisme de l'occident* (Paris, 1896–1902) 1: 35–62.

62. Ibid., 67–68.

63. Delachenal, *Charles V* 5:140–42; H. Kaminsky, *Simon de Cramaud and the Great Schism* (New Brunswick, N.J., 1983), 23–24.

64. Valois, *Schisme*, 1:88–93.

65. Ibid., 96–103.

66. *Chron. des règnes* 2:320–22; Valois, *Schisme* 1:103–4; Delachnal, *Charles V* 5:149.

67. Valois, *Schisme* 1:105 ff.

68. Ibid., 81–82; Autrand, *Charles V*, 830–33; Kaminsky, *Simon*, 25. In the *Songe du Vergier* 1:324–27 (chap. 156), the knight, who generally set forth the views of the Marmousets, argued that it was better for the Pope to reside in France than at Rome, because France was the holiest place in Christendom.

69. *Chron. des règnes* 2:343–44; Christine de Pizan, *Livre des fais* 2:146–48.

70. Delachenal, *Charles V* 5:152–58 gives a convenient summary of the steps in the French endorsement of Clement VII between the fall of 1378 and May of 1379.

71. Valois, *Schisme*, 1:145–51.

72. Ibid., 162–67; Kaminsky, *Simon*, 26.

73. Valois, *Schisme* 1:170–80.

74. A. Blanc, "Le rappel du duc d'Anjou et l'ordonnance du 25 avril 1380," *Bulletin hististorique et philologique du comité des travaux historiques et scientifiques* (1899): 191–95, 197–201, 205–12; *HL* 9:872–79, 892–93, and 10, cols. 1632–39; *ORD* 6:465; *RTF 1356–70*, 298–99. In *Soc. Charles*, 553–54, Cazelles found the recall of Anjou to be part of a pattern of disgraces imposed by Charles V towards the end of his reign, but I do not share this view (see Chapter 6, at note 49).

Chapter 6

1. For these events, see above, Chapter 4.

2. Morice 2, col. 77; Lobineau 2, col. 588.

3. Morice 2, cols. 78–79.

4. Jones, *DB*, 80 (Cf. *RJ IV* 1: 36); Lefranc, *Olivier*, 175; Gicquel, *Olivier*, 95.

5. Morice 2, cols. 79–80.

6. *Chron. Briocense* (Lobineau 2, col. 840).

7. Jones, *DB*, 77–78.

8. Morice 2, cols. 85–86.

9. Frois-SHF 8:195–96, with comments by Luce on p. cxxi; Bouchart, *Grandes chroniques* 2:125.

10. Bouchart, *Grandes chroniques*, 126; Lefranc, *Olivier*, 165–70; Gicquel, *Olivier*, 97; Mazas, *Vies* 4:377; Doucet, *Vallée*, 77; Toudouze, *DCR*, 147–48; G. Gaudu, "La tour de Cesson," *Bulletin de la Société d'Émulation des Côtes-du-Nord* 82 (1953):68. Everyone seems to accept this story, but geography makes it suspect. It seems odd that commanders charged with preventing the duke from taking Saint-Brieuc should have diverted troops as far away as Quimperlé, which is across the peninsula from Saint-Brieuc.

11. Morice 2, cols. 98–99; Jones, *DB*, 78; Delachenal, *Charles V* 4:516–20.

12. BN FR 18698, fol. 433r; Morice 2, col. 99; Lobineau 2, cols. 588–89; Lefranc, *Olivier*, 176–77. Jones, *DB*, 82, implies that Charles V may have missed a chance to split the duke from the English.

13. Lobineau 2, col. 589; Morice 2, col. 86.

14. Morice 2, cols. 172–73.

15. BN FR 22319, pp. 578–79; Gicquel, *Olivier*, 96.

16. AN JJ 113, no. 163.

17. *Cart. Morbihan*, no. 583 (19 July, 1377). It may have been the resolution of this matter that caused the king to send him a message in November (Fonds Grandville en Bringolo, cabinet 28).

18. BMN 1684/1528, no. 1, contains about a dozen documents between 1374 and 1399, one of which, a letter of 25 February 1379, has been partially published by Gicquel, *Olivier*, 191–92. Another ten documents on Blain for the period 1382–90 are in BMN 1694/1538, no. 2. See also Buffé, *Blain*, 63; Gaden-Puchet, "Château de Blain," 7; Lefranc, *Olivier*, 185–86.

19. Lefranc, *Olivier*, 178–87.

20. Jones, *Creation*, 40, notes that a number of Breton castles now had platforms for defensive artillery, but also points out (42) that the improvements to Clisson castle did not employ the latest techniques and may have antedated Olivier IV.

21. Jones, *DB*, 80–84; *Chron. des règnes* 2:182–88, 192; Christine de Pizan, *Livre des fais* 1:231; Lehoux, *Jean de France* 1:400–401. Froissart has Clisson besieging Brest into 1378 before being recalled to Normandy to assist in occupying the lands of Charles the Bad (Frois-B 3:9, Frois-KL 9:60–61).

22. Morice 2, col. 198; *RJ IV*, no. 282; *Calendar of the Close Rolls Preserved in the Public Record Office: Richard II*, 6 vols. (London, 1914; repr. Nendeln, 1972) 2:142.

23. Goodman, *John of Gaunt*, 226–27; Pocquet, "Dernière phase," 159. See Frois-B 3:18–20; Frois-KL 9:77–78.

24. One version has it that John was summoned on 20 June to appear 4 September (Lobineau 2, col. 725); others say that the summons was issued late in July for an appearance on 4 December. See Bréjon de Lavergnée, "Confiscation," 331–32, note 10, and Lobineau 1:418. Lobineau in particular questioned the king's adherence to proper procedure, apparently on the basis of *Chron. Briocense*.

25. Bréjon de Lavergnée, "Confiscation," 340. The basic document, AN X 1a 1471, fols. 133v–136v, was also published by Delachenal in *Chron. des règnes* 3: P.J. 29, pp. 213–19. See also Brown and Famiglietti, *Lit de Justice*, 25.

26. Bréjon de Lavergnée, "Confiscation," 340–42. The passage dealing with the king's ceremonial appearance (AN X 1a 1471, fol. 134v) is omitted by Delachenal in *Chron. des règnes*.

27. Bréjon de Lavergnée, "Confiscation," 342–43; *Chron. des règnes* 3:216–18.

28. Jamison, *Life and Times*, 296n. On the career of one of these, see Pocquet, *Papes*, 380.

29. Bréjon de Lavergnée, "Confiscation," 343; *Chron. des règnes* 3:218.

30. See above, Chapter 3, at note 51.

31. Kerhervé, *État breton*, 584–87; Jones, *DB*, 52–56.

32. On the earlier attempt, see above, Chapter 4, note 90.

33. See above, Chapter 3, at notes 120–30.

34. *Songe* 1:261–63 (chap. 143). Delachenal, *Charles V* 5:237, appreciated the importance of the *Songe du Vergier* in this case but missed a chance to set forth clearly the changes that were made in the original *Somnium* when it was translated

into French in 1378. See also Minois, *Du Guesclin*, 434; Leguay and Martin, *Fastes et malheurs*, 127.

35. Bréjon de Lavergnée, "Confiscation," 332–37 and notes; Lobineau 1: 418–19. See also Roy, *Histoire*, 100–101; Toudouze, *DCR*, 152–53; Plaine, *Jeanne*, 34.

36. Autrand, *Charles V*, 819, insists that Charles never intended to add Brittany to the royal domain, but the length of the legal proceedings suggests that the matter was more complicted than she believes. On this subject of Breton identity, see Jones, *Creation*, 283–307. Arguments against the action of the Parlement are found in the chronicle of Saint-Brieuc (Lobineau 2, cols. 841–43) and that of Guillaume de Saint-André (Saint-André, lines 2540–2627).

37. Pocquet, "Dernière phase," 161, and document cited above, note 25.

38. Pocquet, "Dernière phase," 162–66.

39. Ibid., 166–69. Coville, *Premiers Valois*, 249; Saint-André, lines 2808–2967; Minois, *Du Guesclin*, 440.

40. Pocquet, "Dernière phase," 166.

41. Those portraying Clisson as a Breton partisan and hero have suggested that he experienced anguish over divided loyalties like that which afflicted Du Guesclin (see, for instance, Toudouze, *DCR*, 155–56), but there is no evidence that he ever deviated from his support of the crown's action and opposition to John IV. In contrast, Lefranc, *Olivier*, 195, went so far as to wonder if Clisson supported the royal action in expectation of becoming governor of Brittany.

42. Pocquet, "Dernière phase," 160–61.

43. Morice 2, cols. 214–18; Lobineau 2, cols. 592–96, 732–33, 846–47; *Chronique de Bretagne de Jean de Saint-Paul, chambellan du duc François II*, ed. A. de la Borderie (Nantes, 1881), 34–36; BN Dupuy 635, fol. 141; Bréjon de Lavergnée, "Confiscation," 329; Pocquet, "Dernière phase," 170; Lefranc, *Olivier*, 197–200.

44. Pocquet, "Dernière phase," 170.

45. Ibid., 180–81. See Morice 2, cols. 214–18, for members of the league.

46. Jones, *DB*, 86, citing a safe-conduct of 31 March, indicates that Jeanne and her followers were in contact with John of Blois before the league was actually formed. He may have given it his blessing, perhaps as part of a bargain to gain John IV's support for his release from captivity (Jones, *Creation*, 268, 282). The embassy to John IV a week after the league was formed is in Morice 2, cols. 218–219. For the French efforts to negotiate during May, see below at notes 60 and 61. For a Breton draft treaty with England in July, see Morice 2, cols. 219–23.

47. Bouchart, *Grandes chroniques* 2:130; Saint-André, lines 3062–91. On Du Guesclin's failure to stop the duke, see Jones, *DB*, 86, and Gaillou and Jones, *The Bretons*, 236.

48. Lefranc, *Olivier*, 194; Jamison, *Life and Times*, 2:291; Toudouze, *DCR*, 150; Roy, *Histoire*, 100. See also Palmer, *EFC*, 18.

49. *Soc. Charles*, 557.

50. *Songe* 1:264–66 (chap. 144) and above at note 26.

51. *Songe* 1:266, 268 (chap. 144).

52. Louis of Bourbon was the one royal prince who generally cooperated with the Marmousets, while Coucy, Sancerre, and La Rivière were Clisson's per-

sonal friends. See Pocquet, "Dernière phase," 162–68. On the careers and ties of these men see also Henneman, "Who Were the Marmousets?" passim.

53. Autrand, *Charles VI*, 175, cited above, Chapter 4, note 65. In another work (*Charles V*, 824) she calls Clisson an "activist."

54. G. Minois, *Nouvelle histoire de la Bretagne* (Paris, 1992), 312–14, believes that the recall of John IV was purely a matter of perceived self-interest on the part of the Breton lords and that it would be *abusif* to speak of Breton patriotism.

55. See Chapter 3, at notes 76–78.

56. Bruel, "Inventaire," pp. 223, 241, 242, 244; Lefranc, *Olivier*, 454–55.

57. ADLA E 217, no. 4.

58. On 22 May 1379 the pope's auditor general issued a *monitoire* against Jeanne: Bruel, "Inventaire," 226–27 and note 9; and *Catalogue générale des manuscrits des bibliothèques publiques de France: Départements*, 22:249 (describing a document in BMN 1711/1555). A year later, the dean of Gap ordered her excommunicated for failing to pay her debt of 9,220 francs: BMN 1693/1537, no. 16, after she had failed to respond to a summons in April 1380 (BMN 1703/1547, no. 7). Later in the year she agreed to pay him: BN FR 22325, p. 797.

59. Lefranc, *Olivier*, 177, suggested the importance of this dispute, but it has not been given adequate attention.

60. Moranvillé, *Jean le Mercier*, 73–74.

61. *Chron. Valois*, 283–84.

62. Pocquet, "Dernière phase," 170.

63. Ibid., 170–73. Various prominent Bretons associated with the league wrote conciliatory letters to Anjou in June and July (Morice 2, cols. 223–25). On 10 August, shortly after John IV's landing, Du Guesclin reported to Anjou that all the Breton aristocracy was with him at Dinan except himself and Clisson (Morice 2, cols. 225–26). In August and September, Clisson wrote Anjou several times reporting on the duke's advance and seeking reinforcements (Morice 2, cols. 229–31). Blanchard's notes at Nantes (ADLA 7 JJ 70) refer to this correspondence.

64. Coville, *Premiers Valois*, 250. Autrand, *Charles V*, 823–24, portrays Anjou and Du Guesclin as the moderates on Brittany who were opposed to Clisson and the legists.

65. Lobineau 2, cols. 604–6; Morice 2, cols. 233–34; *RJ IV*, no. 326. Moranvillé, *Jean le Mercier*, 76–77, describes the French side of the negotiations in October 1379, with Coucy and La Rivière heading a mission to the count of Flanders and his mother, still hoping unsuccessfully to find a way to exclude John IV from the duchy.

66. ADLA E 92, no. 2; Pocquet, "Dernière phase," 174–77.

67. *RJ IV*, no. 307, and above, note 45.

68. *CCR Richard II* 1: 267.

69. *RJ IV*, nos. 333, 334.

70. Musters of troops under Clisson's command in Brittany in 1380 are in CL 33, nos. 18 and 20; BN PO 789 doss. 17,879 Clisson, nos. 42 and 43, and Morice 2, cols. 242–65.

71. Lefranc, *Olivier*, 438–39 has published a document of 2 March 1381 by which Charles VI pledged him Pontorson for the money owed by the treasury.

Nine days later (Lobineau 2, cols. 623–24; BN FR 22325, p. 797), the king assigned him revenues expected to be collected from the Jews. In this text he called the debt seventy thousand francs, not eighty thousand.

72. On the revenues of the royal domain in 1374, see Chapter 1 at note 45.

73. See the table in Jones, *DB*, 57–59, and the analysis of it by Gicquel, *Olivier*, 263 ff.

74. Pocquet, "Dernière phase," 174–75.

75. *RJ IV*, no. 320.

76. Morice 2, cols. 281–83; Lobineau 2, col. 621; *RJ IV*, no. 341. See also Pocquet, "Dernière phase," 175–77.

77. Morice 2, col. 228. Rohan's oath to John IV was actually one of the later ones. See ibid. for the oaths of a number of other important Breton lords in the summer and fall of 1379 (evidently from the text now in ADLA E 142, no. 34). Rohan was then still out of favor with the duke, who revoked his rights and privileges (Morice 2, cols. 231–32). See ADIV 1 F 626 for the oath of fidelity to the duke by Alain de la Houssaye, captain of Rennes, on 24 April 1380.

78. Pocquet, "Dernière phase," 185; Delachenal, *Charles V* 5:223, 354–60; *Soc. Charles*, 551–52. *Chronique Cabaret d'Orville*, 113–14, wrote that the dukes of Anjou and Bourbon actually relieved Du Guesclin for favoring the duke of Brittany. Autrand, on the contrary (*Charles V*, 840–43), found no evidence of disgrace or distrust, saying that he was sent to the south because Languedoc was clamoring for a captain to suppress the *routiers* in the Cevennes.

79. *RJ IV*, no. 335; Morice 2, cols. 237–41.

80. Champollion-Figeac, *Lettres* 2:216–20.

81. Delachenal, *Charles V* 5:368–69.

82. Ibid., 371–83.

83. CL 23, nos. 120, 121. Clisson's own contingent numbered only 160, but with him were Jean de Bueil with 200 men and Pierre de Rocherousse with 60.

84. We should not, however, see Charles V as totally opposed to a settlement, for in May 1380 he had addressed a letter to the clergy, barons, nobles, and towns of Brittany, responding favorably to their request for his reconciliation with the duke and promising a pardon to all who supported a treaty that the count of Flanders was proposing: Morice 2, cols. 285–86. Yet according to Bouchart, *Grandes chroniques* 2:136, Charles on his death bed still warned against John IV's pro-English sentiments and urged that the Breton lords be induced to oppose him.

85. Jones, *DB*, 90.

86. Ibid., 94–95.

87. Lobineau 2, cols. 607–10; Morice 2, cols. 294–96; *RJ IV*, no. 349.

88. Jones, *DB*, 90–91.

89. *RJ IV*, no. 354; Bouchart, *Grandes chroniques* 2:141.

90. Jones, *DB*, 91.

91. Jean Juvenal des Ursins, *Histoire de Charles VI, roy de France*, published in Michaud, *Nouvelle collection des mémoires* (Paris, 1836–39) 2:342–43; Lefranc, *Olivier*, 220. Frois-B 3:170–72, Frois-KL 9:308–10, said that the greater Breton lords refused to provide Buckingham with any assistance.

92. Lobineau 2, cols. 610–14; Morice 2, cols. 298–301 (from original in AN

J 240, no. 1). A copy is found in ADLA, enclosed in another document in E 91, fols. 11v–17r.

93. ADLA E 92, nos. 7 (Anjou), 8 (Burgundy), 9 (Bourbon), 11 (Berry), and 12 (Charles VI). See published ratifications in Lobineau 2, col. 622, and Morice 2, cols. 275–80.

94. Lobineau 2, col. 623; ADLA E 92, no. 10. It is probably no coincidence that some weeks after Clisson ratified the treaty, Jeanne de Penthièvre ended her quarrel with him over money by agreeing to pay him what she had owed him since 1371 (BMN 1703/1547, no. 9).

95. Morice 2, col. 273.

96. *RJ IV*, nos. 363, 364, where many of the manuscript versions of these documents are indicated. Another later copy is in AN X 1a 8602, fols. 131v–133r. The second of these documents is published by Lobineau 2, cols. 615–16, and Morice 2, cols. 274–75.

97. Lobineau 2, cols. 619–20; AN J 240, no. 7.

98. The text of the treaty is published by Lobineau 2, cols. 610–14, and Morice 2, cols. 298–301.

99. Lobineau 2, col. 624; Morice 2, cols. 280–81 (11 April 1381). The exemption was put in writing a week later, on the nineteenth, when it was specified that the duke's new alliance with Charles VI did not require him to fight the English personally but did require him to prevent his vassals from assisting the English: ADLA E 113, fol. 37r.

100. Jones, *DB*, 91–92. The duke's promise to pay Buckingham twenty thousand francs to withdraw is found in BN FR 22319, p. 355 and *RJ IV*, no. 362.

101. Jones, *DB*, 91 described John IV as pulling off a coup.

102. Palmer, *EFC*, 18.

103. Ibid., 19. On the English reaction, see Jones, *DB*, 98: "nothing, in their eyes, could absolve John from his treachery in 1381." It appears from *CCR Richard II* 2:391 that the English again seized Richmond.

104. Palmer, *EFC*, 19; Jones, *DB*, 94–95.

105. *RJ IV*, no. 365 (from ADLA E 179, no. 1).

106. ADIV 1 F 626; ADLA 7 JJ 23.

107. ADLA E 179, no. 2; AN P 1339, no. 438. Anjou also began pressing his mother-in-law for unpaid portions of her daughter's dowry: *Journal de Jean Le Fèvre, évêque de Chartres* . . . , ed. H. Moranvillé (Paris, 1887), 4.

108. BN NAF 7619, fols. 99r–v; AN J 243, no. 62 (see H. du Halgouet, *Répertoire sommaire des documents manuscrits de l'histoire de Bretagne antérieures à 1789 conservées dans les dépots publics de Paris* [Saint-Brieuc, 1914], 229).

109. *RJ IV*, no. 367; Lobineau 2, col. 626; Morice 2, cols. 370–71; BN PO 789, doss. 17,879 Clisson, no. 46.

110. *RJ IV*, no. 402; Lobineau 2, col. 632; Morice 2, col. 379. It was only at this point, according to Lefranc, *Olivier*, 234, that the French relinquished the last strongholds they held in Brittany.

111. Lobineau 2, cols. 624–26; Morice 2, cols. 371–72.

112. ADIV 1 E 9, no. 5; ADLA E 92, no. 14.

113. The promise of safe-conduct is enclosed in Anjou's letters cited in the

next note and there are manuscript copies in BN FR 22319, p. 526, and ADLA
E 92, no. 15.

114. Morice 2, cols. 373–74.

115. ADLA E 92, no. 18.

116. Lobineau 2, cols. 629–32; Morice 2, cols. 376–78.

117. *RJ IV*, no. 389.

118. ADLA E 104, no. 3

119. ADLA E 108, no. 8.

Chapter 7

1. Frois-KL 9:237–28. Moranvillé, *Jean le Mercier*, 69, and Delachenal,
Charles V 5:237–38, both tell of Charles V's visit to Coucy in March of 1379.
This great baron had emerged as a member of the king's circle even before finally
renouncing his allegiance to England in 1377.

2. Lefranc, *Olivier*, 217–19.

3. Lehoux, *Jean de France* 2:14–15.

4. See above, Chapter 5, at notes 37–42.

5. Lehoux, *Jean de France* 2:13, note 1.

6. *RSD* 1:26.

7. Coville, *Premiers Valois*, 269–70.

8. Lehoux, *Jean de France* 2:14–15.

9. N. Grévy-Pons and E. Ornato, "Qui est l'auteur de la chronique latine de
Charles VI dite du religieux de Saint-Denis?" *BÉC* 134 (1976): 85–102.

10. *RSD* 1:24–26. The chronicler does not name this person, but presumably
the office was still held by Pierre de Villiers, lord of L'Isle-Adam, who had held it
since 1372. See Anselme de Sainte-Marie, *Histoire généalogique et chronologique de
la maison de France*, 3d. ed. (Paris, 1726–33) 8:204.

11. Lefranc, *Olivier*, 211–12 (270, for his friendship with Coucy and La Rivière); Juvenal des Ursins, *Histoire* (Michaud ed.) 2:341; Toudouze, *DCR*, 173.
Two old works also associate Clisson with another important figure, Louis, duke
of Bourbon, the king's maternal uncle, calling Bourbon and Coucy the two "sages"
of the period (Roy, *Histoire*, 112; Mazas, *Vies* 4:388).

12. Bibliothèque de l'Arsenal 5424, p. 151.

13. Morice 2, cols. 296–97; Lobineau 2, col. 610; BMN 1694/1538, no. 1;
BN FR 22339, fol. 88r–v.

14. Lefranc, *Olivier*, 212; Roy, *Histoire*, 115; Toudouze, *DCR*, 172.

15. BMN 1690/1534, no. 3. Lefranc, *Olivier*, 216, thought the fact that
Berry owed him money made it hard for the duke to resist Clisson's appointment,
but it seems more likely that Clisson won Berry's support by promising to lend
him money. Buteau, "Naissance," 72, suggested that his wealth was a major factor
in Clisson's appointment, as did Toudouze, *DCR*, 173, and Gicquel, *Olivier*, 169,
both of whom noted that the crown's debt to him climbed from 44,320 pounds
on 1 October 1380 to eighty thousand three months later. Gicquel (ibid., 107)
offered two other reasons besides wealth that might have recommended Clisson:

his great military knowledge and his connection with Brittany, a major source of fighting men.

16. Lehoux, *Jean de France* 2:13.

17. Moranvillé, *Jean le Mercier*, 84; Lefranc, *Olivier*, 217. On Charles VI's dislike of La Grange, see *Chron. Valois*, 283.

18. Juvenal des Ursins, *Histoire* (Michaud ed.), 342; *RSD* 2:36–40. Frois-B 3:166, Frois-KL 9:303, also mentioned Luxembourg's return to favor. Cf. Lefranc, *Olivier*, 99, 217–19; and Moranvillé, *Jean le Mercier*, 113, for Clisson's ties with La Rivière. Moranvillé also mentions Philip of Burgundy's efforts in the 1370s to make La Rivière and Le Mercier his clients (37–38). Their lack of enthusiasm for his offers of pensions may have earned his hostility.

19. S. Babbitt, *Oresme's Livre de Politiques and the France of Charles V* (Philadelphia, 1985), 88–89; *Songe du Vergier* 1:229–31, 233–34, 240–42 (chaps. 135–37, 140). Oresme seemed to regard all extraordinary taxes as tyranny, a view more extreme than that of the clerk in the *Songe*. The position of the Marmousets presumably coincided with that of the knight in the *Songe*, and was more in the mainstream of legal thought, namely that taxes were legitimate in specified situations. See the discussion of Autrand, *Charles V*, 681–85, and also that of Cazelles, who noted the preoccupation with restoring the royal domain (*Soc. Charles*, 560) and added that Charles V seemed more concerned with the suffering of the people after 1378 (566).

20. *ORD* 7:710–11; *Mandements*, no. 1955; AN P 2296, pp. 25–26; L. Finot, "La Dernière Ordonnance de Charles V," *BÉC* 50 (1889): 164–67; Coville, *États*, 122; H. A. Miskimin, "The Last Act of Charles V: The Background of the Revolts of 1382," *Speculum* 38 (1963): 433–42; E. A. R. Brown, "Taxation and Morality in the Thirteenth and Fourteenth Centuries: Conscience and Political Power and the Kings of France," *French Historical Studies* 8 (1973): 24–25.

21. L. Mirot, *Les Insurrections urbaines au debut de règne de Charles VI (1380–1383): Leurs causes, leurs conséquences* (Paris, 1906), 27–34 and notes; Coville, *États*, 123. The contemporary suspicions of Louis of Anjou were voiced a generation later by Christine de Pizan (*Livre des fais* 1:136).

22. *RSD* 2:44–52; Frois-B 3:165–66, Frois-KL 9:300–303; *ORD* 6: 527–28; Mirot, *Insurrections*, 37–40; Coville, *États*, 124.

23. Mirot, *Insurrections*, 39–44.

24. BN NAF 7619, fols. 5r–8v, 9r–13v; *ORD* 6: 552–54, 564–65; *Chron. Valois*, 294; Mirot, *Insurrections*, 45–49.

25. Coville, *États*, 124, 127–28, 192, 391–93; Mirot, *Insurrections*, 52–61.

26. Mirot, *Insurrections*, 64–70, 75, 87–90.

27. Ibid., 91–95, 113–15, 179, 189, 197–98, 209–13.

28. D. Nicholas, *Town and Countryside: Social, Economic, and Political Tensions in Fourteenth-Century Flanders* (Bruges, 1971), 333 ff.; R. Vaughan, *Philip the Bold: The Formation of the Burgundian State* (Cambridge, Mass., 1962), 19 ff.

29. *ORD* 6:529–32; AN J 188[B], no. 8; Lehoux, *Jean de France* 2: 16–18.

30. Autrand, *Charles VI*, 113–15; *HL* 9: 899–913; C. Portal, "Les Insurrections des Tuchins dans les pays de Langue d'oc, vers 1382–1384," *Annales du Midi* 4 (1892): 433–74; Lehoux, *Jean de France* 2:57–58.

31. For Anjou's decision and departure, we have the comments of his chancellor: *Journal Le Fèvre*, 8–14, 24. See also Lehoux, *Jean de France* 2:60–61.

32. Palmer, *EFC*, 227–28, 245–47. For more on the Anglo-Flemish diplomatic contacts, see D. Nicholas, *The Van Arteveldes of Ghent: The Varieties of Vendetta and the Hero in History* (Ithaca, 1988), 178–81.

33. *Chron. des règnes* 3:7–9, 25, 31; Vaughan, *Philip*, 25–27; Autrand, *Charles VI*, 126–34; Nicholas, *Van Arteveldes*, 184–85; Lefranc, *Olivier*, 237–43; Juvenal des Ursins, *Histoire* (Michaud ed.), 354–56.

34. Mazas, *Vies* 4:393–417; Toudouze, *DCR*, 174. See also the remarks of Lefranc, *Olivier*, 263–64. One chronicler did not give Clisson credit for the victory but gave the glory to Bourbon and Coucy: *Chronique Cabaret d'Orville*, 165–75.

35. Gicquel, *Olivier*, 168; Lefranc, *Olivier*, 248–49, 278. The revolt of 1379–85 ultimately damaged severely the great prosperity of Flanders, but the French campaign did part of the damage. The king specifically awarded Clisson all English goods seized on the campaign (AN JJ 128, no. 78).

36. Palmer, *EFC*, 22.

37. Autrand, *Charles VI*, 105–12. For the royal entry into Paris on 11 January 1383, see *Chron. des règnes* 3:39. Two weeks later the crown abolished the office of *prévôt des marchands*, the Parisian equivalent of a mayor: BN NAF 7619, fols. 134r–137v; AN P 2296, pp. 89–92.

38. Lefranc, *Olivier*, 254; Mazas, *Vies* 4:419–420; Toudouze, *DCR*, 175–76.

39. Rey, *Domaine*, 166–67. Documents re-establishing the fiscal machinery are AN P 2296, pp. 81–87; *ORD* 7:746–52.

40. Vaughan, *Philip*, 28–31; Palmer, *EFC*, 47–49. The politics of the schism were an important secondary theme in the ongoing revolt in Flanders. It is significant that soon after his victory at Roosebeke, Olivier de Clisson sent a message to Clement VII at Avignon reporting on the battle (Lefranc, *Olivier*, 247).

41. ADLA E 104, nos. 6, 7; BN FR 22319, p. 405.

42. *RJ IV*, no. 425; ADLA E 92, no. 20, and E 104, no. 5.

43. *RJ IV*, no. 465; ADLA E 104, nos. 9, 10.

44. ADLA E 104, no. 8; E 236, fol. 94.

45. *RJ IV*, no. 459.

46. *RJ IV*, no. 455.

47. BN FR 32510, fols. 264r, 270v; BN FR 7858, fols. 221v, 226v, 227r, 228r.

48. The payroll for this royal army is found in BN FR 7858, fols. 221r–53v. From individual pay records found in BN PO 789 dossier 17,879 Clisson, we have one of Clisson's musters (no. 44) and a receipt for one month's salary (no. 9), which had been set at two thousand francs since October 1380 (AN K 53, nos. 17, 17²). Another payment to Clisson is in CL 33, p. 2437, no. 22.

49. Lefranc, *Olivier*, *P.J.* 11, p. 440 (from AN JJ 128, no. 78). See above, note 35.

50. ADLA 7 JJ 70 (citing document of 13 January 1383).

51. Lefranc, *Olivier*, *P.J.* 12, p. 441 (from AN J 400, no. 70). See also Buteau, "Naissance," 73.

52. Moranvillé, *Jean le Mercier*, 92.

53. Ibid., 95–96; Frois-KL 10: 265–72; Juvenal des Ursins, *Histoire* (Michaud ed.), 360. John IV, whose monthly salary of three thousand francs (BN FR 20405, nos. 4–7, 20590, nos. 28, 39) was 50 percent more than that of the constable, nevertheless was under Clisson's military command, and Toudouze thought he felt slighted and therefore conspired with the uncles to bring about a truce (*DCR*, 176).

54. Lehoux, *Jean de France* 2:85–86. The relevant royal documents are in BN FR 20403, nos. 19 (pay order of 28 October 1383) and 20 (instructions to Berry dated 7 November).

55. BN FR 20403, no. 18.

56. BN FR 20416, fol. 23 renumbered 31, and 20403, nos. 21–22.

57. *Foedera* 3 pt. 3: 162–163.

58. BN FR 20416, fol. 24 renumbered 32; CBourg 53, fol. 226v.

59. Lefranc, *Olivier*, 262.

60. Rey, *Finances*, 608.

61. Lefranc, *Olivier*, 267, and *P.J.* 13, pp. 441–42 (from AN K 53, no. 24, not no. 17^2 as Lefranc claimed).

62. Lefranc, *Olivier*, 279, cites a document at the Vatican indicating a loan from Clisson to Clement VII in June of 1384.

63. Ibid., 269, on Clisson's troubles with Berry over the taxes. See also Autrand, *Charles VI*, 176, and Gicquel, *Olivier*, 228–29. Lefranc (*Olivier*, *P.J.* 14, p. 442, from BN PO 789 doss. 17,879 Clisson, no. 8) has published a document of early February 1384, showing that even after receiving 4,000 francs (two months' salary), Clisson still was owed 52,300 francs in back pay.

64. Lehoux, *Jean de France* 2:201.

65. A copy of the ratification of 20 July in BMN 1689/1533, no. 9, may be the one found among Clisson's documents at his death (Bruel, "Inventaire," p. 224). The agreement of 11 July is in Lefranc, *Olivier*, *P.J.* 15, pp. 443–44 (from AN J 382, no. 7), AN X^{1c} 49, no. 22, and BN FR 22325, p. 894.

66. BMN 1690/1534, no. 5.

67. *Cart. Morbihan*, no. 595.

68. This well-known document (AN J 187, no. 10; ADLA E 177, no. 6) has been published in *RJ IV*, no. 483; L. C. Douet-d'Arcq, *Choix de pièces inédits relatives au règne de Charles VI* (Paris, 1863–64) 1: 54; Frois-KL 18:564–66. See also Palmer, *EFC*, 19. A later copy of this alliance, bearing a date somewht later in the month, is in BN FR 22319, p. 361. Pocquet, *Deux féodaux*, 29, believed the treaty to be directed against Clisson and the Marmousets.

69. Morice 2, col. 446.

70. *RJ IV*, no. 485.

71. *RJ IV*, no. 508; Lobineau 2, cols. 645–48; Morice 2, cols. 456–59; BN FR 16654, no. 26, fols. 165–68; Halgouet, *Répertoire*, 229 (a rather detailed analysis of two documents in AN J 243).

72. Morice 2, cols. 427, 428. Gicquel, *Olivier*, 127–28, refers to the bishop as Clisson's "creature." For further background on the duke's quarrel with the bishop, see Pocquet, *Papes*, 389, and Jones, *Creation*, 37–38.

73. Morice 2, cols. 466–68; Lobineau 2, cols. 654–56; Jones, *Creation*, 342.

A group of Breton bishops and barons, Clisson among them, was named to arbitrate the dispute between John IV and Saint-Malo. The bishop's nephew Jean, viscount of Rohan, who had been the duke's chancellor, was discharged from this office in May of 1384 (Morice 2, col. 449).

74. Palmer, *EFC*, 57.

75. Vaughan, *Philip*, 32–38; Palmer, *EFC*, 57–62.

76. Vaughan, *Philip*, 41, 86–87; Autrand, *Charles VI*, 152.

77. Palmer, *EFC*, 90. The crown had been generous with Burgundy, giving the duke a hundred thousand francs over and above all previous gifts, to help pay his expenses in taking over Flanders (CBourg 53, fol. 226v, 1 February 1384).

78. Palmer, *EFC*, 77–80.

79. Lehoux, *Jean de France* 2:201, and Coville, *Premiers Valois*, 290–96, both emphasized Berry's opposition to invasion plans and believed he was particularly involved in the failure of 1386.

80. Frois-J 2:201–3.

81. Palmer, *EFC*, 77–78, draws attention to a specific error regarding Berry in 1386. See Chapter 11 for Froissart's errors regarding Berry's whereabouts in the summer of 1392. En route to southwestern France in 1389, the chronicler fell in with a local knight who charmed him with stories about the count of Foix, including his feud with the Armagnacs and their patron, the duke of Berry (Frois-J 2:90–94). Perhaps it was on this journey that Froissart formed the negative opinion of Berry that colored his treatment of the duke in the chronicle and influenced posterity.

82. Jones, *DB*, 99–103. Ducal embassies to England in this period received little satisfaction, in part because of the competing factions at the English court (on these see also Goodman, *John of Gaunt*, 99–100). Meanwhile, the old friction between English and Breton merchants was in evidence when the English government, in July 1384, ordered the arrest of various Bretons: *CCR Richard II* 2: 463.

83. See above, Chapter 3, for the provisions of the treaty. Toudouze, *DCR*, 178, notes Clisson's belief that the duke's failure to obtain the release of John of Blois was a serious breach of promise. On the captive heir, see M. Jones, "The Ransom of Jean de Bretagne, Count of Penthièvre: An Aspect of English Foreign Policy, 1386–88," *BIHR* 14, no. 111 (May 1972): 9–11. This piece has been republished in Jones, *Creation*, but citations here will be to the original article. On the Breton refusal to accept his younger brother Henry, see above, Chapter 6.

84. Lefranc, *Olivier*, 229; Goodman, *John of Gaunt*, 186–87.

85. Bruel, "Inventaire," no. 376 and note 8; Lefranc, *Olivier*, 271–72, note 2.

86. Morice 2, cols. 480–81 (ADLA E 151, no. 14); Roy, *Histoire*, 136; Jones, "Ransom," 13; Lefranc, *Olivier*, 272.

87. *Journal Le Fèvre*, 56.

88. P. Timbal, "La Confiscation dans le droit français des XIIIe et XIVe siècles," *Revue Historique du Droit Français et Étranger* série 4, 22:47, pointed out, however, the danger of using the term "confiscation" imprecisely, since there was a clear legal distinction between confiscation and a temporary seizure that did not deprive the holder of seisin. Jones, *DB*, 99–101, thinks John IV was able to seize the Penthièvre strongholds because he was assured of fairly broad support since

former followers of the Blois-Penthièvre party had become his men since 1379. Some doubtless did shift their allegiance permanently, but the quick military successes achieved against the duke later in 1384, 1387, and 1393 suggest the survival of a strong core of nobles devoted to the Penthièvre cause. What may have facilitated John IV's successful occupation in September 1384 was the belief that it was a temporary act, incident to the transfer of the fief.

89. Reynaud, "Maison d'Anjou," 181; *Journal Le Fèvre*, 66, 68, 70.

90. *Journal Le Fèvre*, 74–75.

91. Bouchart, *Grandes chroniques* 2:150.

92. Morice 2, cols. 482–83; Lobineau 2, cols. 677–78; Bouchart, *Grandes chroniques* 2: 149–50; BN FR 22325, pp. 787 ff.

93. *RJ IV*, no. 551.

94. *Journal Le Fèvre*, 89

95. Rey, *Finances*, 592–93.

96. *Journal Le Fèvre*, 91–93.

97. Ibid., 96.

98. Historians differ as to which reasons most influenced Clisson. Leguay and Martin, *Fastes et malheurs*, 129, emphasize the duke's failure to honor his promise to work for his cousin's liberation. Doucet, *Vallée*, 82, emphasizes the constable's personal animus, his desire to "rendre Jean IV fou de colère."

99. Jones, "Ransom," 15–16. John of Gaunt, en route to Castile in 1386, broke John IV's siege of Brest (Goodman, *John of Gaunt*, 227).

100. *RJ IV*, no. 551.

101. Gicquel, *Olivier*, 145. Gicquel overstates the case in saying that Jeanne was "above all" a Valois.

102. J. Carrasco, "Le Royaume de Navarre et le duché de Bretagne au cours du denier tiers du XIVe siècle: Politique matrimoniale et circulation monétaire," in *1491: La Bretagne, terre d'Europe* (Brest, 1992), 207–9; Jones, *Creation*, 175–78, 195–96. The contract for the Navarrese marriage was dated 5 August 1386 (*RJ IV*, no. 597).

103. Lobineau 2, col. 850 (*Chron. Briocense*); Jones, *DB*, 120; Gicquel, *Olivier*, 25 (note 2) and 215. Bouchart, *Grandes chroniques* 2:171, mistakenly placed the marriage in December 1388.

104. *ORD* 7:123; Bruel, "Inventaire," 227. Gicquel, *Olivier*, 177, follows the faulty arithmetic of Buteau, "Naissance," 116, and says that Clisson realized 405,000 pounds from this transaction, whereas the real total was in the area of 41,000 *l.t.* By contrast, Lefranc, *Olivier*, 277, erred by a factor of ten in the opposite direction.

105. Juvenal des Ursins, *Histoire* (Michaud ed.), 363–67; Frois-J 2:41–47, 52–57; Palmer, *EFC*, 60; Terrier de Loray, *Jean de Vienne*, 179–205.

106. Lehoux, *Jean de France* 2:181–83; Palmer, *EFC*, 67–85; Juvenal des Ursins, *Histoire* (Michaud ed.), 368; ADLA 7 JJ 70 (order from Clisson dated 7 September 1386 to Blaisy and Montmor); BN FR 20590, nos. 45, 46; BN FR 25765, no. 55; BN NAF 7620, fols. 56r–57v.

107. For the royal tax, see Terrier de Loray, *Jean de Vienne*, *P.J.* 119; for that in Burgundy: CBourg 53, fol. 79. With Philip the Bold now controlling Flanders, the

proposed embarkation point, the crown thought it wise to revoke the constable's permission to profit from plunder in Flanders (AN JJ 128, no. 78, fol. 52)!

108. Seventy-one musters from 1386 preserved in AN K 53, no. 45, are analysed in J. Tardif, *Monuments historiques* (Paris, 1866). On 8 September, Charles VI promised to respect the liberties of Brittany because the duke had sent troops to the planned invasion (ADLA E 104, no. 13). The indications of Breton lords mustering with the French army under Clisson's command are in BN NAF 8604, pp. 78–83; BN FR 7858, fols. 261r, 288v, 292v, 293; BN FR 32510, fol. 295r.

109. Palmer, *EFC*, 77–80. One of those who adhered to the view that Palmer opposes was Toudouze, *DCR*, 179.

110. Frois-J 2:201–3; Juvenal des Ursins, *Histoire* (Michaud ed.), 370.

111. Lehoux, *Jean de France* 2:177, 183.

112. Palmer, *EFC*, 95, 231–32.

Chapter 8

1. BN FR 25765, no. 117; BN FR 20590, no. 47.

2. Palmer, *EFC*, 98. Military pay vouchers issued by the constable during these preparations are in BN PO 789 doss. 17,879 Clisson, nos. 10, 11. On the preparations, see also Juvenal des Ursins, *Histoire* (Michaud ed.), 372.

3. *Journal Le Fèvre*, 179, 181, 214, 245, 327, 328, 330.

4. Lefranc, *Olivier*, 284–85; Jones, "Ransom," 16–17.

5. *Journal Le Fèvre*, 312–15.

6. Ibid., 330–31. Clisson, meanwhile, turned to his friends among the Marmousets for help in raising the ransom (ibid., 332–33).

7. Lefranc, *Olivier*, 311.

8. *RJ IV*, no. 620; Morice 2, col. 534.

9. ADLA E 177, no. 5 (excerpt in *RJ IV*, no. 621, and indicated in BN NAF 7620, fol. 110).

10. Lefranc, *Olivier*, 311.

11. Jones, "Ransom," 16–17; Jones, *DB*, 105.

12. Frois-J 2:259, Frois-KL 12:218.

13. For the events described below, see Frois-J 2:239–49, Frois-KL 12:152–81, Frois-SHF 13:229–52.

14. It was Coville, *Premiers Valois*, 293, who called Clisson naive for attending the assembly, but Bouchart, *Grandes chroniques* 2:152, long ago recognized that he could not have honorably refused to attend.

15. Morice 2, cols. 540–42; Lobineau 2, cols. 678–80; Frois-KL 12:382; BN FR 22325, pp. 799–800; BN FR 22339, fols. 25v–29r; ADLA E 166, no. 1, fols 1–3, and E 166, no. 3; AN K 53 B, no. 70.

16. Palmer, *EFC*, 97.

17. Clisson's ratification (Morice 2, col. 542) was dated at Moncontour on 4 July. Toudouze, *DCR*, 181, thought a false date and place had been written on the document a week earlier in Vannes. According to Lefranc, *Olivier*, 306, the purpose of having the ratification dated in this way was to make it harder for Clis-

son to claim that the agreement was invalid by reason of extortion. The constable's subordinates, Blaisy and Montmor, were at Moncontour, where as late as 10 July they were acknowledging receipt of pay for mustering men for the aborted English expedition (Fonds Grandville en Bringolo, cabinet 28).

18. *RSD* 2:482–84. Bouchart, *Grandes chroniques* 2:152–60, largely followed Froissart, but downplayed the role of Laval and said that John IV actually ordered the execution and was much relieved the next day when he found that his subordinate had not obeyed. Juvenal des Ursins, *Histoire* (Michaud ed.), 372–73, was closer to Pintoin. The chronicler of Saint-Brieuc (Lobineau 2, cols. 852–53) stressed Clisson's offenses against the duke and said the barons intervened to secure his release, but did not imply that the duke intended from the start to secure the castles. Gicquel, *Olivier*, 118–22, characteristically emphasizing Clisson's desire to set himself up as a rival power in Brittany, treats the duke's actions in the light of that threat.

19. *RSD* 2:482–84.

20. Lefranc, *Olivier*, 309–10. Various authors have remarked upon the speed with which the cash for Clisson's ransom was assembled: Buteau, "Naissance," 79; Lefranc, *Olivier*, 307; Gicquel, *Olivier*, 169–70.

21. Lehoux, *Jean de France* 2:211–12, generally following Frois-KL 13:248–51.

22. Lefranc, *Olivier*, 310–11; Frois-J 2:248. In Provence, Marie of Blois was also shocked at the news of Clisson's capture, which she first learned about on 11 July, roughly the same time that the pope was informed, and within three days had dispatched a messenger to the uncles and her Breton supporters expressing her displeasure at the news: *Journal Le Fèvre*, 365–67.

23. Lefranc, *Olivier*, 312–13. Interestingly enough, on 25 July, exactly a month after the constable was seized, the keeper of the seal of the *prévôté* of Paris appended his *vidimus* to the duke of Brittany's letter of 17 February 1382 promising his protection to Clisson (BMN 1703/1547, no. 8³). It is probable that Clisson deliberately had his copy of this document authenticated and then brought it to the attention of the king and his advisers.

24. Henneman, "Who Were the Marmousets?" 29. On the attachment between the constable and young Louis, see Lefranc, *Olivier*, 265, 329.

25. Autrand, *Charles VI*, 177.

26. Lehoux, *Jean de France* 2:211–12.

27. Planiol, *Institutions* 3:124–25 has pointed out that the Estates of Brittany in this period were not distinct from the duchy's judicial parlement. Presumably the general Parlement of 1387, for which no proceedings survive (ibid., 137–38), was the body that Clisson attended just before his capture, but no source gives any hint that the ducal government brought charges before this assembly.

28. Palmer, *EFC*, 99. He concludes (101) that John did not approach the English until after arresting Clisson. Autrand, *Charles VI*, 175, notes that John may have been within his rights in strictly feudal terms but failed to understand that seizing the person of a great officer of the French crown was sure to be regarded as *lèse majesté* at the French court. Lefranc, *Olivier*, generally follows Froissart's account of the entire incident (above, note 13).

29. *AHP* 21:370, note 1, referring to AN J 186ᴬ, no. 69 (published by Lefranc, *Olivier*, *P.J.* 17, pp. 445–50). Clisson's men had seized property belonging to Guy de la Forget, preventing his heirs from taking possession of it.

30. On this dispute see above, Chapter 7, note 63. Clisson was blocking the collection of royal taxes even though Berry had agreed to share the proceeds with him (source cited next note).

31. Lefranc, *Olivier*, 445–50 (AN J 186ᴬ, no. 69); Lehoux, *Jean de France* 2:212.

32. Lefranc, *Olivier*, 450 (AN J 186ᴬ, no. 69²); Douet d'Arcq, *Choix de pièces* 1:80.

33. Palmer, *EFC*, 101. It is interesting, however, that Philip of Burgundy, on 5 August, dispatched his secretary on a seven-week trip to Poitou and Touraine "for business of the duke of Berry against the lord of Clisson, constable of France" (Petit, *Itinéraires*, 525).

34. Jones, "Ransom," 18. On 1 October 1387, De Vere and the duchess of Anjou reached agreement on the payment of the second sixty thousand francs (BMN 1707/1551, no. 2, pc. 1). A list of those standing surety for the ransom is in Morice 2, col. 528, and in Lobineau 2, col. 684.

35. *Journal Le Fèvre*, 411, 418, 468; Lefranc, *Olivier*, 315–16; BN FR 22319, p. 523; ADLA E 217, no. 6; BMN 1689/1533, no. 10; 1690/1534, no. 6. On the mortgaging of Mayenne and Champtoceaux to Clisson, see *Journal Le Fèvre*, 469, 478; *AHM* 5:343–44 (no. 321).

36. Jones, *DB*, 106, and "Ransom," 19. Some of De Vere's receipts of payments in late 1387 and 1388 are in Lobineau 2, cols. 684–85; Morice 2, cols. 528–29; and BMN 1707/1551, no. 2, pc. 2. Clisson guaranteed twelve thousand francs promised by various Breton lords (ibid., pc. 3) and added ten thousand francs in July 1388 in the name of Enguerrand de Coucy, to whom he owed the money (BN FR 22319, p. 525; ADLA E 217, no. 7, and De Vere's receipt of 12 September in BN FR 22325, p. 894). About the same time, the king had to order those who had promised money to pay what they owed (BMN 1707/1551, no. 2, pc. 4). A later installment reached De Vere on 10 September 1389 (BN FR 22319, p. 614 and ADLA E 120, no. 10. On 5 January 1390, John of Blois still owed Coucy a thousand francs (ADLA E 218, no. 8).

37. ADLA E 166, no. 7.

38. Lefranc, *Olivier*, 314–15; Mazas, *Vies* 4:443; Palmer, *EFC*, 101. This campaigning was damaging to the seigneurial economy of northern Brittany (ADCA E 79, no. 3, fol. 25r). Recovery of Clisson's own strongholds farther south evidently took longer, for it appears that a ducal garrison was still at Blain in December 1387 (ADIV 1 F 626).

39. Lefranc, *Olivier*, 297, addresses the nobles' reaction.

40. Ibid., 313–14; Lehoux, *Jean de France* 2:216.

41. Lefranc, *Olivier*, 316; Morice 2, cols. 544–45; BN NAF 23634, no. 10. Bernard de la Tour was paid fifteen francs per day (AN K 53ᴮ, no. 682). On Jean de Bueil, see Moranvillé, *Jean le Mercier*, 113, note 5.

42. Morice 2, col. 545.

43. Bouchart, *Grandes chroniques* 2:163.

44. *Chron. Briocense* (Lobineau 2, col. 852). This reference may refer to the earlier embassy headed by the bishop of Langres, since the chronology is not entirely clear.

45. *RJ IV*, nos. 646–47; Lobineau 2, cols. 680–84; Morice 2, cols. 543–547 (archival sources are ADLA E 166, no. 1, fols. 3v–7r, and E 166, no. 4).

46. Palmer, *EFC*, 96, 232. Palmer shows that the defiance attributed to William of Guelders was actually drawn up by the English and passed off as William's own pronouncement.

47. Ibid., 122–31; Lehoux, *Jean de France* 2:215–17; Jones, "Ransom," 21. Froissart (Frois-J 2:300–362; Frois-KL 13:1–39) devoted considerable attention to the duke of Guelders and his quarrel with Brabant.

48. Jones, *DB*, 121. The duchess of Anjou, who had returned from Provence, was reunited with her brother and attended the king at Orléans in her usual search for royal financial aid: *Journal Le Fèvre*, 516–20. The crown put her off on 24 April, promising an answer by Ascension Day (7 May), in Paris (ibid., 521). The king and court finally left Orléans on the twenty-seventh because of an epidemic (ibid., 522)

49. *RSD* 1:506–8; Palmer, *EFC*, 127.

50. Juvenal des Ursins, *Histoire* (Michaud ed.), 374.

51. Palmer, *EFC*, 131–33. The timetable of events led Palmer to conclude that the council must have decided to send the embassy around 12 May. When it convened on that date to hear the Angevin requests for help regarding Sicily, Clisson and the uncles were present (*Journal Le Fèvre*, 523), but there is no mention of Coucy, La Rivière, or the admiral, who may have already left. Bouchart, *Grandes chroniques* 2:166, said that the duke of Brittany *aymoit moult* Enguerrand de Coucy, who must have been the pivotal figure in the embassy.

52. Lefranc, *Olivier*, 321; Frois-J 2:337–40; Frois-KL 13:116–26. Palmer, *EFC*, 131, thought these instructions should have encouraged John IV to resist further, but he wouldn't because Lancaster in Aquitaine was not showing much interest in a coordinated coampaign. Bouchart, *Grandes chroniques* 2:164–65, reported that the uncles laid the groundwork for this mission by sending the count of Étampes to John IV as their special envoy.

53. Palmer, *EFC*, 132. Bouchart, *Grandes chroniques* 2:167–68, described the deliberations of the ducal council, which advised John IV to return the rest of the castles he had taken.

54. Jones, "Ransom," 21.

55. *RSD* 1:506–13; Bouchart, *Grandes chroniques* 2:170; Frois-J 2:343–46; Frois-KL 13:136–43; Palmer, *EFC*, 132. Reconstructing the timetable of events in May and June (*EFC*, 235–36), Palmer underscores the urgent need of Philip of Burgundy for a negotiated settlement. A military response would have required a campaign in Brittany where Clisson would have the limelight and his interests would be advanced. Campaigns in the Low Countries, by contrast, placed Philip in this role. Bouchart, *Grandes chroniques* 2:163–64 noted that the princes on the royal council wanted an expedition to Guelders, not Brittany.

56. This important document is found in many places, among them Lobineau 2, cols. 685–88; Morice 2, cols. 552–55; BN NAF 7620, fols. 177r–190v; Bibliothèque de l'Arsenal 5424, pp. 152–58; BN PO 789, doss. 17,879 Clisson,

no. 72; BN FR 16654, fols. 242r–245v (no. 37). The royal decision was registered at the Châtelet on 28 July (ADLA E 166, no. 5). See also the comments of Lefranc, *Olivier*, 323, and Gicquel, *Olivier*, 129–30.

57. *RJ IV*, no. 672; BN FR 22319, p. 358.

58. *RJ IV*, no. 673; Jones, *DB*, 212–14. Lehoux, *Jean de France* 2:223, thought that the king's pronouncement was one of the most severe shocks England had received, but this statement seems very exaggerated. Unless their intelligence had completely broken down, the English cannot have been totally surprised at the royal decision, and the shock surely was not comparable to that caused by the second treaty of Guérande.

59. It is not clear why Lehoux, *Jean de France* 2:222, should have considered Charles VI's decision "contrairement à toutes les previsions."

60. On this point I concur entirely with Lehoux (ibid., 212), who saw the attack on Clisson as provoking the split between the uncles and the Marmousets.

61. See above, notes 46–47. The duchess of Brabant had designated her relative, the duchess of Burgundy, to inherit her duchy (*RSD* 1:520).

62. Palmer, *EFC*, 92 ff.

63. AN P 2296, pp. 439–516 (reduction of salaries of royal officers in February 1388), 531–34 (restriction of number and perquisites of certain officers in July); *ORD* 7:186–89, 764–67 (or the royal *taille* and *aides*); BN FR 22451, nos. 7–11 (on the subsidy to support troops in Normandy, August–September 1388).

64. *RSD* 1:522–38; Frois-J 2:377–82, Frois-KL 13:258–73. Clisson was receiving his two-thousand-franc monthly salary on this campaign (BN PO 789 doss. 17,879 Clisson, no. 14). Musters of his troops are found in the same dossier (ibid., nos. 5, 17, 19), as is one of his pay receipts (no. 16). A list of the commanders who went on the campaign to Guelders (BN FR 20683, no. 44) has been published by E. Jarry, *La Vie politique de Louis de France, duc d'Orléans, 1372–1407* (Paris, 1889), *P.J.* 11, pp. 414–415.

65. *RSD* 1:546–47.

66. *RSD* 1:552–53.

67. Juvenal des Ursins, *Histoire* (Michaud ed.), 376–77; *RSD* 1:556–58 (the cardinal's speech) and 558–62 (what followed in the meeting). Lehoux, *Jean de France* 2:229–30, observed that people expected Charles to assume personal rule fairly soon but not to dismiss his uncles so abruptly. *RSD* 1:566 reported the efforts of the uncles to change the king's mind. Autrand, *Charles VI*, 164–65, points out that the meeting at Reims was staged on the anniversary of the king's coronation.

68. Document quoted in Frois-KL 13:353 and A. Coville, *Gontier et Pierre Col et l'Humanisme en France au temps de Charles VI* (Paris, 1934), 26. Cf. Lehoux, *Jean de France* 2:230–31.

69. *RSD* 1:562–63; Moranvillé, *Jean le Mercier*, 118–19.

70. On these earlier power struggles, the best analysis is that of Cazelles (*Soc. Philippe*, 201 ff., 261; *Soc. Charles*, 211 ff.).

71. Autrand, *Charles VI*, 170.

72. See note 70 for reference to the problems Philip VI and John II had with their respective heirs. On Charles VI's relations with his son, see R. C. Famiglietti, *Royal Intrigue: Crisis at the Court of Charles VI, 1392–1420* (New York, 1986), esp.

190, 195. Admittedly, the precarious mental condition of Charles VI made his reign a special case, but it is worth noting that the Treaty of Troyes in 1420 was the one instance in which a king actually disinherited an estranged son. The most bitter of the father-son feuds in the Valois family was that between Charles VII and his son, the future Louis XI. In all these cases, the son had a powerful following yet won few successes in his father's lifetime.

73. Frois-KL 15:2.

74. Autrand, *Charles VI*, 191, followed by Chauvernon, *Des maillotins*, 147.

75. Frois-J 2:521.

76. Lefranc, *Olivier*, 329, note 1.

77. L. Lalanne, *Dictionnaire historique de la France*, 2d ed. (Paris, 1877), 1223; *Grand Larousse encyclopédique* (Paris, 1963) 7:104.

78. Autrand, *Charles VI*, 191. Gicquel, *Olivier*, 231–32, has noted the irony of a man of Clisson's wealth and lineage being associated with a term used to insult *petits gens*.

79. Henneman, "Who Were the Marmousets?" 27.

80. Autrand, *Charles VI*, 193.

81. *Soc. Charles*, 428, 446, 466–68; Autrand, *Charles VI*, 191, 211.

82. Henneman, "Who Were the Marmousets?" 22, 51–52.

83. Ibid., 40–47 and notes. See also Coville, *Premiers Valois*, 297; *RSD* 1: 570, 580.

84. Henneman, "Who Were the Marmousets?" 40–62.

85. *RSD* 1:568; Frois-J 2:407, 410.

86. Lefranc subjected the royal council of this period to considerable analysis (*Olivier*, 329–33 and notes). Cf. Rey, *Finances*, 581; Coville, *Premiers Valois*, 297; Moranvillé, *Jean le Mercier*, 125.

87. Frois-KL 15:2.

88. *RSD* 1:569.

89. Autrand, *Charles VI*, 191–92; Coville, *Premiers Valois*, 297. Moranvillé, *Jean le Mercier*, 113, details the ties that linked Clisson and La Rivière and those that linked La Rivière with Le Mercier, then argues that the events of 1387 and 1388 had brought them even closer together.

90. Autrand, *Charles VI*, 165.

91. Ibid., 167.

92. See above, Chapter 7, at notes 19 and 20, for the concern about taxes at the end of Charles V's life. Juvenal des Ursins, *Histoire* (Michaud ed.), 383, wrote of dissensions and hatreds over fiscal exactions ten years later.

93. Rey, *Finances*, 571–72. See in particular Rey's discussion of the king's private coffers, where Charles V had maintained a sizable reserve (ibid., 446) which had been suppressed at his death in 1380 (449) then revived under the Marmousets in 1388 (449–50).

94. Rey, *Domaine*, 236–44, 325–26.

95. *ORD* 7:186–89.

96. *Foedera* 3 pt. 4: 39–42; Lehoux, *Jean de France* 2:246–47.

97. Lefranc, *Olivier*, 333, note 1.

98. *ORD* 7:768.

99. *ORD* 7:225 (AN P 2296, pp. 793–94), 5 February 1389. Another enactment (*ORD* 7:290) specifically prohibited the Parlement from taking into consideration letters issued in the king's name that were known to be contrary to the rulings of ordinary judges. According to Lefranc, *Olivier*, 333, such letters had been abused by the uncles in recent years.

100. AN P 2296, pp. 793–834.

101. Ibid., 599–634

102. *ORD* 7:245–249.

103. AN P 2296, pp. 659–78.

104. *ORD* 7:236–43; Rey, *Domaine*, 102–3; Moranvillé, *Jean le Mercier*, 123 ff.

105. Chauvernon, *Des maillotins*, 147–56.

106. Autrand, *Charles VI*, 228–29; Juvenal des Ursins, *Histoire* (Michaud ed.), 377–78.

107. Moranvillé, *Jean le Mercier*, 122; Rey, *Domaine*, 100–103, 175.

108. Autrand, *Charles VI*, 199–200.

109. Ibid., 206–10; Chauvernon, *Des maillotins*, 146. On election, see also *Soc. Charles*, 508–9.

110. Moranvillé, *Jean le Mercier*, 125. The University was probably ill-disposed towards the Marmousets from a much earlier date. Never really reconciled to Charles V's decision to support Clement VII, the theologians in Paris must have recognized the role of certain Marmousets in the events that created the schism in 1378.

111. M. Nordberg, *Les Ducs et la royauté: Études sur la rivalité des ducs d'Orléans et de Bourgogne, 1392–1407* (Uppsala, 1964), 40.

112. AN P 2296, pp. 793–94. See the discussion by Rey, *Finances*, 580.

113. Autrand, *Charles VI*, 205.

114. Rey, *Finances*, 572–74.

115. Lehoux, *Jean de France* 2:254–55; Autrand, *Charles VI*, 249; Moranvillé, *Jean le Mercier*, 136.

116. Autrand, *Charles VI*, 242–44. Cf. *HL* 9:938–941. Rey, *Domaine*, saw a twofold purpose in Charles VI's trip—to restore public order and to restore financial order.

117. Autrand, *Charles VI*, 250; Moranvillé, *Jean le Mercier*, 134, note 4; *HL* 9:941–43.

118. Lehoux, *Jean de France* 2:259; Autrand, *Charles VI*, 251–53. Lacking a legitimate son, Foix thought to leave his lands to the king for a price of one hundred thousand francs. He was also involved in the negotiations relating to the duke of Berry's second marriage.

119. Autrand, *Charles VI*, 242.

120. AN J 188ᴮ, no. 14 (1 September 1389).

121. *RSD* 1: 646–49; Moranvillé, *Jean le Mercier*, 136.

122. AN X¹ᵃ 8602, fols. 123–125.

123. Petit, *Itinéraires*, 534.

124. Autrand, *Charles VI*, 37–38, 264–65; Lehoux, *Jean de France* 2:256 (noting that Louis supported the Marmousets) and 230 (indicating the sharp in-

crease in favors to Louis after the Marmousets came to power). Various payments to Louis in 1390 and 1391 are indicated in BN FR 20586, nos. 47–50. See also Rey, *Finances*, 602.

125. Coville, *Premiers Valois*, 297–98, gave Louis a considerable role in the coup of 1388 and called him their patron.

126. Lehoux, *Jean de France* 2:230.

127. After an excellent survey of the many Orleanists in the field administration, (Nordberg, *Ducs*, 41–51), Nordberg seems to convey the impression that Louis had placed his men in these positions (ibid., 52).

128. BN PO 922 doss. 20,385 Craon, nos. 19, 20, 32; PO 1280 doss. 28,818 Garencières, nos. 51, 52; BN NAF 3638, nos. 116, 127; Moranvillé, *Jean le Mercier*, 136, 140, 362–66; Jarry, *Vie politique*, 42–43.

129. BN FR 6210, no. 247; BN FR 26028, no. 2408; BN FR 26029, no. 2638; PO 61 doss. 1340 Albret, no. 16; PO 494 doss. 11,108 Braquemont, no. 16; PO 875 doss. 19,660 Coucy, nos. 26, 27; PO 2883 doss. 64,022 Trie, no. 52. Also see Chapter 11, note 16.

130. Lehoux, *Jean de France* 2:248. A month after the wedding, Louis formally ratified the arrangements regarding her dowry: BN FR 3863. no. 25 (fols. 154–59).

131. Jarry, *Vie politique*, 82–88. Châtillon's closest relative and potential heir was Clisson's son-in-law, the count of Penthièvre, and in Brittany some felt that he had been deprived of his inheritance: Bouchart, *Grandes chroniques* 2:180.

132. Jarry, *Vie politique*, 89–92; *ORD* 7:467–72; and below, Chapter 11.

Chapter 9

1. J. J. N. Palmer, "English Foreign Policy, 1388–99," in *The Reign of Richard II: Essays in Honour of May McKisack*, ed. F. R. H. DuBoulay and C. M. Barron (London, 1971), 94.

2. On Berry's zeal to end the schism, see Kaminsky, *Simon*, 33–34.

3. Palmer, *EFC*, 142–45 (on the continuing peace talks and the French plan to invade Italy); Rey, *Finances*, 449–50 (on rebuilding the royal coffers).

4. On the newer attitudes towards war and military discipline, see G. W. Coopland, ed., *The Tree of Battles of Honoré Bonet* (Cambridge, Mass., 1949), 129–44, 153–54. For Charny's *Livre de Chevalerie*, see Frois-KL 1 pt. 2:463–533.

5. N. A. R. Wright, "The Peasant Lobby at the Court of the Valois Kings" (paper, Adelaide, 1990). The voices of such intellectuals grew louder over the next fifteen years. See K. L. Forhan, "Reflecting Heroes. Christine de Pizan and the Mirror Tradition," in *The City of Scholars: New Approaches to Christine de Pizan*, ed. M. Zimmermann and D. De Rentiis (Berlin, 1994), 189–96.

6. Jones, *DB*, 121; Autrand, *Charles VI*, 263 calls attention to the recurring strife between Foix and Armagnac which was fueled by the availability of employable fighting men.

7. Autrand, *Charles VI*, 256, and 25–30 on the king's education; Moranvillé, *Jean le Mercier*, 139.

8. Autrand, *Charles VI*, 258.

9. Ibid.; Moranvillé, *Jean le Mercier*, 137; Frois-J 2:446–49, 465–77, 481–84; Frois-KL 14:151–59, 212–52; *Chronique Cabaret d'Orville*, 220–57. A royal order to pay a number of lords who accompanied Louis of Bourbon is in BN FR 20590, no. 68.

10. Autrand, *Charles VI*, 261. For Clisson's support of the Angevin venture, see *Journal Le Fèvre*, 523 ff.

11. The definitive work on Louis of Orléans remains Jarry, *Vie politique*. See also the nice summary of his Italian schemes in Palmer, "English Foreign Policy," 90–92, and the comments of J. d'Avout, *La Querelle des Armagnacs et les Bourguignons* (Paris, 1943), 37.

12. Autrand, *Charles VI*, 260, argues that Charles VI saw an expedition to Rome to end the schism as a Christian work that substituted for a crusade. Apparently the Marmousets encouraged him to think in these terms (Moranvillé, *Jean le Mercier*, 139, and Frois-J 2:485).

13. Frois-J 2:261.

14. Palmer, "English Foreign Policy," 86–88. For Charles VI's support of the house of Anjou under the Marmousets, see also Autrand, *Charles VI*, 248–49; Lehoux, *Jean de France* 2:265; Palmer, *EFC*, 192–94; and *AHM* 5:398 (no. 376).

15. Autrand, *Charles VI*, 261; Lehoux, *Jean de France* 2: 265 ff.

16. Autrand, *Charles VI*, 261–62; Avout, *Querelle*, 36; but see especially Palmer, "English Foreign Policy," 95–100. Lehoux, *Jean de France* 2: 275 ff., also sees the intervention of Richard II as the crucial action in aborting the Italian plan.

17. Lehoux, *Jean de France* 2:268–69. On 28 November 1390, Armagnac concluded an arrangement with the king's representative, Jean de Blaisy, for clearing the fortresses occupied by "English" (doubtless meaning *routiers* in this case): BN Collection Languedoc 87, fols. 127r–v.

18. Autrand, *Charles VI*, 263. For English and Breton overtures to Armagnac early in 1391, see Palmer, "English Foreign Policy," 97–98. See also Lehoux, *Jean de France* 2:270–74. Armagnac was closely related and politically aligned to the duke of Berry, and according to Lehoux, Berry had not counted on his "obstinacy" in choosing Florence over Milan. Yet the Saint-Denis chronicler, in reporting Armagnac's campaign and death in Italy in 1391, clearly saw his sister's marriage to Carlo Visconti as a major factor in Armagnac's Florentine sympathies. *RSD* 1: 710–19. This marriage dated back to 1382: BN FR 6537, pp. 55–58.

19. The future John V was born on 24 December 1389 (Jones, *DB*, 120).

20. Autrand, *Charles VI*, 265–66.

21. Jones, *Creation*, 246–52.

22. Lefranc, *Olivier*, 336–37, note 1; La Borderie, *Histoire* 4:81. See also Jones, *Creation*, 251–52 for evasion of the payment owed to Clisson. At this very time (1391) the duke was collecting taxes earmarked for this payment (BN FR 22319, pp. 373–74).

23. Morice 2, col. 557; Lobineau 2, cols. 688–89; *RJ IV*, no. 683.

24. *RJ IV*, no. 700; see also Jones, *DB*, 121.

25. ADIV 1F 626; BN FR 20405, no. 10.

26. *RJ IV*, no. 740; ADLA E 186, nos. 4, 5; E 236, fol. 72v.; Lehoux, *Jean de France* 2:261–62.

27. Lefranc, *Olivier*, 340–41.

28. BN FR 22319, p. 397. This contract of sale actually executed an agreement reached earlier, on 25 February (ibid.). Jones, *DB*, 121, discusses this matter briefly.

29. AN P 1339, no. 439 (original parchment of November 1392, enclosing a copy of this transaction).

30. Morice 2, cols. 573–74. An archivist assigned the date of c. 1384 to the manuscript in ADLA E 104, no. 11, which contains the duke's arguments and his instructions to his envoys to the French court, but the document seems to belong to the dispute of 1390.

31. Jones, *DB*, 121; Lehoux, *Jean de France* 2:268. La Borderie and Pocquet seem not to have understood that the duke's seizure of Champtoceaux was motivated by Clisson's custody of the fortress (La Borderie, *Histoire* 4:81). Juvenal des Ursins, *Histoire* (Michaud ed.), 386, thought that Clisson had provoked a crisis because the duke had not lived up to his engagements. Tensions had already been increased when the duke's men regained La Roche-Derrien in September 1390 while wrangling with John of Blois over homage for the place: ADCA E 1, fourth liasse. This dispute was resolved the following spring (ibid., sixth liasse).

32. ADLA E 104, no. 12; BN FR 20885, nos. 77–79; Autrand, *Charles VI*, 266.

33. Morice 2, cols. 555–56, and discussion in Jones, *DB*, 124.

34. ADIV 1F 626; BN FR 20405, no. 14.

35. *RJ IV*, nos. 779. 780. See Palmer, "English Foreign Policy," 97, and Jones, *DB*, 125.

36. Jones, *DB*, 123; *RJ IV*, no. 786

37. ADLA E 108, nos. 10, 12, 13.

38. ADLA E 108, nos. 14, 19, 20.

39. ADLA E 108, no. 11

40. Morice 2, cols. 483–84.

41. ADLA E 108. nos. 15–18.

42. *RJ IV*, no. 783. The same representatives were to try to have quashed a suit brought by Jeanne Chabot, lady of Rais, before the Parlement in Paris. See Chapter 12, note 11, for a summary of the sources for this lengthy litigation.

43. *RJ IV*, no. 786; Autrand, *Charles VI*, 266.

44. Jones, *DB*, 124, note 3.

45. Lefranc, *Olivier*, 342, thought the uncles were encouraging John IV.

46. ADLA E 92, no. 22, partially published in Morice 2, cols. 577–78, and Lobineau 2, cols. 750–52.

47. BN NAF 7269, fol. 74v; Jones, *RJ IV* 1:69 note 1; Autrand, *Charles VI*, 267; Coville, *Premiers Valois*, 305.

48. *RJ IV*, no. 795.

49. ADLA E 8, no. 3.

50. *RJ IV*, no. 797; Morice 2, cols. 578–80; Lobineau 2., cols. 753–56.

51. *RJ IV*, no. 798. See Bouchart, *Grandes chroniques* 2:174–77, for a generally sympathetic summary of the duke's position and his responses to the crown.

52. *RJ IV*, nos. 799, 800; Morice 2, cols. 590–93; ADLA E 8, nos. 4, 7, 8. Bouchart, *Grandes chroniques* 2:178–79.

53. Morice 2, cols. 581–85; Lobineau 2, cols. 757–60; ADIV 1E 16, no. 2; ADCA E 1, seventh liasse.

54. AN JJ 142, no. 308, fols. 172v–173v; BN FR 22319, p. 471; Morice 2, cols. 586–88; Lobineau 2, cols. 761–63; BMN 1689/1533, no. 11; ADLA E 166, no. 17. The amounts these lords were assessed may indicate their relative wealth. By far the two biggest contributors (at 16,000 *l.t.* apiece) were Guy de Laval (Clisson's brother-in-law) and Charles de Dinan, lord of Châteaubriant. Clisson gave Laval a receipt for his share on 18 July (ADIV 1F 1527, no. 40; BN FR 22325, p. 353). Of the 80,000 *l.t.* deposited in accordance with this treaty, some 77,000 was still at Josselin in sealed bags when Clisson died fifteen years later (Bruel, "Inventaire," 202–4). It would seem that the duke evaded restitution to the end. See also Lefranc, *Olivier*, 343, and La Borderie *Histoire* 4:81.

55. ADLA E 166, nos. 1 (fols. 7r–8r), 11, 13, 15, some of which are cited in *RJ IV*, nos. 803–4.

56. The document naming these castellanies—Saint Père en Rais, Hede, Duault, Huelgouet, Châteauneuf du Fou, Gourein, Châteaulin en Cornoaille, Lannion, and La Guerche—is published in *RJ IV*, no. 805; Morice 2, col. 585; and Lobineau 2, col. 760. It appears from ADLA E 166, no. 9, that a prominent neutral Breton lord, Charles de Dinan, had custody of two of these places while their revenues were being determined, just as he had administered Champtoceaux while waiting for the duke of Bourbon to take possession. Although John of Blois promised to relinquish the nine castellanies once the revenues were provided for in some other way (ADLA E 166, no. 14), he and John IV soon were wrangling over the actual value of the revenues of Châteaulin (ADLA E 166, nos. 8, 10; BN FR 22319, p. 297).

57. *RJ IV*, no. 802; Morice, cols. 580–81; Lobineau 2, cols. 756–57.

58. For the duke's agreement at Tours to hold such an inquiry, see *RJ IV*, no. 798. The inquiry was accomplished by late March (*RJ IV*, no. 809). Autrand, *Charles VI*, 267, feels that the duke really gave no ground on any of the major issues.

59. Jones, *DB*, 127, has a disappointingly abbreviated disscussion of the issues and arrangements involved in the treaty of Tours.

60. *RSD* 1: 732–33; Autrand, *Charles VI*, 268.

61. See Frois-B 6:34–42; Frois-J 2:516–20; Frois-KL 14:376–90; *RSD* 1: 734–43. On 12 March, Charles granted the duke of Burgundy 3000 *l.t.* per month for his assistance at the conference in Amiens (CBourg 53, fol. 224r). See also Lefranc, *Olivier*, 343–44; Famiglietti, *Royal Intrigue*, 1–2, and notes. Lehoux, *Jean de France* 2:284–86, places the end of the conference around 8 April and the king's return to Paris in early May, but it is hard to trust her dating since she found no trace of the duke of Berry's whereabouts between late March and late May and was evidently unaware that he had also fallen sick at Amiens.

62. Jones, *DB*, 127–28.

63. *RJ IV*, no. 814.

64. Coville, *Premiers Valois*, 305.

65. *AHM* 5:108–9, 112–18, 122–36 (nos. 140, 142–44, 148–49, 151–52) from documents in AN T 159[18]. For a brief sketch of Craon's career, see R. C. Famiglietti, *Tales of the Marriage Bed from Medieval France (1300–1500)* (Providence, 1992), 315–18.

66. Autrand, *Charles VI*, 277; J. Pichon, "Mémoire de Pierre de Craon," *Mélanges de litterature et d'histoire recueillis et publiés par la Société des Bibliophiles françois*, pt. 1 (Paris, 1856): 95–97. Among the documents placing him in the service of Louis of Orléans (then duke of Touraine) in 1389 and 1390 are BN NAF 3653, nos. 387, 388, 391, 392, 404, 416–18; BN PO 922 doss. 20,385 Craon, nos. 32, 37, 48. 51–55, 57. By March of 1389, he was also a chamberlain of the king: BN NAF 3638, no. 124; BN PO 922 doss. 20,385 Craon, nos. 19, 20.

67. Pichon, "Mémoire," 98; A. Bertrand de Broussillon, *La Maison de Craon, 1050–1480, étude historique, accompagnée du cartulaire de Craon* (Paris, 1893) 2: 247 (no. 1219).

68. *Journal Le Fèvre*, 113, 117, 141, 142, 145, 192, 193.

69. Ibid., 201–2, 205–6; Juvenal des Ursins, *Histoire* (Michaud ed.), 363; Pichon, "Mémoire," 99–102.

70. Pichon, "Mémoire," 103.

71. For the Angevin acquisition of Sablé in the 1370s, the principal documents are AN P 1334¹, no. 6, fol. 3, and P 1344, nos. 586, 587, 589–91, and 593. Pierre repurchased Sablé in June of 1390 for fifty thousand francs: AN P 1344, nos. 594, 595. For Pierre de Craon's favor at court, see Bouchart, *Grandes chroniques* 2:172.

72. *RSD* 2:2–5, the version apparently preferred by Autrand, *Charles VI*, 284; Juvenal des Ursins, *Histoire* (Michaud ed.), 388. According to Pichon, "Mémoire," 103–4, Craon spent four months at the abbey of Saint-Denis in 1395 and could have told this story to the royal historian there. See also the comments of Autrand, *Charles VI*, 277.

73. Frois-J 2:496–97; Frois-KL 14:315–23, followed by Lefranc, *Olivier*, 346–48.

74. *RSD* 1:338–41. See above, note 69.

75. La Borderie, *Histoire* 4:83.

76. Frois-J 2:497.

77. Bouchart, *Grandes chroniques* 2:173; Lefranc, *Olivier*, 356–57.

78. Frois-J 2:498. Somewhat more mysterious is Froissart's assertion that Craon and John IV had maintained a lively, and rather seditious, correspondence in the days when Craon was still in favor at court (ibid., 496). Nobody has produced documentary evidence of this correspondence. Jones, *DB*, 129, points out that there is no proof of a clear connection between Craon's actions and the duke of Brittany, but he does not rule it out, and John IV did lend him ten thousand francs in September 1391 (BN FR 11531, p. 120; BN FR 22319, p. 530).

79. Autrand, *Charles VI*, 284.

80. Pichon, "Mémoire," 106–7.

81. *RSD* 2:2–4.

82. BN FR 22319, fol. 361; AN P 1344, nos. 596, 597; Reynaud, "Maison d'Anjou," 183; Pichon, "Mémoire," 105; *RJ IV*, no. 812. Craon is said to have explained the sale with an announcement that he planned a pilgrimmage to the Holy Land: Mazas, *Vies* 4:450.

83. *RSD* 2:8–9.

84. Jones, *DB*, 128.

85. Pichon, "Mémoire," 105–6.

86. *RSD* 2:4–5. This account is to be preferred to that of Frois-J 2:523, who has Pierre using as his base Sablé, which was no longer in his hands and was, in any case, much farther from Paris than Porchefontaine. See also Bouchart, *Grandes chroniques* 2:181–83; AN K 54 no. 20; Lehoux, *Jean de France* 2:290; La Borderie, *Histoire* 4: 84–85; Moranvillé, *Jean le Mercier*, 148; Pichon, "Mémoire," 107–12; and Toudouze, *DCR*, 185–86.

Chapter 10

1. *RSD* 2:6–7; BN NAF 7621, fols. 21r–23v.

2. *RSD* 2:6–7; *AHM* 5:493. See below, note 4. On Craon's escape, see Pichon, "Mémoire," 113–14.

3. AN J 359, no. 20; Lefranc, *Olivier, P.J.* 19, pp. 450–52; AN J 179, no. 13; AN PP 109, p. 595; AN U 785, fols. 191–93; BN FR 3876, no. 21 (fols. 186–87); BN FR 2836, fol. 17v; AN K 54, no. 20; BN NAF 7621, fols. 38r–45v.

4. AN K 54, nos. 21 and 21². This award to Louis may have followed the council in which he supported the Beton expedition (see below at nn. 9–10). Six months later, the crown confirmed Louis in possession of the site of Craon's demolished Parisian town house (AN JJ 144, no. 17, fols. 7r–v) and noted pointedly that the attack on Clisson occurred while he was returning from the royal residence.

5. AN P 2296, pp. 909–16, 919–22; BN NAF 7621, fols. 15–19, 28–37; AN K 54, no. 19; and above, Chapter 9, note 130.

6. Frois-J 2:526, 528.

7. Berry's name is conspicuously missing from the list of leading commanders who were paid for the abortive campaign of August 1392 (BN FR 7858, fol. 309v). Lehoux, *Jean de France* 2:289–92, placed Berry at Lyon on 29 July (290), at Pont-Saint-Esprit on 23 August (291), and back at Creil by 13 September (292). A document published by J. Petit et al., *Essai de restitution des plus anciens mémoriaux de la chambre de comptes de Paris* (Paris, 1899), 117, indicates that it took a representative from Lyon eleven days to reach Paris for a court appearance. Such a person, paid by the day, was expected to travel fast and would have covered the ground more rapidly than a royal prince on a diplomatic mission. Berry could not have left Paris after 18 July and probably departed several days earlier. Petit, *Itinéraires*, 229, shows the duke of Burgundy at Amiens on the seventeenth and reaching Saint-Denis only on 20 July. Thus these two royal uncles were not in the same place, and would have been unable to work in concert, for several months prior to September 1392. The council that decided to attack Brittany clearly met when neither duke was in town and had made its decision by 15 July, when Charles VI assigned a thousand francs to Marshal Boucicaut, then captain of Tours, to pay his expenses for a forthcoming voyage to Le Mans. See D. Lalande, *Jean II Le Meingre, dit Boucicaut (1366–1421)* (Geneva, 1988), 43, citing CL 73, no. 96.

8. BN FR 11531, p. 117; B. Pocquet du Haut-Jussé, "Les séjours de Philippe le Hardi, duc de Bourgogne, en Bretagne (1372, 1394 et 1402)," *MSHAB* 16 (1935): 11.

9. *Chron. Briocense* (Lobineau 2, col. 859).

10. *RSD* 2:8–9

11. Bouchart, *Grandes chroniques* 2:185; *Chron. Briocense* (Lobineau 2, col. 859).

12. *RSD* 2:16–19.

13. Ibid., 10–11.

14. Ibid.; Bouchart, *Grandes chroniques* 2:186–89; Juvenal des Ursins, *Histoire* (Michaud ed.), 388–89; Moranvillé, *Jean le Mercier*, 148; Autrand, *Charles VI*, 282. See ibid., 273, for a summary of how the attack on Clisson could be treated — as an attack on his office and therefore *lèse majesté*, or as an episode in a purely private war.

15. *RSD* 2:10–11. According to the always suspect later narrative of *Chronique Cabaret d'Orville*, 261–63, the duke of Bourbon argued against the expedition after learning that Clisson and La Rivière had broken the treaty of Tours. The chronicler makes no mention of Craon or the assassination attempt.

16. BN FR 7858, fols. 309v–320v. The leading followers of the duke of Orléans were present, however (C. Lannette-Clavérie, *Collection Joursanvault, sous-series 6-J* [Orléans, 1976] 9–11, nos. 40–42, 51, 56–58). Despite the government's belief in John IV's culpability, the agreements made with him at Tours in January were by no means a dead letter. Early in June, he reached agreement with the count of Penthièvre on a number of points (ADLA E 166, no. 19), and on 18 July Clisson received some money promised in that agreement (above, Chapter 9, note 54).

17. Famiglietti, *Royal Intrigue*, 2 and notes; Autrand, *Charles VI*, 284; Frois-J 2:533.

18. Bouchart, *Grandes chroniques* 2:193–94. Bouchart's actual account does not inspire confidence since he followed Froissart in thinking that Berry was present, but Burgundy was quick to inform John IV when the mission was indeed halted (below, note 21).

19. Jones, *DB*, 128–29.

20. Lefranc, *Olivier*, 361–62; Moranvillé, *Jean le Mercier*, 151–52; Frois-B 6: 60–71; Frois-J 2:530–36; Frois-KL 15:35–48; *RSD* 2:20–21. Bouchart, *Grandes chroniques* 2:188, 197–98; Juvenal des Ursins, *Histoire* (Michaud ed.), 389–90.

21. Lefranc, *Olivier*, 354, citing BN FR 4482. Philip also quickly obtained a royal order (on 7 August) authorizing payment of nearly 5,000 *l.t.* to him for the maintenance of his "estate" during the expedition: CBourg 53, fol. 230v.

22. Avout, *Querelle*, 13.

23. Famiglietti, *Royal Intrigue*, 3–20, brilliantly analyzes the king's successive psychotic episodes and shows how his symptoms resembled those now associated with paranoid schizophrenics.

24. Autrand, *Charles VI*, 289.

25. Jarry, *Vie politique*, 96–99. Cf. Roy, *Histoire*, 168. Lehoux, *Jean de France* 2: 292–93, says that Louis made no effort to defend the Marmousets. Louis did, however, provide some negative support by refusing to attend and lend his endorsement to the session of the parlement that pronounced against the constable (Frois-J 2:545; Frois-KL 15:73).

26. Vaughan, *Philip*, 44.

27. See below at note 34.

28. Lefranc, *Olivier*, 369–70. See Lehoux, *Jean de France* 2:292, for Berry's return. Bouchart, *Grandes chroniques* 2:200–202, noted Berry's lingering resentment over the punishment of Bétizac in Languedoc three years earlier.

29. Lehoux, *Jean de France* 2:292–93; Moranvillé, *Jean le Mercier*, 157. Not surprisingly, a chronicler sympathetic to John IV, *Chron. Briocense* (Lobineau 2, col. 860), associated the disgraced Marmousets with the decision to attack Brittany.

30. Moranvillé, *Jean le Mercier*, 158.

31. Ibid., 159; BN FR 2836, fol. 17r–v; AN PP 109, p. 578.

32. Frois-J 2:540; Frois-KL 15:58; Bouchart, *Grandes chroniques* 2:184, 203; Lefranc, *Olivier*, 357–58; Gicquel, *Olivier*, 173–74; Toudouze, *DCR*, 188–89; Autrand, *Charles VI*, 283. Buteau, "Naissance," 81, thinks that the reported figure was only a slight exaggeration of Clisson's actual fortune.

33. Frois-J 2:540–42; Frois-KL 15:58–61; Bouchart, *Grandes chroniques* 2: 205; Lefranc, *Olivier*, 362–63, 366–67; Toudouze, *DCR*, 192. Although Mazas, *Vies* 4:461, said it was Orléans who let Clisson know of his impending disgrace, other writers attribute his escape to Josselin to Enguerrand de Coucy, the leader of the force sent against him. According to Lefranc, *Olivier*, 354, Coucy was Clisson's brother in arms in the same sense that Du Guesclin had been, and had been one of the first people to visit Olivier after Craon's attack in June.

34. ADLA E 166, no. 20.

35. AN U 785, fols. 7v–8r; *RSD* 2:26–31; Bouchart, *Grandes chroniques* 2: 205; *Chron. Briocense* (Lobineau 2, col. 860); Frois-J 2: 545; Frois-KL 15:73; Coville, *Premiers Valois*, 307; La Borderie, *Histoire* 4:87; Lefranc, *Olivier*, 367–71. The king is said to have ordered subsequently that documents relating to judicial proceedings against Clisson and other Marmousets be destroyed (ibid., 369).

36. Lehoux, *Jean de France* 2:293; BN NAF 7621, fols. 147r–149v. Villaines was released from prison in March 1393 after a fine of twenty thousand francs: AN X1a 11, fols. 159v–160r, 12, fol. 170r.

37. Rey, *Finances*, 577; Perroy, *Hundred Years War*, 195. On the other hand, Lefranc, *Olivier*, 375, considered the changes of late 1392 to be a revolution because, for the first time, the council was largely cleared of the advisers of Charles V.

38. Avout, *Querelle*, 57.

39. Moranvillé, *Jean le Mercier*, 156, note 1; Famiglietti, *Royal Intrigue*, 3; Petit, *Itinéraires*, 229.

40. *RSD* 2:33–34.

41. Avout, *Querelle*, 57–58.

42. Famiglietti, *Royal Intrigue*, 3–4.

43. See citations note 35, above. The count of Eu was Berry's new son-in-law.

44. Autrand, *Charles VI* 268; Rey, *Finances*, 577.

45. Although in power for less than four years, those identified as members of the Marmouset party averaged more than thirty years in royal service: Henneman, "Who Were the Marmousets?" 27.

46. Indeed, Clisson had promised Charles VI another loan of eighty thousand gold francs. A company of sixty men was dispatched to Josselin a day or two before the king's attack to collect the money but returned empty-handed because

Clisson would not hand over the funds once the campaign was canceled: Rey, *Finances*, 412, note 1; Moranvillé, *Jean le Mercier*, 153.

47. *RSD* 2:30.

48. Above, Chapter 9, note 54.

49. ADLA E 166, no. 20.

50. Lobineau 2, col. 763; ADLA E 166, no. 22.

51. Morice 2, cols. 588–90; Lobineau 2, cols. 763–65; BN NAF 7621, fols. 56r–v. On the problem of the hearth assessments (based on very outdated figures), see Kerhervé, *État breton*, 541–42.

52. *RJ IV*, no. 856; BN FR 22319, p. 422. They were still talking in mid-February 1393 (ADLA E 166, no. 18).

53. AN P 1334, no. 6, fol. 4. Other documents relating to Sablé are BN NAF 7269, fol. 103, and *AHM* 5:401–402 (no. 381).

54. AN P 1344, no. 598; ADLA E 179, no. 3.

55. BN FR 22319, p. 405; *RJ IV*, nos. 974, 990; Morice 2. col. 629. The money for this transaction seems to have come from Louis of Orleans and the nobles of his entourage, essentially a pro-Marmouset group: AN P 1344, nos. 599, 600.

56. Jones, *DB*, 130.

57. Aside from Eustache de la Houssaye, who had become a loyal follower of the duke's, his supporters included such former royal commanders as Olivier le Moine (*RJ IV*, nos. 830, 855) and the lord of Tournemine (*RJ IV*, nos. 826, 831). In November 1393, John IV received oaths of loyalty from a number of other important lords: BN FR 11531, p. 163, and Lobineau 2, cols. 768–69). On Clisson's supporters, resources, and the strategic placement of the strongholds under his control, see Lefranc, *Olivier*, 378–79; Roy, *Histoire*, 169; Juvenal des Ursins, *Histoire* (Michaud ed.), 391; B. Pocquet du Haut-Jussé, *Philippe le Hardi, régent de Bretagne (1402–1404). Discours de reception à l'Académie de Dijon prononcé dans la seance du 20 décembre 1933* (Dijon, 1933), 4.

58. Frois-J 2:555.

59. Famiglietti, *Royal Intrigue*, 207, note 12.

60. Frois-J 2:557; *RSD* 2:30–33.

61. *RJ IV*, no. 930. On John IV's negotiations with Lancaster, see Jones, *DB*, 132–35, and Morice 2, cols. 644–45.

62. Lefranc, *Olivier*, 378–79; Frois-J 2:556–58.

63. Lobineau 1: 485; *Chron. Briocense* (Lobineau 2, cols. 861–62); Lefranc, *Olivier*, 379–81; Gicquel, *Olivier*, 138.

64. Morice 2, col. 620; Lobineau 2, col. 768; ADLA E 166, nos. 1 (fols. 8r–v), 25, 26.

65. *RJ IV*, no. 947. Among other things, Clisson had a cannonier at Blain supervising the construction of artillery: M. Jones, "L'utilisation de la poudre à canon et de l'artillerie dans le duché de Bretagne avant 1400: la preuve documentaire," *MSAB* 69 (1992): 166.

66. *Cart. Morbihan*, no. 619.

67. ADLA E 166, nos. 1 (fols. 9v–10r), 27; Morice 2, cols. 622–623; Lobineau 2, col. 769.

68. *RSD* 2:100–105; Juvenal des Ursins, *Histoire* (Michaud ed.), 395; Lefranc, *Olivier*, 382. On 26 January, Charles VI authorized the customary 15 francs per day for the expenses of the bishop of Langres on this mission: AN K 54, no. 27[2].

69. *RJ IV*, no. 962; Lobineau 2, cols. 769–70; Morice 2, cols. 623–24.

70. Juvenal des Ursins, *Histoire* (Michaud ed.), 393.

71. Bouchart, *Grandes chroniques* 2:206, said that Louis of Orléans tried to premote a reconciliation between Clisson and Berry but that it failed.

72. Lefranc, *Olivier*, 382–83; La Borderie, *Histoire* 4:87.

73. Douet d'Arcq, *Choix de pièces* 1:117–19 (from AN X[1a] 8845, fol. 204v, 31 January); Moranvillé, *Jean le Mercier*, *P.J.* 112, pp. 373–74 (from AN X[1a] 12, fols. 204v–205r, 13 February); BN FR 2836, fol. 17r.

74. AN X[1a] 1477, fol. 409v (1 April).

75. Lefranc, *Olivier*, 374; Frois-J 2:353.

76. Morice 2, cols. 626–29; Lobineau 2, cols. 770–73. Royal representatives were ordered to assume control of the town on 20 February 1395 after the bishop transferred his authority to the king (AN J 244[a], no. 82; BN FR 16654, no. 36, fols. 234r–240v; BN FR 6537, pp. 85–96). In July 1395, the crown granted the inhabitants some fiscal privileges (BN NAF 7621, fols. 189r–194v).

77. On the campaigning of 1394, see Gicquel, *Olivier*, 139, and especially Lefranc, *Olivier*, 383–89, who is considerably clearer than La Borderie, *Histoire* 4:88. The accounts of the lordship of Lamballe from September 1393 to August 1394 (ADCA E 79, no. 1) contain gaps because the receipts from some farms were lacking due to the war.

78. Gicquel, *Olivier*, 140; Lefranc, *Olivier*, 388–89, citing chroniclers.

79. Lefranc, *Olivier*, 384–85.

80. Mollat, "Désastres," 173–74; Gaudu, "Tour," 68.

81. Lefranc, *Olivier*, 386–87; Gaudu, "Tour," 68.

82. According to Juvenal des Ursins, *Histoire* (Michaud ed.), 395–96, when the king and council heard the report of the embassy sent to John IV earlier in the year, they regretted not having sent somebody of royal blood.

83. AN J 243, no. 79; BN NAF 7621, fols. 151r–152v. Burgundy received a salary of 3,000 *l.t.* per month, plus expenses (CBourg 53, fol. 230v).

84. CBourg 100, p. 55. The king reimbursed him for their cost two years later: CBourg 53, fol. 227.

85. *RJ IV*, no. 972 (31 August 1394).

86. Ibid., no. 977, excerpt of document published by L. Delisle, "Pièce soustraite au trésor des chartes des ducs de Bretagne," *BÉC* 58 (1897): 379–80.

87. *RJ IV*, no. 982; Morice 2, cols. 629–32 (AN J 243, nos. 75–77); AN J 240, no. 2; BN FR 16654, no. 14 (fols. 84r–97v); BN NAF 7621, fols. 153r–156v.

88. *RJ IV*, nos. 982–983A; Lobineau 2, cols. 783–86.

89. La Borderie, *Histoire* 4:88; Petit, *Itinéraires*, 236–37.

90. ADLA E 167, no. 1.

91. AN J 244[A], no. 81.

92. *RJ IV*, no. 985.

93. *RJ IV*, no. 988 (ADLA E 167, no. 4).

94. Lobineau 2, cols. 773–75.

95. Ibid., col. 773.

96. AN J 243, no. 78; Lobineau 2, col. 786; ADCA E 1, eighth liasse.

97. ADCA E 1, eighth liasse; ADIV 1E 7, no. 5; Lobineau 2, cols. 777–81; *RJ IV*, no. 996 (a portion of the document in Morice 2, cols. 633–43).

98. Morice 2, cols. 643–44.

99. ADLA E 92, no. 21; E 167, nos. 5–10.

100. *RJ IV*, no. 1003.

101. ADLA E 167, nos. 14, 16; BN FR 22319, pp. 295, 298; ADCA E 1, eighth liasse.

102. *Cart. Morbihan*, no. 624.

103. See the accounts in Toudouze, *DCR*, 195–96; Lefranc, *Olivier*, 392–96, and La Borderie, *Histoire* 4:88; cf. Frois-J 2:589–92; Bouchart, *Grandes chroniques* 2:206–9.

104. *RJ IV*, no. 1026.

105. Morice 2, cols. 655–56, summarized in *RJ IV*, no. 1027, and indicated in ADLA E 236, fols. 71v–72r. Toudouze, *DCR*, 197, regarded the peace of Aucfer as a victory for Clisson that enhanced his reputation. As Kerhervé, *État breton*, 56, has pointed out, the settlement did effectively restore the status quo of 1392.

106. See ADLA E 167, nos. 19, 20; ADIV 1E 7, no. 6; BN FR 22319, pp. 293, 611.

107. ADLA E 167, no. 24.

108. Morice 2, col. 657; ADLA E 167, nos. 18, 21, 22; BN FR 22319, p. 295.

109. Above, at notes 63 and 67; Pichon, "Mémoire," 115–16 (where the account is marred by errors such as a reference to 31 April 1393). Again, cf. the sketch of Craon's career by Famiglietti, *Tales*, 315–18.

110. Pichon, "Mémoire," 116.

111. Ibid., 116–17.

112. AN X^{2a} 13, fols. 99v–100r.

113. Ibid., fols. 126r–128r.

114. AN JJ 144, no. 115, fols. 73r–v. Pichon, "Mémoire," 117–18, discusses this letter of remission but cites it as AN JJ 149, fol. 114, no. 115 (perhaps another copy). Roy, *Histoire*, 175, said that this letter was issued at the request of the English.

115. AN X^{2a} 12, fols. 297r–v, and Pichon, "Mémoire," 118–19.

116. Pichon, Mémoire," 119.

117. Famiglietti, *Royal Intrigue*, 4–5.

118. Pichon, "Mémoire," 120.

119. AN X^{2a} 13, fols. 103v–104r.

120. Brown and Famiglietti, *Lit de Justice*, 29. This action is published in full by Pichon, "Mémoire," 120–24.

121. Pichon, "Mémoire," 124.

122. AN X^{2a} 12, fols. 311r–v.

123. Ibid., fols. 311v, 312v; and 13, fols. 147r–v.

124. Ibid., fols. 318r, 320r–325v, entries for five different dates between 4 and

19 December. Bertrand de Broussillon, *Maison de Craon* 2, nos. 1307–1310, gave a somewhat inaccurate summary of these texts.

125. See the discussion of Pichon, "Mémoire," 125–27 which summarizes the material in AN X²ᵃ 12, fols. 318r, 320r–325v.

126. Ibid.

127. AN X²ᵃ 12, fol. 340r.

128. Pichon, "Mémoire," 128; Morice 2, cols. 690–91.

129. AN X²ᵃ 12, fols. 406v–406ᵇⁱˢr, is a short summary of the ruling. The full ruling is found in AN X²ᵃ 13, fols. 278r–284r and BN NAL 2574, no. 13. Palmer, *EFC*, 225, regards this ruling as an action pushed through by Louis of Orléans when the duke of Burgundy was away from court.

130. AN JJ 154, no. 603, fols. 338v–339r.

131. Ibid., no. 686, fols. 388r–389r.

132. On Craon's last years, see Cuttler, *Law of Treason*, 136, 188. He evidently had not paid Clisson the required reparations when the latter drew up his final will in February 1407 (see Chapter 12, note 79), and probably never paid.

Chapter 11

1. Lehoux, *Jean de France* 2:348–49.

2. See above, Chapter 10, at notes 44–46.

3. Chapter 10, notes 35, 60.

4. Lehoux, *Jean de France* 2:298.

5. Avout, *Querelle*, 27.

6. Guenée, *Meurtre*, 145–146.

7. Avout, *Querelle*, 28; Guenée, *Meurtre*, 148.

8. Autrand, *Charles VI*, 315, 323. What made matters worse was that when Charles VI failed to recognize the queen during his psychotic episodes, he still recognized Valentina and called her his beloved sister (*RSD* 2:86–89; Autrand, *Charles VI*, 322). This fueled the gossip about sorcery. Jarry, *Vie politique*, 101, rather indignantly quotes *Chronique normande de Pierre Cochon*, ed. C. de Beaurepaire (Rouen, 1870), 192, as saying that the king was healthy or sick when the duke of Orléans wished.

9. Autrand, *Charles VI*, 315.

10. Avout, *Querelle*, 57–58.

11. *ORD* 7:517–22. See also Brown and Famiglietti, *Lit de Justice*, 29.

12. *ORD* 7:530–38. These ordinances are discussed in Guenée, *Meurtre*, 160. Louis of Orléans then swore an oath of loyalty to the king, queen, and dauphin in late February (AN J 359, no. 19). See above, Chapter 5, for the circumstances of the three similar ordinances of Charles V in 1374.

13. Avout, *Querelle*, 59, and Nordberg, *Ducs*, 64 (writing from quite different points of view).

14. Nordberg, *Ducs*, 231–32.

15. Jarry, *Vie politique*, 280–81.

16. Nordberg, *Ducs*, 41–57.

17. For references to some of the early Orleanists, see Henneman, "Military Class," 960–62; also Moranvillé *Jean le Mercier*, 136. Among the influential royal commanders listed in Appendix I who received salaries or favors from Louis in 1388–89 were "Saquet" de Blaru (BN NAF 3638, no. 128); Jean de Bueil (BN NAF 3653, no. 406; Jarry, *Vie politique*, *P.J.* 13); Hervé le Coich (BN NAF 3638, no. 132; NAF 3653, nos. 408–409); Enguerrand de Coucy (BN PO 875, doss. 19,660 Coucy, no. 14); and Jean de Garencières (BN PO 1280, doss. 28,818 Garencières, nos. 51, 52). In the next four years, during the regime of the Marmousets, the following appeared on the prince's payroll: Alain de Beaumont (BN NAF 3653, no. 460), Robert de Béthune (Lannette-Claverie, *Collection Joursanvault*, pp. 26–27), Guillaume de Braquemont (BN NAF 3653, no. 411), Taupin de Chantemerle (Lannette-Claverie, *Collection Joursanvault*, p. 8), Guillaume de Fayel (BN FR 6211, nos. 54, 55), and Guillaume de Tignonville (BN PO 2828, doss. 62,831 Thignonville, nos. 2, 4).

18. See Chapter 10, at note 25.

19. Avout, *Querelle*, 56; Frois-KL 15:96. Again, see Guenée, *Meurtre*, 146 on Valentina's sense of rank.

20. See Chapter 9 and Palmer, "English Foreign Policy," 94.

21. Avout, *Querelle*, 28. An embassy dispatched to Giangaleazzo in January of 1393 actually included members who were close to the duke of Burgundy (Avout, *Querelle*, 38; Jarry, *Vie politique*, 107).

22. Jarry, *Vie politique*, 134–36. In January 1393, Charles VI sent an embassy to Clement VII to discuss the Italian kingdom for Louis. See Douet d'Arcq, *Choix de pièces* 1:112–17.

23. E. Jarry, *Les Origines de la domination française à Gênes (1392–1402)* (Paris, 1896), 393–97, documents nos. 2 and 3.

24. Nordberg, *Ducs*, 85–86, said that Louis was executing a royal project. Jarry, *Vie politique*, 134–36, 141–42, seems to have adhered to the other view, evidently based on his reading of a document that he published on p. 431, in which Louis was regarded as substituting for the king.

25. Jarry, *Vie politique*, 141.

26. Jarry, *Origines*, 397–400, document no. 4.

27. Jarry, *Vie politique*, 144.

28. AN KK 315, fol. 4v. The appointment was renewed and expanded in November: Jarry, *Vie politique*, 438–39 (*P.J.* 20).

29. Jarry, *Vie politique*, 145–54; BN NAF 3655, pp. 91–163. See Jarry, *Origines*, 403–20, document 7, for the treaty of Savona concluded in mid-November 1394.

30. Jarry, *Vie politique*, 436–37.

31. Palmer, *EFC*, 195–96.

32. Avout, *Querelle*, 39.

33. Ibid., 41.

34. Nordberg, *Ducs*, 95–97.

35. BN FR 26026, no. 1876.

36. AN J 359, no. 20.

37. AN P 2296, pp. 979–82; AN J 359, nos. 21, 22; BN NAF 7621, fols. 159r–164v.

38. Aside from the accounts of Coucy's expedition (AN KK 315), documents indicating expenses of Louis of Orléans in 1394–95, mainly for the Italian campaign, are found in BN FR 26027, nos. 2127, 2129, 2131, 2132, 2139; BN NAF 3638, nos. 199–201, 205, 208, 210; BN NAF 3655, pp. 91–163; Lannette-Claverie, *Collection Joursanvault*, pp. 12–14; and Jarry, *Origines*, 421–22, document no. 8.

39. Jarry, *Vie politique*, 155–58; Jarry, *Origines*, 532–33, document 24; Douet d'Arcq, *Choix de pièces* 1:134–36 (from AN K 55, no. 11).

40. CBourg 53, fols. 224v, 230v.

41. Palmer, *EFC*, 148–49. The process of arranging peace was complicated by events in England, where a revolt in Chestershire had to be put down in the summer of 1394 and a party hostile to Lancaster was becoming more vocal in the Parliament (Goodman, *John of Gaunt*, 153–54).

42. Palmer, *EFC*, 152 ff.

43. Ibid., 160–76. On 15 July, the royal council authorized payment to a distinguished embassy that was to meet Richard at Calais: BN NAF 7621, fols. 278r–283v. Richard did not acknowledge receipt of the first installment of Isabelle's dowry until November 1397 (Champollion-Figeac, *Lettres* 2:296–98).

44. See the various draft agreements in Jarry, *Origines*, 438–45 (documents 12–13), 502–6 (document 18), and 517–32 (document 23); and the comments of Avout, *Querelle*, 42–45. Louis finally received his compensation of three hundred thousand florins in December (Douet d'Arcq, *Choix de pièces* 1:134–36).

45. BN NAF 7621, fols. 311r–313v, 317r–324v. Nordberg, *Ducs*, 102, sees the agreements with Florence as exclusively the work of Queen Isabeau and says that Burgundy had nothing to do with it. It is impossible to suppose, however, that such a reversal of policy could have been executed without Philip's approval.

46. Bouchart, *Grandes chroniques* 2:212; Lehoux, *Jean de France* 2:335. The king and council, on 14 March 1396, granted Louis the proceeds of the aids collected in his lands for one year (BN PO 2153 doss. 48,873 Orléans, no. 206), by now a fairly standard form of largesse to the princes.

47. P. de Mézières, *Letter to King Richard II: A plea made in 1395 for peace between England and France*, ed. and trans. G. W. Coopland (Liverpool, 1975).

48. Palmer, *EFC*, 197–203.

49. Ibid., 204. *RSD* 2: 482–523 describes the campaign in the Balkans. It is treated much more briefly by Juvenal des Ursins, *Histoire* (Michaud ed.), 408–9.

50. *RSD* 2: 30–33 (cited Chapter 10, note 60).

51. BN NAF 3655, no. 89; BN FR 10431, p. 52, no. 316; Lannette-Claverie, *Collection Joursanvault*, pp. 40, 42. Louis had previously made a gift to Clisson's wife (p. 31).

52. BN FR 26029, nos. 2638–40, 2643–45, 2648–50, 2653–55.

53. BN NAF 3639, no. 276.

54. AN K 57, no. 92, published by Lefranc, *Olivier*, P.J. 20 and 21, pp. 452–53, yet another of those private alliances that had become so common in this period (see above, Chapter 4, note 22).

55. Bibliothèque de l'Arsenal 5424, p. 129; BN NAF 7621, fols. 405r–406r; Juvenal des Ursins, *Histoire* (Michaud ed.), 412.

56. Pocquet, *Deux féodaux*, 37.

57. Rey, *Finances*, 580, 603 ff.

58. Famiglietti, *Royal Intrigue*, 24; Nordberg, *Ducs*, 177.

59. Douet d'Arcq, *Choix de pièces* 1:140–142. See Guenée, *Meurtre*, 155, on the hatred of Wenceslas for the Wittelsbachs (which had led him to elevate Milan to a duchy for Giangaleazzo in 1395).

60. Jarry, *Vie politique*, 195–97. Some of the costs of the duke's entourage on a trip to the emperor are indicated in AN K 54, no. 57² (21 February 1398).

61. Lehoux, *Jean de France* 2:374–75 and notes; Nordberg, *Ducs*, 152–53. On 1 June 1398, Louis loaned Wenceslas ten thousand francs: AN K 54, no. 58⁴.

62. Petit, *Itinéraires*, 269–74.

63. Ibid., 274–86.

64. Lehoux, *Jean de France* 2:385–87; Guenée, *Meurtre*, 153. Louis did, however, state his opinion on the subject: Douet d'Arcq, *Choix de pièces* 1:143–44; Jarry, *Vie politique*, 439–43 (*P.J.* 21). On the subtraction of obedience, see also *ORD* 8:258–73; AN K 54, no. 49; Juvenal des Ursins, *Histoire* (Michaud ed.), 413; Kaminsky, *Simon*, 222–24.

65. Douet d'Arcq, *Choix de pièces* 1:157–60; Nordberg, *Ducs*, 111; Palmer, *EFC*, 225; Lehoux, *Jean de France* 2:416; *RSD* 2:700–703; Guenée, *Meurtre*, 112–13.

66. *RSD* 2:732 ff.

67. Petit, *Itinéraires*, 291–94.

68. For a more detailed examination of the Breton situation, see Chapter 12, at notes 31–34.

69. Guenée, *Meurtre*, 139. Orléans continued to develop his network of vassals in the Empire (Nordberg, *Ducs*, 157–76).

70. Lefranc, *Olivier*, *P.J.* 22, pp. 453–54; BN FR 11531, p. 109; BN FR 22319, p. 510. The loan, dated 19 March, 1398/9 is misdated as 1388 (old style) by Gicquel, *Olivier*, 176, note 2.

71. Petit, *Itinéraires*, 286–91.

72. *ORD* 8:331. In December 1400, the king granted the same status to the lordship of Coucy, which Louis had acquired (*ORD* 8:405).

73. *ORD* 8:383–84, 448–49; BN FR 6537, p. 111.

74. See above, note 46.

75. Rey, *Domaine*, 327.

76. *Soc. Charles*, 481–93, and above, Chapter 5, note 10.

77. *ORD* 8:345–48.

78. Nordberg, *Ducs*, 57.

79. *ORD* 8:468–69. See Jarry, *Vie politique*, 265.

80. Nordberg, *Ducs*, 65–66. Tignonville's appointment was 6 June 1401: Douet d'Arcq, *Choix de pièces* 1:203.

81. Petit, *Itinéraires*, 314–19.

82. Douet d'Arcq, *Choix de pièces* 1:203–4.

83. Nordberg, *Ducs*, 65. Douet d'Arcq, *Choix de pièces* 1:212–13.

84. Jarry, *Vie politique*, 262.

85. AN J 359, nos. 23, 23²; Douet d'Arcq, *Choix de pièces* 1:220–26. See also comments by Avout, *Querelle*, 68; Famiglietti, *Royal Intrigue*, 25; Lehoux, *Jean de France* 2:463; Nordberg, *Ducs*, 66–67; and Jarry, *Vie politique*, 262–63.

86. Lehoux *Jean de France* 2:465; Nordberg, *Ducs*, 68. Fearing future crises when he might be incapacitated, Charles VI began to assign an important role to the queen in resolving disputes, such as over the safeguard of the pope (Douet d'Arcq, *Choix de pièces* 1:227–38, 16 March 1402) and over the administration of finances (ibid., 1: 240–43, 1 July 1402).

87. Lehoux *Jean de France* 2:466–67.

88. BN FR 2836, fol. 48; *ORD* 8:494–96; Jarry, *Vie politique*, 265; Nordberg, *Ducs*, 68–69.

89. Jarry, *Vie politique*, 266; Avout, *Querelle*, 69–70; Lehoux, *Jean de France* 2:475.

90. *ORD* 8:518–19; BN PO 2154 doss. 48,873 Orléans, no. 293 and PO 2155 doss. 48,873 Orléans, nos. 294–95 (confirmations of January and February 1403). See also Nordberg, *Ducs*, 69–70; Jarry, *Vie politique*, 267; Lehoux, *Jean de France* 2:476; and Famiglietti, *Royal Intrigue*, 26–27.

91. BN FR 25707, no. 507.

92. Bibliothèque de l'Arsenal 5424, pp. 160–61; 163–65. Famiglietti, *Royal Intrigue*, 27–28, indicates that this appointment blocked that of a Wittelsbach candidate favored by the queen and the uncles, but all three uncles were present at the council that named Albret.

93. See Lehoux, *Jean de France* 2:470–74, 501.

94. Lehoux, *Jean de France* 2:483–84; Jarry, *Vie politique*, 274; Avout, *Querelle*, 52. Ensuing exchanges between Louis and Henry are in AN X¹ᵃ 8602, fols. 170v, 172, 174v, according to the inventory.

95. Jarry, *Vie politique*, 274; Avout, *Querelle*, 52; Lehoux, *Jean de France* 2:484.

96. Juvenal des Ursins, *Histoire* (Michaud ed.), 422–23. See the detailed discussion in the next chapter at notes 42–59; cf. Avout, *Querelle*, 70–71.

97. Pocquet, "Philippe en Bretagne," 49.

98. Lehoux, *Jean de France* 2:508–9.

99. *ORD* 8:593–96. See also Kaminsky, *Simon*, 256.

100. Lehoux, *Jean de France* 2:509–12; Famiglietti, *Royal Intrigue*, 35 and note 84.

101. Jarry, *Vie politique*, 301 and 445–50 (*P.J.* 23–25, three documents from AN J 516).

102. *ORD* 8:577–79, 581–83; BN FR 3910, fols. 176r–177v; Guenée, *Meurtre*, 163–64.

103. Nordberg, *Ducs*, 70–72; Lehoux, *Jean de France* 2:497–98 (attributing to Isabeau the main influence in these changes).

104. Famiglietti, *Royal Intrigue*, 29–31.

105. Nordberg, *Ducs*, 72–73; Avout, *Querelle*, 72; Famiglietti, *Royal Intrigue*, 31. After the death of Philip the Bold, however, Louis did obtain, as a bride for his son, the king's daughter Isabelle, lately queen of England (AN J 359, nos. 25–27).

106. Famiglietti, *Royal Intrigue*, 31–34; cf. Nordberg, *Ducs*, 73–75, and Guenée, *Meurtre*, 165.

107. See the analysis of Jarry, *Vie politique*, 295–300. Vouchers or receipts indicating payments from Orléans to commanders listed in Appendix 1 are found in BN NAF 3655, pp. 255, 256; BN PO 246 doss. 5418 Beaumont, nos. 19–21;

PO 1117 doss. 25,640 Fayel, nos. 30, 31; PO 1561 doss. 35,775 Ivry, nos. 25, 29; PO 1896 doss. 43,692 Mauny, nos. 27, 32–34; PO 2095 doss. 47,746 Neele, nos. 29, 31, 33.

108. Nordberg, *Ducs*, 75, 130.

109. Petit, *Itinéraires*, 341–50.

110. Avout, *Querelle*, 74–77; R. Vaughan, *John the Fearless: The Growth of Burgundian Power* (London, 1966), 30; Jarry, *Vie politique*, 307; Coville, *Premiers Valois*, 322 ff.; Guenée, *Meurtre*, 166. Orléans was allowed to hold Coucy and Soissons as peerages (AN K 55, no. 26), and the king granted him additional lordships (AN J 359, nos. 24, 24²).

111. Guenée, *Meurtre*, 145, 169.

112. BN FR 4768, fols. 5–10.

113. Jarry, *Vie politique*, 324 ff.; Avout, *Querelle*, 78; Nordberg, *Ducs*, 185–95; Famiglietti, *Royal Intrigue*, 46–47. Orléans, on 2 September, publicly denounced Burgundy's forcible return of the Dauphin to Paris (Douet d'Arcq, *Choix de pièces* 1:269–71, 273–83; and BN FR 10237, fols. 48r–52v) and Burgundy soon responded with another manifesto on the health of the king and the state of the realm (BN FR 10237, fols. 53v–57v). The mobilization of followers by Louis of Orleans is in AN KK 267, fol. 109.

114. Nordberg, *Ducs*, 195–204; Avout, *Querelle*, 81; Vaughan, *John the Fearless*, 36; Famiglietti, *Royal Intrigue*, 48–51. The restoration of peace, moreover, did not prevent the dukes of Orléans and Berry from joining in an alliance with the queen on 1 December 1405 (Douet d'Arcq, *Choix de pièces* 1:283–85). Unthinkable just a few years earlier, this alliance illustrates how things had changed since the death of Philip the Bold.

115. Vaughan, *John the Fearless*, 31–43; Jarry, *Vie politique*, 308–13; Rey, *Finances*, 603.

116. Nordberg, *Ducs*, 204–5; Guenée, *Meurtre*, 167.

117. F. Autrand, "De l'Enfer au Purgatoire: La Cour à travers quelques textes français du milieu du XIVᵉ à la fin du XVᵉ siècle," in *L'État et les aristocraties, XIIᵉ–XVIIᵉ siècle, France, Angleterre, Écosse* (ed. P. Contamine, Paris, 1989), esp. 57; Forhan, "Reflecting Heroes," 189–96; N. Grévy-Pons, "Propagande et sentiment national pendant le règne de Charles VI: L'Example de Jean de Montreuil," *Francia* 8 (1980): 127–45; and J. Krynen, *Idéal du prince et pouvoir royal en France à la fin du moyen âge (1380–1440)* (Paris, 1981), esp. 69–71, 142–54.

118. Guenée, *Meurtre*, 168.

119. Nordberg, *Ducs*, 219–21. See also Famiglietti, *Royal Intrigue*, 61; Guenée, *Meurtre*, 177–78.

120. Juvenal des Ursins, *Histoire* (Michaud ed.), 444–45. Famiglietti, *Royal Intrigue*, 61–63, shows that John had actually planned the murder for some months' earlier.

Chapter 12

1. Jones, *DB*, 132. See also Champollion-Figeac, *Lettres* 2:284–86.

2. ADLA E 8, nos. 5, 10; Morice 2, col. 657.

3. Jones, *DB*, 132–34.

4. *RJ IV*, nos. 1097, 1099, 1100; Morice 2, cols. 678–79; Lobineau 2, cols. 793–94; ADLA E 120, no. 1; Champollion-Figeac, *Lettres* 2:279–80, 282–83.

5. *RJ IV*, nos. 1102–3. See also the comments of Jones, *Creation*, 252.

6. Palmer, *EFC*, 176; *RJ IV* no. 1060; Morice 2, cols. 667–68; ADLA E 8, no. 9; BN NAF 7268, fols. 23r–26v; Lobineau 2, cols. 794–96. For a subsequent document covering some of the financial arrangements, see *RJ IV*, no. 1062, Morice 2, cols. 674–75.

7. Jones, *DB*, 134; Palmer, *EFC*, 173.

8. Jones, *DB*, 134; Palmer, *EFC*, 173. *RSD* 2:442–43 and 550–51 considered each of these events a marriage and gave somewhat confused dating. When the duke went to Paris, he is said to have left Olivier de Clisson as his lieutenant in Brittany: Lefranc, *Olivier*, 399; Gicquel, *Olivier*, 144; Pocquet, "Philippe en Bretagne," 16.

9. *RJ IV*, no. 1118. Some of the payments are indicated in ADLA E 108. Finally, in 1409, Charles VI assigned John's successor lands to compensate for those in Nevers and Rethel (ADIV 1 E 5, no. 13).

10. ADLA E 177, no. 1; BN NAF 7621, fols. 439r–440v.

11. Documents relating to this case are published by Blanchard, "Cartulaire," in *AHP* 28, and in Lobineau 2, cols. 797–99. Among the manuscript sources are ADIV 1 E 6, no. 4, and 1 E 15, no. 5; BN FR 22319, pp. 321–322. Hoping to acquire the lordship of Rais, John IV had pressured the childless Jeanne into making some exchanges of property with him and then had seized Rais in 1383. Jeanne's subsequent litigation remained for years an irritant in ducal relations with the crown, and the decision of 1399 finally thwarted the duke's designs. See Jones, *DB*, 135–36; Champollion-Figeac, *Lettres* 2:284–87.

12. John IV's will of 1385 is in Lobineau 2, cols. 802–3 and a codicil of 26 October 1399 is in *RJ IV*, no. 1179.

13. *RJ IV*, no. 1086.

14. Lobineau 2, cols. 796–97.

15. Lefranc, *Olivier*, 398. His will is in Morice 2, cols. 658–60. Clisson and Robert de Beaumanoir were his executors.

16. Contamine, *Guerre*, 587, for service of Alain VIII de Rohan in 1392.

17. *RJ IV* nos. 1058, 1059, 1061; Morice 2, cols. 666–67; BMN 1691/1535, no. 10; BN FR 18698, fol. 429r; BN NAF 7269, fol. 80v. On the *rachat*, see Kerhervé, *État breton*, 480–82. It entitled the duke to collect the revenues of a fief for one year, but it was often convenient to all parties to substitute a lump sum payment that might be a lesser sum but was not necessarily less. In any case, comparative payments for *rachat* can indicate the comparative worth of of different fiefs. A list of ducal *rachats* in this period (BN FR 11531, pp. 320–54) indicates an average payment of about 30 *l.t.*, or 1 percent of what the duke collected for the vast Rohan holdings. Gicquel, *Olivier*, 142–43, reached the dubious conclusion that the transaction of May 1396 was a favor to Clisson, reflecting the duke's new friendship for him.

18. BMN 1692/1536, no. 4. The complaints against ducal officers had been an ongoing issue since John IV received his first tax in 1365. See Kerhervé, *État breton*, 82.

19. BMN 1689/1533, no. 12 (document of July).

20. BMN 1689/1533, no. 13.

21. BMN 1689/1533, no. 12 (document of September).

22. On the Estates, see Lobineau 2, cols. 799–801.

23. BN FR 16654, no. 28, fols. 175r–179v (testimony of John of Blois on 10 April), 180r–181v (testimony of Clisson on the eleventh), and 182r–183v (testimony of Rohan).

24. Ibid. Jones has conveniently summarized the major points in *RJ IV*, no. 1175, and a roll containing much of the same material is in AN J 244A, no. 90.

25. BN FR 22325, p. 870.

26. *Catalogue général des manuscrits . . .* 22: 230, describing BMN 1695/1539.

27. BN PO 789 doss. 17,879 Clisson, no. 47; Lobineau 2, cols. 803–4.

28. Morice 2, cols. 701–3; ADLA E 168, no. 1.

29. ADLA E 90, nos. 7, 8, 9, the last of these dated 5 July 1401.

30. Bouchart, *Grandes chroniques* 2:238–39. Among those who have repeated this story are Mazas, *Vies*, 4:473; Lefranc, *Olivier*, 407–8; La Borderie, *Histoire* 4: 144–45; Toudouze, *DCR*, 200; and Gicquel, *Olivier*, 30.

31. *Chron. Briocense* (Lobineau 2, cols. 870–71).

32. Ibid.; Bouchart, *Grandes chroniques* 2:239–40; Frois-J 2:707. Pocquet, *Philippe régent*, 4–5, and Lehoux, *Jean de France* 2:424, generally follow these chroniclers. After the peace of Aucfer in 1395, the crown had again entrusted Clisson with the custody of Pontorson (BN PO 789 doss. 17,879 Clisson, no. 21).

33. Jarry, *Vie politique*, 232–33. Cf. La Borderie, *Histoire* 4:142.

34. Lehoux, *Jean de France* 2:424, note 3, cites sources showing that Burgundy was in immediate communication with the duchess of Brittany and also exchanging messages with Berry over the desire of avoiding a return of Clisson to power.

35. Clisson's receipts are in ADLA E 168, nos. 2 and 3, and BN FR 22319, p. 501 (fall of 1400). John IV had previously accepted the obligation to pay this money (*RJ IV*, no. 1087, 1 May 1397).

36. Bouchart, *Grandes chroniques* 2:223–24. Henry's letter of appreciation for the duke's gifts is in Champollion-Figeac, *Lettres* 2:302.

37. Pocquet, "Philippe en Bretagne," 19. On the overthrow of Richard II and the dangerous consequences for Anglo-French relations, see Palmer, *EFC*, 225.

38. Toudouze, *DCR*, 200; Lefranc, *Olivier*, 409; and Gicquel, *Olivier*, 25–27, all evidently drawing on the detailed account of the ceremonies in the cathedral of Rennes by *Chron. Briocense* (Lobineau 2, cols. 872–73). Subsequent events do not bear out the contention of Gicquel (*Olivier*, 28) that his role in these ceremonies effectively gave Clisson the regency of Brittany.

39. Pocquet, "Philippe en Bretagne," 19–20.

40. Petit, *Itinéraires*, 297.

41. Pocquet, "Philippe en Bretagne," 20–21; Lehoux, *Jean de France* 2:485, note 2. Both of these authors drew upon material in Archives Départementales, Côte-d'Or, B 1532.

42. Pocquet, "Philippe en Bretagne," 19–20.

43. Famiglietti, *Royal Intrigue*, 25–26. See above, Chapter 11, at notes 87–89.

44. Pocquet, *Philippe régent*, 6.

45. Famiglietti, *Royal Intrigue*, 26–27.

46. Pocquet, "Philippe en Bretagne," 19–20.

47. BN FR 22319, p. 527; ADLA E 104, no. 25; A. de La Borderie, "Lettre de Charles VI, roi de France, aux barons de Bretagne sur la régence du duché (23 Aout 1402)," *RBV* (1889): 473–74.

48. Pocquet, "Philippe en Bretagne," 22.

49. Petit, *Itinéraires*, 330; Pocquet, *Philippe régent*, 8; La Borderie, *Histoire* 4:144. Bouchart's story was that the proxy marriage of the duchess had taken the Breton baronage by surprise and they had asked Burgundy to come (*Grandes chroniques* 2:243). Perhaps the chronicler confused the baronage with the ducal officers who had been in contact with Burgundy.

50. Pocquet, "Philippe en Bretagne," 29–38.

51. Pocquet, *Deux féodaux*, 34. Philip's generosity and hospitality had won over some, but not all, of Clisson's traditional adherents. According to Lefranc, *Olivier*, 409–10, Philip's custody of the young princes won support from most of the bishops, plus the lords of Laval, Châteaubriant, Montfort, Montauban, and La Hunaudaye. The opposition, besides Clisson, Rohan, and Penthièvre, included the lords of Beaumanoir, Derval, Rostrenen, Pont-L'Abbé, and Coëtmen.

52. ADLA E 5, no. 1.

53. Morice 2, col. 722. Manuscript copies are in BMN 1689/1533, no. 14, and 1696/1540, no. 13; BN FR 22340, fols. 31r–v.

54. BN FR 11531, pp. 171–88, indicates captains given the *garde* of various Breton strongholds at this time. Specifically, the one-time royal military commander Alain de la Houssaye was entrusted with Clisson castle and promised to be loyal to the duchess and to Philip of Burgundy: BN FR 22319, p. 398; BN FR 11531, pp. 50, 172.

55. ADLA E 5, no. 2.

56. Morice 2, col. 723; *Lettres et mandements de Jean V, duc de Bretagne*, ed. R. Blanchard (Nantes, 1889–95), vol. 1, no. 1. The manuscript is in ADLA E 177, no. 7. See Lehoux, *Jean de France* 2:485, note 3, and the comments of Pocquet, "Philippe en Bretagne," 40, and *Deux féodaux*, 35.

57. ADLA E 126, no. 14; BN FR 22319, p. 373. See Jones, *Creation*, 339 for useful comments on Burgundy's remodelling of the Breton ducal court to project an impressive image of rulership.

58. Lehoux, *Jean de France* 2:486. The removal of the princes is rightly seen as a victory for French policy since it guaranteed that the future rulers of the duchy would be brought up at the French court rather than at the English court as John IV had been (Lefranc, *Olivier*, 411). Gicquel, *Olivier*, 241, noted that on this occasion Breton interests (those of the barons?) coincided with those of the French in desiring that the princes not be brought up in England. On the other hand, E. Cosneau, *Le Connétable de Richemont (Artur de Bretagne)(1393–1458)* (Paris, 1886), 5, apparently misreading the situation, noted the opposition by Clisson's faction and thought that Philip had to *enlever* the young princes.

59. Pocquet, "Philippe en Bretagne," 19.

60. Pocquet, *Deux féodaux*, 34.

61. Lobineau 2, cols. 811–12.

62. Pocquet, *Deux féodaux*, 39. One of John's first signs of an independent policy came on 24 May 1404 when he empowered an emissary to go to his mother in England and try to arrange the return of his two youngest sisters: *Lettres Jean V*, vol. 1, no. 10.

63. ADLA E 5, no. 4. The duke of Burgundy exacted a price, however, in the form of a *rachat* of fourteen thousand *écus* payable in three installments. The second third had been paid by 29 November 1407 (ADLA E 177 no, 9; BN FR 22319, pp. 526–27).

64. Bouchart, *Grandes chroniques* 2:244; Pocquet, *Deux féodaux*, 39. The account in BN Collection Périgord 58, fol. 326, is rather inaccurate on dates and other facts.

65. *Lettres Jean V*, vol. 1, no. 7. Almost immediately after John's death in January, the duke's men had begun to occupy most of the strongholds in the county of Penthièvre (ADLA E 151, no. 18; ADCA E 11, first liasse) as part of the procedure for exercising the right of *rachat*. *Lettres Jean V*, vol. 1, no. 9, indicates that the county was in John V's hands for this purpose, as do the accounts of Lamballe for 1404–5 (ADCA E 11, second liasse, and E 79, no. 2).

66. For Clisson's role in the defense of Brittany in 1403 and 1404, see Juvenal des Ursins, *Histoire* (Michaud ed.), 426–30; Lobineau 1: 505–6; Toudouze, *DCR*, 200–201; Mazas, *Vies* 4:475–77; and Lefranc, *Olivier*, 412.

67. Juvenal des Ursins, *Histoire* (Michaud ed.), 442; Pocquet, *Deux féodaux*, 39.

68. *Lettres Jean V*, vol. 1, no. 342. In May of 1408, John V would renew this alliance with the duchess Valentina and the young duke Charles of Orléans (ibid., no. 1031; also Douet d'Arcq, *Choix de pièces* 1:309–10; Famiglietti, *Tales*, plate 32).

69. *Lettres Jean V*, vol. 1, no. 323; BN FR 11531, pp. 46–47. In 1408, after the death of Louis of Orléans, Brittany and the count of Armagnac formed an alliance (*Lettres Jean V*, vol. 2, no. 1041, and ADLA E 181, no. 12).

70. *Lettres Jean V*, vol. 2, no. 564 (19 April 1407); BMN 1690/1534, no. 8; BN FR 22340, fols. 48r–v. Subsequent texts dealing with this marriage contract are in BMN 1690/1534, no. 9, and Morice 2, cols. 784–785. See below at notes 93–98.

71. Pocquet, *Deux féodaux*, 41.

72. La Borderie and Pocquet, *Histoire* 4:153, take this position. Clisson's daughters would in fact soon be in litigation over their father's estate, and they had already been in court in the years 1403–6 to reach accords on small inheritances from other sources: BN FR 22340, fols. 40r–41v; BN FR 22319, p. 627; BN FR 18698, fol. 430v; Morice 2, cols. 767–769 (from ADLA E 217, no. 5).

73. BN FR 22340, fols. 43r–44v.

74. Doat 244, fols. 167–72. Two copies of the original transaction of 1403 are found in ADPA E 636.

75. ADCA E 619, second liasse. See Jouve, *Montcontour*, 92–93, and below, at notes 109–21.

76. BN FR 22340, fols. 46r–47r; Morice 2, cols. 778–79; BMN 1708/1552, no. 4; Doat 244, fols. 173r–176v.

77. Morice 2, cols. 779–82 (from ADLA E 217, no. 16); Lobineau 2, cols.

823–26; BMN 1703/1547, no. 10. These appear to be incomplete versions. The most complete version is in BN NAL 2574, no. 15 (Cf. Bruel, "Inventaire," pp. 194–95).

78. BN NAL 2574, no. 15.

79. Lobineau 2, col. 827. Four months after Clisson's will, Craon had still not paid the indemnity owed to the duchess of Anjou, which we may suppose took precedence over his debt to Clisson. The Parlement had to rescind the donation of La Ferté-Bernard to Louis of Orléans to generate income to pay this debt (Bertrand de Broussillon, *Maison de Craon* 2:266, no. 1353, from AN X 1a 54, fol. 200).

80. Bouchart, *Grandes chroniques* 2:246; E. de la Gournerie, "Les villes de Bretagne—Clisson," *RBV* 1865 pt. 1:259; ADLA E 82, no. 19; BMN 1699/1543, second and third pieces (an agreement between Clisson's heirs in 1419).

81. Lefranc, *Olivier*, 417.

82. Bouchart, *Grandes chroniques* 2:246; Juvenal des Ursins, *Histoire* (Michaud ed.), 444.

83. Bruel, "Inventaire," pp. 195–96.

84. AN X 1a 55, fol. 214r.

85. BMN 1703/1547, no. 11, published by Lefranc, *Olivier*, *P.J.* 23, pp. 454–455.

86. Bruel, "Inventaire," pp. 202–4.

87. Ibid., pp. 206–10. For fifty-four items between nos. 39 and 105, I calculate a total of 1424 marks of silver. If the mark was then worth 6.5 *l.t.*, we get a total of 9259, but this is a conservative estimate because it neglects the fact that many of these utensils were in fact gilded and thus had greater value than that of the silver as bullion.

88. Ibid., p. 213.

89. Ibid., pp. 236–37. Besides a total of 45,681 francs, there were amounts of various other gold coins that differed in value from the franc. If we assume, conservatively, that on the average, every four of these was worth three francs, we elevate to 56,400 francs the wealth found at Josselin alone. As indicated in the next paragraph, another large sum was at Blain.

90. BN FR 22340, fols. 53r–54r; Lobineau 1:511 ff. and 2, cols. 822–23; Morice 2, cols. 797–99. See C. Bellier-Dumaine, "L'administration de la duché de Bretagne sous le règne de Jean V (1399–1442)," *Annales de Bretagne* 16:479.

91. Lefranc, *Olivier*, 418–19.

92. La Borderie, *Histoire* 4:153–55.

93. ADLA E 163, no. 3; E 166, no. 1, fols. 10r–12v; BMN 1708/1552, no. 5.

94. *Lettres Jean V*, vol. 2, no. 571; BMN 1694/1538, no. 4 ("l'en espoire plus en luy la mort que la vie"); Lobineau 2, col. 827. Alain and Béatrix also promised to return to the duke the land of Guillac which Charles V had taken from him and given to Clisson in 1373 (BN FR 22340, fols. 50r–51v).

95. Morice 2, cols. 786–87; *Lettres Jean V*, vol. 2, no. 574; ADLA E 168, no. 7 and E 166, no. 1, fols. 13r–v; BN FR 22340, fol. 49.

96. ADLA E 166, no. 1, fol. 14r; BN FR 22325, p. 795.

97. ADLA E 168, no. 8.

98. BMN 1691/1535, no. 14; BN FR 22319, p. 471.

99. A recent popular work (Doucet, *Vallée*, 86–87) gives the most insightful portrait of Marguerite that I have found.

100. ADPA E 636, first document.

101. There are fifteen such documents in BMN 1703/1547, no. 13; three more in BMN 1703/1547, no. 12; as well as BMN 1708/1552, nos. 6–9, 11–13; BMN 1693/1537, nos. 9, 13; Doat 244, fols. 215–16; and those cited below in subsequent notes.

102. Harpedenne held the lordship of Belleville and added some of the adjacent Poitevin lands: BN FR 22340, fols. 71r–72v; Morice 2, cols. 818–19. Several documents of 1413–15 (BMN 1708/1552, no. 10; BN FR 22325, p. 814) deal with the settlement made with Isabeau, the sister and heiress of Amaury II de Clisson.

103. BN FR 22340, fols. 50r–51v.

104. BMN 1699/1543, first two pieces.

105. Above, at note 90.

106. AN X^{1a} 55, fols. 213r–216v, cited above, note 84. Note that this case is recorded in the registers of civil judgments rather than the register dealing with accords and settlements (AN X^{1c}).

107. Doat 244, fols. 178–79. This long notarial instrument (fols. 176r–189v) is a copy of the original in ADPA E 636, second document.

108. Doat 244, fols. 179v–182v.

109. Ibid., fols. 183–86.

110. ADCA E 619, third and fourth liasses; ADLA E 217, nos. 17, 18.

111. Morice 2, cols. 794–97; ADLA E 236, fols. 36r–40v; BN FR 22319, p. 291; BN NAF 7269, fol. 7

112. ADLA E 163, no. 2; Cosneau, *Richemont*, 11–12.

113. La Borderie, *Histoire* 4:155; Morice 2, col. 841. Allegations of "excesses" by Marguerite's officials in 1408 are found in BN FR 22319, p. 422, and ADLA E 168, no. 10.

114. ADLA E 168, nos. 11–28; E 104, no. 27.

115. Morice 2, cols. 815–16.

116. La Borderie, *Histoire* 4:156–58.

117. ADLA E 177, no. 3.

118. Ibid., no. 10.

119. ADLA E 168, no. 29; ADCA E 1317, first and second liasses; BN NAF 7269, fol. 6r; Cosneau, *Richemont*, 13.

120. ADLA E 168, no. 30.

121. Ibid., no. 31; BN FR 22319, p. 291.

122. ADLA E 168, nos. 32, 33.

123. Ibid., no. 34.

124. Ibid., nos. 35, 37, 38; BN FR 22319, p. 582.

125. Jones, *Creation*, 52, 342–43; Kerhervé, *État breton*, 57–58; Doucet, *Vallée*, 88–89; La Gournerie, "Clisson," 253. Among the relevant documents on the Penthièvre coup of 1420 are BN FR 22319, pp. 286, 287; ADCA E 1, eleventh liasse, and E 1567, 1st liasse; BN NAF 7269, fol. 2 (no. 4); Champollion-Figeac, *Lettres* 2:375–78.

Appendix 1

1. Contamine, *Guerre*, 562–93.
2. Henneman, "Military Class," 953, note 28.
3. The principal records are those in BN NAF 7414, 8604; BN FR 7858, 21539, 32510; and the account in BN FR 20684 that was published by Moranvillé, *Jean le Mercier*, 205–79. Besides these, the documentation for this appendix is found in thousands of individual receipts, pay vouchers, and musters preserved in many hundred volumes of the Pièces Originales and in the first 211 volumes of the Clairambault series.

Appendix 2

1. Kerhervé, *État breton*, 720.
2. Anselme, *Histoire* 6:201–4; La Chesnaye-des Bois, *Dictionnaire* 6, cols. 946–47; Levot, *Biographie bretonne* 1:354–76.
3. Consisting of bundles of small cards and slips in ADLA 7JJ, these notes are taken from many published and archival sources. Those concerning the name Clisson (7JJ 70) are arranged roughly in chronological order and make up a very considerable bundle. Items on the Clisson genealogy found in BN Collection Duchesne 55, fol. 38, are much less complete than those collected by Blanchard. I am much indebted to Professor Michael Jones, who examined an early draft of this appendix and helped me by correcting errors and clarifying certain textual problems.
4. Levot, *Biographie bretonne* 1:354, probably drawing on the document published in Morice 1, cols. 384–85.
5. ADLA 7JJ 70. For those that have been published, see Lobineau 2, cols. 116, 180, 185, 259; Morice 1, cols. 441, 451, 512–13.
6. One such document has been published in Lobineau 2, col. 282 and Morice 1, col. 566. Others are mentioned in ADLA 7JJ 70.
7. BN FR 22348, fol. 60r; BN FR 22319, p.270; BN LAT 17092, p. 62; Morice 1, col. 612.
8. BN FR 22319, p. 261; BN LAT 17092, p. 76; Morice 1, col. 637.
9. BN FR 22348, fol. 60r.
10. ADLA 7JJ 70 (note on a document of 1212).
11. Besides two that are undated, Blanchard (ADLA 7JJ 70) lists documents of 1185, 1186, 1189, 1200 (2), 1205 (2), 1206, 1207, 1209, 1211, 1212 (2), 1214, 1215, 1216, and 1217. Others are BN LAT 17092, pp. 84, 216; Morice 1, col. 712. Guillaume also received a charter from King John of England in 1214: Bertrand de Broussillon, *Maison de Craon* 1, no. 213.
12. BN FR 22348, fol. 60r; BN FR 22319, p. 256; BN LAT 17092, p. 65; Morice 1, col. 707. For another of Geoffrey's documents witnessed by Guillaume, see A. de la Borderie, "Recueil des actes inédites des ducs et princes de Bretagne," in *Bulletin et mémoires de la Société archéologique du département de l'Ille-et-Vilaine* (1885–93) 1:117–18 (no. 59, published from ADLA H 23).

13. Morice 1, col. 801; BN LAT 17092, p. 215; BN FR 22348, fol. 60r; also La Borderie, "Recueil" 1:137–38 (no. 72).

14. ADLA H 32, bundle D-16, part 1; BN FR 22348, fol. 60r; BN LAT 17092, p. 77.

15. ADLA H 32, bundle D-16, part 1. Buteau, "Naissance," 9, places the marriage of Gaudin de Clisson and Eustachie in 1160. This name was common in the seigneurial family of Rais, another Eustachie being the mid-thirteenth century heiress whose marriage to Gerard Chabot brought the barony to this new lineage (Blanchard, "Cartulaire," *AHP* 28:lxxx–lxxxi). Three previous lords of Rais had the name Garsire (ibid., lvii, lxxi, lxxvi), which did not appear in the Clisson family until Guillaume I had a son by that name.

16. ADLA H 32, bundle D-16, part 1, includes a document confirming seven previous ones involving members of the Clisson family. Gaudin, son of Guillaume, was mentioned in 1216.

17. ADLA H 74, no. 7. Earlier, in Garsire's lifetime, Flavie and Guillaume had made a donation that mentioned two of their daughters (BN LAT 5480, pp. 430–31).

18. Levot, *Biographie bretonne* 1:355; *Recueil des Historiens des Gaules et de la France* (Paris, 1840–1904) 23: 684, 719.

19. Prevel, "Château de Blain," 39, is one example.

20. The grant itself (BN FR 22319, pp. 230–31) did not mention the Clisson connection, but ADLA H 1, no. 14, is a confirmation by Olivier II, who identifies Constance as his grandmother.

21. Prevel, "Château de Blain," 40.

22. Doucet, *Vallée*, 52–53 and genealogical table, perhaps using the dubious work of La Fontenelle de Vaudoré, indicates that Guillaume II outlived his father by several years and may have died as late as 1223.

23. Blanchard, "Cartulaire," *AHP* 28:lxvi, note 6; and Buteau, "Naissance," 10, note that Guillaume also held the lordship of La Banaste (Benâte). The source of this acquisition (probably an inheritance) is not certain, but it augmented his wealth and prestige.

24. ADLA 7JJ 70; H 32, bundle D-16, part 1.

25. Morice 1, col. 553; Buteau, "Naissance," 15.

26. BN FR 11531, p. 130; Morice 1, col. 958; La Borderie, *Histoire* 3:344; Prevel, "Château de Blain," 39; Buffé, *Blain*, 53–54; Gaden-Puchet, "Château de Blain," 3–5; Buteau, "Naissance," 17–24. At first glance it appears that Olivier received Hervé's property in preference over Hervé's own children, an arrangement that would have been most irregular. The houses of Blain and Pontchâteau, however, were closely connected, and it is possible that the lordship of Blain had belonged to Constance and that Hervé, despite his surname, did not become sire de Blain until his marriage to her.

27. See above, Chapter 2, and Lobineau 2, cols. 403, 404, 405; Morice 1, cols. 976, 980–81, 987; ADLA E 165, no. 1; Prevel, "Château de Blain," 44–45, 132–33. The agreement by which Olivier I retired was dated 1 March 1262.

28. ADLA E 142, no. 1.

29. ADLA 7JJ 70; H 1, no. 14; E 151, no. 4; E 236, fol. 77; BN FR 22319,

pp. 146–47, 254; BN LAT 17092, p. 61; Morice 1, cols. 997, 1037, 1044; Lobineau 2, col. 424.

30. ADLA E 151, no. 4; BN FR 22319, pp. 146–47. See the discussion of *rachat* in Chapter 12, note 17 (citing Kerhervé, *État breton*, 480–82). The origin of the institution in 1276 arose from John I's attempt to exercise the right of *bail*, a form of wardship that gave the duke complete control over the property of a minor heir. The Breton baronage opposed the practice, saying John's father had instituted it against custom. The agreement of 11 January 1276 provided that the duke could claim a succession tax or *rachat* of a year's revenue when lands passed to an heir (whether minor or not), but could not intervene further in the administration of the property. See La Borderie, *Histoire* 3:347 ff.

31. ADLA E 236, fol. 77. See Buteau, "Naissance," 30.

32. Anselme, *Histoire* 6:202 (who believed Olivier II was still pursuing an active military career in 1324!); Levot, *Biographie bretonne* 1:357 (who extended Olivier II's military career to 1341, when he would have been over 100 years old!); BN FR 22348, fols. 55r–56r (which calls Isabelle the *first* wife of Olivier II); and Bertrand de Broussillon, *Maison de Craon* 1:213. This last work includes a cartulary of the Craon family that does not indicate the first name of the Clisson that married Isabelle.

33. Bertrand de Broussillon, *Maison de Craon* 1: 203–13.

34. Morice 1, col. 1291; BN FR 22348, fols. 55r–56r.

35. Olivier last appears in 1293 (above, note 31), and his son was lord of Clisson in 1298 (below, note 37).

36. The best explanation of this marriage and the acquisition of Le Thuit is that of Buteau, "Naissance," 18–22, who has corrected an erroneous genealogy of the Clisson family found in AN X 1c 43, no. 30 (which she reproduces in part) and AN X 1c 38 A, an extract of which is published in Lefranc, *Olivier*, 429, *P.J.* 5.

37. Olivier II had died by 22 July 1298, when a document identifies Guillaume as lord of Clisson but also a minor under the guardianship of another lord (ADLA E 196, no. 1, published in La Borderie, "Recueil" 2: 75). He must therefore have been born in the 1280s, when his father was already middle-aged. The second document, indicating his early death leaving minor children, is mentioned by Blanchard in ADLA 7JJ 70.

38. Buteau, "Naissance," 33–34, followed by Gicquel, *Olivier*, 48, who calls the future constable Olivier V.

39. Bruel, "Inventaire," p. 228, note 3, thought Isabelle then had a son by a third marriage, but a contemporary text in Fonds Grandville en Bringolo, cabinet 28, shows clearly that she was still married to Anthoing when she was past childbearing age.

40. Bertrand de Broussillon, *Maison de Craon* 1:246–63.

41. BN FR 22348, fols. 55r–56r. Beginning with the children of Isabelle de Craon, this document seems entirely trustworthy, since much of its information can be verified elsewhere.

42. Buteau, "Naissance," 34–38. For documents relating to the Clisson-Bouville marriage contract in AN JJ 60, nos. 82–83, see *Registres du Trésor des chartes 2*, ed J. Guérout (Paris, 1966–67), p. 717, nos. 3452, 3453.

43. Roy, *Histoire*, 12; Buteau, "Naissance," 35–37, indicating the Bouville family relationships and litigation over Blanche's estate.

44. Bertrand de Broussillon, *Maison de Laval* 2:228–29. At her death in 1383, Louise held the lordships of Palluau, Montaigu, and Châteaumur, which were part of her mother's inheritance (Buteau, "Naissance," 100).

45. Buteau, "Naissance," 38, citing a dispensation of 30 April 1330 in the Vatican archives.

46. BN FR 22348, fols. 55r–56r; *AHP* 13:111; Gaden-Puchet, "Château de Blain," 5.

47. See above, Chapter 2.

48. BN FR 22348, fols. 55r–56r; Buffé, *Blain*, 60.

49. In 1389, the younger Jean Harpedenne was a royal chamberlain and on the payroll of the king's brother Louis: BN NAF 3653, no. 403; NAF 3638, no. 129.

50. BN FR 22325, p. 795; BMN 1703/1547, no. 2.

51. See above, Chapter 2.

52. BN FR 22325, p. 797; FR 22331, p. 107; PO 789, doss. 17,879 (Clisson), nos. 27–29, 31, 34, 35; *AHM* 5:79–85; A. Joubert, "Le château de Ramefort de Gennes et ses seigneurs aux XIVe et XVe siècles," *RHAM* 22 (1887): 389–93.

53. See above, Chapter 3, at notes 20–21 and 44–45. Although Guy XII de Laval, who had married Clisson's half-sister, played an important role, as male head of the family, in arranging his sister's marriage to Clisson, his mother provided a major part of the dowry and her prestige as a member of the ducal house gave her a greater role in the proceedings than a widowed mother would normally have.

54. Chapter 3, at notes 44–46.

55. See sources cited in Chapter 3, note 20.

56. Y. Gicquel, *Alain IX de Rohan (1382–1462): Un Grand Seigneur de l'âge d'or de la Bretagne* (Paris, 1986), 43, does not furnish concrete evidence of the year of Alain's birth, but thinks 1382 the most probable date, evidently with the blessing of the current head of the Rohan family who wrote an introduction to the book.

57. BMN 1703/1547, no. 6.

58. Lefranc, *Olivier*, 138.

59. BMN 1703/1547, no. 4.

60. Gicquel, *Olivier*, 49; Buteau, "Naissance," 70.

61. Bertrand de Broussillon, *Maison de Laval* 2:294–95; AN JJ 113, no. 163.

62. ADLA H 232, fol. 1v.

63. See above, Chapter 6, at notes 72–75.

64. See above, Chapter 7, at notes 100–101.

65. BMN 1691/1535, no. 8. Roy, *Histoire*, 151–52, who placed Clisson's second marriage after that of his second daughter, is not the most reliable source, but he is probably correct on this point.

66. Gicquel, *Olivier*, 92; Bruel, "Inventaire," p. 226, no. 371 and note 4.

67. Gicquel, *Olivier*, 171, 224–27. Clisson acquired lands from the count of La Marche (*Catalogue générale* 22:230), Jean d'Orange (BN FR 22361, p. 394), Pierre de Tournebu (ADLA E 217, no.5; ADCA E 1380, liasse 1), and Olivier du

Guesclin (Bruel, "Inventaire," p. 226; Buteau, "Naissance," 120). Gicquel, *Olivier*, 178–80, suggests that Clisson may have profited, in some of his transactions, from advanced information on a small alteration of the currency in 1385.

68. Gicquel, *Olivier*, 212, 226, 267. Clisson's lands were rich sources of wine and salt (ibid., 210–11; above, Chapter 2 at note 36, and J.-C. Hocquet, "Le sel des Bretons, la France, et l'Europe aux XVᵉ et XVIᵉ siècles," in *1491: La Bretagne, Terre d'Europe*, ed. J. Kerhervé and T. Daniel [Brest, 1992], 26). As indicated above, Chapter 1, note 61, noble status and trade were not as incompatible in Brittany as elsewhere. Clisson's relatively small expenditures on largesse may, I think, be inferred from the bequests discussed above in Chapter 12 at notes 78–80.

69. Gicquel, *Olivier*, 163. A receipt for part of his salary at Montl'hery in 1386 is in BN FR 22338, fol. 98v.

70. Clisson's control of the county of Penthièvre in 1387 is made clear by the castles he was required to surrender in order to gain his freedom (Chapter 8 at note 15). On his collections of revenues, see the allegations of his daughter Marguerite after his death (Chapter 12 at note 106).

71. Buteau, "Naissance," 100. Part of this inheritance was still being adjudicated in 1397: AN X¹ᶜ 81ᴬ, no. 149.

72. AN P 1334¹, no. 6, fols. 70r–71r.

73. Gicquel, *Olivier*, 202–3, says that Clisson possessed over sixty properties, but this total seems to include everything he ever owned and not his holdings at any particular time. Toudouze, *DCR*, 177, counted seventeen castellanies in Brittany alone at the time of the hearth survey of 1392 mentioned in the next note.

74. Gicquel, *Olivier*, 204; Martin, "Grand seigneur," 59.

75. Chapter 10, note 32.

76. AN X¹ᵃ 55, fols. 213r–216v and the discussion in Chapter 12 at notes 84–85. Buteau, "Naissance," 81, noted that the sum divided between the daughters was liquid cash and did not include any capital. She concluded that 1.7 million francs might have approximated the value of the entire estate.

77. Gicquel, *Olivier*, 189–90. Here and elsewhere, Gicquel seeks to impress upon the reader the magnitude of this fortune in terms of modern gold prices and also in terms of the salaries paid to people in various occupations in Clisson's day.

78. The most comparable wealthy noble of Clisson's time was Gaston Phoebus, count of Foix, who accumulated a fortune at Orthez that exceeded 730,000 florins in local currency (about 470,000 *l.t.*), according to Tucoo-Chala, *Gaston Fébus*, 143–46.

Bibliography

MANUSCRIPTS

Bringolo (Côtes d'Armor): Fonds Grandville (private collection)

Cabinet 28

Chantilly: Musee Condé, Cabinet de Titres

Series B: cart. 117, reg. 126
Series BA: reg. 25, 27
Series CC: cart. 1
Series E: cart. 15

Le Mans: Archives Départementales, Sarthe

Series E: 29, 140, 147, 371, 372
Series H: 1377, 1457

Nantes: Archives Départmentales, Loire-Atlantique

Series B: 1890
Series E (archives of the dukes of Brittany): 5, 6, 8, 17, 56, 82, 90–92, 103, 104,
    108, 113, 120, 126, 142, 151, 154, 163–68, 177, 179, 181, 182, 186, 217,
    218, 225, 232, 233, 236, 245
Series G: 345
Series H: 1, 2, 32, 74, 232
Series 7 JJ (notes of René Blanchard): 23, 23[2], 24, 50, 70

Nantes: Bibliothèque Municipale

Collection Bizeul (documents rescued from the destruction of the archives at
    Blain castle): cartons 1684, 1686, 1689–94, 1696, 1699, 1703, 1707, 1708
    (also called *manuscrits français* 1528, 1530, 1533–38, 1540, 1543, 1547,
    1551, 1552)

Paris: Archives Nationales

Series AA: 60

Series J (documents received by the royal chancery): 179, 186, 188, 214, 240–44, 246, 250, 293, 359, 381, 382, 400, 641, 642, 654

Series JJ (registers of documents issued by the royal chancery): 66, 75, 78, 87, 89, 99, 102–6, 108–11, 113, 122, 128, 129, 142, 144, 149, 150, 154

Series K (cartons of royal documents): 49–51, 53–55

Series KK (financial accounts of kings and princes): 30, 242, 251–53, 267, 315

Series P (records kept by the Chamber of Accounts): 594, 1334, 1339, 1344, 2294, 2296

Series PP: 109

Series U: 785

Series X^{1a} (civil judgments and pleadings before the Parlement of Paris): 29–35, 44–47, 55, 1469–74, 1476–78, 8602

Series X^{2a} (criminal judgments of the Parlement of Paris): 10–13

Series X^{1c} (accords and settlements reached and recorded at the Parlement of Paris): 22, 49, 78A, 78B, 81A 83A, 85C, 89B, 94A, 97C

Paris: Bibliothèque de l'Arsenal

Ms 5424, 6589

Paris: Bibliothèque Nationale

Collection Baluze: 51, 59

Collection Bourgogne: 24–26, 52, 53, 100

Collection Clairambault: 3–8, 10–17, 20–25, 27–37, 39–41, 43–48, 51–53, 55–60, 62–65, 67–76, 83, 87, 86, 93, 138, 159, 161, 166, 167, 173, 176–78, 189, 217, 487, 782, 957–59

Collection Doat: 243, 244

Collection Duchesne: 45, 55, 59, 60, 68

Collection Dupuy: 635

Collection Languedoc: 87

Collection Moreau: 1161, 1162

Collection Périgord: 58

Manuscrits Français: 810, 2836, 3863, 3876, 3910, 4482, 4768, 4995, 5512, 6210–12, 6537, 7858, 10237, 10430–32, 11531, 11550, 16654, 18698, 20372, 20402–5, 20416, 20586, 20590, 20599, 20683, 20684, 20686, 20692, 20880, 20883, 20885, 20888, 21405, 21539, 22222, 22315, 22319, 22325, 22330, 22331, 22338–40, 22348, 22361, 22362, 22451, 22468, 23271, 23952, 25704–8, 25764–66, 25903, 26009, 26012–29, 26271, 26740, 31952, 32510, 32511

Manuscrits Latins: 5381, 5480, 11829, 13868, 17092

Nouvelles Acquisitions Françaises: 3638–40, 3653–55, 7268, 7269, 7413, 7414,
    7919–21, 8603, 8604, 9175, 9179, 9189–91, 20027, 20528, 23634
Nouvelles Acquisitions Latines: 184, 2574
Pièces Originales: A total of 359 volumes between numbers 7 and 3059, consisting
    largely of pay records, most of them for military service, originally collected
    for genealogical purposes and used here primarily to document the material
    in Appendix 1.

Pau: Archives Départementales, Pyrénées Atlantique

Series E: 134, 636, 638, 715 (consulted on microfilm)

Rennes: Archives Départementales, Ille-et-Vilaine

Series 1E: 5–7, 9, 15, 16
Series 1F: 625, 626, 1527, 1535, 1536
Series 2Ea: 48

Saint-Brieuc: Archives Départementales, Côtes d'Armor

Series E: 1, 11, 79, 173, 619, 1317, 1380, 1567, 1834

Printed Sources, Inventories, Chronicles

Anciens mémoire du XIVe siècle sur Bertrand du Guesclin. Published in J. F. Michaud,
    Nouvelle collection des mémoires pour servir à l'histoire de France (Paris, 1836–39)
    1: 437–579.
Bardonnet, A., ed. *Procès-verbal de délivrance à Jean Chandos, commissaire du roi
    d'Angleterre, des places françaises abandonées par le traité de Brétigny, publié
    d'apres le manuscrit de musée Brittanique*. Niort, 1869.
Bertrand de Broussillon, A. "Documents inédits pour servir à l'histoire du Maine
    au XIVe siècle." *AHM* 5 (1905).
———. *La Maison de Craon, 1050–1480, étude historique, accompagnée du cartulaire
    de Craon*, 2 vols. Paris, 1893.
———. *La Maison de Laval, 1020–1605, étude historique*, 3 vols. Paris, 1895–1900.
Bouchart, A. *Grandes chroniques de Bretagne*, 2 vols. Ed. M. L. Auger and G. Jean-
    neau. Paris, 1986.
Calendar of the Close Rolls Preserved in the Public Record Office: Edward III, 14 vols.
    London, 1908.
Calendar of the Close Rolls Preserved in the Public Record Office: Richard II, 6 vols.
    London, 1914; repr. Nendeln, 1972.
Cartulaire du Morbihan. Ed. L. Rosenzweig. Extracts from *Revue historique de
    l'Ouest*, 1893–97.

Catalogue général des manuscrits des bibliothèques publiques de France: Départements. Vol. 22: Nantes, Quimper, Brest. Paris, 1893.

Champollion-Figeac, J. J., ed. *Lettres des rois, reines et autres personnages des cours de France et Angleterre dupuis Louis VII jusqu'à Henri IV, tirées des archives de Londres par Bréquigny.* 2 vols. Paris, 1839–47.

Chaplais, P., ed. "Some Documents Regarding the Fulfilment and Interpretation of the Treaty of Brétigny (1361–1369)." *Camden Miscellany* 19 (1952): 1–84.

Coopland, G. W., ed. and trans. *The* Tree of Battles *of Honoré Bonet.* Cambridge, Mass., 1949.

Chronicon Briocense. Extracts covering the period 1364–1415. See Lobineau 2, cols. 833–91.

Chronique de Bertrand du Guesclin par Cuvelier, trouvère du XIVe siècle. 2 vols. Ed. E. Charrière. Paris, 1839.

Chronique de Bretagne de Jean de Saint-Paul, chambellan du duc François II. Ed. A. de la Borderie. Nantes, 1881.

Chronique de Jean le Bel. 2 vols. Ed. J. Viard and E. Deprez. Paris, 1904–5.

Chronique des quatre premiers Valois (1327–1393). Ed. S. Luce. Paris, 1862.

Chronique des règnes de Jean II et de Charles V. 3 vols. Ed. R. Delachenal. Paris, 1910.

La Chronique du bon duc Loys de Bourbon par Jean Cabaret d'Orville. Ed. A. M. Chazaud. Paris, 1876.

Chronique du Religieux de Saint-Denis contenant le règne de Charles VI de 1380 à 1422. Ed. L. Bellaguet. 5 vols. Paris, 1839–40.

Chronique latine de Guillaume de Nangis 1113–1300, avec les continuations de cette chronique de 1300 à 1368. 2 vols. Ed. H. Géraud. Paris, 1843.

Chronique normande de Pierre Cochon. Ed. C. de Beaurepaire. Rouen, 1870.

Chronique normande du XIVe siècle. Ed. A. Molinier and E. Molinier. Paris, 1882.

Chronographia regnum francorum. 2 vols. Ed. H. Moranvillé. Paris, 1893.

Delisle, L., ed. *Mandements et actes divers de Charles V (1364–1380), recueillis dans les collections de la Bibliothèque Nationale.* Paris, 1874.

————, ed. "Pièce soustraite au trésor des chartes des ducs de Bretagne." *BÉC* 58 (1897): 379–80.

Demay, G. *Inventaire des sceaux de la Collection Clairambault à la Bibliothèque Nationale.* 2 vols. Paris, 1885–86.

Douet d'Arcq, L. C., ed. *Choix de pièces inédits rélatives au règne de Charles VI.* 2 vols. Paris, 1863–64.

Foedera, conventiones litterae et cujuscunque generis acta publica inter reges Angliae et alios quosvis imperatores, pontifices, principes vel communitates. Comp. T. Rymer, 3d ed. 10 vols. Ed. G. Holmes. The Hague, 1739–45.

Froissart, Jean. *The Chronicle of Froissart Translated by Sir John Bourchier, Lord Berners.* 6 vols. London, 1901–3.

————. *Chronicles of England, France, Spain, and the adjoining countries . . . by Sir John Froissart.* 2 vols. Trans. Thomas Johnes. London, 1842.

————. *Chroniques de J. Froissart* (Société de l'Histoire de France). 13 vols. Ed. S. Luce, G. Raynaud, L. Mirot, A. Mirot. Paris, 1869–.

————. *Chroniques. Dernière rédaction du premier livre. édition du manuscrit de Rome Reg. lat. 869.* Ed. G. T. Diller. Paris and Geneva, 1972.

————. *Oeuvres de Froissart*. 25 vols. in 26. Ed. H. Kervyn de Lettenhove. Bruxelles, 1867–77.

Furgeot, H. *Actes du Parlement de Paris: Jugés*. 2 vols. Paris, 1920–60.

Les Grandes Chroniques de France. 9 vols. Ed. J. Viard. Paris, 1920–37.

Guérin, P., et al., eds. "Recueil de documents concernant le Poitou contenus dans les régistres de la chancellerie de France, 1881–1958. *AHP*, 14 vols. (11, 13, 17, 19, 21, 24, 27, 29, 32, 35, 38, 41, 50, 56).

Halgouet, H. du. *Répertoire sommaire des documents manuscrits de l'histoire de Bretagne antérieures à 1789 conservés dans les dépots publics de Paris*. Saint-Brieuc, 1914.

Jones, M., ed. *Recueil des actes de Jean IV, duc de Bretagne*. 2 vols. Paris, 1980.

————, ed. "Some Documents Relating to the Disputed Succession to the Duchy of Brittany, 1341." *Camden Miscellany* 24 (1972): 1–78.

Journal de Jean Le Fèvre, évêque de Chartres, chancelier des rois de Sicile Louis I et Louis II d'Anjou. Ed H. Moranvillé. Paris, 1887.

Juvenal des Ursins, Jean. *Histoire de Charles VI, roy de France* . . . . In *Nouvelle collection des mémoires pour servir à l'histoire de France*, ed. J. F. Michaud, 2:333–569. Paris, 1836–39.

La Borderie, A. de. "Recueil des actes inédites des ducs et princes de Bretagne." *Bulletin et mémoires de la Société Archéologique du Departement d'Ille-et-Vilaine* 17 (1885): 1–87, 341–436; 19 (1889): 155–285; 21 (1892): 91–193; 22 (1893): 181–286.

Lannette-Clavérie, C. *Collection Joursanvault, sous-série 6-J: Inventaire analytique*. Orleans, 1976.

Lettres et mandements de Jean V, duc de Bretagne. 5 vols. Ed. R. Blanchard, *Archives de Bretagne*, vols. 4–8. Nantes, 1889–95.

Maitre, L. *Inventaire sommaire des Archives Départementales anterieures à 1790. Loire-Inférieure 3: Archives Civiles (série E)*. Nantes, 1879.

Merlin-Chazélas, A. *Documents rélatifs au clos de galées en Rouen et aux armees de mer du roi de France de 1293 à 1418*. 2 vols. Paris, 1977–78.

Mézières, Philippe de. *Letter to King Richard II: A Plea Made in 1395 for Peace between England and France*. Ed. and trans. G. W. Coopland. Liverpool, 1975.

Morice, H. *Mémoires pour servir de preuves à l'histoire ecclésiastique et civile de Bretagne*. 3 vols. Paris, 1742–46; repr. 1968.

Ordonnances des roys de France de la troisième race recueillies par ordre chronologique. 21 vols. Ed. E. J. de Laurière, D.-F. Secousse, et al. Paris, 1723–1849.

Petit, J., et al. *Essai de restitution des plus anciens mémoriaux de la chambre des comptes de Paris*. Paris, 1899.

Peyronnet, G. "Les Sources documentaires anglaises de l'histoire mediévale de la Bretagne." *Annales de Bretagne et des pays de l'ouest* 96 (1989): 279–312; 97 (1990): 463–78; 98 (1991): 373–89.

Pizan, Christine de. *Le Livre des fais et bonnes moeurs du sage roy Charles V*. Ed. S. Solente. Paris, 1936.

Plaine, F., ed. *Monuments du procès de canonisation du bienheureux Charles de Blois, duc de Bretagne 1320–1364*. Saint-Brieuc, 1921. Bound in same volume as Plaine's *Histoire . . . Charles de Blois . . .* (listed below under Secondary Works).

Recueil des historiens des Gaules et de la France. 24 vols. Many editors. Paris, 1840–1904.

Régistres du Trésor des Chartes 2: Règnes des fils de Philippe le Bel. 2 vols. Ed. J. Guérout. Paris, 1966–68.

Régistres du Trésor des Chartes 3: Règne de Philippe de Valois. 3 vols. Ed J. Viard and A. Vallée. Paris, 1978–84.

Robertus de Avesbury de gestis mirabilibus regis Edwardi Tertii. In *Rerum Britannicarum medii aevi scriptores,* ed. E. M. Thompson. London, 1889, 279–471.

Saint-André, Guillaume de. *C'est le libvre du bon Jehan, duc de Bretagne.* Ed. E. Charrière in vol. 2 of *Chronique de Bertrand du Guesclin par Cuvelier.* Paris, 1839.

Secousse, D.-F., ed. *Recueil de pièces servent de preuves aux mémoires sur les troubles excités en France par Charles II dit le Mauvais.* Vol. 2 of his *Mémoire pour servir à l'histoire de Charles II, roi de Navarre et comte d'Évreux, surnommé le Mauvais.* Paris, 1755–58.

Le Songe du Vergier. Édite d'après le manuscrit royal 19 C IV de la British Library. Ed. M. Schnerb-Lievre. 2 vols. Paris, 1982.

Le Songe veritable. Pamphlet politique d'un parisien du XVe siècle. ed. H. Moranvillé. *Mémoires de la société de Paris et de l'Ile de France* 17 (1890): 217–438 (text pp. 230–305).

Tardif, J. *Monuments historiques.* Paris, 1866; repr. Nendeln, 1977.

Viard, J. "Documents français remis au gouvernment anglais à la suite du traité de Brétigny." *BÉC* 58 (1897): 155–61.

Secondary Works Cited in the Notes

(Asterisks indicate works that contain important published texts.)

Allmand, C. T. "Changing Views of the Soldier in Late Medieval France." In *Guerre et société en France, en Angleterre et en Bourgogne XIVe–XVe siècle,* ed. P. Contamine, C. Giry-Deloison, M. Keen, 171–88. Lille, 1991.

Anselme de Sainte-Marie, Le Père. *Histoire généalogique et chronologique de la maison de France.* 9 vols. 3d ed. Paris, 1726–33.

Autrand, F. *Charles V le Sage.* Paris, 1994.

———. *Charles VI: La Folie du roi.* Paris, 1986.

———. "De l'Enfer au Purgatoire: la cour à travers quelques textes français du milieu du XIVe à la fin du XVe siècle." In *L'État et les aristocraties, XIIe–XVIIe siècle, France, Angleterre, Écosse,* ed. P. Contamine, 51–78. Paris, 1989.

———. "La déconfiture. La bataille de Poitiers (1356) à travers quelques textes français des XIVe et XVe siècles." In *Guerre et société en France, en Angleterre et en Bourgogne XIVe–XVe siècle,* ed. P. Contamine, C. Giry-Deloison, M. Keen, 93–121. Lille, 1991.

Avout, J. d'. *La Querelle des Armagnacs et des Bourguignons.* Paris, 1943.

Babbitt, S. M. *Oresme's Livre de Politics and the France of Charles V. Transactions of the American Philosophical Society* 75 pt. 1. Philadelphia, 1985.

Bellier-Dumaine, C. "L'administration du duché de Bretagne sous le règne de Jean V (1399–1442)." *Annales de Bretagne* 14 (1898): 562–90; 15 (1899): 162–88, 468–89; 16 (1900–01): 112–29, 246–78, 477–514.

Biou, O. "Notice sur Jeanne de Belleville, poème de M. Emile Pehant." *ASAN* 39 (1868): 189–221.

Blanc, A. "Le Rappel du duc d'Anjou et l'ordonnance du 25 avril 1380." *Bulletin historique et philologique du comité des travaux historiques et scientifiques*, 1899.

*Blanchard, R. "Cartulaire des sires de Rays," 2 vols. *AHP*, 1898–99. Vols. 28, 30.

Bois, G. *The Crisis of Feudalism: Economy and Society in Eastern Normandy, c. 1300–1500*. Cambridge and New York, 1984, a translation of his *Crise de féodalisme* (Paris, 1976).

———. "Noblesse et crise des revenus seigneuriaux en France aux XIVe et XVe siècles: Essai d'interpretation." In *La Noblesse au moyen age, XIe-XVe siècles: Essais à la mémoire de Robert Boutrouche*, ed. P. Contamine. Paris, 1976.

Bonney, R., ed. *Rise of the Fiscal State in Europe, 1200–1815*. Oxford, 1996.

*Bréjon de Lavergnée, J. "La Confiscation du duché en 1378." *MSHAB* 59 (1982): 329–43.

Bridrey, E. *La Théorie de la monnaie au XIVe siècle, Nicole Oresme*. Paris, 1906.

Brown, E. A. R. "Taxation and Morality in the Thirteenth and Fourteenth Centuries: Conscience and Political Power and the Kings of France." *French Historical Studies* 8 (1973): 1–28.

———, and R. C. Famiglietti. *The Lit de Justice: Semantics, Ceremonial, and the Parlement of Paris, 1300–1600*. Beihefte der Francia 31. Sigmaringen, 1994.

Bruel, F.-L. "Essai dur la vie et le rôle d'Olivier IV, sire de Clisson et de Belleville, connétable de France, 1336–1407." *Positions de Thèses, École des Chartes* (1903): 45–50.

*———. "Inventaire de meubles et de titres trouvés au chateau de Josselin à la mort du connétable de Clisson (1407)." *BÉC* 66 (1905): 193–245.

Buffé, M. *Blain de la préhistoire à nos jours*. Nantes, 1968.

Buteau, M. "La Naissance de la fortune de Clisson." *Mémoire de Maîtrise*, University of Vincennes, 1970. Copy at Archives Départementales, Vannes (Morbihan).

Carpentier, E. "Autour de la peste noire: Famines et epidémies dans l'histoire du XIVe siècle." *Annales: Économies, sociétés, civilisations* 17 (1962): 1062–92.

Carrasco, J. "Le Royaume de Navarre et le duché de Bretagne au cours du dernier tiers du XIVe siècle: Politique matrimoniale et circulation monétaire." In *1491: La Bretagne, Terre d'Europe*. Colloque international. Ed. J. Kerverhé and T. Daniel, 205–21. Brest, 1992.

Cassard, J.-C. "Les *Gestes des Bretons* en Italie ou le voyage sans la découverte." In *1491: La Bretagne, Terre d'Europe*. Colloque international. Ed. J. Kerhervé and T. Daniel, 101–17. Brest, 1992.

Cazelles, R. *Étienne Marcel: Champion de l'unité française*. Paris, 1984.

———. "Les Mouvements revolutionnaires du milieu du XIVe siècle et le cycle de l'action politique." *Revue historique* 464 (1962): 279–312.

———. "Le Parti navarrais jusqu'à la mort d'Etienne Marcel." *Bulletin philologique et historique (Comité des travaux historiques et scientifiques)* (1960): 839–69.

———. "Quelques réflexions à propos des mutations de la monnaie royale française (1295–1360)." *Le Moyen Age* 72 (1966): 83–105, 251–278.

———. *La Société politique et la crise de la royauté sous Philippe de Valois*. Paris, 1958.

———. *Société politique, noblesse, et couronne sous Jean le Bon et Charles V*. Genève, 1982.

Charon, P. "Relations entre les cours de la France et de Navarre en 1376–1377." *BÉC* 150 (1992): 85–108.

Chauvernon, R. de. *Des maillotins aux Marmousets: Audoin Chauvernon, prévôt de Paris sous Charles VI*. Paris, 1992.

Chauvin-Lechaptois, M. *Les comptes de la châtellenie de Lamballe (1387–1482)*. Paris, 1977.

Cintré, R. *Les Marches de Bretagne au moyen âge: Économie, Guerre et Société en pays de frontière (XIVᵉ–XVᵉ siècles)*. Pornichet, 1992.

Clément-Simon, G. *La Rupture du traité de Brétigny et ses consequences en Limousin*. Paris, 1898.

Contamine, P. "The French Nobility and the War." In *The Hundred Years War*, ed. K. Fowler. London, 1971.

———. *Guerre, état, et société à la fin du moyen âge*. Paris, 1971.

Cosneau, E. *Le Connétable de Richemont (Artur de Bretagne) (1393–1458)*. Paris, 1886.

Coville, A. *Évrart de Trémaugon et le Songe du Vergier*. Paris, 1933.

———. *Gontier et Pierre Col et l'Humanisme en France au temps de Charles VI*. Paris, 1934.

*———. *Les États de Normandie, leurs origines et leur developpement au XIVᵉ siècle*. Paris, 1894.

———. *Les Premiers Valois et la guerre de Cent Ans*. Vol. 4, part 1 of *Histoire de France*, ed. E. Lavisse. Paris, 1900–11.

Cuttler, S.H. *The Law of Treason and Treason Trials in Later Medieval France*. Cambridge, 1982.

Delachenal, R. *Histoire de Charles V*. 5 vols. Paris, 1909–31.

*Delisle, L. *Histoire du château et des sires de Saint-Sauveur-le-Vicomte*. Valognes, 1867.

*Devic, C., and J. Vaissete. *Histoire générale de Languedoc avec des Notes et les pièces justificatives*, ed. A. Molinier et al., 16 vols. Toulouse, 1872–1904.

Doucet, Y. *Histoire de la vallée de Clisson*. Maulévrier, 1992.

Duboueix, M. "Topographie de la ville de Clisson." *ASAN* 39 (1968): 131–88.

Du Cange, C. de Fresne, sieur. *Dissertations, ou reflexions sur l'histoire de S. Louis, du sire de Joinville*. In *Collection complete des mémoires rélatifs à l'histoire de France*, ed. Petitot, 3: 59–527. Paris, 1819.

Emery, R. "The Black Death of 1348 in Perpignan." *Speculum* 42 (1967): 611–23.

Famiglietti, R. C. *Royal Intrigue: Crisis at the Court of Charles VI, 1392–1420*. New York, 1986.

———. *Tales of the Marriage Bed from Medieval France (1300–1500)*. Providence, 1992.

Favier, J. *La Guerre de Cent Ans*. Paris, 1980.

Favreau, R. *La Ville de Poitiers à la fin du moyen âge: Une Capitale regionale.* Poitiers, 1978.

Finot, L. "La Dernière Ordonnance de Charles V." *BÉC* 50 (1889): 164–67.

Floquet, C. *Châteaux et manoirs bretons des Rohan.* Loudéac, 1989.

Forhan, K. L. "Reflecting Heroes: Christine de Pizan and the Mirror Tradition." In *The* City of Scholars: *New Approaches to Christine de Pizan,* ed. M. Zimmermann and D. De Rentiis, 189–96. Berlin, 1994.

Fowler, K. *The King's Lieutenant: Henry of Grosmont, First Duke of Lancaster (1310–1361).* London and New York, 1969.

Gaden-Puchet, C. "Le Château de Blain." *Mémoire de maîtrise,* University of Paris, 1969. Microfilm at Archives Départementales, Nantes (Loire-Atlantique).

Gaillou, P., and M. Jones. *The Bretons.* Oxford, 1991.

Gaudu, G. "La Tour de Cesson." *Bulletin de la société d'émulation des Côtes-du-Nord* 82 (1953): 63–74.

Gauvard, C. *"De grace especial": Crime, état, et société en France à la fin du moyen âge.* 2 vols. Paris, 1991.

Gicquel, Y. *Alain IX de Rohan (1382–1462): Un Grand Seigneur de l'âge d'or de la Bretagne.* Paris, 1986.

———. *Olivier de Clisson (1336–1407): Connétable de France ou chef de parti breton?* Paris, 1981.

Given-Wilson, C. "The Ransom of Olivier du Guesclin." *BIHR* 129 (1981): 17–28.

Goodman, A. *John of Gaunt: The Exercise of Princely Power in Fourteenth-Century Europe.* Harlow, Essex, 1992.

Grand Larousse encyclopédique, 10 vols. Paris, 1963.

Grévy-Pons, N. "Propagande et sentiment national pendant le règne de Charles VI: L'Example de Jean de Montreuil." *Francia* 8 (1980): 127–45.

———, and E. Ornato, "Qui est l'auteur de la chronique latine de Charles VI dite du religieux de Saint-Denis?" *BÉC* 134 (1976): 85–102.

Guenée, B. *Un Meurtre, une société. L'Assassinat du duc d'Orléans, 23 novembre 1407.* Paris, 1992.

Halgouet, H. du. *La Vicomté de Rohan et ses seigneurs.* Paris and Saint-Brieuc, 1921.

Henneman, J. B. "The Military Class and the French Monarchy in the Late Middle Ages." *American Historical Review* 83 (1978): 946–65.

———. "Nobility, Privilege, and Fiscal Politics in Late Medieval France." *French Historical Studies* 13 (1983): 1–17.

———. "Reassessing the Career of Olivier de Clisson, Constable of France." In *Law, Custom, and the Social Fabric in Medieval Europe: Essays in Honor of Bryce Lyon,* ed. B. Bachrach and D. Nicholas, 211–33. Kalamazoo, 1990.

———. *Royal Taxation in Fourteenth Century France: The Development of War Financing, 1322–1356.* Princeton, 1971.

———. *Royal Taxation in Fourteenth Century France: The Captivity and Ransom of John II, 1356–1370.* Philadelphia, 1976.

———. "Taxation of Italians by the French Crown, 1311–1363." *Mediaeval Studies* 31 (1969): 15–43.

———. "Who Were the Marmousets?" *Medieval Prosopography* 5 (1984): 19–63.

Hocquet, J.-C. "Le Sel des Bretons, la France, et l'Europe aux XVe et XVIe siècles. In *1491: La Bretagne, Terre d'Europe.* Colloque international. Ed. J. Kerhervé and T. Daniel, 23–33. Brest, 1992.

Jamison, D. F. *The Life and Times of Bertrand du Guesclin: A History of the Fourteenth Century,* 2 v. Charleston, 1864.

Jarry, E. *Les Origines de la domination française à Gènes (1392–1402).* Paris, 1896.

———. *La Vie politique de Louis de France, duc d'Orléans, 1372–1407.* Paris, 1889.

Jones, M. *The Creation of Brittany: A Late Medieval State.* London, 1988.

———. "The Diplomatic Evidence for Franco-Breton Relations, c. 1370–1372." *English Historical Review* 93 (1978): 300–319.

———. *Ducal Brittany, 1364–1399.* Oxford, 1970.

———. "Les Capitaines anglo-bretons et les marches entre la Bretagne et le Poitou de 1342 à 1373." In *La "France anglaise" au moyen âge: Actes du 111e Congrès National des sociétés savantes.* Paris, 1986. 1 (1988): 357–75.

———. "Nantes au debut de la guerre civile en Bretagne." In *Villes, bonnes villes, cités et capitales: Mélanges offerts à Bernard Chevalier,* 105–20. Tours, 1989.

———. "The Ransom of Jean de Bretagne, Count of Penthièvre: An Aspect of English Foreign Policy 1386–8." *BIHR* 111 (1972): 7–26.

———. "L'Utilisation de la poudre à canon et de l'artillerie dans la duché de Bretagne avant 1400: la Preuve Documentaire." *MSHAB* 69 (1992): 163–72.

Joubert, A. "Le Château de Ramefort de Gennes et ses seigneurs aux XIVe et XVe siècles, d'apres des documents inédits." *Revue historique et archéologique du Maine* 22 (1887): 387–99.

Jouve, G. *Montcontour de Bretagne.* Saint-Brieuc, 1990.

Kaminsky, H. *Simon de Cramaud and the Great Schism.* New Brunswick, N.J., 1983.

Keen, M. "Brotherhood in Arms." *History* 47 (1962): 1–17.

Kerhervé, J. *L'État breton aux 14e et 15e siècles: Les Ducs, l'argent, et les hommes.* 2 vols. Paris, 1987.

Krynen, J. *Idéal du prince et pouvoir royal en France à la fin du moyen âge (1380–1440).* Paris, 1981.

La Borderie, A. de. *Histoire de Bretagne.* Continued by B. A. Pocquet du Haut-Jussé. 6 vols. Paris and Rennes, 1896–1914.

*———. "Lettre de Charles VI, roi de France, aux barons de Bretagne sur la régence du duché (23 Aout 1402)." *RBV* 62 (1889): 473–74.

La Chesnaye-des Bois, F. A. A. de. *Dictionnaire de la noblesse de la France.* 3d ed. 16 vols. Paris, 1863–76.

La Fontenelle de Vaudoré, A. D. de. *Histoire d'Olivier de Clisson, connétable de France.* 2 vols. Paris, 1826.

La Gournerie, E. de. "Les Villes de Bretagne—Clisson." *RBV* (1865): pt. 1, pp. 249–64.

Lalande, D. *Jean II le Meingre, dit Boucicaut, 1366–1421.* Geneva, 1988.

Lalanne, L. *Dictionnaire historique de la France,* 2d ed. Paris, 1877.

*Langlois, M., and Y. Lanhers. *Confessions et jugements des criminels au Parlement de Paris (1319–1350).* Paris, 1971.

Lefranc, A. *Olivier de Clisson, connétable de France*. Paris, 1898. Leguay, J.-P., and H. Martin. *Fastes et malheurs de la Bretagne ducale (1213-1532)*. Rennes, 1982.

Lehoux, F. *Jean de France, duc de Berri, sa vie, son action politique (1340-1416)*, 4 vols. in 3. Paris, 1966–68.

Leland, J. "Heroine or Lunatic: The Alleged Madness of the Duchess of Brittany." Paper, Bowling Green State University, 1986.

Le Mené, M. *Les Campagnes angevines à la fin du moyen âge: étude economique (vers 1350-vers 1550)*. Nantes, 1982.

Levot, P. *Biographie bretonne, recueil de notices sur tous les bretons qui sont fait un nom*. 2 vols. Vannes and Paris, 1852.

Lewis, P. S. "Of Breton *Alliances* and Other Matters." In *War, Literature, and Politics in the Late Middle Ages*, ed. C. T. Allmand, 122–43. Liverpool, 1976.

*Lobineau, G. A. *Histoire de Bretagne, composée sur les titres et les auteurs originaux*. 2 vols. Paris, 1707; repr. Paris, 1973.

Loirette, G. "Arnaud Amanieu, sire d'Albret, et l'appel des seigneurs gascons en 1368." In *Mélanges historiques offerts à M. Charles Bémont*, 317–40. Paris, 1913.

Luce, S. *Histoire de Bertrand du Guesclin et de son epoque: La Jeunesse de Bertrand (1320-1364)*. Paris, 1876.

Martin, J-L. "Une grand seigneur breton en Ile-de-France: Olivier de Clisson." *Bulletin de la Société d'Émulation des Côtes-du-Nord* 82 (1953).

Mazas, A. *Vies des grands capitaines français du moyen âge*, 2d ed., 4: 349–481 (biography of Olivier de Clisson). Paris, 1838.

Michea, H. "L'Équipement du château de Brest sous Richard II, d'après les comptes du receveur Thomas Norwych (1378-1381)." *MSHAB* 69 (1992): 173–82.

Minois, G. *Du Guesclin*. Paris, 1993.

———. *Nouvelle histoire de la Bretagne*. Paris, 1992.

Mirot, L. *Les Insurrections urbaines au debut du règne de Charles VI (1380-1383): Leurs causes, les conséquences*. Paris, 1906. Miskimin, H. A. "The Last Act of Charles V: The Background of the Revolts of 1382." *Speculum* 38 (1963): 433–42.

Miskimin, H. A. "The Last of Charles V: The Background of the Revolts of 1382." *Speculum* 38 (1963): 433–42.

Mollat, G. "Les désastres de la Guerre de Cent Ans en Bretagne." *Annales de Bretagne* 26 (1910–11): 168–201.

*Moranvillé, H. *Étude sur la vie de Jean le Mercier*. Paris, 1888.

*———. "Rapports à Philippe VI sur l'état de ses finances." *BÉC* 48 (1887): 380–95.

Nicholas, D. M. *Town and Countryside: Social, Economic, and Political Tensions in Fourteenth-Century Flanders*. Bruges, 1971.

———. *The van Arteveldes of Ghent: the Varieties of Vendetta and the Hero in History*. Ithaca, 1988.

Nordberg, M. *Les ducs et la royauté: Études sur la rivalité des ducs d'Orléans et de Bourgogne, 1392-1407*. Uppsala, 1964.

Oexle, G. H. "Christine et les pauvres." In *The* City of Scholars: *New Approaches to Christine de Pizan*, ed. M. Zimmermann and D. De Rentiis, 206–20. Berlin, 1994.

Palmer, J. J. N. *England, France, and Christendom, 1377–1399*. London and Chapel Hill, 1972.

———. "English Foreign Policy, 1388–99." In *The Reign of Richard II: Essays in Honour of May McKisack*, ed. F. R. H. DuBoulay and C. M. Barron, 75–107. London, 1971.

———, ed. *Froissart, Historian*. Woodbridge, 1981.

*Perroy, E. "The Anglo-French Negotiations at Bruges, 1374–1377." *Camden Miscellany* 19 (1952): xix, 95 pp.

———. *The Hundred Years War*. Trans. W. B. Wells. London, 1951.

Petit, E. *Itinéraires de Philippe le Hardi et de Jean sans Peur, ducs de Bourgogne (1363–1419), d'après les comptes de depenses de leur hôtel*. Paris, 1888.

Petit-Dutaillis, C. *Charles VII, Louis XI, et la minorité de Charles VIII*. Paris, 1981 (repr. of *Histoire de France*, ed. E. Lavisse, Paris, 1900–11, vol. 4, pt, 2).

Peyronnet, G. "Les Rélations entre la Bretagne et l'Angleterre sous les ducs de la maison de Montfort d'apres les sources diplomatiques anglaises: État des travaux et directions de recherche." In *1491: La Bretagne, Terre d'Europe*. Colloque international. Ed. J. Kerhervé and T. Daniel, 243–49. Brest, 1992.

*Pichon, J. "Mémoire de Pierre de Craon." *Mélanges de litterature et d'histoire recueillis et publiés par la Société des Bibliophiles françois* 1 (1856): 92–119.

Plaine, F. *Histoire du Bienheureux Charles de Blois, duc de Bretagne et vicomte de Limoges*. Saint-Brieuc, 1921. Bound in same volume with Plaine's *Monuments du proces de canonisation . . .* (listed above under Printed Sources).

———. *Jeanne de Penthièvre, duchesse de Bretagne*. Saint-Brieuc, 1873.

Planiol, M. *Histoire des institutions de la Bretagne*. 3 vols. Reprint. Paris, 1981.

Pocquet du Haut-Jussé, B. "La dernière phase de la vie de Du Guesclin, L'Affaire de Bretagne." *BÉC* 125 (1967): 142–89.

———. *Deux féodaux. Bourgogne et Bretagne (1363–1491)*. Paris, 1935.

———. *Les Papes et les ducs de Bretagne*. 2 vols. Paris, 1928.

———. *Philippe le Hardi, régent de Bretagne (1402–1404)*. *Discours de reception à l'Académie de Dijon prononcé dans la seance du 20 décembre 1933*. Dijon, 1933.

———. "Les Séjours de Philippe le Hardi, duc de Bourgogne, en Bretagne (1372, 1394, et 1402)." *MSHAB* 16 (1935).

Portal, C. "Les Insurrections des Tuchins dans les pays de Langue d'oc, vers 1382–1384." *Annales du Midi* 4 (1892): 433–74.

Prat, G. "Albi et la peste noire." *Annales du Midi* 44 (1952): 15–25.

*Prevel, L. "Le Château de Blain: sa description, son histoire." *ASAN* 40 (1869): 5–149.

Quillet, J. *La philosophie politique du* Songe du Vergier *(1378): Sources doctrinales*. Paris, 1977.

Rey, M. *Le domaine du roi et les finances extraordinaires sous Charles VI, 1388–1413*. Paris, 1965.

———. *Les finances royales sous Charles VI: Les Causes du déficit 1388–1413*. Paris, 1965.

Reynaud, M.-R. "Maison d'Anjou et maison(s) de Bretagne (vers 1360-vers 1434)." In *1491: La Bretagne, Terre d'Europe*. Colloque international, ed. J. Kerhervé and T. Daniel, 177–91. Brest, 1992.

Rohan-Chabot, L. "Le Porhoët, la vicomté, le duché de Rohan." *Association bretonne, Bulletin des comptes rendus* (1976): 40–46.

Rohan, A. de. *Le Château de Josselin*. Rennes, 1985.

Rouquette, J. *Le Rouergue sous les anglais*. Millau, 1887.

Roy, J. *Histoire d'Olivier de Clisson*. Paris, 1872.

Russell, P. E. *The English Intervention in Spain and Portugal in the Time of Edward III and Richard II*. Oxford, 1955.

Samaran, C. "Pour l'histoire des grandes compagnies. Le videment de Château-Gontier par les anglais (1369)." In *Mélanges d'histoire du moyen âge dediées à la mémoire de Louis Halphen*, 641–44. Paris, 1951.

Sherbourne, J. "John of Gaunt, Edward III's Retinue, and the French Campaign of 1369." In *Kings and Nobles in the Later Middle Ages: A Tribute to Charles Ross*, ed. R. Griffiths and J. Sherbourne, 41–61. New York, 1986.

Sumption, J. *The Hundred Years War: Trial by Battle*. London, 1990.

*Terrier de Loray, H. *Jean de Vienne, amiral de France (1341–1396)*. Paris, 1877.

Timbal, P. "La confiscation dans le droit français des XIIIe et XIVe siècles." *Revue Historique du Droit Français et Étranger* série 4, 22 (1943): 44–79; 23 (1944): 35–60.

Touchard, H. *Le commerce maritime breton à la fin du moyen âge*. Paris, 1967.

Toudouze, G. G. *Du Guesclin, Clisson, Richemont*. Paris, 1942.

Tuchman, B. W. *A Distant Mirror: The Calamitous Fourteenth Century*. New York, 1978.

Tucoo-Chala, P. *Gaston Fébus et la vicomté de Béarn 1343–1391*. Bordeaux, 1960.

Vale, M. G. A. "Warfare and the Life of the French and Burgundian Nobility in the Late Middle Ages." In *Adelige Sachcultur des Spätmittelalters: International Kongress Krenis an der Donau, 22. bis 25. September 1980*. Osterreichische Akademie der Wissenschaften. Wien, 1982.

Valois, N. *Le conseil du roi anx XIVe, XVe, et XVIe siècles*. Paris, 1888.

———. *La France et le grand schisme d'occident*, 4 vols. Paris, 1896–1902.

Vaughan, R. *John the Fearless: The Growth of Burgundian Power*. London, 1966.

———. *Philip the Bold: The Formation of the Burgundian State*. Cambridge, Mass., 1962.

Vuitry, A. *Études sur le régime financier de la France avant la Révolution de 1789*. Paris, 1878–83.

Wright, N. A. R. "The Peasant Lobby at the Court of the Valois Kings." Paper, Adelaide, 1990.

Index